Nathan Haskell

Rubáiyát of Omar Khayy am

English, French, and German translations comparatively arranged in accordance

with the text of Edward Fitzgerald's version Band 2

Nathan Haskell

Rubáiyát of Omar Khayy am
English, French, and German translations comparatively arranged in accordance with the text of Edward Fitzgerald's version Band 2

ISBN/EAN: 9783743331112

Hergestellt in Europa, USA, Kanada, Australien, Japan

Cover: Foto ©ninafisch / pixelio.de

Manufactured and distributed by brebook publishing software (www.brebook.com)

Nathan Haskell

Rubáiyát of Omar Khayy am

RUBÁIYÁT OF OMAR KHAYYÁM.

VOLUME II.

Copyright, 1896,
By Joseph Knight Company.

𝔘niversity 𝔓ress:
John Wilson and Son, Cambridge, U.S.A.

CONTENTS OF VOLUME II.

			PAGE
APPENDIX	I.	(Rubáiyát ii, iii, c, note 1)	207
"	II.	(R. iv, notes 2, 3)	213
"	III.	(R. v)	216
"	IV.	(R. ix)	219
"	V.	(R. xi, xii)	221
"	VI.	(R. xiii, lxii)	224
"	VII.	(R. xviii, note 10)	234
"	VIII.	(R. xx)	239
"	IX.	(R. xxiii, xxiv, lxxii)	241
"	X.	(R. xxvi)	242
"	XI.	(R. xxvii)	244
"	XII.	(R. xxix, xxx)	253
"	XIII.	(R. xxxiii, xlix)	254
"	XIV.	(R. xxxvii, note 14)	256
"	XV.	(R. xxxix, note 15)	260
"	XVI.	(R. xli)	261
"	XVII.	(R. li)	268
"	XVIII.	(R. liii)	271
"	XIX.	(R. liv)	272
"	XX.	(R. lv)	276
"	XXI.	(R. lvi, note 18)	278
"	XXII.	(R. lviii, lix)	282
"	XXII *continued*.	(R. lix)	299
"	XXIII.	(R. lxi)	301
"	XXIV.	(R. lxii)	306
"	XXV.	(R. lxiii)	308
"	XXVI.	(R. lxiv, lxv)	311

Contents.

			PAGE
APPENDIX	XXVII.	(R. lxviii, note 21)	315
"	XXVIII.	(R. lxix)	317
"	XXIX.	(R. lxxi)	319
"	XXX.	(R. lxxii)	322
"	XXXI.	(R. lxxv)	328
"	XXXII.	(R. lxxvii)	332
"	XXXIII.	(R. lxxviii)	336
"	XXXIV.	(R. lxxxi)	339
"	XXXV.	(R. lxxxii)	348
"	XXXVI.	(R. lxxxiv, lxxxv)	353
"	XXXVII.	(R. lxxxvii, note 21)	359
"	XXXVIII.	(R. lxxxviii)	365
"	XXXIX.	(R. lxxxix)	366
"	XL.	(R. xci)	367
"	XLI.	(R. xcii)	372
"	XLII.	(R. xciii)	373
"	XLIII.	(R. xciv)	376
"	XLIV.	(R. xcv)	377
"	XLV.	(R. lxv, 1868)	379
"	XLVI.	(R. cvii, 1868)	381
"	XLVII.	(Biographical Rubáiyát)	382
"	XLVIII.	(Versions of H. G. Keene)	414-438
"	XLIX.	(Bibliography)	438-544
"	L.	(Omar Khayyám Club)	544-560
"	LI.	(Legend of the Broken Wine Jar)	561-563
"	LII.	(Omar and his Opponents)	563-571
"	LIII.	(Translations from Omar Khayyám, by Frank Siller)	571-574
"	LIV.	(Dr. Wollheim da Fonseca's Translations)	575-581
"	LV.	(Comparative Table)	581-585

INDEX 587-597

APPENDICES.

APPENDICES.

APPENDIX I.

RUBÁIYÁT II, III, AND C.

In the first edition of FitzGerald's translation the first stanza, or Rubá'iy, had a note numbered 1: referring to the flinging of a Stone into a Cup as a Signal of departure. This note was afterwards expunged. Consequently the note-numbers appearing in the above reprint of the 1859 edition are one digit greater than those of the later editions and here indicated in brackets.

FitzGerald says in his note (1): —

"The '*False Dawn;*' *Subhi Kázib*, a transient Light on the Horizon about an hour before the *Subhi sádik* or True Dawn; a well-known Phenomenon in the East."

In the note (2) to edition 1 (1859), he calls the "False Dawn" *Subhi Khazib*, the True Dawn *Subhi Sádhuk*, and the note ends: —

The Persians call the Morning Gray, or Dusk, "Wolf-and-Sheep-While." "Almost at odds with, which is which."

Tom Moore quotes Scott Waring as follows: —

"The Persians have two mornings, the Soobhi Kazim and the Soobhi Sadig, the false and the real day-break. They account for this phenomenon in a most whimsical manner.

They say that as the sun rises from behind the Kohi Qaf (Mount Caucasus), it passes a hole perforated through that mountain, and that, darting its rays through it, it is the cause of the Soobhi Kazim, or this temporary appearance of daybreak. As it ascends, the earth is again veiled in darkness, until the sun rises above the mountain, and brings with it the Soobhi Sadig, or real morning." — He thinks Milton may allude to this, when he says, —

> " Ere the blabbing Eastern scout,
> The nice morn on the Indian steep
> From her cabined loop-hole peep."

It is mentioned again in : —

Nicolas
(185)
Lorsque l'aurore d'azur se montrera, aie dans ta main la coupe étincelante. On dit que la vérité est amère dans la bouche des humains. C'est une raison plausible pour que le vin soit cette vérité même.

McCarthy
(275)
Seize the sparkling cup in thy hand, as soon as the yellow daybreak appeareth. Truth is sharp, it has been said, in the mouth of mankind, for this cause, it may be, that wine is very truth.

Whinfield
(200)
When false dawn streaks the east with cold grey line,
Pour in your cups the pure blood of the vine ;
  The truth, they say, tastes bitter in the mouth,
This is a token that the " Truth " is wine.

Line 2 in Whinfield, 108 (1882), reads : —
    Arise and quaff the firstfruits of the vine.
In line 4 " *the Truth.*"

Sobald das Morgenrot färbt den Himmelsrand ; **Bodenstedt**
Nimm einen schimmernden Becher zur Hand. (IX. 82)
Man sagt, die Wahrheit geht bitter den Menschen ein ;
Du findest sie schmackhaft in gutem Wein.

This phenomenon is gracefully and whimsically introduced into the following Rubá'iy : —

Hier (avant le jour), en compagnie d'une ravissante **Nicolas**
amie et d'une coupe de vin rose, j'étais assis au bord (333)
d'un ruisseau. Devant moi était placée la coupe, cette
coquille dont la perle (le contenu de la coupe) répandait
un tel éclat de lumière que le héraut du soleil, s'éveillant en sursaut, annonça le réveil de l'aurore.

Yesterday I sat by a stream with a beautiful girl and **McCarthy**
a vessel of wine. Before me stood the shell whose pearl (361)
gave forth such light that the cock crew, believing it
was dawn.

Last night upon the river bank we lay, **Whinfield**
I with my wine-cup, and a maiden gay, (373)
  So bright it shone, like pearl within its shell,
The watchman cried, " Behold the break of day ! "

Gestern sass ich mit der Liebsten am Bachesrand, **Bodenstedt**
Vor mir eine Schale mit rosigem Weine stand, (VI. 13)
Eine Muschel, so strahlend von Perlenpracht,
Als sei schon das Frührot am Himmel erwacht.

Von Schack (221)	Gestern vor der Morgendämm'rung, einen Becher in der Hand, Mir zu Seiten eine Schöne, sass ich an des Baches Rand, Und vom Lichtglanz, den der rote Wein auf einmal rings entzündete, Ward getauscht der Stundenrufer, dass er schon den Tag verkündete.

There seem to be several Rubáiyát from which Fitz-Gerald drew inspiration for the second and third quatrains: and the same thought reappears with slight variation in the next to the last in all editions.

The two Rubáiyát that follow are those that most distinctly suggest themselves:—

Nicolas (255)	Vois l'aurore qui apparaît. Elle a déjà déchiré le voile de la nuit. Lève-toi donc, vide la coupe du matin. Pourquoi cette tristesse ? Bois, ô mon cœur ! bois, car ces aurores se succéderont, la face tournée vers nous, quand nous aurons la nôtre tournée vers la terre.

McCarthy (146)	Behold the dawn appears. She has torn aside the veil of night. Rise, then, and empty the morning's cup. Why so sad ? Drink, heart, drink, for these dawns will follow and follow with their faces turned to us, when our faces shall be turned to the earth.

M. K.	Lo! the dawn breaks, and the curtain of night is torn; Up! swallow thy morning cup — Why seem to mourn? Drink wine, my heart! for the dawns will come and come Still facing to us when our faces to earthward turn !

See! the dawn breaks and rends night's canopy:	Whinfield
Arise! and drain a morning draught with me!	(295)
Away with gloom! full many a dawn will break	(158, 1882)
Looking for us, and we not here to see.	

Sieh, das Frührot zerriss den nächtlichen Schleier	Bodenstedt
Erheb' dich und atme beim Frühtrunke freier.	(IX. 28)
Vertrink Deinen Gram!	
Wie es heute kam,	
So wird das rosige Himmelslicht	
Noch oft uns zeigen sein Angesicht,	
Wenn wir, längst in der Erde geborgen	
Nicht wissen, ob's Nacht ist oder Morgen.	

Le clair de lune a découpé la robe noire de la nuit: **Nicolas**. bois donc du vin, car on ne trouve pas toujours un (94) moment aussi précieux. Oui, livre-toi à la joie, car ce même clair de lune éclairera bien longtemps encore (après nous) la surface de la terre.

The light of the moon has severed the black robe of **McCarthy** the night. Drink wine, therefore, for thou wilt never (47) find a moment so precious. Yea, give thyself up to joy, for this same moon will illumine long after us the face of the earth.

The moon cleaves the skirt of the night — then, oh!	**M. K.**
drink Wine!	
For never again will moment like this be thine.	
Be gay! and remember that many and many a moon	
On the surface of earth again and again will shine!	

Garner
(V. 5)

The Moonlight tears the robe of Night in twain,
Such Moments wilt Thou henceforth seek in vain,—
When we are gone the Moon will still be bright,
So fill Thy Cup, and all its Sweetness drain.

Von Schack
(313)

Sich, wie der Mond die Nacht zerteilt! bei seinen
    Lichtstrahlen froh uns wollen wir ergeh'n;
Ach! oftmals noch wird er auf Erden scheinen,
    Allein vergebens nach uns Beiden späh'n.

FitzGerald's translation of Jami's "Salámán and Absál" has these corresponding lines:—

> Alas for those who having tasted once
> Of that forbidden vintage of the lips
> That, press'd and pressing, from each other draw
> The draught that so intoxicates them both,
> That, while upon the wings of Day and Night
> Time rustles on, and Moons do wax and wane,
> As from the very Well of Life they drink,
> And, drinking, fancy they shall never drain.
> But rolling Heaven from his ambush whispers,
> "So in my license is it not set down:
> "Ah for the sweet societies I make
> "At morning, and before the Nightfall break,
> "Ah for the bliss that coming Night fills up,
> "And Morn looks in to find an empty Cup."

APPENDIX II.

RUBÁIY IV.

The reference here is to the passage in the Koran where Moses on Mount Sinai sees his rod changed by the power of God into a serpent:—

"And God said unto Him, O Moses, draw near and fear not; for thou art safe. Put thy hand into thy bosom, and it shall come forth white, without any hurt."— Koran, Chap. XXVII., entitled "The Ant," pp. 283, 292 (George Sale's Translation).

FitzGerald's notes are as follows:—

(2) New Year. Beginning with the Vernal Equinox, it must be remembered; and (howsoever the old Solar Year is practically superseded by the clumsy *Lunar* Year that dates from the Mohammedan Hijra) still commemorated by a Festival that is said to have been appointed by the very Jamshyd whom Omar so often talks of, and whose yearly Calendar he helped to rectify.

"The sudden approach and rapid advance of the Spring," says Mr. Binning, "are very striking. Before the Snow is well off the Ground, the Trees burst into Blossom, and the Flowers start from the Soil. At *Now* * *Rooz (their* New Year's Day) the Snow was lying in patches on the Hills and in the shaded Vallies, while the Fruit-trees in the Garden were budding beautifully, and green Plants and Flowers springing upon the Plains on every side —

> ' And on old Hyems' Chin and icy Crown
> ' An odorous Chaplet of sweet Summer buds
> ' Is, as in mockery, set — '—

Among the Plants newly appeared I recognized some Acquaintances I had not seen for many a Year: among these, two

* *Naw Rooz* in earlier editions.

varieties of the Thistle; a coarse species of the Daisy, like the Horse-gowan; red and white clover; the Dock; the blue Corn-flower; and that vulgar Herb the Dandelion rearing its yellow crest on the Banks of the Water-courses." The Nightingale was not yet heard, for the Rose was not yet blown: but an almost identical Blackbird and Woodpecker helped to make up something of a North-country Spring.

(3) "The White Hand of Moses." Exodus iv. 6; where Moses draws forth his Hand — not, according to the Persians, "*leprous as Snow*," — but *white*, as our May-blossom in Spring perhaps. According to them also the Healing Power of Jesus resided in his Breath.

FitzGerald translated this quatrain into Latin rhyme, to be read as Monkish Latin he says, like "Dies Irae," etc., retaining the Italian value of the vowels: —

>Tempus est quo Orientis
>   Aurâ mundus renovatur,
>Quo de fonte pluviali
>   dulcis Imber reseratur;
>*Musi-Manus* undecumque
>   ramos insuper splendescit;
>Jesu-spiritusque Salutaris
>   terram pervagatur.

He says in a letter to Professor Cowell (May 7, 1857):

"You will think me a perfectly Aristophanic Old Man when I tell you how many of Omar I could not help running into such bad Latin.

"I should not confide such follies but to you who won't think them so, and who will be pleased at least with my still harping on our old Studies. You would be sorry, too, to think that Omar breathes a sort of Consolation to me. Poor Fellow; I think of him, and Oliver Basselin, and Anacreon; lighter Shadows among the Shades, perhaps, over which Lucretius presides so grimly."

FitzGerald promised to "rub up a few more" of these "lazy Latin Versions," and send them to Cowell for his approval: but apparently only one was preserved.

The "breath of 'Isa," or Jesus, is again introduced in the following Rubá'iy:—

C'est l'effet de ton ivresse qui te fait craindre la mort et abhorrer le néant, car il est évident que de ce néant germera une branche de l'immortalité. Depuis que mon âme est ravivée par le souffle de Jésus, la mort éternelle a fui loin de moi.　　Nicolas (39)

It is but thy drunkenness which makes thee dread death and fear nothingness; for it is clear that from that nothingness the Tree of Immortality shall spring. Since my soul has been resuscitated by the breath of Jesus, eternal death has fled afar from me.　　McCarthy (101)

Death's terrors spring from baseless phantasy,
Death yields the tree of immortality;
　Since 'Isa breathed new life into my soul,
Eternal death has washed its hands of me!　　Whinfield (43)

　Whinfield, 23 (1882), has *foolish fantasy*, *Isa*, and the last line reads:—
　　I wash my hands of fear and dare to die.

The fears of Death from your Illusions rise,
For Death is but the Door to Paradise,
　The Breath of Jesus hath revived my Soul,—
The Tales of Everlasting Death, are Lies.　　Garner (l. 30)

Wie thöricht,* dass Dich Todesbangen quäle!
　Aus jedem Nichts, davor Dir graut, wächst Alles.
Seit Jesu Hauch belebt hat meine Seele,
　Sind Tod und Nichts mir Worte leeren Schalles.　　Bodenstedt (l. 25)

* Wörtlich: Deine Trunkenheit (Unverstand, Kopflosigkeit) macht Dich den Tod und das Nichts fürchten.

Von Schack (93)

Blindheit ist's, ihr Menschen, dass ihr vor dem Tode
    bange seid,
Denn erblüh'n wird aus dem Tode, glaubt mir, die
    Unsterblichkeit!
Seit mit seinem Wunderhauche Jesus meinen Geist
    belebt,
Ward ich von dem ew'gen Tode und der Furcht vor
    ihm befreit.

APPENDIX III.

RUBÁ'IY V.

Djem or Jám signifies *king*: *shed* (*chid* or *shyd*) signifies *sun*. Jamshed is supposed to have founded Persepolis, called in Persian Istakhr, or Tekhté-Djemshid, the Throne of Jamshed. He also instituted the nuruz (Naw Rooz), or new day, the first day of the solar year, as a festival. To him is attributed by some historians the glory of having discovered the virtues of wine.

The cup of Jamshed was the invention of the famous Kai-Kosru, third king of the Keyan or Kaianian dynasty, great-grandson of Kai-Kobad. It was made of metal, and bore the signs of the zodiac and cabalistic letters, whereby its possessor could read the future.

Jamshed and Alexander the Great are fabled to have in turn owned this treasure. Nicolas refers to Genesis xliv. 5, to prove that Joseph possessed a cup of similar power: —

"Is not this [that is to say the silver-cup which Joseph caused to be hidden in Benjamin's sack] it in which my lord drinketh and whereby he indeed divineth?"

See Appendix XI, Nicolas, 103, etc.

Attár in the Bird-Parliament makes effective mention of Joseph's Cup. FitzGerald's Translation runs:—

> " And after death? — that shirk it as we may,
> *Will* come, and with it bring its After-Day —
>
> For ev'n as Yúsuf (when his Brotherhood
> Came up from Egypt to buy Corn, and stood
> Before their Brother in his lofty Place,
> Nor knew him, for a Veil before his Face,)
> Struck on his Mystic Cup, which straightway then
> Rung out their Story to those guilty Ten : —
> Nor to *them* only, but to every one :
> Whatever he have said and thought and done,
> Unburied with the Body shall fly up,
> And gather into Heav'n's inverted Cup,
> Which, stricken by God's Finger, shall tell all
> The story whereby we must stand or fall."

The transitoriness of earthly power and magnificence expressed in the first two lines of FitzGerald, and mention of Jamshyd's cup, are found in the following:—

En philosophie quand tu serais un Aristote, un Bouzourdjméhr; en puissance quand tu serais quelque empereur romain ou quelque potentat de Chine, bois toujours, bois du vin dans la coupe de Djém, car la fin de tout c'est la tombe ; oh! quand tu serais Béhram lui-même, le cercueil est ton dernier séjour. **Nicolas** (430)

Wert thou as wise as Aristotle, wert thou as potent as Roman Caesar, or monarch of Cathay, drink, drink, I say, in the cup of Djemshid, for the grave is the end of all, yea, wert thou Bahram himself, the tomb is thy final abode. **McCarthy** (329)

Whinfield
(465)

Though you should sit in sage Aristo's room,
Or rival Cæsar on his throne of Rúm,
 Drain Jamshed's goblet, for your end 's the tomb,
Yea, were you Bahram's self, your end 's the tomb!

 In Whinfield, 239 (1882), *wise Aristu's room, Bahrám*, and *your end is the tomb*.

Garner
(VI. 3)

With Aristotle wise you may contend,
And Cæsar's Power may e'en transcend, —
 But still drink Wine from Jámshed's Cup
Though Bahrám's self, the Tomb would be your End.

Bodenstedt
(IX. 100)

Wärst Du wie Aristoteles ein Weiser,
An Macht wie Roma's oder China's Kaiser:
Trink Wein aus Dschem's Pokal; des Lebens Lauf
(Wärst Du selbst Behram!) hört im Grabe auf.

Nicolas
(237)

J'ai vu sur les murs de la ville de Thous un oiseau posé devant le crâne de Key-Kavous. L'oiseau disait à ce crâne: " Hélas! que sont donc devenus le bruit des anneaux de ta gloire et le son du clairon?"

McCarthy
(50)

I saw upon the walls of Thous a bird perched in front of the skull of Kai Khosrou. The bird said unto the skull, " Alas, what has become of the clash of the gear of thy glory and the bruit of thy trumpets?"

Whinfield
(277)

I saw a bird perched on the walls of Tús,
Before him lay the skull of Kai Kawús,
 And thus he made his moan, " Alas, poor king!
Thy drums are hushed, thy 'larums have rung truce."

 Whinfield, 153 (1882), Kai Kaiús; line 4, *have sung truce*.

A Bird upon the crumbling walls of Tús,   Garner
Addressed the grinning Skull of Kai-Kaiús:—   (VII. 1)
  "The Rumbling of Thy Drums affright no Ears,
Thy Trumpets now are tarnished from Disuse."

Einen Vogel sah ich sitzen auf der Mauer von Thuss   Bodenstedt
Und hört' ihn sprechen zum Schädel des Key-Kawuss: (VIII. 33)
Ach, wo sind nun die Pauken und Zinken des Ruhms,
Wo der Lärm und Glanz Deines Herrschertums?

Zum Schädel des Kai Kawus auf dem Wall   Von Schack
  Von Tus einst hört' ich sprechen einen Geier: (119)
"Ach! ach! wo ist nun deiner Feste Feier?
Wo blieb nun deiner Kriegsdrommeten Schall?"

Tús was uncle of Kai-Kaiús; it is also the name of a town near Nishápúr. Kai-Kaiús was son and successor of Kai-Kobad, founder of the Kaianian dynasty which displaced the mythical Peshdadians.

See also following Appendix.

APPENDIX IV.

RUBÁ'IY IX.

FitzGerald apparently combined two Persian originals for Rubá'iy IX. The first has been already given.

Voici le bruit du matin, ô idole dont la venue procure   Nicolas
le bonheur! entonne ton refrain et apporte du vin; car   (455)
(tu le sais) cette succession constante du mois de Tir
au mois de Di a renversé sur terre cent mille potentats
comme Djèm, cent mille comme Kéy.

McCarthy (315)	It is dawn, ever welcome, beloved, sing your song, and drink your wine, for the long array of months has overthrown a thousand kings like Djemshid and Kai-Khosrou.
Whinfield (484) (250, 1882)	Angel of joyful foot! the dawn is nigh; Pour wine, and lift your tuneful voice on high, Sing how Jamsheds and Khosraus bit the dust, Whelmed by the rolling months, from Tir to Dai.
Garner (VI. 18)	Come, fill the morning Cup, the Sun is high, Come tune Thy Harp, asleep Thou shouldst not lie, The swift and sure return of Tyr and Dai Has crushed a thousand kings like Jám and Kai.

Von Schack (246)	Auf nun und das Frühlied sing! den Becher voll Weines
	    mir bring;
	Was gäb' es, o mein Idol, auf Erden Besseres wohl,
	   Wo hunderttausend Herrscher das Rad
	   Der rollenden Zeit zermalmt schon hat?

    Tyr and Dai, in the old Iranian calender, correspond to April and December.

    In a letter to Professor Cowell, dated July 3, 1857, Fitz-Gerald says:—

    "Have I previously asked you to observe 486, of which I send a poor Sir W. Jones' sort of Parody which came into my mind walking in the Garden here; where the Rose is blowing as in Persia? . . .

> "I long for wine! oh Saki of my Soul,
> Prepare thy Song and fill the morning Bowl;
> For this first Summer month that brings the Rose
> Takes many a Sultan with it as it goes."

APPENDIX V.

RUBÁIYÁT XI AND XII.

Here with a little Bread beneath the Bough,   **FitzGerald**
A Flask of Wine, a Book of Verse — and Thou   (XII.)
   Beside me singing in the Wilderness —   1868
Oh, Wilderness were Paradise enow.

All a long summer's day here Khayyám lies   **Whinfield**
On this green sward, gazing in Houris' eyes,   (39, 1882)
   Yet Mollas say he is a graceless dog,
Who never gives a thought to Paradise.

The same idea appears in other Rubáiyát; *e. g:*—

   Lorsqu'on possède un pain de froment, deux mèns **Nicolas**
de vin et un gigot de mouton, et qu'on peut aller   (118)
s'asseoir dans quelque lieu en ruine ayant avec soi une
jeune belle aux joues colorées du teint de la tulipe, oh!
c'est une jouissance qu'il n'est pas donné à tout sultan
de se procurer.

   When the hand possesses a loaf of wheaten bread, **McCarthy**
two measures of wine, and a piece of flesh, when seated   (398)
with Tulip-cheeks in some lonely spot, behold such joy
as is not given to all Sultans.

So long as I possess two maunds of wine,   **Whinfield**
Bread of the flower of wheat and mutton chine,   (179)
   And you, O Tulip cheeks to share my hut,
Not every Sultan's lot can vie with mine.

Whinfield
(247, 1882)

Come brim my cup with foaming head of wine,
And bring a hunch of bread, a mutton chine
   And sit you by me, O sweet tulip cheeks:
I would not change the Sultan's state for mine.

Bodenstedt
(X. 23)

Bei einer Hammelkeule, Brot und Wein,
Mit einer tulpenfarbigen Schönen allein
In Einsamkeit den Tag zu verleben,
Ist ein Glück, das nicht jedem König gegeben.

The following contains a quite modern idea of equality: —

Nicolas
(146)

En ce monde, celui qui possède la moitié d'un pain et qui peut abriter son individu dans un nid quelconque, celui qui n'est ni le maître, ni le serviteur de personne, dis-lui de vivre content, car il possède une bien douce existence.

McCarthy
(262)

He who, in this world possesses half a loaf and can shelter himself in any nest, he who is neither the master, or slave of any man, tell him his lot is sweet and tranquil, and he should live content therein.

Whinfield
(168)

Let him rejoice who has a loaf of bread,
A little nest wherein to lay his head,
   Is slave to none, and no man slaves for him, —
In truth his lot is wondrous well bested.

M. K.

He who doth here below but half a loaf possess,
Who for his own can claim some sheltering nook's
   recess,
   He who to none is either lord or thrall —
Go! tell him he enjoys the world's full happiness!

Wer in dieser Welt nur ein halbes Brod hat **Bodenstedt**
Und ein ruhiges Nest bis zu seinem Tod hat, (VIII. 19)
  Wer Keinem zu gehorchen noch zu befehlen braucht,
Der sei froh, da er weder Sorge noch Not hat.

The following Rubá'iy begins in a way that would satisfy a protectionist, and ends with the same idea of independent equality:—

  Pourquoi un homme qui possède un pain lui per- **Nicolas**
mettant de vivre deux jours, qui dans une cruche fêlée (462)
peut puiser une goutte d'eau fraîche, pourquoi un tel
homme doit-il être commandé par un autre qui ne le
vaut pas, ou pourquoi en servirait-il un qui serait son
égal?

Sooner with half a loaf contented be, **Whinfield**
And water from a broken crock, like me, (207)
  Than lord it over one poor fellow man,
Or to another bow the vassal knee.

Sooner with crusts of bread contented be, (114, 1882)
And water from the well of liberty,
  Than crouch and fawn and bend the vassal knee
To one who is nothing worth compared with thee.

Wer ein Brod besitzt, sein Leben nur zwei Tage lang **Von Schack**
    zu fristen, (184)
  Einen Krug, mit dem er Wasser schöpfe, wenn er
    Trank begehrt,
O wie möcht' er Andern dienen, die in Hoffart stolz
    sich brüsten
  Und doch nichts als seines Gleichen, ja geringer sind
    an Wert.

APPENDIX VI.

RUBÁIYÁT XIII AND LXII.

Whinfield, 61 (1882), has the last three lines as follows:—

"But, look you, so is wine sweet, taste and see
Hold fast this cash and let the credit be,"
And shun the din of empty drums with me.

Whinfield, 43 (1882), reads:—

Khayyám his own true lineage cannot tell,
Whether derived from heaven or from hell;
Howbeit he will not renounce his wine,
Nor cash in hand for promised credit sell.

There are many Rubáiyát based on the Horatian idea of seizing the present moment. A few of them follow:—

Nicolas (77) Procure-toi des danceurs, du vin et une charmante aux traits ravissants de houri, si houris il y a; ou cherche une belle eau courante au bord du gazon, si gazon il y a, et ne demande rien de mieux; ne t'occupe plus de cet enfer éteint, car, en vérité, il n'y a pas d'autre paradis que celui que je t'indique, si paradis il y a.

Get thyself dancing girls, wine, and a mistress as fair   McCarthy
as the Houris, if indeed there be Houris, or seek out a   (179)
limpid stream gushing by a meadow, if any meadow be,
and ask for no better lot. Vex yourself no more with
an extinguished Hell, for truly there is no other Paradise than this, if any Paradise there be.

Some Wine, a Houri, (Houris if there be),   Whinfield
A green bank by a stream, with minstrelsy; —   (79)
  Toil not to find a better Paradise,
If other Paradise indeed there be!

If wine and song there be to give thee soul-entrancing   *4
    bliss,
If there be spots where verdant fields and purling
    brooklets kiss,
  Ask thou no more from Providence, nor turn thee in
    despair;
If there be any Paradise for man, 'tis even this.

Lass Dich Tänzer und Wein und Huris erfreuen, wenn's   Bodenstedt
    deren giebt;   (X. 3)
Sieh die Gräser und Blumen am schimmernden Bach
    sich erneuen, wenn's deren giebt,
  Denn nichts Anderes können die Freuden des
    Paradieses Dir bieten,
Dabei lass Dich getrost von den Strafen der Hölle be-
    dräuen, wenn's deren giebt.

Nicolas
(437)

O mon roi! comment un homme comme moi, se trouvant, dans la saison des roses, au milieu d'une joyeuse société, entouré de vin, de danseurs, comment pourrait-il demeurer spectateur passif? Oh! se trouver dans un jardin avec un flacon de vin et une flûte sont des choses préférables au paradis avec ses houris et son Kooucer!

McCarthy
(352)

O my king, how many a man like me in the rose-bower, in the fair fellowship of dancers and drinkers, remains aloof, an onlooker? A garden, a wine-jar, and a lute are better than Paradise with its streams and houris.

Bodenstedt
(VIII. 86)

Bei Wein, Tanz und Rosen mit frohen Genossen,
O Herz, soll ich hier stehn aller Freude verschlossen?
Wein und Lautenklang hier in Garten und Wiese
Gilt mir mehr als die Huris im Paradiese.

Nicolas
(68)

Pourquoi, aujourd'hui que la rose de ta fortune porte ses fruits, la coupe est-elle absente de ta main? Bois du vin, ami, bois, car le temps est un ennemi implacable, et retrouver un jour pareil est chose difficile.

McCarthy
(14)

Why, when to-day the rose of fortune blossoms, is the wine-cup missing from your hands? Drink, my friend, drink red wine, for time is a merciless fellow, and it is hard to find again a day like this.

Now that your roses bloom with flowers of bliss, To grasp your goblets be not so remiss; Drink while you may! Time is a treacherous foe, You may not see another day like this.	**Whinfield** (71)

Da heut' die Rose Deines Glücks erschlossen, Warum lässt Du den Becher ungenossen? Trink, lieber Freund: die Zeit hat flücht'ge Sohlen, Ein Tag wie heute ist schwer einzuholen.	**Bodenstedt** (IX. 57)

Oublie le jour qui a été retranché de ton existence; ne t'inquiète pas de celui de demain, qui n'est pas encore venu; ne te repose pas sur ce qui est ou sur ce qui n'est plus; vis un instant heureux et ne jette pas ainsi ta vie au vent.	**Nicolas** (334)

Do not call to mind the day which has passed from you; do not lament for unborn to-morrow, do not build on the coming and past away, take the fair hour, and do not cast your life to the wind.	**McCarthy** (377)

Ask not the chances of the time to be, And for the past, 'tis vanished, as you see; This ready money breath set down as gain, Future and past concern not you or me.	**Whinfield** (278)

Vergiss die Tage die Dir verloren sind, Fürchte die nicht die noch nicht geboren sind. Geniesse des Augenblicks Gunst und bedenke, Dass, die das Leben in den Wind schlagen, Thoren sind.	**Bodenstedt** (VIII. 50)

Von Shack (124)	Den Tag, der gestern war, vergiss!
	Mach' dir gedanken nicht um Morgen!
	Des Augenblicks, der dir allein gewiss,
	Des jetzigen, geniese ohne Sorgen!

    Compare Horace I. 11.

> tu ne quaesieris (scire nefas) quem mihi, quem tibi finem di dederint, Leuconoë. . . . dum loquimur, fugerit invida aetas: carpe diem, quam minimum credula postero.

Nicolas (214) Voici l'aurore, lève-toi, ô jeune homme imberbe, et remplis vite de ce vin en rubis la coupe de cristal, car (plus tard) tu pourras chercher longtemps sans jamais le retrouver, ce moment d'existence qu'on nous prête dans ce monde de néant.

McCarthy (251) Behold the dawn; arise, O beardless lad, and fill with ruddy wine the clear vessel, for you may seek hereafter, and seek in vain, this fair hour which this world of shadows lends you.

M. K. Up! smooth-faced boy, the daybreak shines for thee:
  Brimm'd with red wine let the crystal goblet be!
    This hour is lent thee in the House of Dust:—
  Another thou may'st seek, but ne'er shalt see!

Von Schack (140) Jüngling, auf! der Freude jage nach bei ihrem Flug,
    dem raschen!
  Fülle mir den Becher! Siehe! wie der Himmel sich
    erhellt!
Später magst du noch so sehr dich müh'n, du wirst ihn
    nie mehr haschen,
  Diesen Augenblick, den flücht'gen, in dem grossen
    Nichts der Welt.

Ne deviens pas la proie du chagrin de ce monde d'iniquité ; ne rappelle pas à ton âme le souvenir de ceux qui ne sont plus ; ne livre ton cœur qu'à une amie aux douces lèvres et à stature de fée ; ne sois jamais privé de vin, ne jette pas ta vie au vent.

Nicolas
(367)

Let not the weight of the world oppress you, do not vex your soul with the thought of those who have passed away, yield not your heart save to the fairest of the fair, never lack good wine nor cast your life to the wind.

McCarthy
(443)

    Yield not to grief, though future prove unkind,
No[r] call sad thoughts of parted friends to mind;
    Devote thy heart to sugary lips, and wine,
Cast not thy precious life unto the wind!

Whinfield
(412)

Opfere nicht den Launen der Zeit Dein Glück,
Rufe nicht, was längst gewesen, zurück,
Öffne Dein Herz nur süsslippigen Feen,
Trink Wein, lass Dein Leben nicht unnütz vergehn!

Bodenstedt
(VIII. 69)

Le temps que nous passons dans ce monde n'a point de prix sans vin et sans échanson ; il n'y a point de prix sans les sons mélodieux de la flûte d'Irak. J'ai beau observer les choses d'ici bas, je n'y vois que la joie et le plaisir qui aient du prix : le reste n'est rien.

Nicolas
(84)

Irak ou Irak-Adjémi, says Nicolas, *province située au midi de la Perse, pays des Persans proprement dit.*

McCarthy (174)   The days of our abiding on this earth are worthless without wine and the cup-bearer, worthless without the soft melodies of Iram's lute. I have studied closely the course of earthly things, and I know that joy and pleasure alone are dear, all else is worthless.

Whinfield (86)
Life, void of wine, and minstrels with their lutes,
And the soft murmurs of Irákian flutes,
  Were nothing worth : I scan the world and see,
Save pleasure, life yields only bitter fruits.

Von Schack (212)
Gäb' es keinen Wein auf Erden, keinen Schall der Irakflöten,
Keine Schenken, o man sollte lieber sich zur Stelle töten!
Auf der Welt, so weit mein Auge sie durchmisst von Ost nach West,
Stich hält nur die Lust bei'm Becher; keinen Deut wert ist der Rest.

The following Rubá'iy is supposed by Whinfield to have been written on the margin of some MS. by some pious reader as an answer to the one above:—

Nicolas (96)   Il n'y a point de bouclier qui tienne contre une flèche lancée par le Destin. Les grandeurs, l'argent, l'or, tout cela ne sert de rien. Plus je considère les choses de ce monde, plus je vois qu'il n'y a de bien que le bien : tout le reste n'est rien.

McCarthy (105)   There is no shield to save you from the spear-cast of destiny. Glory, gold, silver, each avails not. The more I ponder on this world and its gear, the more I am assured that to be good is all ; the rest avails not.

Against death's arrows what are bucklers worth?   Whinfield
What all the pomps and riches of the earth?   (97)
   When I survey the world, I see no good
But goodness, all beside is nothing worth.

With Swift Destruction are Fate's Arrows fraught,   Garner
Nor can this Worldly Wealth avail Thee aught.   (II. 11)
   The more I ponder on this World I see
The Good is Good, and all the rest is Naught.

Kein Schild hält einem Pfeil des Schicksals Stand;   Bodenstedt
Gold, Gut und Rang, ist alles eitler Tand;   (V. 9)
Im Weltlauf merk' ich prüfenden Gesichts:
Gut ist, was gut ist, und sonst gilt mir nichts.

   But "old Omar" has an appropriate reply ready:

   Le vin couleur de rose dans une coupe vermeille est   Nicolas
agréable. Il est agréable, accompagné des airs mélo-   (83)
dieux du luth et des sons plaintifs de la harpe. Le
religieux qui n'a aucune notion des délices de la coupe
de vin est agréable, lui, quand il est à mille farsakhs loin
de nous.

   Sweet is it to drink red wine in a fair cup. Sweet is   McCarthy
it to hear the wedded melodies of lutes and harps.   (178)
The fanatic who recks not of the joys of a cup of wine
is pleasing only when he is a thousand miles away
from us.

Sweet is rose-ruddy wine in goblets gay,   Whinfield
And sweet are lute and harp and roundelay;   (85)
   But for the zealot who ignores the cup,
'Tis sweet when he is twenty leagues away!

Bodenstedt Beim Becher, gefüllt mit rosigem Weine, zu weilen ist
(IX. 60) angenehm;
 Beim Klange der Saiten nicht sehn, wie die Stunden
  enteilen, ist angenehm;
  Selbst der Heilige, der uns verwünscht mit all' unsern
   Freuden,
 Bleibt er fern von uns auf hundert von Meilen, ist ange-
  nehm.

Von Schack Wein, den rosenfarb'gen, lieb' ich, wenn er funkelt in
(45) den Gläsern
 Bei der Laute sanften Tönen und dem Spiel von Flöten-
  bläsern;
 Auch Asceten, Weinverächter lieb' ich, wenn mit ihrem
  Treiben
 Sie nur hundert Farasangen weit mir stets vom Leibe
  bleiben.

And he returns to the charge:—

Nicolas Pendant la saison des fleurs, bois du vin couleur de
(209) rose; bois-en aux sons plaintifs de la flûte, au bruit
 mélodieux de la harpe. Moi, j'en bois et je m'en
 réjouis; puisse-t-il m'être salutaire! Si tu n'en bois
 pas, que veux-tu que j'y fasse? Va donc manger des
 cailloux!

McCarthy In the season of flowers, drink wine the colour of
(185) roses, drink to the plaintive notes of the flute, and the
 melodious sound of the harp. I for my part drink
 thereof and rejoice, and it is congenial to me. If thou
 wilt not drink, what is that to me? Go, then, and eat
 stones.

Whinfield does not translate Nicolas, 209, but 210, which is similar:—

Are you depressed? Then take of *bang* one grain,   Whinfield
Of rosy grape-juice take one pint or twain;   (251)
  Sufis, you say must not take this or that,
Then go and eat the pebbles off the plain.

    Bang, or hashish, is a narcotic made from hemp.

Trink rosigen Wein, wenn die Knospen springen   Bodenstedt
Und lass Flöten und Harfen beim Becher klingen.   (IX. 12)
  Ich selbst mach' es so, mög' es gut mir gedeihn!
Bist Du anderen Sinns, magst Du Steine verschlingen!

Où sont les danseurs? Où est le vin? Vite, que je   Nicolas
fasse honneur à la gourde! Heureux le cœur qui se   (104)
souvient du vin du matin! Oh! il existe en ce monde
trois choses qui me sont chères: une tête prise de vin,
une belle amoureuse et le bruit du matin.

Where are the dancers? where is the wine? Hasten   McCarthy
that I may do honour to the gourd. Happy is the heart   (142)
which remembers the wine in the morning. Oh! there
exist three things in this world which are dear to me —
a head overtaken with wine, a fair mistress, and the
sound of singing.

Wo sind die Sänger? wo ist der Wein? Geschwinde   Von Schack
   nun eingeschenkt!   (247)
Gesegnet sei mir das Herz, das fromm des Morgentrunkes
   gedenkt!
Von Allem auf dieser Erde sind drei Dinge das beste,
   glaubt:
Ein holdes Liebchen, der Morgentrunk und ein Wein-
   benebeltes Haupt.

So also Nicolas, 344: —

Il ne faut point se résoudre a flétrir par le chagrin un cœur joyeux, à broyer sous la pierre des tourments nos instants d'allégresse. Personne ne pouvant nous dire ce qui adviendra, ce qu'il faut donc, c'est du vin, c'est une maîtresse chérie et un repos au gré de nos souhaits.

McCarthy, 433: —

Never wound with sorrow a joyous heart, nor break with the stones of torment one moment of delight. Since none can say what is to come, our needs are wine, a beloved, and desireful ease.

See Whitley Stokes's version 10.

In the same spirit Keats sang: —

> Give me women, wine and snuff
> Until I cry out "hold, enough!"
> You may do so sans objection
> Till the day of resurrection;
> For bless my beard they aye shall be
> My beloved Trinity.

APPENDIX VII.

RUBÁ'IY XVIII.

Bahrám-Gur, one of the Sassanian kings of Persia, was a cruel persecutor of the Christians, and also an ardent huntsman. It is said that one day while chasing wild asses on the plain of Veramin he was swallowed up, together with his horse, in a quicksand or marsh. In the original Persian this Rubá'iy has a curious play on words, the word for wild ass and tomb being *gur*.

FitzGerald's note (10), with its variants, is as follows:

Persepolis: call'd also *Takht-i-Jamshyd* — THE THRONE OF JAMSHYD, "*King Splendid*," of the mythical *Peshdádian* [Peeshdádian] Dynasty, and supposed [with Shah-náma Authority] (according to the Shâh-náma) to have been founded and built by him. Others [though others] refer it to the Work of the Genie King, Ján Ibn Ján [Jann] — who also built the Pyramids — before the time of Adam.

[Ed. 1: It is also called *Chehl-minar* — *Forty-column;* which is Persian, probably, for *Column-countless;* the Hall they adorned or supported with their Lotus Base and taurine Capital indicating double that Number, though now counted down to less than half by Earthquake and other Inroad. By whomsoever built, unquestionably the Monument of a long extinguished Dynasty and Mythology; its Halls, Chambers and Galleries, inscribed with Arrow-head Characters, and sculptured with colossal, wing'd, half human Figures like those of Nimroud; Processions of Priests and Warriors — (doubtful if any where a Woman) — and kings sitting on Thrones or in chariots, Staff or Lotus-flower in hand, and the *Ferooher* — Symbol of Existence — with his wing'd Globe, common also to Assyria and Ægypt — over their heads. All this, together with Aqueduct and Cistern, and other Appurtenance of a Royal Palace, upon a Terrace-platform, ascended by a double Flight of Stairs that may be gallop'd up, and cut out of and into the Rock-side of the *Koh'i Ráhmet*, *Mountain of Mercy*, where the old Fire-worshiping Sovereigns are buried, and overlooking the Plain of Merdasht.

Persians, like some other People, it seems, love to write their own Names, with sometimes a Verse or two, on their Country's Monuments. Mr. Binning (from whose sensible Travels the foregoing Account is mainly condens't) found several such in Persepolis; in one Place a fine Line of Háfiz: in another "an original, no doubt," he says, "by no great Poet, however right in his Sentiment." The Words somehow looked to us, and the "halting metre" sounded, familiar; and on looking back at last among the 500 Rubáyiát of the

Calcutta Omar MS. — *there* it is: old Omar quoted by *one* of his Countrymen, and here turned into hasty Rhyme, at any rate —

"This Palace that its Top to Heaven threw,
  And Kings their Forehead on its Threshold drew —
  I saw a Ring-dove sitting there alone,
  And 'Coo, Coo, Coo,' she cried, and 'Coo, Coo, Coo.'"

So as it seems the Persian speaks the English Ring-dove's *Pehlevi*, which is also articulate Persian for "Where?"]

BAHRÁM GÚR. — *Bahrám of the Wild Ass* [from his Fame in hunting it] — a Sassanian Sovereign — had also his Seven Castles (like the King of Bohemia!) each of a different Colour: each with a Royal Mistress within [side; each of whom recounts to Bahrám a Romance, according to one of]; each of whom tells him a Story, as told in one of the most famous Poems of Persia, written by Amír Khusraw: all these Sevens also figuring (according to Eastern Mysticism) the Seven Heavens; and perhaps the Book itself that Eighth, into which the mystical Seven transcend, and within which they revolve. The Ruins of Three of those Towers are yet shown by the Peasantry; as also the Swamp in which Bahrám sunk, like the Master of Ravenswood, while pursuing his *Gúr*.

  The Palace that to Heav'n his pillars threw,
  And Kings the forehead on his threshold drew —
  I saw the solitary Ringdove there,
  And "Coo, coo, coo," she cried; and "Coo, coo, coo."

This Quatrain Mr. Binning found, among several of Háfiz and others, inscribed by some stray hand among the ruins of Persepolis. The Ringdove's ancient *Pehlevi Coo, Coo, Coo*, signifies also in Persian "*Where? Where? Where?*" [note of 1859 edition ended with these words]. In Attár's "Bird-parliament" she is reproved by the Leader of the Birds for sitting still, and for ever harping on that one note of lamentation for her lost Yúsuf.

Apropos of Omar's Red Roses in Stanza XIX I am reminded of an old English Superstition that our Pulsatilla, or purple "Pasque Flower," (which grows plentifully about the Fleam Dyke, near Cambridge,) grows only where Danish Blood has been spilt.

Various versions of the Ring-dove Rubá'iy follow :—

Ce château qui par sa splendeur rivalisait avec les   **Nicolas**
cieux, ce château où les souverains se succédaient à   (350)
l'envi, nous avons vu une tourterelle s'y poser et sur ses
créneaux en ruine crier : " Kou, kou, kou, kou."

That palace which touched the heavens, before whose   **McCarthy**
door kings bowed the head, we saw the ring-dove on its   (364)
battlements, resting and crying, " Coo, coo, coo, coo."

Yon palace, towering to the welkin blue,   **Whinfield**
Where kings did bow them down, and homage do,   (392)
   I saw a ring-dove on its arches perched,   1889
And thus she made complaint, " Coo Coo, Coo, Coo ! "

Yon palace whose roofs touch the empyreal blue,   (206)
Where kings bowed down and rendered homage due,   1882
   The ringdove is its only tenant now,
And perched aloft she wails, " Coo Coo, Coo Coo."

Yon fallen Palace once with Heaven vying,   **Garner**
Where Kings bowed down, is now in ruin lying,   (I. 9)
   The Ring-dove haunts its desolated courts,
And wails *coo-coo, coo-coo*, forever crying.

Coo, or *ku*, is a contraction of the Persian word *kuja, where*. The German versions paraphrase the meaning:—

Bodenstedt Jenes Schloss, drin die mächtigsten Herrscher gethront,
(VIII. 60) Das zum Himmel aufglänzte, ward doch nicht verschont.
Eine Turteltaube ruft auf den Zinnen jetzt:
Wo sind, die einst hausten darinnen, jetzt?

Von Schack Dies Schloss, wie der Himmel so leuchtend, einst
(189) strotzend von Gold und von Schätzen,
In dessen prangenden Sälen der Könige viele gethront,
Auf seine zerfallenen Zinnen jetzt seh'n wir die Taube sich setzen;
Sie girrt, als wollte sie sagen: "Wo blieben sie, die hier gewohnt?"

In the Mantik-ut-tair (Mantik et Teyr), or "Bird-Parliament," there is a pretty passage about the "Ring Dove." FitzGerald's version runs:—

Then from a Wood was heard unseen to coo
The Ring Dove — "Yúsuf! Yúsuf! Yúsuf! Yú"—
(For thus her sorrow broke her Note in twain,
And, just where broken, took it up again)
"— suf! Yúsuf! Yúsuf! Yúsuf!" — But one Note,
Which still repeating, she made hoarse her throat:—

Till checkt — "Oh You, who with your idle Sighs
Block up the Road of better Enterprize:
Sham Sorrow all, or bad as sham if true,
When once the better thing is come to *do*:
Beware lest wailing thus you meet *his* Doom
Who all too long his Darling wept, from whom
You draw the very Name you hold so dear,
And which the World is somewhat tired to hear."

APPENDIX VIII.

RUBÁ'IY XX.

It would be difficult to decide which Rubá'iy Fitz-Gerald took for his original,— the one already given (pp. 40, 41), or the following: —

Avant toi et moi, il y a eu bien des crépuscules, bien des aurores, et ce n'est pas sans raison que le mouvement de rotation a été imprimé aux cieux. Sois donc attentif quand tu poseras ton pied sur cette poussière, car elle a été sans doute la prunelle des yeux d'une jeune beauté.   Nicolas (29)

Before ever you or I were born, there were dawns and twilights and it was not without design that the revolutions of the skies were sanctioned. Be careful, then, how you tread upon this dust, for it was once, no doubt, the apple of some fair girl's eye.   McCarthy (75)

Days changed to nights, ere you were born, or I,
And on its business ever rolled the sky;
  See you tread gently on this dust, perchance
'T was once the apple of some beauty's eye.   Whinfield (33)

Before us twain were many Nights and Days,
The Stars have long pursued their Heavenly ways, —
  But tread with Lightest Foot upon this Dust,
'T was once an Eye that beamed with Loving Rays.   Garner (V. 9)

Bodenstedt (III. 4)	Vor Dir und mir gab's Morgenröten und Dämmerungen, Und haben sich leuchtende Sterne auf himmlischen Bahnen geschwungen. Wohin Du auch wandelst, Du trittst auf die Augen einst blühender Mädchen, Die wieder zu Staube geworden, wie einst sie dem Staube entsprungen.
Von Schack (263)	Oft vor dir und mir hienieden ward es Tag und wieder Nacht, Keine Dauer gönnt die Erde ihren Töchtern, ihren Söhnen, Drum, wenn deines Fusses Sohle diesen Staub berührt, hab' Acht! Sicher war er einst das Auge einer jugendlichen Schönen.

So Theognis sings:—

ἡβώοις, φίλε θυμέ· ταχ' ἄν τινες ἄλλοι ἔσοιντο
ἄνδρες, ἐγὼ δὲ θανὼν γαῖα μέλαιν' ἔσομαι.

APPENDIX IX.

RUBÁIYÁT XXIII, XXIV, AND LXXII.

Ô mon cœur! puisque ce monde t'attriste, puisque ton âme si pure doit se séparer de ton corps, va t'asseoir sur la verdure des champs et réjouis-toi pendant quelques jours, avant que d'autres verdures jaillissent de ta propre poussière.

Nicolas (72)

Oh, my heart, since this world grieves thee, since thy pure soul must so soon be severed from thy body, sit thee down in the grassy fields and make merry awhile, before other grasses spring from thy very dust.

McCarthy (57)

O Freund, da Dich der Gedanke durchschauert,
Dass die Seele im Körper nicht lange dauert,
Erfreu' Dich des Lebens im frischen Grün,
Eh' Blumen aus Deinem Staube erblühn.

Bodenstedt (VI. 25)

O Freund, da einmal solches Los das Schicksal dir
   bestimmt
Und dich nach kurzer Erdenrast von hinnen nieder
   nimmt,
Erfreu dich ein'ge Tage lang an Blumenduft und
   Grün,
Eh and're Blumen wiederum aus deinem Staub
   erblüh'n.

Von Schack (72)

See Appendix XXX.

APPENDIX X.

RUBÁ'IY XXVI.*

"The firmament," says Nicolas, in explanation of this Rubá'iy, "is here compared by the poet to a bowl reversed on the head of human beings, as a sign of despair at failing to reach the eternal Truth. Wise men are no farther advanced in their researches than the firmament itself, the movement of which around the earth and its influence on men's destiny proceed directly from God."

In this and the following appendix are gathered several Rubáiyát reflecting on the futility of human knowledge and the brevity of human life : —

Nicolas (384) Ceux qui sont partis avant nous, ô échanson! sont couchés dans la poussière de l'orgueil; va boire du vin, va, écoute la vérité que je te dis : tout ce qu'ils ont avancé n'est que du vent, sache-le, ô échanson.

McCarthy (340) Those that have gone hence before us, O cup-bearer, are lapped in the dust of pride, O cup-bearer; drink then thy wine, and hear the truth I tell; the words they whispered were but wind, O cup-bearer.

---

* The quatrain numbered XXVI in the first edition (1859) of FitzGerald corresponds to LXIII in the later editions, and will be found on page 122.

They that have passed away, and gone before,   Whinfield
Sleep in delusion's dust forevermore;   (428)
  Go, boy, and fetch some wine, this is the truth,   (222, 1882)
Their dogmas were but air, and wind their lore!

Alle, die uns schon verlassen haben, o Freund!   Bodenstedt
Sind im Staube ihres Stolzes begraben, o Freund!   (VII. 41)
  Trinke Wein und vernimm meine Worte der Wahrheit:
Wind war Alles, was sie geredet haben, o Freund!

O Schenke! Alle, die vor uns dahingegangen sind,   Von Schack
Voll leeren Dünkels waren sie, an Geist sie alle blind!   (160)
  Giess Wein mir ein und glaube mir, dass ich die Wahrheit sage,
"Was irgendwie sie vorgebracht, war nichts als eitel Wind."

"I applied my heart to know wisdom, and to know madness and folly: I perceived that this also was a striving after wind. . . . Then I looked on all the works that my hands had wrought, and on the labour that I had laboured to do: and, behold, all was vanity and a striving after wind, and there was no profit under the sun. . . . For of the wise man, even as of the fool, there is no remembrance for ever; seeing that in the days to come all will have been already forgotten. And how doth the wise man die even as the fool! So I hated life; because the work that is wrought under the sun was grievous unto me: for all is vanity and a striving after wind."—*Ecclesiastes* i. 17, 18; ii. 11, 16, 17.

APPENDIX XI.

RUBÁ'IY XXVII.

In Whinfield, 143 (1882), line 2, *Towards a higher seat* stands for the later *Up to a higher nest*; and in line 4, *the same door where through* reads *that same door through which*.

Garner XI, 1, might well have found its place on p. 55, but it has no sparrow-hawk:—

> Within the Maze of Human Faith and Doubt
> I erst while loved to wander round about,
>   But No One have I met the way to clear,
> And through the Entrance Door I passed Without.

A number of illustrative or analogous Rubáiyát follow:—

Nicolas (113)

En ce moment, où mon cœur n'est pas encore privé de vie, il me semble qu'il y a peu de problèmes que je n'aie résolus. Cependant, quand j'appelle l'intelligence à mon aide, quand je m'examine avec soin, je m'aperçois que mon existence s'est écoulé et que je n'ai encore rien défini.

Whinfield (142)

Whilom, ere youth's conceit had waned, methought
Answers to all life's problems I had wrought;
  But now, grown old and wise, too late I see
My life is spent, and all my lore is naught.

Jetzt, wo noch mein Aug' und Odem auf den Schein der   **Bodenstedt**
    Dinge stösst.   (III. 11)
Scheint mir, wenig Lebensrätsel geb' es, die ich nicht
    gelöst;
Doch mich gründlich prüfend find' ich an der Summe
    des Erkennens:
Was mir klar im dunklen Leben wurde, ist nicht wert
    des Nennens.

Oft wohl denk' ich, jetzt, da ich noch fröhlich lebe,   **Von Schack**
Dass es nichts mehr, was ich nicht begriffen, gebe,   (268)
Aber bald besinn' ich mich, dass ich dem Grabe
Nah schon stehe, doch noch nichts begriffen habe.

   Dis, ami, qu'ai-je pu acquérir des richesses de ce   **Nicolas**
monde? Rien. Que m'a laissé dans la main le temps   (103)
qui s'est écoulé? Rien. Je suis le flambeau de la
joie; mais une fois ce flambeau éteint, je ne suis plus
rien. Je suis la coupe de Djèm, mais cette coupe une
fois brisée, je ne suis plus rien.

   Tell me, friend, what have I acquired of the riches   **McCarthy**
of this world? — Nothing. What has fleeting time left   (145)
in my hands? — Nothing. I am the torch of joy, but
once the torch is extinct I exist no longer. I am the
cup of Jamshid, but the cup once broken I exist no
more.

See! from the world what profit have I gained?   **Whinfield**
What fruitage of my life in hand retained?   (133)
   What use is Jamshed's goblet, once 'tis crushed?
What pleasure's torch, when once its light has waned.

   For the sake of the reference to "Jamshed's goblet," I
quoted Whinfield, 133, in illustration of FitzGerald, V, p. 11.

Bodenstedt
(X. 6)
	Was hab' ich von den Schätzen dieser Erde gewonnen?
	    Nichts!
	Was blieb in der Hand von der Zeit, die entronnen?
	    Nichts!
	Ich bin ein Freudenfeuer, doch kommt es zum Sterben — Nichts!
	Ich bin ein Lebensbecher, doch bricht er in Scherben — Nichts!

Von Schack
(34)
	Was von allem Erdenreichtum hab' ich nun gewonnen?
	    nichts.
	Was bedeutet nun die Zeit mir, die dahingeronnen?
	    nichts.
	Lustig lodert meines Lebens Fackel, doch, wenn sie erlischt,
	Bin ich selber und sind alle die genoss'nen Wonnen nichts.

Nicolas (76)	Ô homme insouciant! Ce corps de chair n'est rien, cette voûte composée de neuf cieux brillants n'est rien. Livre-toi donc à la joie dans ce lieu où règne le désordre (le monde), car notre vie n'y est attachée que pour un instant, et cet instant n'est également rien.
McCarthy (104)	Heedless man, thy fleshly body is naught, yon vault built up of seven shining heavens is naught. Give thyself up to all delight in this kingdom of misrule, for our life is only bound to it for a moment, and that moment itself is nothing.
Whinfield (79)	O foolish one! this moulded earth is naught, This particoloured vault of heaven is naught; Our sojourn in this seat of life and death Is but one breath, and what is that but naught?

Unwissender Mensch! Dieser Leib, aus Staub **Bodenstedt**
    gewoben, ist Nichts;   (III. 7)
Auch jenes Glanzgewölbe mit seinen neun Himmeln
    dort oben, ist Nichts.
  Darum geniesse die Freuden des flüchtigen Lebens,
Denn auch dies atmende Sein, schnell wie gekommen,
    zerstoben, ist Nichts.

Menschen, o ihr Thoren, Alles, was ihr thut und seid, **Von Schack**
    ist nichts!   (163)
Über euch der sieben Himmel Strahlenherrlichkeit ist
    nichts!
  Drum in dieser Welt, der tollen, weiht der Fröhlich-
    keit eu'r Leben;
Eine Spanne Zeit nur währt es und auch diese Zeit ist
    nichts.

  Suppose que tu aies vécu dans ce monde au gré de **Nicolas**
tes désirs; eh bien! après? Figure-toi que la fin de   (372)
tes jours est arrivée; eh bien! après? J'admets que
tu aies vécu durant cent ans entouré de tout ce que ton
cœur a pu désirer, imagine à ton tour que tu aies cent
autres années à vivre; eh bien! après?

  If in this life you feasted full, what then? Suppose **McCarthy**
the latest of your days has come, what then? If you   (461)
have lived a hundred happy years and have yet a
hundred years to live, what then?

Suppose the world goes well with you, what then?   **Whinfield**
When life's last page is read and turned, what then?   (415)
  Suppose you live a hundred years of bliss,
Yea, and a hundred years besides, what then?

Whinfield, 212 (1882), reads: —

> Suppose you hold the world in fee, what then?
> When life's last page is read and turned, what then?
> You may outlive the present century,
> And haply see the next, but what comes then?

Von Schack (92)
> Nimm an, du wärst zum Ziel gelangt mit allem Streben
> — was alsdann?
> Nimm an, verronnen wäre dir das süsse Leben — was
> alsdann?
> Ich setze, tausend Jahre schon nach Wunsche hättest
> du gelebt,
> Und weit're hundert wollte Gott noch Frist dir geben —
> was alsdann?

Nicolas (47)
> Tu as parcouru le monde, eh bien! tout ce que tu y as vu n'est rien; tout ce que tu y as vu, tout ce que tu y as entendu n'est également rien. Tu es allé d'un bout de l'univers à l'autre, tout cela n'est rien; tu t'es recueilli dans un coin de ta chambre, tout cela n'est encore rien, rien.

McCarthy (66)
> You have wandered upon the face of the earth, but all that you have known is nothing, all that you have seen, all that you have heard, is nothing. Though you travel from world's end to world's end, all that is nothing, although you abide in a corner of your house, all that is nothing.

Whinfield (50)
> You see the world, but all you see is naught,
> And all you say, and all you hear is naught.
> Naught the four quarters of the mighty earth,
> The secrets treasured in your chamber naught.

Hast seen the world? All thou hast seen is naught,   *(16)
All thou hast said, all thou hast heard or wrought,
  Sweep the horizon's verge from pole to pole, t is vain;
Even all thou hast in secret done is naught.

Du sahst die Welt, doch was im Weltenall   **Bodenstedt**
  Zu Deinen Augen kam, ist blosser Schein;   (III. 6)
Du sahst und hörtest viel, doch auch der Schall
  Wie ihn Dein Ohr vernahm, ist blosser Schein;
Von einem Ende dieser Welt zum andern
  Trug Dich Dein Fuss —
Nun ruhst Du aus, sinnst über manchen Fall —
  Was darin wundersam, ist blosser Schein.

Was irgend du hören und seh'n magst, es Alles, Alles   **Von Schack**
  ist nichts!   (138)
Wohin auf Erden du geh'n magst, es Alles, Alles ist
  nichts!
Ob du das Weltall durchfliegest, es Alles, Alles ist nichts!
Ob im Winkel des Stübchens du liegest, es Alles, Alles
  ist nichts!

This ignorance extends beyond "the veil." There are several fine Rubáiyát which might also serve to illustrate Fitz-Gerald's 32nd stanza:—

Personne n'a accès derrière le rideau mystérieux des   **Nicolas**
secrets de Dieu, personne (pas même en esprit) ne peut   (44)
y pénétrer; nous n'avons point d'autre demeure que le
sein de la terre. Ô regret! car c'est là aussi une énigme
non moins difficile à saisir.

McCarthy (19)	No one has ever passed behind the veil that masks the secrets of God. No one shall ever pass behind it; there is no other dwelling-place for us than the bosom of the earth. Woe's me that this secret, too, should be so short.
Whinfield (47)	All mortal ken is bounded by the veil, To see beyond man's sight is all too frail; Yea! earth's dark bosom is his only home;— Alas! 't were long to tell the doleful tale.

Whinfield, 25 (1882), is quite different:—

> Still doth the "veil" man's utmost ken impede,
> And all our fond conjecturings mislead:
> Our only prospect is earth's quiet breast;
> 'Tis given to none the dark beyond to read.

Bodenstedt (IV. 1)	Kein Mensch kann den Schleier der Schöpfung heben, Uns ward nur ein Obdach auf Erden gegeben, Die auch von Geheimnissen so erfüllt, Dass keines Menschen Geist sie enthüllt.
Von Schack (110)	Keiner hat vom Weltgeheimnis je den Schleier noch gehoben; Uns'res Geistes Auge, ringshin ach! mit Nacht ist es umwoben; Einen sichern Wohnort haben wir allein, im Erdenschoss; Ach! wie viel wir sinnen mögen, dieses Rätsel ist zu gross.

And again:—

Personne n'a eu accès derrière le rideau du destin ; **Nicolas**
personne n'a eu connaissance des secrets de la Provi- (177)
dence. Durante soixante et douze ans j'ai jour et nuit
réfléchi ; je n'ai pourtant rien appris, et l'énigme est
restée inexpliquée.

No one has ever drawn aside the veil of Fate. To **McCarthy**
no one are the hidden things of the divine wisdom made 284)
known. For seventy-two years I have thought thereon,
by day and night, but I have learned nothing, and the
enigma remaineth unsolved.

What eye can pierce the veil of God's decrees, **Whinfield**
Or read the riddle of earth's destinies? (192)
   Pondered have I for years threescore and ten,
But still am baffled by these mysteries.

Whinfield, 104 (1882), has in line 1, *heaven's decrees*.

The Ways of God are veiled from Human Ken, **Garner**
Yes, Night and Day, 'tis three score years and ten, (VIII. 2)
   That I have pondered o'er them,—but in vain,—
My Thoughts have ne'er been cleared by Tongue or
    Pen.

Niemand kann hinter den Vorhang des Schicksals **Bodenstedt**
   sehen, (IV. 11)
Niemand der Vorsehung Ratschluss verstehen.
Zweiundsiebzig Jahre lang forscht' ich eifrigen Strebens,
Ohne zu lernen, ohne zu lösen die Rätsel des Lebens.

Von Schack
(117)

Hinter den geheimnissvollen Vorhang drang noch nie
    ein Blick.
Keiner hob noch je den Schleier, der verhüllt das
    Weltgeschick;
Zweiundsiebzig Jahre hab' ich Tag und Nacht darob
    gesonnen,
Doch das Rätsel blieb mir dunkel und mein Leben ist
    verronnen.

Compare with the above this fine passage from Victor Hugo in his description of the Charnel-house at Bordeaux:—

Ils savent ce qu'il y a derrière la vie. Ils connaissent le secret du voyage. Ils ont doublé le promontoire. Le grand nuage s'est déchiré pour eux. Nous sommes encore, nous, dans le pays des conjectures, des espérances, des ambitions, des passions, de toutes les folies que nous appelons sagesses, de toutes les chimères que nous nommons vérités. Eux, ils sont entrés dans la région de l'infini, de l'immuable, de la réalité.

(They know what there is behind life. They have learned the secret of the long journey. They have doubled the cape. For them the mighty veil is torn. We are still in the land of conjectures, of hopes, of ambitions, of passions, of all the follies which we call wisdom, of all the illusions which we designate as truths. They have entered into the region of the infinite, of the immutable, of reality.)

This may be contrasted with the hopelessness of Psalm cxv. 17:—

    "The dead praise not the Lord,
    Neither any that go down into silence;"

or of Ecclesiastes (Koheleth) viii. 4, 5, 10:—

"For to him that is joined with all the living there is hope: for a living dog is better than a dead lion. For the living know that they shall die: but the dead know not anything, neither have they any more a reward; for the memory of them is forgotten ... for there is no work, nor device, nor knowledge, nor wisdom, in the grave whither thou goest."

APPENDIX XII.

RUBÁIYÁT XXIX AND XXX.

Whinfield, 80 (1882), is quite different from 145 (1883):

> They bring us hither to our sore undoing,
> And while we stay, we find but grief and rueing;
> And last we go against our wills, nor know
> The reason of our coming, nor our going.

Puisque les choses ne doivent pas se passer suivant nos désirs, à quoi servent nos desseins et nos efforts? Nous sommes constamment à nous tourmenter et à nous dire en soupirant de regret: Ah! nous sommes arrivés trop tard, trop tôt il nous faudra partir! — **Nicolas** (41)

Since life seldom answers to our heart's desire, of what avail are all our hopes and all our strivings? Our spirits are always vexed, always are we saying in sighing, "Too late we came, too soon we must depart." — **McCarthy** (16)

Facts will not change to humour man's caprice.
So vaunt not human powers, but hold your peace;
Here must we stay, weighed down with grief for this,
That we were born so late, so soon decease. — **Whinfield** (45)

Von Hammer-Purgstall	Da Nichts nach unserm Wunsche geht im Leben Was nützen Müh', Gedanken und Bestreben! Ich sitz gedankenvoll darob in Wehen; Dass ich seit langem kam, und schnell muss gehen.
Bodenstedt (V. 3)	Da die Dinge nicht werden nach unsern Entwürfen, Und wir selbst nicht recht wissen, was wir bedürfen, So klagen wir stets bei verlorener Müh': Wir kamen zu spät und wir scheiden zu früh.
Von Schack (324)	Da die Dinge sich auf Erden nie nach unser'm Wunsch gestalten, Was bemüh'n wir uns und ringen wider des Geschickes Walten? Immer seufzen wir und klagen, hadernd mit des Himmels Schlüssen: "Ach dass wir zu spät gekommen! dass zu früh wir scheiden müssen."

APPENDIX XIII.

RUBÁIYÁT XXXIII AND XLIX.

Persia being an inland country, Omar rarely refers to the ocean; the following fine Rubá'iy is the principal one among 500:—

Nicolas (365)	La goutte d'eau s'est mise à pleurer en se plaignant d'être séparée de l'Océan. L'Océan s'est mis à rire en lui disant: "C'est nous qui sommes tout; en vérité, il n'y a point en dehors de nous d'autre Dieu, et si nous sommes séparés, ce n'est que par un simple point presque invisible."

The drop of water sorrowed to be sundered from the   **McCarthy**
ocean. Ocean smiling said, "We are all in all, God   (439)
is within and around us, and we are divided but by
an imperceptible point.

The drop wept for his severance from the sea,   **Whinfield**
But the sea smiled, for " I am all " said he,   (410)
  " The Truth is all, nothing exists beside,
That one point circling apes plurality."

In Whinfield, 210 (1882), the last two lines read :—

    " And naught exists outside my unity,
      My one point circling apes plurality."

Der Tropfen hat ob seiner Trennung vom Weltmeer **Bodenstedt**
    geklagt,   (I. 1)
Drauf hat lächelnd das Weltmeer zum Tropfen gesagt :
Wir sind Eins in der Gottheit, in Wahrheit untrennbar,
Was zu trennen uns scheint, ist ein Punkt kaum
    erkennbar.

Der Wassertropfen klagte, dass getrennt er sei vom **Von Schack**
    Ocean,   (120)
Doch lachend sprach der Ocean : "Um was du klagst,
    das ist ein Wahn,
Denn ich bin Alles, was da ist ; kein and'rer Gott ist
    ausser mir ;
Und, wenn getrennt wir sind, so trennt mich nur ein
    kleiner Punkt von dir."

A similar idea occurs in Attár's Bird-Parliament:

> "The Sun of my Perfection is a Glass,
> Wherein from *Seeing* into Being pass
> All who, reflecting as reflected see
> Themselves in Me and Me in Them: not *me*
> But all of Me, that a contracted Eye
> Is comprehensive of Infinity:
> Nor yet *Themselves:* no Selves but of The All
> Fractions, from which they split and whither fall.
> As Water lifted from the Deep, again
> Falls back in individual Drops of Rain
> Then melts into the Universal Main."
> *FitzGerald's Translation.*

In the Persian the words for *separated* and *God* are distinguishable only by a dot, or point, placed in the one under, in the other over, the initial letter. Hence the point of the Rubá'iy, which is untranslatable. Moreover, the Table Land of *One* and *Wonder* blazes with such a sun of unity that it both

> "blinds and reveals
> The Universe that to a Point Congeals."

The same or a similar pun is found in Rubá'iy XLIX, p. 98.

APPENDIX XIV.

RUBÁ'IY XXXVII.

FitzGerald says in his note (14) : —

"One of the Persian Poets — Attár, I think — has a pretty story about this. A thirsty Traveller dips his hand into a Spring of Water to drink from. By-and-by comes another who draws up and drinks from an earthen bowl, and then departs, leaving his Bowl behind him. The first Traveller takes it up for another draught; but is surprised to find that the same Water which had tasted sweet from his own hand tastes bitter from the earthen Bowl. But a Voice — from Heaven, I think — tells him the clay from which the Bowl is made was once *Man*; and, into whatever shape renew'd, can never lose the bitter flavour of Mortality."

Here is FitzGerald's own translation of the passage in question:—

> One day the Prophet on a River Bank,
> Dipping his Lips into the Channel, drank
> A Draught as sweet as Honey. Then there came
> One who an earthen Pitcher from the same
> Drew up, and drank: and after some short stay
> Under the Shadow, rose and went his Way,
> Leaving his earthen Bowl. In which, anew
> Thirsting, the Prophet from the River drew
> And drank from: but the Water that came up
> Sweet from the Stream, drank bitter from the Cup.
> At which the Prophet in a still Surprise
> For Answer turning up to Heav'n his Eyes,
> The Vessel's Earthen Lips with Answer ran —
> " The Clay that I am made of once was *Man*,
> Who dying, and resolved into the same
> Obliterated Earth from which he came
> Was for the Potter dug and chased in turn
> Through long Vicissitude of Bowl and Urn:
> But howsoever moulded, still the Pain
> Of that first mortal Anguish would retain,
> And cast and re-cast, for a Thousand years
> Would turn the sweetest Water into Tears."
>   *Mantik-ut-tair*, or *Bird-Parliament*.

The human clay transformed into a pot, conscious or unconscious of its origin, is a favorite conceit with Omar, and several forms of it, in various versions, follow. Rubá'iy XXXVIII has the same thought also.

Ô potier! sois attentif, si tu possèdes la saine raison; jusques à quand aviliras-tu l'homme en pétrissant sa boue? C'est le doigt de Féridoun, c'est la main de Kéy-Khosrov que tu mets ainsi sur ta roue. Oh! à quoi penses-tu donc ?   **Nicolas** (395)

McCarthy (460)	O Potter, have a care if you are wise, how long will you degrade the clay of man? It is the finger of Feridoun, it is the hand of Kai-Khosrou, that you place upon the wheel. What are you thinking of?
Whinfield (437) (225, 1882)	Ah, potter, stay thine hand! with ruthless art Put not to such base use man's mortal part! See, thou art mangling on thy cruel wheel Faridun's fingers, and Kai Khosrau's heart!
Garner (VII 4)	The Potter heeds no silent Tongue's appeal, His Hands no Tender Mercy ever feel, Though 't is Feridun's Heart,— Kai-Kosrú's Head, That whirls in Anguish on his rapid Wheel.
Bodonstedt (VIII. 75)	O Töpfer, bedenk', was Du thust, wenn Du klug bist, Da Du so mit Entwürdigung des Menschen im Zug bist: Du räderst die Glieder der Weltbezwinger, Kai Chossrew's Hand und Feridun's Finger!
Von Schack (107)	O Töpfer! halt ein mit deinem Frevelthun! Zu schänden den Menschenstaub, ist das erlaubt? Jetzt knetest du den Finger des Feridun! Jetzt trittst du mit Füssen des grossen Kai Chosru Haupt!

Nicolas (404)	Hier au soir j'ai brisé contre une pierre la coupe en faïence. J'étais ivre en commettant cet acte d'insensé. Cette coupe semblait me dire: — " J'ai été semblable à toi, tu seras à ton tour semblable à moi."

Last eve I broke against a stone an earthen cup,   McCarthy
drunk in the doing of this foolish deed. Methought   (395)
the cup protested unto me "I was like thee, thou wilt
be like to me."

Last night I dashed my cup against a stone,   Whinfield
In a mad drunken freak, as I must own,   (449)
  And lo! the cup cries out in agony,
"You too, like me, shall soon be overthrown."

  Whinfield, 231 (1882), reads:—
    And lo! the cup cried, "You who treat me so
    One of these days you shall be overthrown."

Last Night I broke my Cup against a stone,   Garner
An Act of Madness I must e'er bemoan;—   (II. 1)
  'Ah, knowest thou not, that I was once a Man?'
The Fragments asked of me in plaintive tone.

Einen Krug zerschlug ich gestern an einem Steine,   Bodenstedt
Ich war berauscht von desselbigen Kruges Weine.   (VIII. 77)
Der Krug schien zu sagen: Du, durch den ich verletzt
    bin,
Ich war einst wie Du, Du wirst sein, wie ich jetz bin.

Meinen thongeformten Becher brach ich gestern Nacht   Von Shack
    entzwei;   (42)
Trunken bin ich wohl gewesen, und mir däuchte, einen
    Schrei
Hört' ich durch des Bechers Scherben, die am Boden
    lagen, schleichen:
"Deinesgleichen war ich ehmals; morgen bist du mein-
    esgleichen."

  See the Rubáiyát in the Kúza-náma, or Book of Pots
(LXXXII-XC), and appendices.

APPENDIX XV.

RUBÁ'IY XXXIX.

FitzGerald's note (15) is as follows: —

The custom of throwing a little Wine on the ground before drinking still continues in Persia, and perhaps generally in the East. Mons. Nicolas considers it "un signe de libéralité, et en même temps un avertissement que le buveur doit vider sa coupe jusqu'à la dernière goutte." Is it not more likely an ancient Superstition; a Libation to propitiate Earth, or make her an Accomplice in the illicit Revel? Or, perhaps, to divert the Jealous Eye by some sacrifice of superfluity, as with the Ancients of the West? With Omar we see something more is signified; the precious Liquor is not lost, but sinks into the ground to refresh the dust of some poor Wine-worshipper foregone.

Thus Háfiz, copying Omar in so many ways: "When thou drinkest Wine pour a draught on the ground. Wherefore fear the Sin which brings to another Gain?"

The quotation from Nicolas is found in a note to his translation of Rubá'iy 247: —

Nicolas (247)   Bien que le vin soit défendu, bois-en sans cesse, bois en soir et matin, bois-en au bruit des chansons, au son de la harpe. Quand tu pourras t'en procurer, de celui-là qui brille comme le rubis, jettes-en une goutte à terre et bois tout le reste.

Although wine is forbidden, cease not to drink thereof. **McCarthy**
Drink, by morning and eventide, drink to the sound of (136)
song, and to the melody of the harp. When thou hast
procured wine glowing like the ruby, pour one drop on
the earth, and drink the rest.

Though wine is banned, yet drink, forever drink ! **Whinfield**
By day and night, with strains of music drink ! (286)
  Where'er thou lightest on a cup of wine,
Spill just one drop, and take the rest, and drink !

Ob der Wein auch verboten, trink Du ohne Zwang. **Bodenstedt**
Am Morgen und Abend, bei Spiel und Gesang. (IX. 24)
Wo rubinfarb'ner Wein Dich ladet zum Fest
Giess einen Tropfen zu Boden und trinke den Rest.

APPENDIX XVI.

RUBÁ'IY XLI.

It is quite possible that FitzGerald combined two Rubáiyát into number XLI. The following have the same idea variously expressed: —

Pour toi, ce qu'il y a de mieux, c'est de fuir l'étude **Nicolas**
des sciences et la dévotion ; c'est de t'accrocher à la (359)
chevelure d'une ravissante amie ; c'est de verser dans
la coupe le sang de la vigne avant que le temps ait versé
le tien.

McCarthy
(508)

Flee from the lessons of learning and piety, turn to the tresses round the lovely face, spill the blood of the vine in your cup before time spills thy blood on the earth.

Whinfield
(426)

Vain study of philosophy eschew!
Rather let tangled curls attract your view;
And shed the bottle's life-blood in your cup,
Or e'er death shed your blood, and feast on you.

Bodenstedt
(VIII. 62)

Flieh' den Bücherstaub und die Heuchlerpest,
Und halte Dich an den Locken der Schönheit fest.
Eh die Zeit Dein eignes Blut vergiesst,
Sorg', dass Dir das Blut der Rebe noch fliesst.

Von Schack
(241)

Der Arbeit und der Frömmigkeit den Rücken kehren das ist gescheit;
Die Zeit verbringen bei schönen Frau'n, die Huld uns gewähren, das ist gescheit
Verrinnen lassen wird in den Staub die Zeit bald unser Lebensblut,
Darum den Becher voll Rebenblut zuvor zu leeren, das ist gescheit.

A somewhat similar figure occurs in the following Rubá'iy, which has an untranslatable pun; the Persian word for tresses (*boucles*) and that for sinews (*articulations*) being the same:—

Nicolas
(155)

Bois du vin avant que ton nom ait disparu de ce monde, car dès que ce nectar sera entré dans ton cœur, le chagrin en sortira. Dénoue boucle par boucle les cheveux d'une charmante idole, avant que les articulations de tes propres os soient elles-mêmes dénouées.

Drink wine, before thy name has vanished from the world, for when that nectar floweth into thy heart, care will depart therefrom. Unbind the tresses of the loved one's hair before the sinews of thy own bones are themselves unbound. — **McCarthy** (282)

Trink Wein, der Dir das Herz erhellt, — **Bodenstedt** (VIII. 25)
Eh' Dein Name verschwindet aus dieser Welt.
Löse der jungen Huldinnen Locken,
Eh' Deine Glieder die Grabwürmer locken.

Trink Wein, so lang dein Name noch nicht aus der Welt verschwunden ist, — **Von Schack** (112)
Verscheuchen wird der Himmelstrank die Trübsal dir nach kurzer Frist!
Locke an Locke löse sanft auf einer Schönen Haupt das Haar,
Eh Glied an Glied in Staub gelös't dein Leib sich hat für immerdar!

See also Appendix XLII to Rubá'iy XCIII.

The cypress was a favorite tree with the Oriental poets. Here are several of the Rubáiyát in which it is effectively introduced:—

Lorsque tu seras en compagnie d'une belle à taille de cyprès, au teint plus frais que la rose nouvellement cueillie, ne t'éloigne pas des fleurs de la prairie, ne laisse point échapper la coupe de ta main ; (fais cela) avant que l'aquilon de la mort, semblable au vent qui disperse les feuilles de roses, mette en lambeau l'enveloppe de ton être. — **Nicolas** (257)

McCarthy (228)	When you find yourself in the fellowship of some cypress-slender girl, more tender-tinted than the early rose, do not hold aloof from the flowers of the meadow, do not let the cup fall from your hand before the Angel of death, like unto the wild wind that scatters abroad the rose-leaves, tears asunder the veil of thy existence.
Whinfield (298)	With maids stately as cypresses, and fair As roses newly plucked, your wine-cups share, Or e'er Death's blasts shall rend your robe of flesh Like yonder rose leaves, lying scattered there!
Bodenstedt (IX. 20)	In frischer Menschenblumen Geleit Lass auch Wein und die Blumen der Flur nicht weit! Eh der Todeswind Dein Lebensgewand Wie die Blumen zerreisst mit rauher Hand.

Nicolas (45)	J'ai bien longtemps cherché dans ce monde d'inconstance qui nous sert un moment d'asile ; j'ai employé dans mes recherches toutes les facultés dont je suis doué ; eh bien! j'ai trouvé que la lune pâlit devant l'éclat de ton visage, que le cyprès est difforme à côté de ta taille élancée.
McCarthy (5)	Long time I sought in this shifting world for a moment's halting-place. I spent in my endeavours all my wit, and lo! I learn that the moon is but a pallid wheel beside thy beauty, that the cypress, by thy slender form, seems a grotesque deformity.

This faithless world, my home, I have surveyed, Whinfield
Yea, and with all my wit deep question made, (48)
   But found no moon with face so bright as thine,
No cypress in such stateliness arrayed.

Durchforscht hab' ich die unbeständige Welt, Bodenstedt
   Die wir so kurz bewohnen, ohne Ruh, (VI. 1
Doch fand ich keinen Stern am Himmelzelt,
   Auf Erden keine Blume schön wie Du!

In dieser Welt, wo Alles vorbei uns flieht in hurtiger Von Schack
   Flucht, (31)
Hab' ich mit Eifer und emsigen Blick geforscht und
   umhergesucht;
Und was ich gefunden ist dies: der Mond erbleicht
   vor deinem Gesichte,
Plump ist, verglichen mit deinem Wuchs, die schlankste
   Bergesfichte.

   Bien que ma personne soit belle, que le parfum qui Nicolas
s'en exhale soit agréable, que le teint de ma figure (13)
rivalise avec celui de la tulipe, et que ma taille soit
élancée comme celle d'un cyprès, il ne m'a pas été
démontré, cependant, pourquoi mon céleste peintre a
daigné m'ébaucher sur cette terre.

   Although my body may be comely, although its odour McCarthy
may be suave, although my colour may mock the tulip, (26)
and my figure shame the cypress, it is not clear to me,
nevertheless, why my heavenly painter has deigned to
limn me on this world.

M. K.	Howe'er with beauty's hue and bloom endow'd I be,
	Of tulip-cheek and cypress-form though proud I be;
	Yet know I not why the Limner chose that, here, in this
	Mint-house of clay, amid the painted crowd I be!
Whinfield	What though 'tis fair to view, this form of man,
(12)	I know not why the heavenly Artisan
	Hath set these tulip cheeks and cypress forms
	To deck the mournful halls of earth's divan.
(6, 1882)	What though 'tis fair to see, this form of man,
	What caused Thee, O heavenly Artisan,
	To paint these tulip cheeks and cypress forms
	Here on the lowly walls of earth's divan?
Bodenstedt	Schlank wie die Cypresse seh ich Dich prangen,
(VI. 3)	Von gutem Geruch, zart wie Tulpen die Wangen,
	Doch bleibt mir's ein Rätsel, warum in die Wildnis
	Des Lebens der Schöpfer gezaubert Dein Bildnis.
Von Shack	Sei noch so schön ein Menschenbild, an Anmut und an Zierde reich,
(6/6)	Sei wie die Tulpe sein Gesicht, sein hoher Wuchs cypressengleich,
	Nicht Einer doch, so viel du fragst, kann Antwort geben dir zuletzt,
	Aus welchem Grund sein Bildner es auf diese Erde hat versetzt.

Nicolas	Sais-tu pourquoi le cyprès et le lis ont acquis la réputation de liberté dont ils, jouissent parmi les hommes? C'est que celui-ci, ayant six langues, reste muet, et que celui-là, possédant cent mains, les tient raccourcies.
(373)	

Knowest thou why the lily and the cypress have such **McCarthy**
fair renown with men? Because the one, with ten (462)
tongues, is silent; because the other with a hundred
hands, keeps them from picking and stealing.

How is it that of all the leafy tribe, **Whinfield**
Cypress and lily men as " free " describe? (416)
This has a dozen tongues, yet holds her peace,
That has a hundred hands which take no bribe.

Whinfield, 213 (1882), begins:—
   Alone of all the vegetable tribe,
and ends:—
   And that as many hands which grasp no bribe.

Weisst Du, warum die Cypresse wird Baum der Freiheit **Bodenstedt**
 genannt? (V. 29)
Und warum auch die Lilie als Blume der Freiheit
 bekannt?
Hundert Arme hat jene und greift doch nicht um sich,
Und zehn Zungen hat diese und hält doch stumm sich.

Whinfield quotes Sadi's "Gulistan," translated by
Eastwick (p. 306).

" They asked a philosopher why, when God Most High had
created so many famous fruitful trees, the cypress alone was
called 'free,' which bore no fruit? He replied, 'Every tree
has its appointed time and season wherein it flourishes, and
when that is past it droops. But the cypress is not exposed
to either of these vicissitudes, and is at all times fresh and
green, and this is the condition of the free.' "

APPENDIX XVII.

RUBÁ'IY LI.

The following Rubá'iy should, of course, have accompanied FitzGerald's fifty-first stanza. "M. K." says that the original is not found, and G. C. M. Smith, who, July 23, 1889, contributed to *The Academy* a very frequently misleading parallel between McCarthy's and FitzGerald's versions, ignores it. To atone for the too-late discovery, I venture to repeat FitzGerald's quatrain from his second edition : —

FitzGerald
(LII.)
1868

Whose secret presence, through Creation's veins
Running, quicksilver-like eludes your pains;
   Taking all shapes from Máh to Máhi; and
They change and perish all — but He remains.

Nicolas
(73)

Ce vin qui, par son essence, est susceptible d'apparaître sous une foule de formes, qui se manifeste tantôt sous la forme d'un animal, tantôt sous celle d'une plante, ne va pas croire pour cela qu'il puisse ne plus être et que son essence puisse être anéantie ; car c'est par elle qu'il est, bien que les formes disparaissent.

McCarthy
(58)

Although this wine in its essence is capable of taking a thousand shapes, assuming now the form of an animal, now the form of a plant, do not therefore believe that it can ever cease to be, and that its essence can be destroyed, for there is the reality when the shadows disappear.

The very wine, a myriad form sustains, **Whinfield**
And to take shapes of plants and creatures deigns; (75)
   But deem not that its essence ever dies,
Its forms may perish, but its self remains.

This Spirit which the Universe contains, **Garner**
Shines in the Rose, then in the Lion reigns, (IX. 1)
   Although the Outward Forms may pass away,
The Spirit still remains, yes still remains.

Dieser Wein, dessen Geist vielgestaltiger Art **Bodenstedt**
In der Pflanze sich gleichwie im Tier offenbart, (I. 32)
Bleibt immer derselbe, ein ewiges Eins,
Nur wechselnd die Formen des schwingenden Seins.

Dieser Wein, der in verschied'nen Formen sich den **Von Schack**
    Sinnen weis't, (52)
Bald als Saft in Reben, bald in Menschenadern kreis't,
Fürchte nicht, dass er verschwinden jemals könne
    sonder Spur,
Seine Wesenheit ist ewig, seine Formen wechseln nur.

The comparison of quick-silver apparently comes from the following: —

   Mets une coupe de vin dans ma main, car mon cœur **Nicolas**
est enflammé, et cette vie fuit comme fuit le vif-argent. (54)
Lève-toi donc, car la faveur de la fortune n'est qu'un
songe; lève-toi, car le feu de la jeunesse s'échappe
comme l'eau du torrent.

   (Or: le réveil de la fortune n'est qu'un sommeil.)

McCarthy
(37)

Place the wine-cup in my hand, for my heart is all afire and life slips from us swift as quicksilver. Arise, my beloved, for the favour of fortune is but a cheating dream, arise, for the flame of youth gushes like the water of the torrent.

Whinfield
(57)

Bring wine! my heart with dancing spirits teems,
Wake! fortune's waking is as fleeting dreams;
 Quicksilver-like our days are swift of foot,
And youthful fire subsides as torrent streams.

Bodenstedt
(IX. 51)

Füll' mir den Becher, mein Herz steht in Flammen,
Und wie Quecksilber nur hält das Leben zusammen.
Des Glückes Erwachen ist nur ein Traum,
Und das Feuer der Jugend zerstiebt wie Schaum.

Von Schack
(55)

Den Wein her! ich kann ihn erwarten kaum,
 Denn ach! wie währt das Leben so kurz!
Auf! auf! das Glück ist nichts als ein Traum,
 Und die Jugend verrauscht wie ein Wogensturz.

In line 3, "Mah to Mahi": this expression means "from Fish to Moon." "God," says Attar, — quoted by FitzGerald in a note to his translation of the Mantik-ut-Tair, — "God has placed the Earth on the back of the Bull: and the Bull on the Fish; but the Fish on what? On Nothing; but nothing comes of Nothing, and therefore all this is nothing." In other words, "all the visible and material Universe merges into an abstract essence of Deity." In other versions the Bull bears the earth on one of its horns.

The same expression appears in Garner (VI. 20):—

Away with all that grieves the soul, for soon
We leave this World, where Wine the richest Boon
  Of Mortals is, a single Draught outvies
Whatever lies betwixt the Fish and Moon.

See Rubá'iy LXXV and Appendix XXXI.

APPENDIX XVIII.

RUBÁ'IY LIII.

The following Rubá'iy has an equally melancholy note, but a finer, more powerful image:—

Que de gens plongés dans le sommeil je vois sur la surface de cette terre! Que de gens j'aperçois déjà enfouis dans son sein! Quand je jette les yeux sur le désert du néant, que de gens j'y vois qui ne sont pas encore venus! que de gens qui sont déjà partis! — Nicolas (274)

How many men do I behold plunged in the sleep of ignorance upon the earth, how many already buried in its bosom! When I cast my eyes over this desert of nothingness, how many souls do I see who have not yet arrived — how many who have already departed! — McCarthy (243)

On earth's green carpet many sleepers lie,
And hid beneath it others I descry;
  And others, not yet come, or passed away,
People the desert of Nonentity! — Whinfield (317)

Bodenstedt Wie viel schläfrige Menschen seh' ich auf Erden hier!
(VIII. 91) Wie viele Schläfer ruhen schon unter ihr!
Wie viel werden noch schläfrigen Angesichts
Wandern durch diese Wüste des Nichts!

Von Schack Auf der Erde wie viel Menschen seh' ich, die in
(230) Schlummer liegen!
Unter ihr wie Viele, welche schon in's Grab hinabgestiegen!
Und im Nichts, der grossen Wüste, der Gewesenen wie viel
Sieht mein Auge! o von Solchen, die noch kommen, welch Gewühl!

See also last four Rubáiyát in Appendix XI.

APPENDIX XIX.

RUBÁ'IY LIV.

M. K. declares the original of this quatrain is "not found;" it may be compounded of several. There is a hint of it in the following:—

Nicolas Tu ne peux te flatter aujourd'hui de voir le jour de
(26) demain; penser même à ce demain serait de ta part pure folie; si tu as le cœur éveillé ne perds pas dans l'inaction cet instant de vie (qui te reste) et pour la durée duquel je ne vois aucune preuve.

McCarthy You cannot assure yourself to-day that you shall
(76) behold tomorrow's dawn; even to dwell upon tomorrow is mere madness; if your heart is wide awake, do not waste in torpor this little pinch of life, for there is no proof how long it shall abide with you.

To-day is thine to spend, but not to-morrow, **Whinfield**
Counting on morrows breedeth naught but sorrow; (30)
 Oh! squander not this breath that heaven hath lent
   thee,
Nor make too sure another breath to borrow!

 In Whinfield, 15 (1882), line 2 has *bankrupt sorrow*, line 4
begins: *Make not too sure.*

No, From the Future, Hope thou ne'er shouldst borrow, **Garner**
The very Thought would fill thy Heart with Sorrow, (II. 9)
 Lose not the Present Moment in Repining,
For 'tis not known that we shall see the Morrow.

Nicht hoffe heute auf den nächsten Tag! **Von Schack**
Ein Thor ist wer an ihn nur denken mag. (273)
 Den Atem nütze, den du eben thust,
Denn bald vielleicht stockt deines Herzens Schlag!

The following illustrate the first two lines of the FitzGerald stanza:—

Garde-toi de soumettre ton corps aux chagrins et à la **Nicolas**
douleur dans le but d'acquérir de l'argent blanc et de (187)
l'or jaune. Mange en compagnie de tes amis, avant
que ton tiède souffle se refroidisse, car après toi ce sont
tes ennemis qui mangeront.

Give not thyself over to care and to grief in the hope **McCarthy**
of gaining yellow or white money in the end. Enjoy (93)
thyself with thy companions, before thy warm breath
becomes cold, for thy enemies will feast in thy room
when thou art departed.

Whinfield
(201)

O burden not thyself with drudgery,
Lord of white silver and red gold to be;
   But feast with friends, ere this warm breath of thine
Be chilled in death, and earthworms feast on thee.

Bodenstedt
(VIII. 31)

Quäle nicht zu sehr Leib und Sinn
Um weissen Silbers und gelben Goldes Gewinn.
Speis' mit Freunden, eh' Dir der Odem vergangen;
Später werden Deine Feinde zum Speisen gelangen.

Von Schack
(234)

Mit Freunden, statt dich um Gold und Silber zu mühen,
   Sei froh bei'm Weine! noch bist du lebensfrisch,
Bald aber wird dein süsser Odem entfliehen,
   Und deine Feinde setzen sich an den Tisch.

In the same spirit old John Heywood gayly sings:—

    Let the world slide, let the world go;
    A fig for care, and a fig for woe!
    If I can't pay, why I can owe,
    And death makes equal the high and low.

Compare Bion: Εἰδύλλιον V:—

εἰ δὲ θεοὶ κατένουσαν ἕνα χρόνον ἐς βίον ἐλθεῖν
ἀνθρώποις καὶ τόνδε βραχὺν καὶ μῄονα πάντων
ἐς πόσον ἆ δειλοὶ καμάτως κ' εἰς ἔργα πονεῦμες;

    And if the gods have granted unto man
    To live but one life's brief unavailing span,
      How long, alas, shall we hapless slaves of fate
    Be forced in strenuous endeavor to labor and plan!

And says "the Preacher": "He that loveth silver shall not be satisfied with silver; nor he that loveth abundance with increase: this also is vanity" (v. 10). But a little later he says: "Go thy way, eat thy bread with joy, and drink thy wine with a merry heart; for God hath already accepted thy works. Let thy garments be always white and let not thy head lack ointment" (ix. 7, 8). Strange echoes thundering down from dim and distant ages! But listen to Omar again:—

Ô toi qui es le résumé de la création universelle! Nicolas
cesse donc un instant de te préoccuper de gain ou de (319)
perte; prends une coupe de vin, de la main de l'échanson éternel, et affranchis-toi ainsi à la fois et des soucis
de ce monde et de ceux de l'autre.

O thou, the quintessence of the sum of existence, McCarthy
cease a moment to think upon evil gain, take one cup (415)
of wine from the Eternal Saki, and set thyself free
from the care of both worlds.

O man, who art creation's summary, Whinfield
Getting and spending too much trouble thee! (362)
   Arise, and quaff the Etern Cupbearer's wine,
And so from troubles of both worlds be free!

   Whinfield, 190 (1882), has the following variant:—

> O man, creation's glorious summary,
> Gaining and spending . . .
> And live from life's annoys forever free.

(Wordsworth: "The world is too much with us.")

Bodenstedt (VIII. 30)

Mensch, der Du ein Auszug der ganzen atmenden Welt bist,
Was soll's, dass Du nur auf Gewinn und Verlust gestellt bist?
Nähr' Deinen Geist mit Wein aus der Hand des ewigen Schenken,
Und hör' auf in Sorgen an Himmel und Erde zu denken.

Von Schack (70)

O du, der Schöpfung Inbegriff, lass ab vom nieder'n Tand,
Und an Gewinn und an Verlust denk ferner nicht auf Erden!
Empfang den Becher, den dir heut des ew'gen Schenken Hand,
Um von den Sorgen dieser Welt und jener frei zu werden!

APPENDIX XX.

RUBÁ'IY LV.

The law of the Koran allows one of the faithful to marry a woman for the third time after he has twice repudiated her. See Koran, chapter entitled "The Cow."

Ye may divorce *your wives* twice, and then either retain *them* with humanity, or dismiss them with kindness. . . . But if *the husband* divorce her *a third time*, she shall not be lawful for him again, until she marry another husband. But if he *also* divorce her, it shall be no crime in them if they return to each other, if they think they can observe the ordinances of God! — Chap. II. p. 24 (*George Sale's Translation*).

The wine is the daughter of the grape or of the vine.
The same idea recurs in : —

Ne donne point dans ton esprit libre accès à des **Nicolas**
pensées impossibles. Bois du vin durant des années, (250)
et toujours la coupe pleine jusqu'au bord. Sois em-
pressé auprès de la fille de la vigne et réjouis-toi, car
il vaut mieux user de la fille défendue que de la mère
permise.

(Mussulman mollahs allow the faithful to eat grapes, a fruit
which in the poetic language of the Orient is to the wine what a
mother is to its daughter.)

Do not suffer vain thoughts to enter the gate of **McCarthy**
your mind. Drink while the years drive by, let the (232)
cup be always full to the lips. Pay your court to the
daughter of the vine, and be glad, for it is better to
enjoy the forbidden daughter than the permitted
mother.

Cast off dull care, O melancholy brother! **Whinfield**
Woo the sweet daughter of the grape, no other; (299)
   The daughter is forbidden, it is true,
But she is nicer than her lawful mother!

Verwirre Dein Hirn nicht durch unnützes Gegrübel. **Bodenstedt**
Such immer nur im Wein die Heilung aller Übel. (IX. 31)
Ein von der Tochter der Rebe heimlich geraubter Kuss
Ist besser als ein von der Mutter Jedem erlaubter Kuss.

Compare :—

'T is well to drink, and leave anxiety **Whinfield**
For what is past, and what is yet to be ; (308)
   Our prisoned spirits, lent us for a day,
A while from reason's bondage shall go free!

Von Schack
(228)

Der Gegenwart nicht denkend, noch an das Vergang'ne,
  Lasst uns bei'm Trunk, ihr Freunde, der Lust uns weih'n,
Damit wir unsere Seele, die arme Gefang'ne,
  Auf kurz von den Fesseln der Vernunft befrei'n!

APPENDIX XXI.

RUBÁ'IY LVI.

FitzGerald's note numbered 14 to quatrain XLI of the first edition was merely these words: "A laugh at his mathematics perhaps," in previous editions. He afterwards amplified it as follows (18):—

A Jest, of course, at his Studies. A curious mathematical Quatrain of Omar's has been pointed out to me; the more curious because almost exactly parallel'd by some Verses of Doctor Donne's, that are quoted in Izaak Walton's Lives! Here is Omar: "You and I are the image of a pair of compasses; though we have two heads (sc. our *feet*) we have one body; when we have fixed the centre for our circle, we bring our heads (sc. feet) together at the end." Dr. Donne:

> If we be two, we two are so
>   As stiff twin-compasses are two;
> Thy Soul, the fixt foot, makes no show
>   To move, but does if the other do.
>
> And though thine in the centre sit,
>   Yet when my other far does roam,
> Thine leans and hearkens after it,
>   And grows erect as mine comes home.

> Such thou must be to me, who must
> Like the other foot obliquely run;
> Thy firmness makes my circle just,
> And me to end where I begun.

Professor C. E. Norton, in his copy of Edition II, makes marginal corrections of the quotation from Dr. Donne. In Stanza I, line 4, *does* should be *doth*, and the second stanza should read:—

> And though it in the center sit,
> Yet when the other far doth roam,
> It leans and hearkens after it,
> And grows erect as that comes home.

The compass quatrain may be read in various versions:—

Ô mon âme! nous formons à nous deux le parallèle d'un compas. Bien que nous ayons deux pointes, nous ne faisons qu'un corps. Actuellement, nous tournons sur un même point et décrivons un cercle, mais le jour final viendra où ces deux pointes se réuniront. **Nicolas** (283)

Oh, my soul, thou and I together are like unto a compass. We form but one body, having two points. Truly, we move but from the one point, and make the round of the circle; but the day cometh, and is not far off, when the two points must reunite. **McCarthy** (187)

In these twin compasses, O Love, you see
One body with two heads, like you and me,
 Which wander round one centre, circlewise,
But at the last in one same point agree. **Whinfield** (323)

Whinfield, 183 (1882), has *O soul*, instead of *O Love*, and no comma after *centre*.

Bodenstedt (I. 21)

O Hort meiner Seele, einem Compass gleichen wir Beiden:
Im Körper der Nadel geeint, deren Pole sich scheiden.
Um Einen Punkt drehen wir uns, die jetzt gesondert erscheinen,
Doch es kommt einst der Tag, wo die beiden Pole sich einen.

Here is one that shows a more serious mood: —

Nicolas (347)

Ô Dieu ! délivre-moi de ce calcul sur le plus ou le moins (des choses de ce monde), fais que je me préoccupe de toi, en m'affranchissant de moi-même. Tant que j'ai ma saine raison, le bien et le mal me sont connus : rends-moi ivre et débarrasse-moi ainsi de cette connaissance du bien et du mal.

McCarthy (122)

Lord, free me from this puzzle of the more and less. Absorb me in thee and free me from myself. While I can reason I know good and evil: intoxicate me, and free me from knowledge of good and evil.

Whinfield (385)

O Lord! from self-conceit deliver me,
Sever from self, and occupy with Thee!
This self is captive to earth's good and ill,
Make me beside myself, and set me free!

Bodenstedt (V. 27)

O Herr, von der Sorge um mehr oder minder befreie mich!
Dir zu Liebe würd' ich gern zum Selbstüberwinder; befreie mich!
Nüchternen Blickes, erkenn' ich zu klar das Falsche und Ächte;
Lass mich im Rausch vergessen das Böse und Schlechte: befreie mich!

Similar jests at his studies are to be found in various quatrains.

De la cuisine de ce monde [ou, monde-cuisine] tu n'absorbes que la fumée. Jusques à quand, plongé dans la recherche de l'être et du néant, seras-tu la proie du chagrin ? Ce monde ne contient que perte pour ceux qui s'y attachent. Dérobe-toi à cette perte, et tout pour toi deviendra bénéfice. **Nicolas** (397)

In the kitchen of life, you savour only the smoke. How long will you study in sorrow the problem of being and not being ? This world is loss to those that cling to it. Cast it adrift, and lo ! the loss is gain. **McCarthy** (454)

From this world's kitchen crave not to obtain
Those dainties, seeming real, but really vain,
   Which greedy worldlings gorge to their own loss ;
Renounce that loss, so loss shall prove thy gain. **Whinfield** (139) (226, 1882)

Von der Weltküche soll nichts als Rauch Dein
   Gericht sein.
Wie lange wirst Du Dich noch quälen um Sein und
   Nichtsein ?
Diese Welt bringt nur Verlust jedem weltlichen Sinn,
Befrei' Dich davon, und der Verlust wird Gewinn ! **Bodenstedt** (V. 34)

Wie lang noch von dieser niederen Welt einatmen
   willst du den Rauch
  Und, brütend über das Sein und das Nichts, die
   Beute der Kummers sein ?
So lang dir der Sinn an der Erde hängt, schafft Gram
   dir jeglicher Hauch,
  Und wenn von ihr du dich abgewandt, erst atmest
   du Frieden ein. **Von Schack** (78)

APPENDIX XXII.

RUBÁIYÁT LVIII AND LIX.

M. K. calls FitzGerald's stanza "a tolerably close paraphrase of the Persian *words*, but conveying a totally different sense." The *angel shape* appears in several Rubáiyát, but for the most part greatly disguised, "an angel unawares":—

Nicolas
(78)

Ayant aperçu un vieillard qui sortait ivre de la taverne, portant le sedjadèh sur ses épaules et un bol de vin dans sa main, je lui dis : Ô chéikh ! que signifie donc cela ? Il me répondit : Bois du vin, ami, car le monde, c'est du vent.

McCarthy
(169)

Once, seeing an old man stagger from the wine-shop, with his prayer mat on his shoulders, and his flagon in his hand, I said to him, "What means this, oh, my master?" And he made answer to me, "Drink wine, my brother, for this world is but a breath of wind."

Whinfield
(80)

To the wine-house I saw the sage repair,
Bearing a wine-cup, and a mat for prayer;
 I said, " O Shaikh, what does this conduct mean ? "
Said he, " Go drink ! the world is naught but air."

Einen Greiss, den ich sah berauscht aus der Schenke **Bodenstedt**
    treten, (III. 8)
Einen Krug in der Hand, auf der Schulter den Teppich
    zum Beten,
Fragt' ich : was soll das bedeuten ? Und er sprach:
    trinke Wein.
Denn die Welt ist nur Wind sonst und staubiger
    Schein.

Heut aus der Schenke sah ich einen Trunknen taumeln **Von Schack**
Und von der Schulter ihm den Andachtteppich (25)
    baumeln.
Ich sprach zu ihm : "O Scheich! bist du nicht bei
    Verstand?"
Doch er rief aus : "Trink Wein! die Welt ist eitel
    Tand."

Hier, en passant ivre devant une taverne, j'ai ren- **Nicolas**
contré un vieillard pris de vin et portant une gourde (244)
sur son dos. Je lui ai dit: "Ô vieillard! n'as-tu pas
peur de Dieu?" Il me répondit: "La miséricorde
vient de lui, va, bois du vin."

Yesterday, passing drunken before the tavern door, **McCarthy**
I beheld an old man, full of wine, bearing a gourd upon (117)
his back. I spake to him and said, "Oh, old man, dost
thou not fear God?" He answered me, "There is
mercy with him — go, therefore, and drink."

Last night, as I reeled from the tavern-door, **Whinfield**
I saw a sage, who a great wine-jug bore; (284)
  I said, "O shaikh, have you no shame?" Said he,
"Allah hath boundless mercy in his store."

Bodenstedt (IX. 21)	Gestern traf ich auf eignen weinseligen Pfaden Einen Greis, mit einem grossen Weinkrug beladen. Ich frug: hast Du vor Gott weder Furcht noch Scham? Er sprach: Gott ist gnädig gar wundersam.

Nicolas (112)	J'ai vu un sage dans la maison d'un homme ivre de la veille. Je lui ai demandé s'il ne pouvait me donner des nouvelles des absents. Il m'a répondu: "Bois du "vin, ami, car beaucoup, semblables à nous, sont partis "et ne sont pas revenus."
McCarthy (313)	I met a wise man in a drunkard's house, and asked him tidings of the absent ones. He answered, "Drink your wine, for many like us have gone hence, and not returned again."
Bodenstedt (VIII. 70)	In der Schenke fragt' ich einen weinfrohen Greis: Wo sind nun, die fehlen in unserm Kreis? Er sprach: es sind Viele dahin genommen, Wohin wir auch gehn, um nicht wieder zu kommen.
Von Schack (118)	In eines Weinwirts Hause that an einen Greiss ich jüngst die Frage: "Was aus den Abgeschied'nen ward, kannst du mir das berichten? sage!" Zur Antwort gab er: "Freund, trink Wein! gar Viele gingen schon hinweg, Allein zurückgekehrt ist noch kein Einz'ger bis zum heut'gen Tage."

See also Rubáiy LXIV and Appendix XXVI.

Une nuit, je vis en songe un sage qui me dit: Le **Nicolas**
sommeil, ami, n'a fait épanouir la rose du bonheur de (48)
personne : pourquoi commettre un acte si semblable à
la mort ? bois du vin plutôt, car tu dormiras bien assez
sous terre.

One night I beheld in a dream a sage who said to **McCarthy**
me, "In sleep, O my friend, the rose of joy has never (67)
blossomed for any man. Why do you do a deed so
like to death ? Arise, and drink wine, for you will sleep
sound enough beneath the earth."

I dreamt a sage said, "Wherefore life consume **Whinfield**
In sleep ? Can sleep make pleasure's roses bloom ? (51)
   Forgather not with death's twin-brother sleep,
Thou wilt have sleep enough within thy tomb!"

I dreamed a Sage exclaimed to me, "Oh Son, **Garner**
In Sleep, 'the Rose of Fortune' blooms for none, (XI. 5)
   Why sleep, when Sleep is but a Twin to Death ?—
Ah, Thou shalt sleep enough when Life is done."

Im Traum scholl eine Stimme mir in's Ohr : **Bodenstedt**
Im Schlaf erblüht Dir nicht des Glückes Rosenflor. (IX. 49)
Trink lieber Wein ! Schlaf gleicht dem Todeszustand,
Du hast noch Zeit dazu im ewigen Ruhstand.

Ein Weiser erschien mir im Traum und sprach : **Von Schack**
" Was ahmst du den Tod im Schlafe nach ? (130)
Nicht schaffst du also dir Gutes in's Haus ;
Hier oben trinke, dort unten schlaf' aus ! "

A similar thought is found in the following:—

Nicolas
(33)

La fausse monnaie n'a pas cours parmi nous. Le balai en a déblayé entièrement notre joyeuse demeure. Un vieillard revenant de la taverne me dit: Bois du vin, ami, car bien des existences succéderont à la tienne durant ton long sommeil.

McCarthy
(80)

No false money circulates with us. The broom has cleanly swept our happy home. An old man coming from the tavern said, counselling me, "Drink, friend, drink wine, for many lives will follow yours during your long sleep."

Whinfield
(37)

No base or light-weight coins pass current here,
Of such a broom has swept our dwelling clear;
   Forth from the tavern comes a sage, and cries,
"Drink! for ye all must sleep through ages drear."

Bodenstedt
(IX. 46)

In unserm Kreise gilt kein falsch Gepräge.
Ein Greis sprach zu mir auf dem Schenkenwege:
Lass uns des Lebens Bestes nicht versäumen,
Eh wir den langen Traum im Grabe träumen.

Von Schack
(211)

Wer falsche Münzen in Umlauf bringt, schwer sollte den man strafen!
   Längst hat aus unserem fröhlichen Haus sie weggekehrt der Besen.
   Ein Greis kam aus der Schenke und sprach: "Froh bin ich heute gewesen;
   Trink Wein auch du! Zeit hast du nachher, im Grabe auszuschlafen!"

(See also Rubá'iy XIII.)

In the following, life's *leaden metal* is transmuted into a golden chain:—

Ô échanson! mets dans ma main de ce vin délicieux, de ce jus aux attraits d'une charmante idole, de ce nectar enfin qui, semblable à une chaîne dont les anneaux se tordent et se retordent sur eux-mêmes, tient et les fous et les sages dans une si douce captivité.
  Nicolas (374)

Give me delightful wine, O cup-bearer, that divine juice which, like a chain of linked rings, holds fools and sages in sweet servitude.
  McCarthy (357)

Cupbearer! bring my wine-cup, let me grasp it!
Bring that delicious darling, let me grasp it!
 That pleasing chain which tangles in its coils
Wise men and fools together, let me grasp it!
  Whinfield (417)

Come bring the Juice whose dazzling Brightness vies
With these same Houris' merry sparkling eyes,
 And which, like a Chain with Links of Iron, holds
Within its strong embrace, both Fools and Wise.
  Garner (I. 32)

Bring mir den Wein der mir das Herz belebt,
Hold, wie ein Bild der Schönheit, mich erhebt;
Der einer Kette gleich mit losen Ringen,
Die Weisen wie die Thoren weiss zu zwingen.
  Bodenstedt (IX. 93)

O Schenke, den Becher, die Zierde der Welt, bring' her!
Den Trank, der mit Wonne die Herzen schwellt, bring' her!
 Den Wein, die Kette, welche in süsser Haft
Die Weisen zugleich und die Thoren hält, bring her!
  Von Schack (19)

There are many of the Rubáiyát which extol the value of wine above all other earthly things. M. Nicolas invariably interprets this idea of wine as the Holy Spirit. And it must be said, if by wine Khayyám understands fermented grape juice, such an extravagant sentiment does not reflect much credit on his understanding: if he means the TRUTH it is understandable.

Nicolas (94)
Une coupe de vin vaut cent cœurs, cent religions; une gorgée de ce jus divin vaut l'empire de Chine. Qu'y a-t-il, en effet, sur la terre de préférable au vin? C'est un amer qui vaut cent fois la douceur de la vie.

McCarthy (242)
One cup of wine is worth a hundred hearts, a hundred faiths; one drop of wine is of more value than the empire of kings! What is there in truth to be named before it? Its bitterness is beyond all the sweets of life.

Bodenstedt (IX. 6)
Ein Glas Wein wiegt hundert Herzen auf,
  Mit hundert Religionen im Kauf.
Nicht um das Kaiserreich China gebe
  Ich preis die herbe Tochter der Rebe.
Was kann von den Schätzen auf Erden
  Mit *ihr* verglichen werden?
Was uns das trübe Leben gewährt
  Hat Wert nur, wenn durch sie verklärt.[1]

[1] Im Urtext: Wein ist eine Bitterkeit, die tausend süsse Huldinnen aufwiegt.

The last line of Whinfield, 28, is the same, but the Persian original is different from that of Nicolas:—

    Chide not at wine for all its bitter taste,
    Its bitterness sorts well with human life!

The following has the same Oriental extravagance of
expression, but the last couplet is fine : —

Une gorgée de vin vaut mieux que le royaume de **Nicolas**
Kavous; elle est préférable au trône de Kobad, à (61)
l'empire de Thous. Les soupirs auxquelles le matin un
amoureux est en proie sont préférables aux gémisse-
ments des dévots hypocrites.

A mouthful of wine is worth more than the kingdom **McCarthy**
of Kai Khosrou; it is more desirable than the throne (129)
of Kai Kobad or the empery of Thous. The sighs
with which a lover disturbs the dawn are preferable to
the howlings of sanctimonious hypocrites.

One draught of wine outweighs the realm of Tús, **Whinfield**
Throne of Kobád and crown of Kai Kawús; (64)
   Sweeter are sighs that lovers heave at morn,
Than all the groanings zealot breasts produce.

Kobad's Thron und Thus' und Kavus' Reich **Bodenstedt**
Kommt einem guten Glas Wein nicht gleich. (IX. 53)
Der Liebenden Seufzer und Klagetöne
Sind besser als heuchlerisch Andachtsgestöne.

Mehr dünkt ein Zug aus der Flasche mich wert, als aller **Von Schack**
   Erdenruhm, (260)
Als Kobad's mächtiger Herrscherthron, als Chosru's
   Königtum;
Mehr wert ist ein Seufzerhauch, der leis von Munde
   Verliebter weht,
Als aller Mönche und Derwische Geplapper und Gebet.

The Hungarian version numbered the same as Nicolas (61) is: —

> Egy korty ital Kavusz király birtokánál többet ér,
> Értte adnám Kobád trónját s nem adnám Thusz földeér.
> Többet ér a szerelmes szív sóhaja,
> Mintha álszent kebelét felszakasztja.

Kobad, or Kai Kobad, living among the mountains of Elbourz, was invited by Zal, the father of the celebrated Rustem, in the name of the principal men of Persia, to take the place of their incapable king, Guerchasp, and drive from the realm the invader Afrasiab, king of Turan, or Turkestan, who had killed Noouzer, the tenth king of the Pishdadians. Kobad defeated Afrasiab, and having restored the realm to quiet, became renowned for his justice. His son was Kavous, or Kai Kavous. Thous was son of Noouzer, and uncle to Kai Kavous.

The same idea occurs also in the following: —

Nicolas (215)
Une gorgée de vin est préférable à l'empire de Djèm; l'odeur de la coupe est préférable aux aliments de Marie. Le soupir qui le matin s'échappe de la poitrine d'un homme pris de vin de la veille est préférable aux lamentations de Bou-Saïd et à celles d'Adhèm.

McCarthy (155)
A draught of wine is better than the empery of Jamshid. The perfume of the cup is better than the gifts of Hatim Tai. The sigh which slips at dawning from the breast of him who went drunk to bed, is better than the lamentations of Majnun.

Oh! wine is richer than the realm of Jam,   Whinfield
More fragrant than the food of Miriam;   (253)
   Sweeter are sighs that drunkards heave at morn
Than strains of Bu Sa'íd and Bin Adham.

Line 2 in Whinfield, 138 (1882), begins, *More luscious.*

Guter Wein ist dem Reiche Dschem's vorzuziehn,   Bodenstedt
Selbst der himmlischen Speise, Maria verlieh'n;   (IX. 17)
Bu-Said's und Adhem's erbauliche Klagen
Wollen wir minder als Seufzer beim Weine behagen.

    Bou-Saïd and Adhèm, two Persian sovereigns reigning at different epochs, who, being struck by the vanities of this world, abdicated in order to contemplate divine things. Bou-Saïd composed quatrains which Nicolas says the Persians prefer to Omar's. By the "aliments de Marie," or "food of Miriam," is meant the miraculous fruit which suddenly filled the tree under which, according to the Persian fable, the angel Gabriel found the Virgin Mary when she had gone to starve herself to death rather than allow her shame to be known. The Koran, which is supposed by some writers to confound Mary the daughter of Imrân with Miriam the sister of Moses, whose father was also Imrân, says that when she was serving in the temple under the charge of Zacharias, whenever he went to her chamber he found provisions with her; and the commentators add that none went into Mary's apartment but Zacharias himself, and that though he locked seven doors upon her, yet he found that she had always winter fruits in summer and summer fruits in winter!

Omar never wearies of returning to the same extravagant comparison:—

Nicolas
(552)

Une gorgée de vin vaut mieux qu'un nouvel empire. Ce qu'il y a de mieux à faire c'est de rejeter tout ce qui n'est pas vin. Une coupe de ce nectar est cent fois préférable au royaume de Féridoun. La brique qui couvre la jarre est plus précieuse que le diadème de Key-Khosrov.

McCarthy
(402)

A mouthful of wine is better than empire. Abjure all save wine. One cup of wine is better than the kingdom of Feridoun. The tile which covers the mouth of the wine jar is more precious than the crown of Kai-khosrou.

Bodenstedt
(VII. 39)

Guter Wein gilt mir mehr als ein neues Reich,
Nichts kommt in der Welt seinem Werte gleich.
Ein Krug steht an Wert über Feridun's Throne,
Und der Deckel des Krugs über Kai Chossrew's Krone.

Von Schack
(85)

Wahren Weisen ziemt es, Allem, was nicht Wein ist
  zu entsagen;
Höher viel ist, als ein neues Reich, ein Weinschluck
  anzuschlagen,
Höher viel ein voller Becher, als der Erdenherrscher
  Throne,
Höher selbst des Weinkrugs Deckel, als Kai Chosru's
  Königskrone.

Nicolas says Feridoun was the seventh king of the second or Pishdadian dynasty. A blacksmith of Ispahan, named Gaveh, placed him on the throne, after rallying his countrymen to revolt against Zohak the Cruel. Gaveh's leather apron, improvised as the standard of liberty, became historic, and was adorned by Feridoun and his successors with precious stones. Feridoun, when at the summit of his glory, divided his realm among his three sons, and spent the rest of his days in divine contemplation. In the eyes of the Persian poets he was the model of a Shah. Saadi thus sings his praise :—

Feridoun the Fortunate was not of birth divine;
Nor did his earthly form indeed with musk and amber shine;
His justice and his generous heart acquired him his renown;
Practise these virtues and thou'lt be a very Feridoun.

Kai-Khosru (sometimes identified with Cyrus) was the third king of the Kaianian dynasty. His father, Siavoush, was put to death by Afrasiab, king of Turkestan, whose daughter he had married. Kai-Khosrou escaped to Persia, and mounted the throne of his grandfather, Kai-Kavous. Then he waged war against Afrasiab, and put him to death. Having avenged his father, Kai-Khosrou abdicated, and consecrated the rest of his life to religious meditation. Like Charlemagne, he never died, but is still alive somewhere, waiting the time to resume the government.

Vendons le diadème du Khan, la couronne de Key, vendons, pour racheter le son de la flûte, vendons le turban, la soutane de soie, oui, pour une coupe de vin, vendons le chapelet qui à lui seul contient une armée d'hypocrisie.

Nicolas
(279)

McCarthy
(191)

I would sell the diadem of the Khan, the crown of the king, to purchase the song of the flute girl. Let us sell the turban, yea, and the garment of silk, for a cup of wine; let us sell the chaplet which alone contains a multitude of hypocrisy.

Bodenstedt
(VII. 21)

Mehr als Persiens und China's Thron
  Gilt mir eine Flöte mit gutem Ton,
Mehr als Turban und Seidengewand
  Gilt mir ein gutes Glas Wein in der Hand.
Fort mit dem Heiligenglanz,
Fort mit dem Rosenkranz,
Der eine ganze Heuchlerwelt.
An seiner Schnur zusammenhält.

Von Schack
(177)

Des Königs Krone würd' ich gern, den Kajanidenthron verkaufen;
  Den Turban und den Kaftan lasst uns für der Flöte Ton verkaufen!
    Den Rosenkranz, den Inbegriff von Dummheit und von Heuchelei,
  Lasst uns für klaren, goldnen Wein, den edlen Rebensohn, verkaufen!

And lastly, here are four Rubáiyát which reflect Omar's sense of humor:—

Nicolas
(220)

Ô toi qui domines tous les grands de l'univers! Sais-tu quels sont les jours où le vin réjouit l'âme? Ce sont: le dimanche, le lundi, le mardi, le mercredi, le jeudi, le vendredi, et le samedi, en plein jour.

O thou, who lordest over the lords of the earth, dost **McCarthy**
thou know the days when wine delighteth the heart? (163)
They are in good sooth the Monday, the Tuesday, the
Wednesday, the Thursday, the Friday, the Saturday,
and the Sunday to boot.

Illustrious Prophet ! whom all kings obey, **Whinfield**
When is our darkness lightened by wine's ray? (260)
  On Sunday, Monday, Tuesday, Wednesday, Thursday,
Friday, and Saturday, both night and day!

O Du, der den Mächtigen auf Erden gebeut, **Bodenstedt**
Weisst Du, wann der Wein unsre Herzen erfreut? (II. 13)
  Jeden Tag in der Woche, ganz ausnahmlos,
Und das immer so oft sich die Woche erneut.

O Herr der Herren, heiliger Prophet, willst du, dass **Von Schack**
  ich dir künde, (329)
  An welchen Tagen gern der Mensch am Weingenuss
    sich laben mag?
  Am Sonntag und am Montag ist's, am Dienstag,
    Mittwoch, Donnerstag,
Freitag und Samstag; und du willst verpönen den
  Genuss als Sünde?

  Une montagne elle-même danserait de joie si tu **Nicolas**
l'abreuvais de vin. Il n'y a qu'un insensé qui puisse (179)
mépriser la coupe. Tu oses m'ordonner de renoncer à
ce jus de la treille ! Sache donc que le vin est une âme
qui perfectionne l'homme.

McCarthy
(259)

The very hills would leap for joy did you but wash their steeps with wine. Only a fool is scornful of the flagon. You who bid me renounce the juice of the vine, learn that wine is the soul, the complement of man.

Whinfield
(186)

A draught of wine would make a mountain dance,
Base is that churl who looks at wine askance ;
Wine is a soul our bodies to inspire,
A truce to this vain talk of temperance !

Bodenstedt
(IX. 77)

Ein Berg selbst würde tanzen, hätt' er von diesem Wein getrunken,
Mir scheint ein Mensch, der ihn verschmäht, in Thorheit ganz versunken.
Drum sprich mir von Entsagung nicht in gläubiger Verschwommenheit:
Der Geist des Weines zeigt den Weg zu menschlicher Vollkommenheit.

Von Schack
(85)

Ein Berg selbst tanzte vor Lust, wenn mit Wein er würde begossen,
Und wer den Becher verschmäht, den muss man des Wahnsinns zeih'n.
Den Saft der Reben zu flieh'n, o Frömmler, mich mahnst du verdrossen ;
Doch wisse! den Menschen erzieht und bildet zum Guten der Wein.

Nicolas
(364)

J'ai de mes moustaches balayé le seuil de la taverne. Oui, j'ai renoncé à réfléchir sur le bien et le mal de ce monde et de l'autre. Je les verrais, semblables à deux boules, rouler dans un fossé que, quand je dors pris de vin, je ne m'en préoccuperais pas plus que si je voyais rouler un grain d'orge.

I have swept the threshold of the tavern with my **McCarthy**
hair, I have given the good-bye to thoughts of good (302)
and ill, of this world and the other. When I am drunk,
they might both roll into a ditch, without my heeding
them more than two barley-corns.

I sweep the tavern threshold with my hair, **Whinfield**
For both worlds' good and ill I take no care; (409)
   Should the two worlds roll to my house, like balls,
When drunk, for one small coin, I'd sell the pair!

Mit meinem Schnurrbart hab' ich die Schwelle der **Bodenstedt**
   Schenke gefegt, (VIII. 67)
Vergessend, was Böses und Gutes das Diesseits und
   Jenseits bewegt.
Säh' ich beide Welten wie Kugeln in einen Abgrund
   stürzend zertrümmern,
Es würden im Rausche mich beide nicht mehr als ein
   Gerstenkorn kümmern.

Der ich mit meinem Barte gefegt den Staub vom **Von Schack**
   Boden der Schenke, (122)
Gott strafe mich, wenn ich an diese Welt und jene noch
   ferner gedenke!
Und gingen, während berauscht ich bin, sie alle beide
   zu Trümmern,
Nicht mehr, als um ein Waizenkorn würd' ich um
   beide mich kümmern.

La succession constante du printemps et de l'au- **Nicolas**
tomne fait disparaître les feuilles de notre existence. (402)
Bois du vin, ami, car les sages l'ont bien dit, les
chagrins de ce monde sont un poison, et l'antidote de
ce poison c'est le vin.

McCarthy
(300)

The steady march of springs and autumns sweep the leaves from our life's trees. Drink wine, friend, for the wise have wisely said, "Life's cares are a poison, and wine its best antidote."

Whinfield
(411)

Winter is past, and spring-tide has begun,
Soon will the pages of life's book be done!
　Well saith the sage, "Life is a poison rank,
And antidote, save grape-juice, there is none."

Bodenstedt
(VIII. 76)

Des Frühlings und Winters kommen und gehen,
Macht die Blätter von unserm Lebensbaum wehen,
Der Weltschmerz — sagen die Weisen rätlich —
Ist ein Gift, doch guter Wein macht's unschädlich.

Von Schack
(256)

Das Rad der Zeit in seinem ewigen Kreisen
　Macht, dass vom Baume des Lebens das Laub uns fällt,
Drum trinke Wein! Gedenke des Spruchs der Weisen:
Wein ist das Gegengift für den Kummer der Welt.

Still keener the satire in the following, which I will give in only two versions: —

Nicolas
(280)

Le jour où le jus de la vigne ne fermente point dans ma tête, l'univers m'offrirait un antidote, que ce serait du poison pour moi. Oui, le chagrin des choses de ce monde est un poison, son antidote, c'est le vin. Je prendrai donc de l'antidote pour n'avoir pas à craindre le poison.

On the day when the juice of the grape does not turn my brain, this world has nothing to give but that which is poison to me. Yes, the misery of this wretched world is a poison — wine is its only antidote. To escape then from the terror of the poison, I will take the antidote. **McCarthy** (213)

APPENDIX XXII (*Continued*).

RUBÁ'IY LIX.

By the expression "the Two-and-Seventy Sects" may here be meant all the people on earth. Omar speaks of them again : —

La diversité des cultes divise le genre humain en soixante et douze nations environ. Au milieu de tous ces dogmes, j'ai choisi celui de ton amour. Que signifient ces mots : Impiété, islamisme, culte, péché ? Mon véritable but, c'est toi. Loin de moi donc tous ces vains prétextes (indifférents !) **Nicolas** (248)

The multitude of creeds has divided mankind into seventy-two nations. Of all these doctrines I have chosen that of thy love. Of what meaning are the words : Impiety, Islam, faith, sin ? Thou art my sole desire. Away from me all these vain pretences. **McCarthy** (138)

> Although the creeds number some seventy-three.
> I hold with none but that of loving Thee ;
>   What matter faith, unfaith, obedience, sin ?
> Thou 'rt all we need, the rest is vanity.

Whinfield (287) (157, 1882)

Garner
(X. 5)
: The Two and Seventy Wrangling Sects contend,
And ever strive their Crumbling Creeds to mend,
: But I have cast them, One and All away,
And Thou, Oh Allah, art my only End.

Bodenstedt
(I. 16)
: So etwa zweiundsiebzig Sekten die Welt der Gläubigen zählt,
Als einziges aller Dogmen hab' ich die Liebe zu Dir erwählt.
Was ist mir Glaub' und Ketzerei? mein einziges Ziel bist Du!
Mag Jeder glauben, was er will: ich strebe Die nur zu!

Von Schack
(47)
: Von wohl siebzig Religionen hör' ich, die's auf Erden giebt;
Doch die wahre Religion ist die nur, dass der Mensch dich liebt.
Islam, Gottesdienst und Glaube — ferne mag dies Possenspiel,
Dieses eitle, stets mir bleiben! Du nur, du nur bist mein Ziel.

And so Hafiz in his Divan, translated by Nicolas:—

"Considère les discussions des soixante et douze nations comme autant de prétextes, car, comme elles n'ont pas vu la vérité éternelle, elles n'ont fait que débiter des fables."

Whinfield, in a note in his 1882 edition, quotes a saying of Muhammad: "It shall come to pass that my people shall be divided into three-and-seventy sects, all of which, save only one, shall have their portion in the fire." (Pocock's "Specimen Historiæ Arabum," p. 210.)

Sharastáni, according to Whinfield, says "the reason why the prophet pitched on the number seventy-three was that the

Magians were divided into seventy sects, the Jews into seventy-one, and the Christians into seventy-two." He also quotes Hafiz (ed. 1882) :—

"Consider the battle of the seventy-two sects as mischief;
Since they see not Truth, they give way to fables."

APPENDIX XXIII.

RUBÁ'IY LXI.

M. K. asserts that the original which inspired Fitz-Gerald's quatrains (numbered LXII and LXIII in the 2nd edition (1868), and LX and LXI in the succeeding) are "not found." The correlatives of LXI are certainly not own cousins, but several times removed. Nevertheless, the family resemblance may be traced by the subtle mind. The blasphemy of the wine is mentioned in the following Rubá'iy :—

Puisque c'est aujourd'hui mon tour de jeunesse, j'entends le passer à boire du vin, car tel est mon bon plaisir. N'allez pas, à cause de son amertume, médire de ce delicieux jus, car il est agréable, et il n'est amer que parce qu'il est ma vie. — Nicolas (24)

Since the day brings with it a consciousness of youth. I mean to wile [sic] it away with wine even to my heart's delight. Do not blaspheme, on account of its bitterness, this glorious juice, for it is a delight to drink, and bitter only because it is my life. — McCarthy (53)

Whinfield (28)	Now with its joyful prime my age is rife, I quaff enchanting wine and list to fife; Chide not at wine for all its bitter taste, Its bitterness sorts well with human life!

The first two lines of Whinfield, 13 (1882), read: —

> Now with its joyous prime my spring is rife,
> I quaff this wine, and list to lute and fife.

Bodenstedt (IX. 45)	Weil ich heut noch das Kleid der Jugend trage, Mach' ich den Tag mir zum Festgelage. Schmäht nicht die herbe Tochter der Rebe, Sie verklärt mir hold meine bitteren Tage.

The conceit of the reversed wine-cup appears again in the following: —

Nicolas (221)	Ô être adorable, plein de mignardises et d'espiègleries ! assieds-toi, apaise ainsi le feu de mille tourments et ne te relève plus. Tu m'enjoins de ne point te regarder ; mais c'est comme si tu m'ordonnais d'incliner la coupe en me défendant d'en répandre le contenu.

Nicolas calls on Orientalists to verify the first word of this Rubá'iy, which propriety forbids him to translate literally. At the same time he says: "Our poet addresses all these tendresses to the Divinity!" It was the same imaginative spirit that supplied the headings to the chapters of Solomon's Song in King James's Version of the Bible!

Oh, my beloved, full of graces and witcheries, seat **McCarthy**
thyself; and thus, quenching the flames of a thousand (21)
desires rise not up again. Thou forbiddest me to gaze
upon thee, but thou might [*sic!*] as well command me to
turn down the cup, without spilling the contents thereof.

O turn away those roguish eyes of thine! **Whinfield**
Be still! seek not my peace to undermine! (261)
  Thou say'st, "Look not." I might as well essay
To slant my goblet, and not spill my wine.

Du holdes Geschöpf voll süsser Schelmereien, **Bodenstedt**
Sitz' nieder, mein gefangenes Herz zu befreien. (VI. 6)
Dein Reiz zwingt mich sonst, das Auge zu schliessen,
Wie den Becher zu senken, ohne Wein zu vergiessen.

There is also possibly a hint of the thought of Rubá'iy LXI in the following little dialogue between Omar and Muhammad:—

Présentez le salut de ma part à Mostapha, et ensuite **Nicolas**
dites-lui, avec tout le respect qui lui est dû: "Ô seigneur (316)
Hachemite! pourquoi, suivant le chèr'e, le doug aigre
est-il licite et le vin pur défendu?"

Présentez le salut de ma part à Khèyam, et ensuite (317)
dites-lui: "Ô Khèyam! tu es un ignorant. Quand
donc ai-je dit que le vin est défendu? Il est licite pour
les hommes intelligents, il n'est défendu que pour les
ignorants."

Bear greeting from me to Mustapha, and then with **McCarthy**
all respect enquire thus, "Why, O Lord All wise, does (404)
Alkoran make the sour salted curds and water lawful
and pure wine unlawful?"

McCarthy (396)	Bear greeting from me to Khayyam, and then say, "Oh, inexperienced Kayyam, when then have I said that wine is unlawful? To the foolish it is unlawful, but to the wise it is lawful."
Whinfield (318)	Khayyam's respects to Mustafa convey, And with due reverence ask him to say, Why it has pleased him to forbid pure wine, When he allows his people acid whey?

        Whinfield, 183 (1882), reads:—

           Present my Compliments to Mustafa,
           And ask if he will condescend to say,
             Why it has pleased him to prohibit wine
           When he allows us all to drink sour whey?

(319) (184. 1882.)	Tell Khayyam, for a master of the schools, He strangely misinterprets my plain rules; Where have I said that wine is wrong for all? 'T is lawful for the wise, but not for fools.
Bodenstedt (II. 15)	Verehrungsvoll grüsst von mir den Propheten: Zu offenbaren mir sei er gebeten, Warum uns saure Milch mit Salz und Eis erlaubt, Und reiner Wein verboten überhaupt?
(II. 16)	Bringt meinen Gruss Chajjam und redet so: Unwissender, wann sagt' ich Dir und wo, Der Wein sei nicht erlaubt? Nur dummen Tröpfen Gilt mein Verbot, nicht aber klugen Köpfen.

Grüsst ehrfurchtsvoll von mir den Muhammed,   **Von Schack**
  Und sprecht: " Herr der Lebendigen und Toten!   (29)
Sag' an, warum erlaubst du den Sorbet
  Und hast den reinen, klaren Wein verboten?"

"Dir, Chijam, bietet seinen Gruss der Herr der Toten   (30)
  und Lebend'gen,
Doch, Ignorant, wie missverstehst du meines Wein-
  verbots Natur!
Erlaubt hab' ich den Wein für die Verständ'gen
  Und ich verbot ihn für die Dummen nur."

Mostapha means "the chosen. Hachemite is explained by Nicolas as the family name of Mohammed. The chèr'e is the law of the Koran; *doug*, or *dugh*, is a drink prepared by the Persians with water, *mast*, sour milk, salted and cooled with ice.

There is possibly also a hint of the same thought in the following: —

Dieu nous a promis du vin dans le paradis. Dans ce   **Nicolas**
cas, comment nous l'aurait-il défendu dans ce monde?   (121)
Un jour, un Arabe en état d'ivresse trancha d'un coup de sabre les jarrets de la chamelle de Hèmzèh. Ce n'est que pour lui que notre Prophète a rendu le vin illicite.

God hath promised us wine in paradise. Therefore,   **McCarthy**
how can it be denied to us in this world? An Arab, a   (204)
prey to drunkenness, one day severed with his sword the legs of a certain camel. It is for this cause, that the prophet has declared wine forbidden.

Whinfield (148)	Allah hath promised wine in Paradise, Why then should wine on earth be deemed a vice? An Arab in his cups cut Hamzah's girths, — For that sole cause was drink declared a vice.
Bodenstedt (II. 14)	Gott hat uns Wein verheissen im Paradiese; Taugt Wein für jene Welt, warum nicht für diese? Ein trunkner Araber schlug Hamsa's Kameele ein Bein ab, Zur Sühne dafür hält der Prophet uns vom Wein ab!

    Koran, Chap. XLVII., entitled Mohammed (or War). "The description of paradise which is promised unto the pious: — therein *are* rivers of incorruptible water; and rivers of milk, the taste whereof changeth not; and rivers of wine, pleasant unto those who drink, and rivers of clarified honey: and therein shall they have *plenty* of all *kinds* of fruit; and pardon from their LORD." Again in Chap. LII. entitled "The Mountain": "They shall present unto one another therein a cup of *wine*, wherein there shall be no vain discourse, nor any incitement unto wickedness. And youths, appointed to *attend* them, shall go round them; *beautiful* as *pearls* hidden *in their shell*." (Sale's Translation).

    Hamza was Muhammad's uncle, killed at the battle of Ohod.

APPENDIX XXIV.

RUBÁ'IY LXII.

    In Stanza LXII FitzGerald recurs to the favorite idea of present enjoyment in opposition to that "ascetic holiness which waits for joy in the next world." It is not certain what Rubá'iy he took for his original.

The following has evident relationship. The second chapter of the Koran, entitled "The Cow," probably suggested to Omar the blood-thirsty ending. It will be noticed that McCarthy follows Nicolas into an evident mistranslation, whereby the wit of the original escapes.

Je bois du vin, et ceux qui y sont contraire viennent de gauche et de droite pour m'engager à m'en abstenir, parceque, disent-ils, le vin est l'ennemi de la religion. Mais, pour cette raison même, maintenant que je me tiens pour adversaire de la foi, je veux, par Dieu, en boire, car il est permis de boire le sang de son ennemi. **Nicolas** (93)

I drink of the wine, and they who oppose it come about me on the right hand and on the left, to persuade me to renounce it, saying that wine is the enemy of religion. But, therefore, because I hold myself an adversary of the faith, I wish by Allah to drink thereof, for it is permitted to drink the blood of one's enemy. **McCarthy** (316)

From right and left the censors came and stood,
Saying, "Renounce this wine, this foe of good!"
But if wine be the foe of holy faith,
By Allah, right it is to drink its blood! **Whinfield** (95)

In line one, Whinfield, 44 (1882), *grave Mollas came and stood*, and the last two lines read:—

> But if wine be my foe, as they declare
> I swear by Allah I must drink his blood.

A somewhat similar idea occurs in Whinfield, 326:—

> No more let fate's annoys our peace consume,
> But let us rather rosy wine consume;
> The world our murderer is, and wine its blood,
> Shall we not then that murderer's blood consume?

Bodenstedt
(VII. 1)

   Ich trinke Wein und die Gegner klagen
      Von links und rechts mich an und sagen,
   Es sei der Wein des Koran Feind;
      Da ich das auch bin, wie mich scheint,
   Will ich erst recht am Wein mich laben,
      Da wir im Koran gelesen haben
   Der Feinde Blut zu trinken, sei
      Erlaubt — und ich bin gern dabei.

Von Schack
(70)

   Ihr sagt, dass für mein Zechen einst mir schwere
      Strafen droh'n
   Und flieh'n müss' ich den Rebensaft, den Feind der
      Religion;
   Doch eben deshalb will erlaubt der Weingenuss mich
      dünken;
   Der Glaubensfeinde Blut befiehlt ja der Prophet zu
      trinken.

      See Rubá'iy XIII, and Appendix VI.

APPENDIX XXV.

RUBÁ'IY LXIII.

"M. K." says the original of FitzGerald LXIII is not found. The two following Rubáiyát contain the antithesis of the first line:—

Nicolas
(60)

Chaque cœur que (Dieu) a éclairé de la lumière de l'affection, que ce cœur fréquente la mosquée ou la synagogue, s'il a inscrit son nom dans le livre de l'amour il est affranchi et des soucis de l'enfer et de l'attente du paradis.

Every heart in which heaven hath set the lamp of   **McCarthy**
love, whether that heart incline to mosque or syna-   (121)
gogue, if its name be written in the book of love,
it is freed from the fear of hell and the hope of
paradise.

Hearts with the light of love illumined well,   **Whinfield**
Whether in mosque or synagogue they dwell,   (63)
   Have *their* names written in the book of love,   (32, 1882)
Unvexed by hopes of heaven or fears of hell.

Ein jegliches Herz, das die Liebe verklärt,   **Bodenstedt**
Gleichviel welcher Glaube die Andacht nährt,   (I. 31)
Hat die Leuchte zum Ziel alles Höchstes gefunden,
Hat Himmel und Hölle in sich überwunden.

Wenn in deines Herzens Tiefen nur die Sat der Liebe   **Von Schack**
   spriesst,   (2)
Gleich ist's, ob du in Moscheen oder Götzentempeln
   kniest;
Hast du in das Buch der Liebe deinen Namen
   eingeschrieben,
Nicht mehr denkst du dann an Strafe oder an Beloh-
   nung drüben.

Dans la Mosquée, dans le medressèh [école qui est   **Nicolas**
annexée aux mosquées], dans l'église et dans la   (46)
synagogue, on a horreur de l'enfer et on recherche
le paradis; mais la semence de cette inquiétude n'a
jamais germé dans le cœur de celui qui a pénétré les
secrets du Tout-Puissant.

McCarthy
(62)

In mosque, in school, in church, in synagogue, men fear for hell and hope for paradise, but the seed of this uncertainty has never sprouted in the soul of him who has penetrated the secrets of the All-wise.

Whinfield
(49)

In synagogue and cloister, mosque and school,
Hell's terrors and heaven's lures men's bosoms rule,
But they who master Allah's mysteries,
Sow not this empty chaff their hearts to fool.

Line 3 in Whinfield, 26 (1882), reads:—

But they who pierce the secrets of " The Truth."

Bodenstedt
(V. 5)

Um Höllenfurcht und Himmelshoffnung drehn
Sich Kirchen, Synagogen und Moscheen;
Doch wer gedrungen bis zum Quell des Lichts
Macht sich aus Himmel und aus Hölle nichts.

Von Schack
(133)

In den Kirchen und den Klöstern, den Moscheen und Synagogen,
Bebt man vor der Hölle Schrecken, hofft man auf das Paradies;
Doch von solchem Truggebild wird nimmer dessen Geist betrogen,
Den der Herr in das Geheimnis aller Dinge schauen liess.

Nicolas
(43)

Ô Khèyam! pourquoi tant de deuil pour un péché commis? Quel soulagement plus ou moins grand trouves-tu à te tourmenter ainsi? Celui qui n'a point péché ne jouira pas de la douceur du pardon. C'est pour le péché que le pardon existe; dans ce cas, quelle crainte peux-tu avoir?

O Khayyam, why so much mourning for your sin? **McCarthy**
What consolation can you find in thus plaguing your- (18)
self? He who has never sinned can never taste the
sweet of forgiveness. Mercy was made for the sake of
sin, therefore why are you afraid?

Khayyam! Why weep you that your life is bad? **Whinfield**
What boots it thus to mourn? Rather be glad. (46)
He that sins not can make no claim to mercy,
Mercy was made for sinners — be not sad.

The last two lines of Whinfield, 24 (1882), read: —

> He that sins not, no title makes to grace,
> Sin entails grace, then prithee why so sad?

Was quälst Du Dich um Schuld, die längst geschah? **Bodenstedt**
Ist Gnade doch nur für die Schuld'gen da. (II. 8)
Drum, wer sich rühmt, dass er vom Tugendpfade.
Sich nie verirrt, der findet keine Gnade.

APPENDIX XXVI.

RUBÁIYÁT LXIV AND LXV.

There are a number of the Rubáiyát that treat variously of the great mystery of death. The one that
follows goes well in nobility and dignity of tone with
the two last quoted: —

Nicolas
(227)

Ils sont partis, ces passagers, et aucun n'est revenu te dire un mot des secrets cachés derrière le rideau. Ô dévot ! C'est par l'humilité que tes affaires spirituelles prendront une tournure favorable et non par la prière, car qu'est-ce qu'une prière sans sincérité et sans humilité ?

McCarthy
(80)

These travellers have departed, and of them all, not one has returned to tell us of the hidden things concealed behind the veil. Oh, devout man, it is by a humble heart, and not by prayer, that the things which concern thy soul, will be brought to a favourable issue, for prayer is of no avail to a man without sincerity and contrition.

Whinfield
(266)

They go away, and none is seen returning,
To teach that other world's recondite learning:
'T will not be shown for dull mechanic prayers,
For prayer is naught without true heartfelt yearning.

The second line in Whinfield, 145 (1882), is better:—
To teach the after-life's mysterious learning.

Bodenstedt
(VII. 14)

Noch Keiner ist wiedergekommen
    Von Allen, die uns genommen,
Uns zu sagen, wie ihm geschehn ist
    Und was hinter dem Vorhang zu sehn ist.
O Frömmler, die Demut allein,
    Führt Dich in's Himmelreich ein,
Auf Gebete ist nicht zu zählen,
    Wo Demut und Wahrheit fehlen.

But quickly comes the pessimistic answer in another mood: —

Va jeter de la poussière sur cette voûte des cieux et bois du vin; recherche les belles personnes, car où vois-tu sujet de pardon, sujet de prière, puisque, de tous ceux qui sont partis, aucun n'est revenu? — **Nicolas** (228)

Fling dust to the skies, and drink deep of the wine-flagon; seek ever the fairest women. To what end dost thou sue for pardon, to what end dost thou pray, seeing that of all those departed hence, not one has returned? — **McCarthy** (68)

Go to! Cast dust on those deaf skies, who spurn
Thy orisons and bootless prayers, and learn
  To quaff the cup, and hover round the fair;
Of all who go, did ever one return? — **Whinfield** (267)

In line 2, Whinfield, 146 (1882), *bootless cries;* and line 3 runs: —
    To drain the wine-cup and adore the fair.

Lass den Himmel mit seinem Geheimnis in Frieden,
Trink Wein und erfreu' Dich des Schönes hienieden:
Noch Keiner kam wieder aus jenen Bezirken,
Zu melden, wie unsre Gebete dort wirken. — **Bodenstedt** (IX. 18)

Gieb einen Fusstritt dem Himmel! Lass ab
  Von Andacht und Fasten und von Gebet;
Denn keiner der Toten jemals gab
  Dir Kunde, wie es drüben steht. — **Von Schack** (18)

And here is somewhat the same thought in a Rubá'iy which I will give in only two versions:—

Nicolas (343)

Méprise les paroles des femmes coquettes, mais accepte du vin limpide de la main de celles dont la toilette est irréprochable. (Tu le sais,) tous ceux qui ont fait leur apparition en ce monde sont partis les uns à la suite des autres, et il n'est pas donner à personne de t'en montrer un seul qui soit revenu.

McCarthy (362)

Do not heed the speech of frivolous women but seize the cup of clear wine from the hands of the comely. All who ever trod this earth have vanished one by one, and who can say that one has e'er returned?

But the melancholy mood returns:—

Nicolas (125)

Ô regret! le capital (de la vie) nous échappe des mains. Hélas! bien des cœurs ont été par la mort noyés dans le sang, et personne ne revient de l'autre monde pour que je puisse lui demander des nouvelles des voyageurs partis.

McCarthy (221)

Woe's me for the best that slips between our fingers; woe's me for all the hearts that death has drowned in blood; woe's me that none return from the hither world with tales of those who have departed thence.

Whinfield (152)

Ah! wealth takes wings, and leaves our hands all bare,
And death's rough hands delight our hearts to tear;
   And from the nether world let none escape
To bring us news of the poor pilgrims there.

Our Life slips from our Grasp, we soon shall swell   **Garner**
The Ranks of Those who in Death's Kingdom dwell,— (V. 6)
   And of Them All not one has e'er returned,
The Secrets of that Peaceful Realm to tell.

O wie das Capital des Lebens   **Bodenstedt**
   Uns durch die Hände gleitet! (VIII. 11)
O wie im Tod die Qual des Lebens
   Zu blutigem Ende gleitet!
Und Keiner der Geschiedenen kehrt aus jener Welt, zu
   melden,
Wie dort im Himmelsal des Lebens
   Die Schicksalswende gleitet.

O Jammer! täglich schwindet unser Leben!   **Von Schack**
   Wie vieler Herzen brach schon das Geschick, (262)
   Und Keiner kam von drüben je zurück,
Von den Geschied'nen Nachricht uns zu geben!

APPENDIX XXVII.

RUBÁ'IY LXVIII.

   Nicolas explains this lantern (fánús-i-khayál) by the word *fanal*, which he says is made of two copper-plated basins separated about a meter apart by *une chemise de calicot ciré*. The lower one contains the candle and the upper one has a handle for the arm of the ferrásh who carries it. When the lantern is closed the calicot chemise falls into the box thus made by the two basins. Ornaments are often, he says, painted on the cloth, and it is to the vacillation of these figures, as the ferrásh changes from one arm to the other, that Omar compares our fate here below!

FitzGerald says in his note (21) : —

"*Fánúsi khiyál*, a Magic-lanthorn still used in India ; the cylindrical Interior being painted with various Figures, and so lightly poised and ventilated as to revolve round the lighted Candle within."

Professor Cowell explains it as "a lanthorn which revolves by the smoke of the candle within, and has on the sides of it figures of various animals." The editor of the "Calcutta Review" adds in a note : —

These lanthorns are very common in Calcutta. They are made of a tall cylinder with figures of men and animals cut out of paper and pasted on it. The cylinder, which is very light, is suspended on an axis, round which it easily turns. A hole is cut near the bottom, and the part cut out is fixed at an angle to the cylinder, so as to form a vane. When a small lamp or candle is placed inside, a current of air is produced, which keeps the cylinder slowly revolving.

The same idea recurs in the following : —

McCarthy (15)
Man is like unto a flagon and his soul is the wine therein : his mould is like unto a reed, and his soul is the sound therein. What is earthly man, O Khayyam but a paper lantern of fancy and a lamp therein?

Whinfield (491)
Man is a cup, his soul the wine therein,
Flesh is a pipe, spirit the voice within ;
  O Khayyam, have you fathomed what man is ?
A magic lantern with a light therein!

Diesen Himmel, der uns blendet durch Glanz der **Bodenstedt**
    Ferne,   (III. 2)
Können wir füglich vergleichen mit einer Laterne.
Das Licht ist die Sonne, das Gehäuse die Welt,
Wir beugen uns staunend vor dem, was sie enthält.

APPENDIX XXVIII.

RUBÁ'IY LXIX.

There is an astrological reference in the following Rubá'iy :—

Il ne faut pas sans nécessité aller frapper à chaque **Nicolas**
porte. Il faut s'accommoder du bien comme du mal   (27)
d'ici-bas, car on ne peut jouer que d'après le nombre de
points que nous présente la surface des dés jetés par le
destin sur le damier de ce petit bol céleste.

Nicolas calls attention to the graceful condensation of the Persian: "destiny-dice," "heaven-cup," "bow-brows," and "moon-face."

Do not heedlessly beat at every portal. We must learn **McCarthy**
to take the good with the bad in this life, for we can   (74)
only play the game according to the number of dots on
the face of the dice which destiny throws into the hollow
of this heavenly cup.

'Tis labour lost thus to all doors to crawl,   **Whinfield**
Take thy good fortune, and thy bad withal;   (31)
  Know for a surety each must play his game,
As from heaven's dice-box fate's dice chance to fall.

Garner
(III. 5)
> Why strive to know the Hidden Cause of All?
> Enjoy the Sweet, and bravely take the Gall,
>   For on this Checkered Board of Life we Men
> Are moved by Fate, the Skies our Souls enthrall.

Bodenstedt
(V. 15)
> Man muss nicht unnütz an jede Pforte pochen!
> Gute Tage versöhnen mit schlimmen Wochen;
> Die goldenen Kugeln, die Deine Blicke
> Dort oben erspähn, werfen deine Geschicke.

Whinfield, 16 (1882), begins:—
> Art not ashamed thus to all doors to crawl?

and ends:—
> As fortune's dice from heaven's dice-box may fall.

Quite opposite in thought is this, which, like the Calvinistic Creed, makes man the principal object in creation:—

Nicolas
(304)
> C'est nous qui sommes le véritable but de la création universelle; c'est nous qui, aux yeux de l'intelligence, sommes l'essence du regard divin. Le cercle de ce monde ressemble à une bague, et, sans aucun doute, c'est nous qui en sommes le chaton gravé.

McCarthy
(409)
> We are the keys of the scheme of existence, we to wise eyes are the very essence of divinity. Is not the hoop of the world like unto a ring, and are not we the wrought gems thereof?

Whinfield
(316)
> Man is the whole creation's summary,
> The precious apple of great wisdom's eye;
>   The circle of existence is a ring,
> Whereof the signet is humanity.

Ja, wir sind der ganzen Schöpfung Zweckbegriff und **Bodenstedt**
    höchstes Ziel,   (VIII. 36)
Sind der Stern im Aug' des Geistes, drauf das Licht des
    Himmels fiel;
Einem Ringe zu vergleichen ist die Welt, und zweifels-
    ohne
Bilden wir auf diesem Ringe das Gepräge mit der
    Krone.

APPENDIX XXIX.

RUBÁ'IY LXXI.

This splendid quatrain — worth a hundred sermons — has several prototypes in which the inevitableness of the past is portrayed.

Restreins ton envie des choses de ce monde, si tu **Nicolas**
veux être heureux; brise les liens qui t'enchaînent au   (176)
bien et au mal d'ici-bas; vis content, car ce mouvement
périodique des cieux suivra sa marche, et cette vie ne
sera de longue durée.

Be not desirous of the things of this world. If you **McCarthy**
would live in happiness, break in sunder the bonds which   (279)
hold you captive to earthly joys and sorrows. Be content, for the heavens move in their accustomed course,
and your life is of short duration.

Crave not of worldly sweets to take your fill,   **Whinfield**
Nor wait on turns of fortune, good or ill;   (191)
  Be of light heart, as are the skies above,
They roll a round or two, and then lie still.

Whinfield (103, 1882)	Would you be happy, curb your carnal will, Sigh not for lack of good or stress of ill; Take heart, these heavens have their date like you, They roll a round or two and then lie still.

Bodenstedt (IV. 10)	Willst Du leben in Frieden,
	   Lern' Entsagung hienieden,
	Lern die Bande zerreissen,
	   Die Gutes und Böses heissen;
	Siehe: nichts hemmt in der Ferne
	   Den ewigen Kreislauf der Sterne,
	Doch unser Lebenslauf
	   Hört bald im Grabe auf.

      Compare the German proverb: —

          Schweig, leid und lach' —
          Geduld überwindet all sach'!

          Be silent, laugh and endure —
          Patience all trials will cure!

Nicolas (411)	Résigne-toi à la douleur si tu veux y trouver un remède, ne te plains pas de tes souffrances si tu veux en guérir. Dans ta pauvreté remercie la Providence, si tu veux qu'un jour enfin les richesses deviennent ton partage.
McCarthy (151)	Be resigned to sorrow if you wish to escape it, do not complain of your hurts if you would have them healed. If you would fain taste the joys of riches, then thank Providence for your poverty.
Whinfield (451)	To find a remedy, put up with pain, Chafe not at woe, and healing thou wilt gain; Thou poor, be ever of a thankful mind, 'T is the sure method riches to obtain.

Such durch Selbstüberwindung den Schmerz zu lindern, **Bodenstedt**
Durch Klagen wirst Du ihn nicht heilen noch mindern. (VIII. 78)
In Deiner Armut danke dem Himmel auf Erden,
Sollen einst seine Schätze zu Teil Dir werden.

And here is wise advice from the old Persian:—

Dans ce monde, cette maison d'escamoteurs, il est **Nicolas**
inutile de compter sur un ami. Écoute le conseil que (423)
je te donne et ne le confie à personne : Supporte tes
souffrances, n'y cherche aucun remède, sois heureux dans
tes chagrins, ne cherche pas à les faire partager.

In this juggling house of life, friendship is a vain **McCarthy**
thing; be wise and trust none. Bear thy pains, seek (351)
no remedy, be cheerful in thy sorrows, and seek not to
share them with others.

Never in this false world on friends rely, **Whinfield**
(I give this counsel confidentially,) (460)
 Put up with pain, and seek no antidote,
Endure your grief, and ask no sympathy!

In dieser Gauklerbude, der Welt, **Bodenstedt**
 Sei Dein Hoffen auf keinen Freund gestellt. (VIII. 82)
Hör' von mir diesen guten Rat
 Und mach' ihn ganz geheim zur That:
Trage geduldig Dein Schmerzenteil,
 Du findest bei keinem Andern Heil,
Dein Glück kannst Du nur von innen,
 Von aussen nicht gewinnen.

APPENDIX XXX.

RUBÁ'IY LXXII.

The wheel of heaven, the pitiless vault, stands as the type of Fate. The Rubáiyát which contain complaints of its tyranny, of the world's injustice, of the loss of friends, and of man's limited faculties, are classed by Whinfield under the Persian title of Shikáyat-i-Rozgár. Many specimens have already been given. In Nicolas there are upwards of twenty in which "the wheel" is mentioned: 21, 42, 107, 127, 137, 193, 195, 219, 228, 231, 251, 254, 263, 267, 273, 326, 332, 348, 393, 418, 436. One or two must suffice.

Perhaps Vergil refers to "the wheel of heaven," in the line: —

Aspice convexo nutantem pondere mundum:

"Behold the world staggering under the weight of the wheel."

Nicolas
(21)

Ô roue du destin! la destruction vient de ta haine implacable. La tyrannie est pour toi un acte de prédilection que tu commets depuis le commencement des siècles, et toi aussi, ô terre, si l'on venait à fouiller dans ton sein, que de trésors inappréciables n'y trouverait-on pas!

Oh, wheel of fate, destruction falls from thy unconquerable hate. Tyranny has been thy purpose and thy pleasure from the beginning of things. And thou too, O earth, if we but digged into thy breast, what treasures should we not find therein! **McCarthy** (29)

Ah! Wheel of heaven to tyranny inclined, **Whinfield** (25)
'T was e'er your wont to show yourself unkind;
   And, cruel earth, if they should cleave your breast,
What store of buried jewels they would find!

Whinfield, 11 (1882), has, line 1:—
   Ah! wheel of heaven, who run a course so blind,

and it ends:—
     if one should cleave your breast
    What store of buried jewels would he find!

O Schicksalsrad, dein Rollen ist Verderben, **Bodenstedt** (V. 42)
Das Herrlichste und Schönste lässt Du sterben;
Grausamer als die Erde noch bist Du,
Die so viel Schätze deckt mit Erde zu!

In the following appears the cynical humor characteristic of Omar:—

Ô roue des cieux! tu es d'une ingratitude à toute épreuve. Tu me tiens constamment nu comme un poisson. La roue du tisserand tisse des habits pour les humains : elle est donc plus charitable que toi, ô roue des cieux! **Nicolas** (251)

McCarthy (143)	O wheel of heaven, heedless of bread and salt, you leave me ever naked as a fish. The wheel of the weaver weaveth clothes for men, therefore it is more charitable than thou, O wheel of Heaven.
Whinfield (292)	O wheel of heaven! no ties of bread you feel, No ties of salt, you flay me like an eel! A woman's wheel spins clothes for man and wife, It does more good than you, O heavenly wheel!
Bodenstedt (V. 21)	O Himmel, Du denkst weder an Saltz noch Brot, Nackt wie ein Fisch bin ich durch Dich in der Not. Der Weber sorgt doch, das wir Kleider tragen, Soll ein Weber an Fürsorge Dich überragen?

A deeper melancholy sobs through this:—

Nicolas (193)	Pas une seule fois la roue des cieux ne m'a été propice, jamais un seul instant elle ne m'a fait entendre une douce voix, pas un seul jour je n'ai respiré une seconde de bonheur, sans que ce jour-là même elle ne m'ait replongé dans un abime de chagrins.
McCarthy (233)	Not once has the wheel of the heavens been favourable to me. Never for one moment have I listened to a sweet voice, never for one day have I tasted a fleeting happiness, but therefor I have been overwhelmed in an abyss of woe.

For me heaven's sphere no music ever made,   **Whinfield**
Nor yet with soothing voice my fears allayed;   (206)
  If e'er I found brief respite from my woes,
Back to woe's thrall I was at once betrayed.

   The last three lines of Whinfield, 113 (1882), read:—

   Nor jarring discords in my life allayed;
      Nor granted me one moment's peace, but straight
   Into the hands of grief again betrayed.

Nicht einmal ward mir im Leben   **Bodenstedt**
  Ein Tag reinen Glückes gegeben.   (VIII. 32)
Drang mir bis zum Herzensgrunde
  Eine Stimme aus süssem Munde,
Oder fühlt' ich mich sonst gesegnet,
  Weil Holdes mir begegnet,
So ward sicher ein Leidensabgrund
  Meinem Glücke sogleich zum Grabgrund.

———— - - -

   The following Rubá'iy is in illustration of our proverb that "misfortunes never come singly."

   Cette Roue de si haute structure, dont le métier est   **Nicolas**
d'exercer la tyrannie, n'a jamais dénoué pour personne   (127)
le nœud d'aucune difficulté. Partout où elle a entrevu
un cœur ulcéré, elle est venue y ajouter plaie sur plaie.

   That high and ominous wheel whose trade it is to   **McCarthy**
play the tyrant has never solved for anyone the knot   (229)
of any perplexity. Where'er it sees a bleeding heart
it speeds to grind upon the open wound.

Whinfield
(154)

The wheel on high, still busied with despite,
  Will ne'er unloose a wretch from his sad plight;
    But when it lights upon a smitten heart,
Straightway essays another blow to smite.

Bodenstedt
(V. 12)

Dieser hochragender Himmelskreis,
  Der nur zu plagen und placken weiss,
Ist noch nie einem menschlichen Wesen.
  Ein Schwierigkeitslöser gewesen,
Hat kein Unglück verhindert,
  Keine Leiden gemindert,
Doch wo er blutende Herzen gefunden,
  Ihnen geschlagen noch neue Wunden.

Von Schack
(27)

Dieser Himmel, der tyrannisch droben wälzt sein ew'ges Rad,
  Giebt es Einen, dem des Lebens Mühsal er erleichtert hat?
  Nein; doch wo auf seinem Kreislauf er ein blutend Herz gefunden,
  Neue Wunden ihm geschlagen hat er zu den alten Wunden.

And then once more the bitter jest:—

Nicolas
(195)

La roue des cieux ne fait que multiplier nos douleurs! Elle ne pose rien ici-bas qu'elle ne vienne aussitôt l'arracher. Oh! si ceux qui ne sont pas encore venus savaient quelles sont les souffrances que nous inflige ce monde, ils se garderaient bien d'y venir!

The wheel of the heavens only increaseth our woes   **McCarthy**
beyond measure. She giveth nothing to us here that   (249)
she doth not as soon snatch away. Oh, if those who
have not yet come into the world did but know the
miseries which await them, truly they would never come.

Heaven multiplies our sorrows day by day,   **Whinfield**
And grants no joys it does not take away;   (240)
  If those unborn could know the ills we bear,
What think you, would they rather come or stay?

Der Himmel scheint nichts zu thun als uns zu quälen   **Bodenstedt**
    und grämen,   (V. 13)
Er beut seine schönsten Gaben blos um sie wieder zu
    nehmen.
Die noch nicht Geborenen kennen des Lebens Qual
    und Gefahr nicht,
Wenn sie dies Dasein kennten, sie kämen in's Dasein
    gar nicht.

Nur Leiden schafft der Himmel uns armen Verlornen,   **Von Schack**
  Die Sat zerstörend, wenn kaum der Acker bestellt;   (192)
Ach kennten unser Geschick die Ungebor'nen,
  Sie kämen sicher nimmer auf diese Welt.

And in the following he recurs to the thought already
expressed in FitzGerald LXIV and Appendix XXVI:—

Cette roue des cieux, qui ne dit ses secrets à per-   **Nicolas**
sonne, a tué impitoyablement mille Mahmouds, mille   (219)
Ayaz; bois du vin, car elle ne restituera la vie à personne. Hélas! nul de tous ceux qui ont quitté ce
monde n'y reviendra plus!

Mahmúd, first of the Ghaznavite sultans; Ayaz, a simple
peasant, who became his favorite, and attained highest honors.

McCarthy
(162)

That heavenly wheel, which tells its tale to no man, has mercilessly slain a thousand monarchs and a thousand favorites; drink wine, then, for it gives back life to none. Alas, no one of those that quit this world will e'er come back to it.

Whinfield
(259)

Dark wheel! how many lovers thou hast slain,
Like Mahmud and Ayáz, O inhumane!
Come, let us drink, thou grantest not two lives,
When one is spent, we find it not again.

Bodenstedt
(IV. 15)

Der Himmel gab sein Geheimnis noch Keinem kund,
Schloss aber schon Tausenden von Königen den Mund.
Trink Wein, Freund: vom Tod kommt kein Leben zurück,
Und es giebt kein Glück als genosses Glück.

APPENDIX XXXI.

RUBÁ'IY LXXV.

Parwin is mentioned in the following Rubá'iy, which would have delighted the soul of Carlyle: —

Nicolas
(138)

Il existe dans les cieux un taureau nommé Pérvïn (Pléiades), un autre taureau qui est caché sous la terre. Ouvre donc les yeux de l'intelligence comme ceux qui vivent dans la certitude, et regarde-moi cette poignée d'ânes placés entre deux bœufs.

There is a bull in heaven named Parwín, there is **McCarthy**
another bull that bears the earth; open the eyes of (381)
knowledge and behold this drove of asses placed
between two bulls.

In heaven is seen the bull we name Parwín, **Whinfield**
Beneath the earth another lurks unseen; (377)
    And thus to wisdom's eyes mankind appear
A drove of asses, two great bulls between!

Whinfield explains the bulls as the constellation Taurus,
and that which supports the earth.

  In his version of 1882 (199) the first two lines read: —

      One bull is seen in heaven named Parwín,
      Another lurks beneath the earth unseen —

In the last line, *fat* takes the place of *great*.

Am Himmel ist ein Sternbild "der Stier" genannt, **Bodenstedt**
Ein andrer Stier ist unter der Erde bekannt; (VIII. 54)
Du öffne die Augen, um klar zu sehn,
Wieviel Esel zwischen diesen beiden Ochsen stehn!

Ein Stier ist, der drunten auf seinem Horne die Erde **Von Schack**
    hält, (286)
Ein anderer Stier strahlt hell dort oben am Himmels-
    zelt,
Und o! an die Menge von Eseln denk' ich mit Grausen,
Die zwischen den beiden Stieren hausen!

The Pleiades are frequently mentioned in Persian literature.

"When one grows poor, his Friends, heretofore compact as the Pleiades, disperse wide asunder as the Mourners." So says the Anvári Soheili, quoted by FitzGerald in a note to "Salámán and Absál." By the Mourners he understands the stars of Ursa Major.

The sky is picturesquely depicted in a few lines farther on in the same poem:—

> He [Salámán] halted on the Seashore; on the shore
> Of a great Sea that reaching like a floor
> Of rolling Firmament below the Sky's
> From Káf to Káf, to Gau and Máhí down
> Descended, and its Stars were living eyes.
> The Face of it was as it were a range
> Of moving Mountains; or a countless host
> Of Camels trooping tumultuously up,
> Host over host, and foaming at the lip.
> Within, innumerable glittering things
> Sharp as cut Jewels, to the sharpest eye
> Scarce visible, hither and thither slipping,
> As silver scissors slice a blue brocade;
> But should the Dragon coil'd in the abyss
> Emerge to light, his starry countersign
> Would shrink into the depth of Heav'n aghast.

The fourth line is thus explained:—

"He first made the Mountains; then cleared the Face of the Earth from Sea; then fixed it fast on Gau; Gau on Máhí; [that is Bull on Fish] and Máhí on Air; and Air on what? on NOTHING; Nothing on Nothing, all is Nothing—Enough," Attár quoted in note. By "the Dragon coil'd in the abyss" is meant the Eclipse-dragon, whose head devours the Sun and Moon.

Possibly the reference in Stanza LXXVI to the superiority of the drunkard to the dervish may have been derived from the following Rubá'iy:—

Ô moufti de la ville ! je suis plus laborieux que toi. **Nicolas**
Tout ivre que je suis, je possède plus de saine raison (264)
que toi ; car toi, tu bois le sang des humains et moi
celui de la vigne. Sois juste et dis-moi qui de nous
deux est le plus sanguinaire ?

I am more industrious than thee [*sic*], thou sage of the **McCarthy**
town. Though I be drunk, I am better than thee, for (209)
thou drinkest human blood, and I the blood of the
vine. Be just and pronounce which of us two is the
most sanguinary.

O City Mufti, you go more astray **Whinfield**
Than I do, though to wine I do give way ; (307)
  I drink the blood of grapes, you that of men :
Which of us is the more bloodthirsty, pray ?

O Mufti, Richter der Stadtbezirkung ! **Bodenstedt**
  Meine Wirkung ist besser als Deine Wirkung ; (VII. 19)
Treibst Du Dein Geschäft auch zünftiger,
  Treib' ich meins doch, im Rausch selbst, vernünftiger.
Du trinkst das Blut Aller, die an Dich glauben,
  Und ich trinke nur das Blut der Trauben.
Richte gerecht, um zu unterscheiden,
  Wer der Blutgierigste ist von uns Beiden.

Von Schack (58)	Vergieb, o Mufti, wenn ich stolz mich über dich erhebe! Im Rausch selbst mehr Vernunft, als du, noch hab' ich in der That. Nach Menschenblute dürstest du, ich nach dem Saft der Rebe; Sag an, wer bessern Geschmack da von uns Beiden hat?

APPENDIX XXXII.

RUBÁ'IY LXXVII.

Nicolas (303)	C'est le bord de la jarre que nous avons choisi pour lieu de prière; c'est en faisant usage du vin que nous nous sommes rendus dignes du nom d'homme; c'est dans la taverne que nous pourrons rattraper le temps perdu dans les mosquées.
McCarthy (406)	We made the mouth of a jar our place of prayer, the ruby wine made us seem truly men; it is better to be in the street of the tavern, than to leave life to wither in the mosque.
Whinfield (330) (1879, 1882)	We make the wine-jar's lip our place of prayer, And drink in lessons of true manhood there, And pass our lives in taverns, if perchance The time misspent in mosques we may repair.
Bodenstedt (VII. 29)	Wir haben uns den Weinkrug zum Betpult erlesen, Denn der Wein erst schafft menschenwürdiges Wesen, Und im Weinhaus nur ist Ersatz zu sehn Für die Zeit, verloren in den Moscheen.

Wir haben den Weinkrugrand zur Andachtstätte erkoren, **Von Schack**
   Durch Trinken machen wir uns erst würdig, Menschen (165)
     zu sein;
Die Zeit, die nutzlos vordem wir in dem Moscheen
     verloren,
   Wir holen vielleicht durch Besuch der Schenke sie
     wieder ein.

In contrast to the above is the following prayer, which Nicolas takes to be satirical:—

Ô Dieu ! sois miséricordieux pour mon pauvre cœur **Nicolas**
prisonnier ; sois miséricordieux pour mon sein, sus- (346)
ceptible de contenir le chagrin ; pardonne à mes pieds,
qui me conduisent à la taverne ; pardonne à ma main,
qui saisit la coupe !

Oh Lord, have mercy on my captive heart, have mercy **McCarthy**
on my sorrow-laden breast, have mercy on my tavern- (423)
turning foot, and on my hand that catches at the cup.

O Lord ! pity this prisoned heart, I pray, **Whinfield**
Pity this bosom stricken with dismay ! (384)
   Pardon these hands that ever grasp the cup,
These feet that to the tavern ever stray !

O Herr, mit meinem gefangenen Herzen hab' Erbar- **Bodenstedt**
   men ! (V. 26)
Mit meiner Brust voll Bangen und Schmerzen hab'
   Erbarmen.
   Mit meinen Füssen, die mich immer zum Weinhaus
     lenken,
Mit meiner Hand, die den Becher hebt, mich zu tränken,
     hab' Erbarmen !

Von Schack O Herr! schenk meiner Seele meinem armen
(164) Von Gram gebeugten Herzen schenk Erbarmen!
Verzeih dem Fuss, der mich zum Weinhaus trägt,
Der Rechten, die das Glas zum Mund bewegt!

The following is quite opposed in sentiment to FitzGerald, but it is interesting in itself, and worth remembering:—

Nicolas Dans la région de l'espérance attache-toi autant de
(15) cœurs que tu pourras; dans celle de la présence lie-toi avec un ami parfait, car, sache-le bien, cent kaabas, faites de terre et d'eau, ne valent pas un cœur. Laisse donc là ta kaaba et va plutôt à la recherche d'un cœur.

McCarthy In the kingdom of hope win all the hearts you can,
(28) in the kingdom of the Presence, bind to thyself a perfect soul, for, be sure, a hundred kaabas, blent of earth and water, are not worth a single heart. Give then thy kaaba the go-by, and seek a heart instead.

Whinfield Young wooer, charm all hearts with lover's art,
(18) Glad winner, lead thy paragon apart!
A hundred Ka'bas equal not one heart,
Seek not the Ka'ba, rather seek a heart!

The first two lines of Whinfield, 7 (1882), read:—

At first ensnare all hearts with kindly art,
Then let thine heart seek its pure counterpart.

So viel Herzen such' zu fesseln wie du irgend fesseln **Von Schack**
  kannst! (22)
Glücklich du, wenn du auf Erden einen treuen Freund
  gewannst!
Minder wert sind hundert Kaaba's, als ein Herz von
  guter Art,
D'rum nach einem Herzen richte, stat nach Mekka,
  deine Fahrt!

The Kaaba is the sanctuary at Mecca where is preserved the black stone which pilgrims kiss religiously. It is broken in many pieces. Mohammedans believe it a precious stone fallen from Paradise.

And the following is also fine and broad in its way: —

Le temple des idoles et la kaaba sont des lieux **Nicolas**
d'adoration, le carillon des cloches n'est autre chose (30)
qu'un hymne chanté à la louange du Tout-Puissant.
Le mehrab, l'église, le chapelet, la croix sont en vérité
autant de façons différentes de rendre hommage à la
Divinité.

The temples of the gods and kaabas are places of **McCarthy**
praise, the chiming of bells is naught but a hymn raised (78)
in praise of the all Potent. The pulpit, the church, the
beads, the cross, are all but different symbols of the
same homage to the same lord.

Whinfield (34)	Pagodas, just as mosques, are homes of prayer, 'Tis prayer that church-bells chime unto the air, Yea, church and Ka'ba, Rosary and Cross Are all but divers tongues of world-wide prayer.

Whinfield, 19 (1882), reads:—

> Pagodas are, like mosques, true homes of prayer;
> 'T is prayer that church bells waft upon the air;
> Kaaba and temple, rosary, and cross,
> All are but divers tongues of world-wide prayer.

Bodenstedt (I. 24)	Zur Ka'ba treibt's die Gläubigen des Propheten, Den Kirchenglocken folgt der Christ zum Beten. Kreuz, Rosenkranz und Kanzel will ich preisen Wo sie den Weg zu Gott und Wahrheit weisen.

APPENDIX XXXIII.

RUBÁ'IY LXXVIII.

The comfortable doctrine of predestination lies at the bottom of Rubá'iy LXXVIII and the two that follow. Similar ideas are found in many. Here are two characteristic examples:—

Nicolas (268)	Tu m'as formé d'eau et de terre, qu'y puis-je faire? Cette laine ou cette soie, c'est toi qui l'as tissée, qu'y puis-je faire? Le bien que je fais, le mal que je commets, c'est toi qui m'y as prédestiné; qu'y puis-je faire?

Thou hast fashioned me of water and clay; how then **McCarthy**
can I alter it? Whether I be made of wool or of silk, it (237)
is thou who hast woven; how then can I alter it? Thou
hast predestined my good and evil days — how can I
alter it?

Who was it that did mix my clay? Not I. **Whinfield**
Who spun my web of silk and wool? Not I. (311)
Who wrote upon my forehead all my good,
And all my evil deeds? In truth not I.

In Whinfield, 166 (1882), line 2 reads:—

Who wove my web of silk and dross? Not I.

In the last line, *sooth* takes the place of *truth*.

Du hast mich erschaffen aus Wasser und Erde; was **Bodenstedt**
    kann ich dazu? (II. 2)
Du schufst Alles, womit ich bekleidet werde;[1] was kann
    ich dazu?
All mein Gutes und Böses hast Du vorausbestimmt;
Ob und wie ich nun Leib und Seele gefährde, was kann
    ich dazu?

Wie du mich aus Wasser und Erde geformt, so hab' ich **Von Schack**
    gelebt, was kann ich dafür? (307)
Ob niedrige Wolle, ob pracht'ger Brokat, du hast mich
    gewebt, was kann ich dafür?
  Mir im Voraus auf die Stirne schon geschrieben
    hast du mein Lassen und Thun,
Drum ob ich böse Thaten verübt, ob Gutes erstrebt,
    was kann ich dafür?

[1] Wörtlich: Diese Wolle, diese Seide (die ich trage) hast
Du gewoben.

Nicolas (380)	Tu as imprimé à notre être (ô Dieu !) une bien singulière fantasmagorie (d'inconséquences) et tu en fais surgir de bien étranges phénomènes. Je ne puis, moi, être meilleur que je ne suis, car tu m'as retiré tel quel du creuset (de la création).
McCarthy (342)	Thou hast stamped us with a strange seal, thou hast made us do strange deeds. How can I be better than I am, for such as I am, you drew me from the void?
M. K.	The wayward caprices my life that have tinted All spring from the mould on my Being imprinted: Nought else and nought better my nature could be — I am as I came from the crucible minted!
Whinfield (421)	This is the form Thou gavest me of old, Wherein Thou workest marvels manifold ; Can I aspire to be a better man, Or other than I issued from Thy mould?
Garner (III. 1)	I am as from Thy Crucible I came, A Base Alloy, and though I feel my shame, I cannot hope to mend my erring ways, — 'T is Thine, Oh Allah, and not mine, the Blame.
Bodenstedt (II. 5)	Du hast unser Dasein hier seltsam geprägt Und die seltsamsten Wahnbilder dadurch erregt. Wie kann ich mich bessern? Ich trage Dein Siegel, Bin, wie ich hervorging aus Deinem Tiegel.

Ein seltsam Siegel, wahrlich, hast du unser'm Wesen Von Schack
    aufgedrückt,   (109)
Und staunen muss man hundertmal wie sehr dein
    Schöpfungswerk geglückt!
Nicht besser machen kann ich mich, trüg' ich danach
    auch viel Verlangen!
Denn, wie ich bin, just so bin ich aus deiner Hand
    hervorgegangen.

In a similar spirit writes the author of the "Imitation":—

I had rather be poor for thee than rich without thee; I rather choose to be a pilgrim on earth with thee than without thee to possess heaven. Where thou art, there is heaven, and where thou art not there is death and hell.

APPENDIX XXXIV.

RUBÁ'IY LXXXI.

M. K. considers that FitzGerald made up this Rubá'iy from the same sources as LXXVIII–LXXX, and partly from Nicolas, 375. "But," he says, "the original does not contain the idea of Man's forgiveness give and take." See Appendix LV.

The various versions follow:—

Ô regret que la vie se soit passée en pure perte! que Nicolas
nos bouchées aient été illicites et nos corps souillés.   (375)
J'ai la figure noire (ô Dieu !) de n'avoir pas fait ce que
tu as ordonné. Que sera-ce donc d'avoir fait ce que
tu n'as pas ordonné ?

McCarthy (164)	Woe's me for wasted life, for prohibited pleasures, and contaminated bodies. My face is blackened for not having done what thou hast ordered. How then if I had done what thou hast not ordered?
M. K.	Woe! that life's work should be so vain and hollow: Sin in each breath and in the food we swallow! Black is my face that what was Bid, undone is: — If done the Unbidden, ah! what then must follow?
Whinfield (418)	Alas! my wasted life has gone to wrack! What with forbidden meats, and lusts, alack! And leaving undone what 't was right to do, And doing wrong, my face is very black.
Bodenstedt (VIII. 73)	Weh, dass mir mein Leben zum Unheil verflossen, Weil ich verbotene Speisen und Getränke genossen! Mein Antlitz ward schwarz, weil ich nicht that, was geboten, Wie wird's erst, weil ich that, was nicht ge- noch verboten?

Nicolas (391)	Ô toi, dont la mystérieuse essence est impénétrable à l'intelligence, toi qui ne te soucies pas plus de notre obéissance que de nos fautes, je suis ivre de péchés, mais la confiance que j'ai en toi me rend la raison. Je veux dire par là que je compte sur ta miséricorde.
McCarthy (455)	Oh, thou whose essence is unknowable to mind, thou who heedest neither our faults nor our virtues, I am drunk with sins, but my trust in thee makes me sober, I count upon thy clemency.

To Thee, whose essence baffles human thought,   Whinfield
Our sins and righteous deeds alike seem naught;   (433)
    May Thy grace sober me, though drunk with sins,
And pardon all the ill that I have wrought!

Du, dessen heilig Geheimnis wir nicht verstehn,   Bodenstedt
Siehst nicht auf unsern Gehorsam noch unsern Vergehn.
Die Sünde beugt mich, die Hoffnung erhebt mich,
Das Vertraun zu Dir, Allbarmherziger, belebt mich.

Somewhat allied to the above is this fine Rubá'iy on justice:—

La justice est l'âme de l'univers; l'univers est un   Nicolas
corps. Les anges sont les sens de ce corps; les cieux,   (328)
les éléments, les créatures en sont les membres; voilà
unité éternelle. Le reste n'est que tromperie.

Justice is the soul of the world, and the world is a   McCarthy
body. The angels are its senses, the skies its elements,   (426)
humanity its limbs. This is the eternal unity, all else
is delusion.

This world a body is, and God its soul,   Whinfield
And angels are its senses, who control
    Its limbs — the creatures, elements, and spheres;
The ONE is the sole basis of the whole.

In Whinfield, 195 (1882), the last line reads:—
    Such Unity informs and rules the whole.

Bodenstedt (III. 17)

Gerechtigkeit ist die Seele der Welt,
   Die das Weltall als Körper zusammenhält.
Die Engel dienen als Sinne nur,
   Und alle sonstige Kreatur,
Sammt Urstoff, drin Alles sich auflöst wieder,
   Bildet des Weltenleibes Glieder.
Das ist das ewige Eins im All,
   Und alles Andre Trug und Schall.

The following are also noble in thought and feeling: —

Nicolas (282)

Je suis en guerre continuelle avec mes passions, mais que faire ? Le souvenir de mes actes me cause mille douleurs, mais que faire ? J'admets que dans ta clémence tu me pardonnes mes fautes, mais la honte de savoir que tu sais ce que j'ai fait, cette honte-là reste, que faire ?

McCarthy (217)

I wage a warfare without end against my passions, but what can I do ? The remembrance of my iniquities is like a sore burden, but what can I do ? I believe truly, that in thy mercy thou wilt blot out my sins. But the knowledge that my dishonour is not hid from thee remaineth — what can I do ?

Whinfield (322)

Against my lusts I ever war, in vain,
   I think on my ill deeds with shame and pain;
     I trust Thou wilt assoil me of my sins,
But even so, my shame must still remain.

   Whinfield, 172 (1882), has, in line 1, *I war alas! in vain;* line 2 reads: *And grievous overthrow ever sustain;* and in line 3, *my shame will still remain.*

Ich bin in stetem Kampf mit meinem Herzen, — was Bodenstedt
    soll ich thun? (I. 2)
Erinn'rung früh'rer Schuld macht mir viel Schmerzen —
    was soll ich thun?
  Verzeihst Du, Herr, auch gnädig meine Sünden:
Das Schuldbewusstsein ist nicht auszumerzen, — was
    soll ich thun?

  Tous tes secrets sont connus du savant des cieux Nicolas
(Dieu); il les sait cheveu par cheveu, veine par veine. (158)
J'admets qu'à force d'hypocrisie tu puisses tromper les
hommes, mais que feras-tu devant lui, qui connaît (de
tes méfaits) tous les détails un à un?

  All hidden things are known to the eternal wisdom, McCarthy
who numbereth every hair of our head, and hath (196)
fashioned all our members. By hypocrisy thou canst
deceive mankind, but how wilt thou deceive the All-
knowing?

The heavenly Sage, whose wit exceeds compare, Whinfield
Counteth each vein, and numbereth every hair; (177)
  Men you may cheat by hypocritic arts,
But how cheat Him to whom all hearts are bare?

Alle Geheimnisse kennt der Herr von Himmel und Erde, Bodenstedt
Jegliches Haar auf dem Haupt und im Antlitz jede (I. 36)
    Geberde;
  Magst Du durch Heucheln, o Thor, auch thörichte
    Menschen betrügen:
Glaubst Du, dass auch der Herr des Wissens getäuscht
    von Dir werde.

Von Schack　Einer ist im Himmel droben, der dein Tiefgeheimstes
(283)　　　　kennt,
　　　　　　Jeden Tropfen deines Blutes, auf dem Haupt dir
　　　　　　　　jedes Har;
　　　　　　Magst du täuschen auch die Menschen, welche man die
　　　　　　　　klügsten nennt,
　　　　　　Sprich, was nützt vor dem dein Heucheln, welchem
　　　　　　　　Alles offenbar?

Nicolas　Bien que je n'aie jamais percé la perle de l'obéis-
(229)　　　sance qu'on te doit, bien que jamais de mon cœur je
　　　　　n'aie balayé la poussière de tes pas, je ne désespère
　　　　　point d'arriver au seuil du trône de ta miséricorde, car
　　　　　jamais de mes plaintes je ne t'ai importuné.

McCarthy　Although, truly, I have never pierced the pearl of
(72)　　　obedience which we owe to Thee, although I have
　　　　never swept the dust of Thy steps from my heart, I
　　　　do not despair of reaching to the foot of the throne of
　　　　Thy mercy, for I have never worried Thee with my
　　　　importunate prayers.

Whinfield　Though Khayyam strings no pearls of righteous deeds,
(268)　　　Nor sweeps from off his soul sin's noisome weeds,
　　　　Yet will he not despair of heavenly grace,
　　　　Seeing that ONE as two he ne'er misreads.

　　　　In Whinfield, 147 (1882), line 1 reads:—
　　　　　　Khayyám strings not the fair pearls of good deeds,
　　and line 3,
　　　　　　Nevertheless he humbly hopes for grace.
　　In line 4, One is in italics.
　　The last line in Whinfield is from another MS. See Fitz-
Gerald's preface.

Mit der Perle des Gehorsams ward ich nicht geeinigt,   **Bodenstedt**
Vom Staub Deiner Füsse ward mein Herz nicht gerei-   (1. 19)
    nigt :
Und doch hoff' ich vor den Thron Deiner Gnade zu
    treten,
Da ich nie Dich geplagt habe mit Klagegebeten.

    Wörtlich: Obgleich ich die Perle des Gehorsams nie durchbohrt habe, u. s. w.

Reference to the Pearl is made in the following :—

Nicolas says the precious pearls represent the mysteries of creation. The one pierced is the one truth revealed.

Nous voilà parti et le temps est attristé de notre   **Nicolas**
départ ; car de cent perles précieuses il n'y en a qu'une   (152)
de percée. Hélas ! c'est grâce à l'ignorance des hommes
que cent mille idées d'un sens profond sont restées
inexprimées.

Behold, we have fled, and the season sighs for our   **McCarthy**
going ; for out of a hundred pearls, but one is thridded.   (239)
Alas, it is owing to the ignorance of mankind that a
hundred thousand noble thoughts remain unuttered.

Soon shall I go, by time and fate deplored,   **Whinfield**
Of all my precious pearls not one is bored ;   (173)
    Alas ! there die with me a thousand truths
To which these fools fit audience ne'er accord.

Oft wider Gott wohl hab' ich gefehlt,   **Von Schack**
Doch, wenn mich noch immer die Hoffnung beseelt,   (193)
    Er werde mir huldvoll sein, so ist's,
Weil ich ihn nie mit Gebeten gequält.

The following Rubá'iy brings before us as vividly as any the personality of old Omar: —

Nicolas
(200)

Des dogmes de la religion n'admets que ce qui t'oblige envers la Divinité. Cette bouchée de pain que tu possèdes, ne la refuse pas à autrui; garde-toi de la médisance, ne recherche le mal de personne, et alors c'est moi qui te promets la vie future : apporte du vin.

McCarthy
(323)

The commandments of religion only insist on the fulfilling of thy obligations to the deity. Refuse not thy morsel of bread to another, refrain thy tongue from slander, and seek not to render evil to thy neighbour. If thou doest this, I myself promise thee the future life. — Bring hither the wine.

Whinfield
(241)

Heed not the Sunna, nor the law divine;
If to the poor his portion you assign,
   And never injure one, nor yet abuse,
I guarantee you heaven, and now some wine!

In Whinfield, 135 (1882), the first two lines read: —

If you fulfil the ordinance divine,
If to the poor the legal tithes assign.

Bodenstedt
(II. 12)

Von den Dogmen glaub nur solche, die den Geist zu
   Gott erheben.
Von dem Brote, das Du hast, wirst Du gern auch
   Andern geben.
Sprich nichts Böses, thu nur Gutes, suche keines
   Menschen Pein,
Und Du wirst das ewige Leben haben, sag ich Dir.
   Nun bring mir Wein!

Ouvre-moi la porte, car ce n'est que toi qui peux Nicolas
l'ouvrir ; montre-moi le chemin, car c'est toi qui mon- (409)
tres la voie du salut. Je ne donnerai ma main à aucun
de ceux qui voudront me relever, car tous sont péris-
sables, il n'y a que toi d'éternel.

Open the gate, for only Thou canst open it ; show me McCarthy
the road, for only Thou canst show it. I will reach no (302)
hand to those who would fain uplift me, for Thou alone
art eternal.

Open the door! O entrance who procurest, Whinfield
And guide the way, O Thou of guides the surest! (149)
  Directors born of men shall not direct me,
Their counsel comes to naught, but Thou endurest!

  Line 1 in Whinfield, 233 (1882), reads : —

    Open the door of Truth, O usher purest!

Öffne die Pforte mir, Du kannst es allein! Bodenstedt
Zeig mir den Weg, der zu Dir führt ein! (I. 6)
Aller Sterblichen Hülfe ist mir unzulänglich,
Nur Du führst zum Heil, das, wie Du, unvergänglich!

  Bodenstedt also translates the same literally : —

Öffne die Pforte, denn der Eröffnende bist Du!
Zeige den Weg, denn der Wegzeigende bist Du!
  Ich werde meine Hand keinem Handnehmenden
    geben,
Denn vergänglich sind Alle, der Unvergängliche bist
    Du!

Von Schack
(68)

Das Thor zu öffnen hast nur du die Macht — lass mich denn ein!
Den Weg des Heiles zeige mir, denn du kennst ihn allein!
Nicht Einem, der mich leiten will, vertrau ich mich zur Führung;
Vergänglich sind sie allgesammt; nur du hast ew'ges Sein!

APPENDIX XXXV.

RUBÁ'IY LXXXII.

Ramazán, or Ramadán, the ninth in the calendar, is the sacred month among Mohammedans. Says the Korán:—

"The month of Ramadán *shall ye fast*, in which the Korán was sent down from heaven, a direction unto men, and declarations of direction, and the distinction *between good and evil*. Therefore let him among you who shall be present in this month [that is, at home and not in a strange country where the fast cannot be performed, or on a journey] fast the same *month*: but he who shall be sick, or on a journey, *shall fast* the *like* number of other days. God would *make this* an ease unto you, and would not *make it* a difficulty unto you."

Omar more than once refers to it:—

Nicolas
(66)

Le mois de Rèmèzan est venu, la saison du vin est finie, oui les jours de ce vin limpide et de nos habitudes, si simples ont fui loin de nous. Hélas! notre provision de vin nous reste intacte, et les jeunes femmes que nous avons recontrées sont dans une cruelle attente.

The month of Ramazan has come, the time of the wine is over. Yes, the days of that delicious drink and of our easy life, hath fallen far from us. Woe's me for the wine that waits undrunken in the jar, and the eyes of the fair women that burn for us in vain.
  McCarthy (150)

Now Ramazan is come, no wine must flow,
Our simple pastimes we must now forego,
 The wine we have in store we must not drink,
Nor on our mistresses one kiss bestow.
  Whinfield (69)

Der Monat Ramasan ist gekommen,
Der strengste Fastenmond für die Frommen:
Nun hat ihr Wein im Keller Ruh'.
Vielleicht gar die lieben Weiblein dazu!
  Bodenstedt (IX. 56)

Ach böser Fastenmond! Hin ist die Zeit, in der wir tranken,
Die Zeit, in der wir an die Brust von schönen Mädchen sanken!
Fast platzen will das Fass vom Wein, den wir nicht trinken sollen,
Und schmachtend seh'n die Frau'n uns an, die gern geküsst sein wollen.
  Von Schack (254)

The following, Whinfield says, is attributed also to Jalal 'Asad Bardi:—

On nous annonce que la lune de rèmèzan va apparaître et qu'il ne faut pas plus penser au vin. C'est bien, mais alors je veux, à la fin de celle de chè'èban, en boire une quantité telle que je puisse demeurer ivre jusqu'au jour de la fête.
  Nicolas (172)

McCarthy (269)	They tell us that the moon of Ramazan is close at hand, that we must forswear wine. Well and good, then I propose at the end of the feast to drink so deep that I shall be drunken to the very end of the sacred month.
Whinfield (188)	The moon of Ramazan is risen, see! Alas, our wine must henceforth banished be; Well! on Sha'bán's last day I'll drink enough To keep me drunk till Bairam's jubilee.
Bodenstedt (IX 78)	Man sagt, bald scheint der Mond des Ramasan Und mit ihm hebt das strenge Fasten an Nun wohl, dann trinken wir vorher soviel, Dass es noch vorhält bis zum Fastenziel.
Von Schack (59)	Ihr sagt mir: "morgen hebt er an, der heil'ge Mond der Fasten, Und in der Schenke darfst du nicht hinfort beim Weine gasten"; Wohlan denn! heut trinkt' ich so viel, dass, selig hinge-sunken, Den ganzen Fastenmond hindurch ich lieg' am Boden trunken.

Nicolas (159)	Le vin donne des ailes à ceux qui sont atteints de mélancolie; le vin est un grain de beauté sur la joue de l'intelligence; nous n'en avons pas bu durant le rèmèzan qui s'est écoulé, mais nous voici arrivés à la nuit de la féte du mois de chéval (nous allons donc nous dédommager).

Wine giveth wings to the heavy-hearted. Wine is a **McCarthy**
mole on the cheek of Wisdom. We have not drunk of (197)
it during the Ramazan which has fled, but behold now
the night of the month of the drinking of wine has
arrived.

Ah! wine lends wings to many a weary wight, **Whinfield**
And beauty spots to ladies' faces bright; (178)
   All Ramazan I have not drunk a drop,
Thrice welcome then, O Bairam's blessed night!

Fittige leihet der Wein dem, der in Trauer befangen, **Bodenstedt**
Schönheit leuchtet vom Wein auf des Genius blitzende (IX. 75)
   Wangen;
   Da wir nuchtern geblieben, so lange der Ramasan
     währte,
Trinken wir nun um so mehr, nachdem er endlich
     vergangen.

On m'engage à ne point boire du vin durant le mois **Nicolas**
de chèèban, parce que c'est défendu, ni même pendant (65)
le mois de rèdjèb, parce que c'est un mois consacré
à Dieu. C'est juste; ces deux mois appartiennent à
Dieu et au Prophète; buvons-en donc dans le mois de
rèmèzan, puisque c'est un mois qui nous est réservé.

They bid me drink no wine during this month, for **McCarthy**
this month is the Prophet's, nor yet in that month for (135)
that is the month of God. Very well, leave those two
months to God and his prophet, and let us drink deep
in the month of Ramazan, since that month is reserved
to us.

Whinfield
(68)

'T is wrong, according to the strict Korán,
To drink in Rajab, likewise in Sha'bán,
   God and the Prophet claim those months as theirs;
Was Ramazan then made for thirsty man?

Bodenstedt
(IX. 55)

Ich soll nicht Wein trinken in der Fastenzeit,
Weil diese drei Monde dem Herrn geweiht;
   Nun wohl! Ich trinke dem Herrn zum Preise
Mögt Ihr ihn verehren in Eurer Weise.

Rajab, or Redsheb, is the seventh, Shabân the eighth, and Ramazán the ninth month of the Mohammedan calendar. As the Faithful were not allowed to eat in the daytime during their Lent, some of them made up for the prohibition by feasting at night. Such hypocrisy aroused all Omar's scorn:—

Nicolas
(356)

Si j'ai mangé pendant les jours du rèmèzan, ne va pas croire que je l'aie fait par inadvertance. Les dures fatigues du jeûne avaient si bien transformé mes journées en nuits, que j'ai toujours cru manger le repas du matin.

McCarthy
(410)

If I feed in famine-hunted Ramazan, it is not through forgetfulness, but because the clinging fasts have changed my days to nights, and deluded me into believing that I ate the morning meal.

Whinfield
(312)

If so it be that I did break the fast,
Think not I meant it; no! I thought 'twas past;—
   That day more weary than a sleepless night,—
And blessèd breakfast-time had come at last!

Hab' ich an den Tagen des Ramasan Speise genossen, **Bodenstedt**
Glaub' nicht, dass ich sie unbedachtsamer Weise ge- (VII. 30)
    nossen:
Die Fastenqual hatte den Tag mir in Nacht verwandelt,
Und so hab' ich am Tage wie sonst in der Nacht gehan-
    delt.

Verzeih mir, O Gott, wenn ich an des Ramadhan Tagen **Von Schack**
    getrunken! (312)
  Allein so arg hat die Zeit der Fasten mir mitgespielt,
Dass ich, in die tiefste Trübsal versunken,
  Auch ihre Tage für Nächte hielt.

APPENDIX XXXVI.

RUBÁIYÁT LXXXIV AND LXXXV.

M. K. considers that FitzGerald drew his inspiration for Rubáiyát LXXXIV and LXXXV both from Nicolas, 38, which I have placed under LXXXV. The connection between FitzGerald, LXXXIV, and Nicolas, 349, is almost too subtle: nevertheless, I have ventured to put them together. Whinfield has one that is more closely allied:—

There is a chalice made with wit profound, **Whinfield**
With tokens of the Maker's favour crowned; (290)
  Yet the world's Potter takes his masterpiece,
And dashes it to pieces on the ground!

  Whinfield compares Job:—

"Is it good unto thee that thou shouldest despise the labour of thine hands?"

  But the point is lost in the Revised Version.

I here add several Rubáiyát which might have been included in Kúza-náma.

Nicolas (139)
Passe joyeusement ta vie, car bien d'autres voyageurs défileront par ce monde; l'âme criera après le corps dont elle sera séparée, et ce crâne de la tête, siége des passions, sera foulé aux pieds des potiers.

McCarthy (207)
Enjoy thy life while it remaineth to thee, for many other wayfarers will journey through the world. The soul crieth out after the body has been torn away from it, and the crown of thy head will be trampled under the feet of potters.

Bodenstedt (VIII. 15)
Getrosten Muts durch's Leben wandre,
    Dir folgen werden viele Andre.
Die Seele wird nach dem Körper schrei'n,
    Den sie verlassen in Todespein,
Und der Schädel aus Deinem Haupt,
    Seines feurigen Willens beraubt
Durch seinen eignen Schöpfer,
    Wird zerstampft von den Füssen der Töpfer.

There are several interesting Rubáiyát containing the same general idea of the responsibility of the Creator in relation to man: the world-problem facing the old Persian even as it faced the old Hebrew Preacher:—

Nicolas (359)
Quel est l'homme ici-bas qui n'a point commis de péché, dis? Celui qui n'en aurait point commis, comment aurait-il vécu, dis? Si, parce que je fais le mal, tu me punis par le mal, quelle est donc la différence qui existe entre toi et moi, dis?

Say, what man on earth has never sinned? Say, who could live and never sin? If, therefore, because I do ill you punish me by ill, say, then, where is the difference between thee and me?	McCarthy (425)
Was e'er man born who never went astray? Did ever mortal pass a sinless day? If I do ill, do not requite with ill! Evil for evil how can'st Thou repay?	Whinfield (398)
Wo ist der Mensch, der nie gesündigt hienieden? Das sage mir! Wie lebte der, der alle Sünde gemieden? Das sage mir! Thu' ich Böses, und Du vergiltst es mit Bösem, Wodurch sind wir Beide denn unterschieden? Das sage mir!	Bodenstedt (II. 7)
Nie war ein Mensch noch sündenlos, ob Weib nun oder Mann, Da, ohne Sünden zu begeh'n, man nimmer leben kann. Wenn du für Böses, das ich that, mit Bösem mich bestrafst, Wo ist denn zwischen mir und dir der Unterschied? sag an!	Von Schack (250)

Si dès le commencement tu avais voulu me faire connaître à *moi-même*, pourquoi ensuite m'aurais-tu séparé de ce *moi-même*? Si au premier jour ton intention n'avait pas été de m'abandonner, pourquoi m'aurais-tu jeté tout ébahi au milieu de ce monde?	Nicolas (397)

McCarthy
(457)

If from the first you made me know myself, why after would you sunder me from myself? If from the first it was your purpose to abandon me, why did you fling me helpless into the middle of this world?

Whinfield
(440)

This soul of mine was once Thy cherished bride,
What caused Thee to divorce her from Thy side?
Thou didst not use to treat her thus of yore,
Why then now doom her in the world to abide?

In Whinfield, 228 (1882), the last two lines read:—

Is it Thy purpose to forsake her quite,
That Thou dost doom her in this world to abide?

Von Schack
(173)

Was, wenn zuerst ein Teil ich war von deinem Wesen,
Bestimmte dich, nachher mich von ihm abzulösen?
Wohl schon von Anfang musst' es deine Absicht sein,
Dass hülflos durch die Welt ich irrte und allein.

Nicolas
(190)

Le dévot ne saurait apprécier aussi bien que nous ta divine miséricorde. Un étranger ne peut te connaître aussi parfaitement qu'un ami à toi. (On prétend) que tu as dit: Si vous commettez des péchés, je vous conduirai en enfer. Va donc dire cela à quelqu'un qui ne te connaisse pas.

McCarthy
(172)

The devout man can never value the divine mercy as we do. A stranger can never understand thee like thine own familiar friend. Thou sayest, "If thou sinnest, I will send thee to Hell." Go, tell that to one who knoweth thee not.

Can alien Pharisees Thy kindness tell,   **Whinfield**
Like us, Thy intimates, who nigh Thee dwell?   (204)
  Thou say'st, "All sinners will I burn with fire."
Say that to strangers, we know Thee too well.

Whinfield, 111 (1882), has, in line 1, *Thy Sweetness*; in line 3,
   "All sinners will I burn in hell!"

O Herr, kein Frömmler kann Dich hier   **Bodenstedt**
  In Deiner Gnade schätzen wie wir.   (I. 11)
Ein Fremder kann Dich nicht erkennen,
  Wie die sich Deine Freunde nennen.
Man sagt, dass Du die Sünde rächtest
  Und alle Sünder zur Hölle brächtest;
Wir glauben das nicht, trotz unsrer Schuld,
  Und bauen fest auf Deine Huld.

Dein göttliches Erbarmen kennt der Fromme nicht,   **Von Schack**
   denn er ist blind;   (292)
Nicht kennt ein Fremder dich so gut, wie wir, die deine
   Freunde sind.
Du hast gesagt: "Wer Sünden thut, der soll einst in
   der Hölle brennen;"
Doch geh! sag einem Andern das, nicht Solchen, die
   dich kennen.

Ô mon Dieu! tu es miséricordieux, et la miséricorde,   **Nicolas**
c'est de la clémence. Pourquoi donc le premier pé-   (101)
cheur a-t-il été mis hors du paradis terrestre? Si tu me
pardonnes parce que je t'ai obéi, ce n'est point là de la
miséricorde. La miséricorde existerait si tu me par-
donnais, tout pécheur que je suis.

McCarthy
(133)

Dear my God, you are merciful, and mercy is pity. Why then has the greatest sinner been shut off from paradise? If you only pardon me because I have obeyed you, what mercy is that? It would be merciful to forgive me, sinner that I am.

Whinfield
(102)

If grace be grace, and Allah gracious be,
Adam from Paradise why banished He?
Grace to poor sinners shown is grace indeed;
In grace hard earned by works no grace I see.

Bodenstedt
(I. 30)

O Allmächtiger! Du übst Gnade, und die Gnade ist
   Erbarmen;
Warum denn aus Edens Garten jagt'st Du Adam fort,
   den Armen?
Ist das Gnade, nicht zu strafen, wer nach Deiner Vor-
   schrift handelt?
Gnade ist, dem zu verzeihen, der verbotene Wege
   wandelt.

Von Schack
(205)

O Gott, wenn du barmherzig bist, wie das der Gläub'ge
   von dir sagt,
Was hast den ersten Sünder du denn aus dem Paradies gejagt?
Dass du an Fromme Gnade schenkst, nicht nenn' ich
   das barmherzig sein;
Wer sich Erbarmer heissen lässt, muss argen Sündern
   selbst verzeih'n.

APPENDIX XXXVII.

RUBÁ'IY LXXXVII.

FitzGerald's note (24) to Stanza LXXXVII is applicable to the whole "Book of Pots":—

This Relation of Pot and Potter to Man and his Maker figures far and wide in the Literature of the World, from the time of the Hebrew Prophets to the present; when it may finally take the name of "Pot theism," by which Mr. Carlyle ridiculed Sterling's "Pantheism." *My* Sheikh, whose knowledge flows in from all quarters, writes to me —

"Apropos of old Omar's Pots, did I ever tell you the sentence I found in 'Bishop Pearson on the Creed'? 'Thus are we wholly at the disposal of His will, and our present and future condition framed and ordered by His free, but wise and just, decrees. *Hath not the potter power over the clay, of the same lump to make one vessel unto honour, and another unto dishonour?* (Rom. ix. 21.) And can that earth-artificer have a freer power over his *brother potsherd* (both being made of the same metal), than God hath over him, who, by the strange fecundity of His omnipotent power, first made the clay out of nothing, and then him out of that?'"

And again — from a very different quarter — "I had to refer the other day to Aristophanes, and came by chance on a curious Speaking-pot story in the Vespæ, which I had quite forgotten.

Φιλοκλέων.   Ἄκουε, μὴ φεῦγ᾽· ἐν Συβάρει γυνή ποτε
             κατέαξ᾽ ἐχῖνον.

Κατήγορος.   Ταῦτ᾽ ἐγὼ μαρτύρομαι.

Φι.   Οὑχῖνος οὖν ἔχων τιν᾽ ἐπεμαρτύρατο.
             Εἶθ᾽ ἡ Συβαρῖτις εἶπεν. εἰ ναὶ τὰν κόραν
             τὴν μαρτυρίαν ταύτην ἐάσας. ἐν τάχει
             ἐπίδεσμον ἐπρίω. νοῦν ἂν εἶχες πλείονα.

"The Pot calls a bystander to be a witness to his bad treatment. The woman says, 'If, by Proserpine, instead of all this "testifying" (comp. Cuddie and his mother in 'Old Mortality!') you would buy yourself a rivet, it would show more sense in you!' The Scholiast explains *echinus* as ἄγγος τι ἐκ κεράμου."

One more illustration for the oddity's sake from the "Autobiography of a Cornish Rector," by the late James Hamley Tregenna. 1871.

"There was one odd Fellow in our Company — he was so like a Figure in the 'Pilgrim's Progress' that Richard always called him the 'ALLEGORY,' with a long white beard — a rare Appendage in those days — and a Face the colour of which seemed to have been baked in, like the Faces one used to see on Earthenware Jugs. In our Country-dialect Earthenware is called '*Clome*'; so the Boys of the Village used to shout out after him — 'Go back to the Potter, Old Clomeface, and get baked over again.' For the 'Allegory,' though shrewd enough in most things, had the reputation of being '*saift-baked*,' i. e., of weak intellect."

Compare Browning's "Rabbi Ben Ezra": —

This I was worth to God, whose wheel the pitcher shaped.

Ay, note that Potter's wheel,
That metaphor! and feel
Why time spins fast, why passive lies our clay, —
Thou to whom fools propound,
When the wine makes its round,
"Since life fleets, all is change; the Past gone, seize to-day!"

Fool! all that is, at all,
Lasts ever past recall:
Earth changes, but thy soul and God stand sure:
What entered into thee,
That was, is, and shall be:
Time's wheel runs back or stops: Potter and clay endure.

I gather a number of the Rubáiyát containing the same or a similar conceit: —

Livre-toi à la gaieté, car le chagrin sera infini. Les étoiles se réuniront encore sur un même point du firmament, et les briques que l'on fera de ton corps serviront à construire des palais pour d'autres. **Nicolas** (138)

Abandon thyself to enjoyment, for sorrow is without end. The stars will assemble in the heavens in their former courses, and of the bricks which they make from thy body will they build palaces for others. **McCarthy** (215)

Take heart! Long in the weary tomb you'll lie.
While stars keep countless watches in the sky,
   And see your ashes moulded into bricks,
To build another's house and turrets high. **Whinfield** (162)

Überlass Dich der Freude Lauf,
  Der Gram drängt sich selber auf,
Ist jedem Menschen erblich
  Und in der Welt unsterblich.
Die Sterne kreisen noch oben,
  Wenn längst unser Leib zerstorben,
Wenn man unserm Staub zu Backsteinen schichtet
  Und Paläste für Andre daraus errichtet. **Bodenstedt** (VIII. 14)

Sei fröhlich jetzt, denn bald folgt schwere Leidensnacht;
  Der Sterne Stand kann man mit Angst nur schauen,
Und mit den Ziegeln, die aus deinem Staub man macht,
  Wird man für Andere Paläste bauen. **Von Schack** (111)

Nicolas
(277)

Jusques à quand serons-nous esclaves de notre raison de tous les jours ? Qu' importe que nous restions cent ans en ce monde, ou que nous n'y demeurions qu'un jour ? Va, apporte du vin dans un bol avant que nous soyons transformés en cruche dans l'atelier du potier.

McCarthy
(312)

No longer, O Reason, will I continue to be thy slave; wherefore should I care if in this world I remain for fifty years, or but one day is left to me? Come, let us drink wine from the flagon before we ourselves become pots in the shop of the potter.

Whinfield
(320)

Let us shake off dull reason's incubus,
Our tale of days or years cease to discuss,
   And take our jugs, and plenish them with wine,
Or e'er grim potters make their jugs of us!

   Whinfield, 171 (1882), has in line 2, *years or days*, and line 4 begins, *Before grim potters*.

Garner
(XI. 3)

How Long will Reason's Chains oppress my Soul?
What boots it whether One Day or Hundreds roll
   Above my Head, come fill the Cup, my Clay
The Potter soon will shape into a Bowl.

Bodenstedt
(IX. 87)

Wie lange sollen wir täglich vor dem Verstande beben?
Was macht's, ob wir hundert Jahr oder einen Tag nur
   leben?
Lasst uns fröhlich beim Wein unsern Schöpfer loben,
Eh' unsern Staub als guten Thon die Töpfer loben.

Nicolas
(6)

Lève-toi, viens, viens, et, pour la satisfaction de mon cœur, donne-moi l'explication d'un problème: apporte-moi vite une cruche de vin, et buvons avant que l'on fasse des cruches de notre propre poussière.

Rise and come hither, and for mine heart's ease solve at least one problem: bring swiftly here a flask of ancient wine, that we may drink our fill before folk make flagons of our clay. **McCarthy**
(7)

Hither! come hither, love! my heart doth need thee; **M. K.**
Come, and expound a riddle I will read thee.
   The earthen jar bring too,—and let us drink, love!
Ere, turned to clay, to earthenware they knead thee!

Arise! and come, and of thy courtesy **Whinfield**
Resolve my weary heart's perplexity, (5)
   And fill my goblet, so that I may drink,
Or e'er they make their goblets out of me.

O Schenke, lass flehen uns nicht vergebens! **Von Shack**
Komm'! zünd' uns ein Licht im Dunkel des Lebens!
Sei aus den Krügen uns Wein in's Glas zu schenken
     bedacht,
Eh' wieder aus unserem Staub der Töpfer Krüge macht!

Prends dans tes mains la coupe, emporte la gourde, **Nicolas**
ô charme de mon cœur! et va explorer les prairies, les (354)
bords des ruisseaux, car bien des idoles, semblables à
la lune par l'éclat de leurs beaux visages, ont été cent
fois transformées en coupes, cent fois elles ont été des
gourdes.

Take cup and flagon in thy hands, beloved, let us **McCarthy**
hasten to the fields and streams, for many maidens (430)
lovely as the moon have been turned at last into cups
and flagons.

Whinfield (376)	"Take up thy cup and goblet, Love," I said, "Haunt purling river bank, and grassy glade; Full many a moon-like form has heaven's wheel Oft into cup, oft into goblet made!"

Von Schack (35)	Nimm den ird'nen Krug, Geliebte, nimm den Becher in die Hand,
	  Und auf grünen Wiesen wandelnd an der Silberbäche Rand.
	  Denk, wie viele mondgesicht'ge Mädchen, schön wie du, mein Kind,
	  Krüg' und Becher hundert Male schon vordem gewesen sind.

Nicolas (368)	Jusques à quand me parleras-tu de mosquée, de prière, de jeûne? Va plutôt à la taverne et énivre-toi, dusses-tu pour cela demander l'aumône. Ô Khèyam! bois du vin, bois, car de cette terre dont tu es composé on fera tantôt des coupes, tantôt des bols, tantôt des cruches.
McCarthy (370)	A fig for mosques, prayers, fastings; hie thee to the tavern and get drunk, even if thou hast to beg for it. Drink, my Khayyam, for soon that earth of thine will be fashioned into cups and bowls and jars.
Whinfield (403)	Of mosque and prayer and fast preach not to me, Rather go drink, were it on charity! Yea, drink, Khayyam, your dust will soon be made A jug, or pitcher, or a cup, may be!

Wie lange soll ich noch hören von Moscheen und Beten und Fasten?		**Bodenstedt** (VIII. 70)

Such' lieber in der Schenke Dein beladenes Herz zu
  entlasten.
O Chajjam, trink Wein! Dein Staub wird behandelt
Und in Becher, Krüge und Schalen verwandelt.

   Compare "Hamlet," Act V. sc. 1:—

      Imperious Cæsar, dead, and turned to clay,
      Might stop a hole to keep the wind away.

   See also Appendices XXXIX and XL.

APPENDIX XXXVIII.

RUBÁ'IY LXXXVIII.

Here is the personal application of Omar's faith:—

Le jour où les cieux seront confondus, où les étoiles s'obscurciront, je t'arrêterai sur ton chemin, ô idole! et, te prenant par le pan de ta robe, je te demanderai pourquoi tu m'as ôté la vie (après me l'avoir donnée).	**Nicolas** (50)
Though heaven and earth were blent together, though all the lustre of the stars went out, I would wait in your path, O beloved, and ask of you why you have taken away my life.	**McCarthy** (70)
On that dread day, when wrath shall rend the sky, And darkness dim the bright stars' galaxy, I'll seize the Loved One by His skirt, and cry, "Why hast Thou doomed these guiltless ones to die?"	**Whinfield** (83)

Bodenstedt
(l. 13)

Wenn die Himmel sich spalten,
　Wenn die Sterne erkalten,
Dann auf Deinem Pfade,
　Herr der Strafe und Gnade,
Will ich Dich fragen,
　Du sollst mir sagen:
Warum nahmst Du das Leben,
　Das du selbst mir gegeben?

Von Schack
(135)

Dereinst am Tag des Gerichts, wenn die Sterne droben
　　erblassen
　Und der Himmel zusammenbricht, wie das der Gläu-
　　bige glaubt,
　An deines Gewandes Saum, o Liebchen, werd' ich dich
　　fassen
　Und fragen, warum du mir grausam das Leben geraubt.

Compare the refrain in Bayard Taylor's song:—

　　　When the stars grow old,
　　　And the sun grows cold
　　　And the leaves of the Judgment-book unfold.

APPENDIX XXXIX.

RUBÁ'IY LXXXIX.

Omar Khayyam, and his imitators, are fond of repeating his conceits:—

Nicolas
(115)

Lorsque l'arbre de mon existence sera déraciné, lorsque mes membres seront dispersés, que l'on fera des cruches de ma poussière et que l'on remplira ces cruches de vin, alors cette poussière revivra (par le vin qu'elle contiendra.)

When the tree of my existence is uprooted, when my   **McCarthy**
members are scattered, let them make pitchers of my   (192)
dust, and let them fill the pitchers with wine; thus
shall the dust be quickened again.

When Death shall tread me down upon the plain,   **Whinfield**
And pluck my feathers, and my life-blood drain,   (330)
   Then mould me to a cup, and fill with wine;
Haply its scent will make me breathe again.

Wenn entwurzelt wird meines Daseins Baum   **Bodenstedt**
Und meine Gebeine zerstreut im Raum,   (IX. 65)
Wird man Krüge aus meinem Staube machen
Und dieser durch Wein neu zum Leben erwachen.

APPENDIX XL.

RUBÁ'IY XCI.

There are a number of quaint Rubáiyát in which
*Omar, as in his will, provides for the appropriate dis-
position of his body:—

Lorsque je serai mort, lavez-moi avec le jus de la   **Nicolas**
treille; au lieu de prières, chantez sur ma tombe les   (?)
louanges de la coupe et du vin, et si vous désirez me
retrouver au jour dernier, cherchez-moi sous la poussière du seuil de la taverne.

When I am dead, wash me with vintage juice; instead   **McCarthy**
of prayers recite over my tomb hymnals of wine and   (8)
flagons, and if you seek me at the latter day, look for
me in the dust upon the tavern threshold.

M. K.

    Wash me when dead in the juice of the vine, old friends!
    Let your funeral service be drinking and wine, old friends!
        And if you would meet me again when the Doomsday comes,
    Search the dust of the tavern, and sift from it mine, old friends!

Whinfield
(6)

    When I am dead, with wine my body lave,
    For obit chant a bacchanalian stave,
        And, if you need me at the day of doom,
    Beneath the tavern threshold seek my grave.

Garner
(I. 11)

    When I am dead, my body wash with Wine,
    Sing o'er my tomb the praises of the Vine,
        And when the Day of Resurrection dawns,
    Commingled with the Tavern's dust, seek Mine.

Bodenstedt
(IX. 36)

    Wenn ich tot bin, so wascht mit Wein meine Glieder,
    Und am Grab, statt Gebete, singt lustige Lieder;
        Und forscht Ihr nach mir am jüngsten Tage,
    Ihr findet im Staub vor der Schenke mich wieder.

Von Schack
(44)

    Wenn tot ich bin, so sollt ihr den Leib mit Saft der Traube mir waschen;
    Anstatt zu beten, preiset den Wein und klirrt mit Gläsern und Flaschen,
        Und wenn ihr am jüngsten Tage dereinst mich suchen wollt, ich denke:
    Am sichersten findet ihr mein Gebein im Staub am Thore der Schenke.

Au moment où je fuirai la mort, où, semblables aux **Nicolas**
feuilles desséchés, les parcelles de mon corps se déta- (266)
cheront des branches de la vie, oh, alors ! avec quelle
joie ne passerais-je pas l'univers à travers un crible,
avant que le maçon vienne y passer ma propre poussière !

At the moment when my soul shall be delivered from **McCarthy**
death, when my members shall be scattered from the (250)
tree of my life like dry leaves before the wind, O, then,
with what joy I shall pass out of this world through a
sieve, before my own dust is passed through it by the
builder.

When Khayyam quittance at Death's hand receives, **Whinfield**
And sheds his outworn life, as trees their leaves, (309)
   Full gladly will he sift this world away,
Ere dustmen sift his ashes in their sieves.

Wenn der Tod mich einst weckt vom Erdentraume **Bodenstedt**
  Und die Hüllen sich lockern am Lebensbaume, (III. 14)
Um allgemach ganz zu verwettern
  Und abzufallen gleich dürren Blättern,
Dann wird durch das Sieb des Körpers dringen
  Die Seele, sich jauchzend nach oben zu schwingen,
Bevor noch ein Maurer sich fühlt getrieben,
  Mein Körperstand hier unten zu sieben.

Le jour où l'on m'aura rendu étranger à moi-même, **Nicolas**
et où l'on parlera de moi comme d'une fable, alors je (154)
désire, (oserai-je le dire ?) que de ma boue l'on fasse
un pot à vin destiné au service de la taverne.

McCarthy (236)	The day when I shall no longer be known to myself, and when they speak of me as a tale that is told: then my heart's desire is that from my ashes may be formed a wine jar for the tavern.
Garner (VI. 19)	Yes, when within the Ground my Dust is laid, And Name and Memory to a Story fade, Ah, Brother mine, I humbly beg of Thee, That Drinking Vessels from My Clay be made.
Bodenstedt (VII. 24)	Einst, wenn ich nicht mehr bin, was ich gewesen, Und man gleichwie von einem Fabelwesen Von mir wird sprechen, — sammelt mein Gebein, Macht einen Krug daraus, füllt ihn mit Wein.
Von Schack (67)	Einst, wenn zur Fabel ich auf Erden ward Und von mir selber nichts mehr weiss, Möcht' ich als Krug, zu dem mein Staub geformt. Die Runde machen in der Zecher Kreis.

Nicolas (173)	Si vous êtes mes amis, mettez un terme à vos discours frivoles et, pour adoucir mes chagrins, versez-moi du vin. Lorsque je serai redevenu terre, faites de moi une brique, et placez cette brique dans quelque fissure d'un des murs de la taverne.
McCarthy (265)	If you are indeed my friends, silence your vain discourse, and soften my sorrows by filling my cup with wine. When I am turned to dust, mould of my dust a brick, and place that brick in some gap in the walls of a tavern.

If Friends of mine you are, come cease your brawl,   **Garner**
Then fill your Cups, and when in Death I fall,   (VI. 4)
  I pray you take my Clay and mould a Brick,
To stop a hole within the Tavern's wall.

Wenn Ihr mich liebt, so hört auf mit den feichten   **Bodenstedt**
    Geschwatzen,   (IX. 79)
Nur der Wein kann mich in bessere Laune versetzen.
Wird mein Körper zu Staub, so macht einen Backstein
    daraus,
Irgend ein Loch zu stopfen in diesem weinseligen Haus.

Statt eitles Gerede zu pflegen, kredenzt mir Wein   **Von Schack**
Und, werd' ich wieder in Erde zerfallen sein,   (282)
  So formt aus mir einen Ziegelstein
Und in die Wand der Schenke mauert ihn ein!

  Quand je serai mort, aplanissez aussitôt au niveau du   **Nicolas**
sol la poussière de ma tombe, et faites que je serve ainsi   (136)
d'exemple aux hommes. Ensuite, pétrissez avec du vin
la terre de mon corps et faites-en un couvercle de jarre.

  When I am dead, smooth my tomb down to the level   **McCarthy**
of the earth without delay, and make me in this wise   (224)
an example to mankind. Then knead the ashes of
my body with wine, and make thereof the cover of a
jar.

When I am dead, take me and grind me small,   **Whinfield**
So that I be a caution unto all,   (160)
  And knead me into clay with wine, and then   (89, 1882)
Use me to stop the wine-jar's mouth withal.

Von Schack Kein Hügel soll auf meinem Grab sich erheben,
(239)   Nein allen Menschen lasst mich als Vorbild dienen:
Netzt meine Staubesreste mit Saft der Reben
    Und formt dann einen Weinkrugdeckel aus ihnen!

APPENDIX XLI.

RUBÁ'IY XCII.

The extravagant humor of the original of FitzGerald's ninety-second quatrain (toned down in his version) appears in slightly different form in the following: —

Nicolas Ô vin limpide, vin plein d'émail! je veu, foux que je
(439) suis, te boire en quantité telle, que quiconque m'apercevra de loin puisse, confondant mon identité avec la tienne, me dire: "Ô maître vin! dis-moi, d'où viens-tu?"

McCarthy Clear comely wine, I fain would drink so deep of thy
(386) divinity that those beholding me from afar should blend my being with thine and say, "O Lord Wine, whence comest thou?"

Whinfield O wine, most limpid, pure, and crystalline,
(472)   Would I could drench this silly frame of mine
    With thee, that passers by might think 't was thou,
    And cry, "Whence comest thou, fair master wine?"

Bodenstedt O Wein voll Reinheit und Perlenglanz!
(IX. 2) Dein Geist soll mich Thoren erfüllen, dass ganz
Ich werde wie Du — und man ruft mir zu:
Guten Morgen, Herr Wein! woher so rein?

O funkelnder Wein! so viel lass mich zechen,
  Bis sich in dein Wesen verwandelt mein Sein
Und Alle, die mir begegnen, sprechen:
  "Wo kommst du her, o meister Wein?"

Von Shack
(216)

APPENDIX XLII.

RUBÁ'IY XCIII.

In the following he explains the "base metal" of quatrain LXXVI, and shows how he "drowned his glory in a shallow cup."

Le monde ne cesse de me qualifier de dépravé. Je ne suis cependant pas coupable. Ô hommes de sainteté ! examinez-vous plutôt vous-mêmes et voyez ce que vous êtes. Vous m'accusez d'agir contrairement au chèr'e (loi du Koran); je n'ai cependant pas commis d'autres péchés que l'ivrognerie, la débauche et l'adultère.

Nicolas
(88)

Nicolas says of the next to the last noun of this Rubá'iy that it replaces the *mot énergique* which the poet employs, and which propriety prevents him from rendering literally.

The world upbraids me as a debauchee, and yet I am not guilty. Ye holy men, look upon yourselves, and learn what ye truly are. You charge me with violation of the holy law, but I have committed no other sins than riot, drunkenness, and adultery.

McCarthy
(96)

M. K.	Wicked, men call me ever; yet blameless I!
	Think how it is, ye Saints! — My life, ye cry,
	Breaks all Heaven's laws — Good lack! I have no sin,
	That needs reproach, save wenching and drink! — then, why?
Whinfield (90)	O men of morals! why do ye defame,
	And thus misjudge me? I am not to blame.
	Save weakness for the grape, and female charms,
	What sins of mine can any of ye name?
Bodenstedt (VII. 12)	Verlästert mich der Menschen Mund,
	Geb' ich dazu doch keinen Grund.
	O Heilige, seht Euch selbst in's Herz,
	Statt fromm zu äugeln himmelwärts.
	Ihr lästert mich und klagt mich an,
	Ich lebe nicht als Muselmann,
	Und doch hab' ich keine Sünde begangen,
	Die nicht an Wein und Liebe hangen.

But here is his excuse: —

Nicolas (380)	Nous avons violé tous les vœux que nous avions formés; nous avons fermé sur nous la porte de la bonne et celle de la mauvaise renommée. Ne me blâmez point si vous me voyez commettre des actes d'insensé, (car, vous le voyez) nous sommes ivres du vin de l'amour, ivres tous tant que nous sommes.
McCarthy (339)	We have broken all our vows, we have closed the gates of good and evil fame; do not blame us for being foolish in our folly, for we are drunk with the wine of love.

Wir haben alle Gelübde der Entsagung gebrochen,   **Bodenstedt**
Wollen weder auf guten noch auf schlechten Ruf pochen;   (VII. 38)
Drum schmäht nicht zu sehr unser seltsam Getriebe:
Da wir Alle berauscht sind vom Wein hoher Liebe.

And having confessed, he grows more reckless : —

   Voici l'aurore, viens, et, la coupe pleine de vin rose   **Nicolas**
en main, respirons un instant. Quant à l'honneur, à la   (204)
réputation, ce crystal fragile, brisons-le contre la pierre.
Renonçons à nos désirs insatiables, bornons-nous à jouir
de l'attouchement des longues chevelures des belles et
du son harmonieux de la harpe.

   Behold the dawn arises. Let us rejoice in the present   **McCarthy**
moment with a cup of crimson wine in our hand. As   (283)
for honour and fame, let that fragile crystal be dashed
to pieces against the earth. [Last half missing.]

'T is dawn ! my heart with wine I will recruit,   **Whinfield**
And dash to bits the glass of good repute ;   (332)
   My long-extending hopes I will renounce,
And grasp long tresses, and the charming lute.

Lasst trinken uns nun beim Morgenrot! Sagt an, was   **Von Schack**
   kann es uns kümmern,   (87)
Wenn Ehre und Ruf, dies vergängliche Glas, zu Scher-
   ben sich wandeln und Trümmern ?
Nichts wünschen lasst auf Erden uns mehr, nein mit den
   lieblichen Tönen.
Der Harfe wollen zufrieden wir sein und den wallenden
   Locken der Schönen.

APPENDIX XLIII.

RUBÁ'IY XCIV.

M. K. says that Rubáiyát XCII, XCIII, and XCIV of FitzGerald are not found in the original. After repeated search in Von Shack and Bodenstedt, I failed to find the stanza corresponding to McCarthy, XII, Whinfield, 425; it is certainly not in Nicolas. Nor was I more successful in finding in Whinfield or Bodenstedt the stanza corresponding to Nicolas, 162, McCarthy, 113, and Von Schack, 278.

The following have also a decided bearing on Fitz-Gerald, XCIV, and may possibly have inspired a part of it:—

Nicolas (452) Nous possédons du vin, ô échanson! nous jouissons de la présence de la bien-aimée (la Divinité) et du bruit du matin. Qu'on n'attende pas de notre part la renonciation de Nèssouh, ô échanson! Jusques à quand parleras-tu de l'histoire de Noé, ô échanson? Apporte, apporte-moi gentiment le repos de l'âme (du vin) ô échanson.

(*La renonciation de Nèssouh*, est un vœu formel dont on ne peut se faire relever.)

We have wine, and the well-beloved, and the morn- **McCarthy**
ing, O Cup-bearer. Not from us cometh renunciation, (330)
O Cup-bearer. How long wilt thou tell the tales of
old, O Cup-bearer? Bring me sweetly the peace of the
soul, O Cup-bearer.

Yes! here am I with wine and feres again! **Whinfield**
I did repent, but, ah! 'twas all in vain; (481)
   Preach not to me of Noah and his flood,
But pour a flood of wine to drown my pain!

   The second line of Whinfield, 249 (1882), ends, *cannot
refrain;*

Die Geliebte ist da, der Wein und der Morgen. **Bodenstedt**
Nun mache Enthaltsamkeit uns keine Sorgen! (X. 27)
Wie oft willst Du die Sage von Noah erzählen?
Schenk' ein, hör' auf meine Seele zu quälen!

APPENDIX XLIV.

RUBÁ'IY XCV

(Je l'ai déjà dit), le monde entier, semblable à une **Nicolas**
boule, roulerait dans un creux que, lorsque je dors ivre- (442)
mort, je ne m'en soucierais pas plus que si j'y voyais
rouler un grain d'orge. Hier au soir je me suis laissé
mettre en gage dans la taverne pour une coupe de vin.
Le marchand de vin ne cessait de dire : " Ô l'excellent
gage que je tiens là ! "

McCarthy
(105)

When I am drunk, the whole world might roll like a ball into a hole, and I should not care more than for a barley-corn. Yestere'en I pawned myself at the tavern for a stoup of wine, "Lo, what an excellent gage!" says the tapster.

Whinfield
(474)

If, like a ball, earth to my house were borne,
When drunk, I'd rate it at a barley-corn;
Last night they offered me in pawn for wine,
But the rude vintner laughed that pledge to scorn.

Bodenstedt
(X. 10)

Wenn der Erdball, während ich schliefe,
  Versänke in grundlose Tiefe;
Es kümmerte mich nicht mehr,
  Als ob es ein Gerstenkorn wär'!
Gestern blieb ich als Pfand in der Schenke
  Wegen Schuld für genoss'ne Getränke,
Und der Wirt sprach immer zu mir:
  Welch' kostbares Pfand hab' ich hier!

Von Schack
(305)

Lieg' ich im Rausch, so wüsst' ich nicht, was es mich
    kümmern sollte,
Wenn kugelgleich die ganze Welt in einen Abgrund
    rollte.
Mich selbst verpfändet' ich für Wein erst gestern in der
    Schenke;
Da sprach der Wirt: "Ein sich'res Pfand! das liegt
    doch fest, ich denke!"

APPENDIX XLV.

RUBÁ'IY LXV, 1868.

The humorous suggestion that the soul has control of its own disposal appears in several Rubáiyát: —

Boire du vin et rechercher les beaux visages est un parti plus sage que celui d'user d'hypocrisie et d'apparente dévotion. Il est évident que, s'il existe un enfer pour les amoureux et les buveurs, personne ne voudra du paradis. — **Nicolas** (342)

To drink and delight in fair faces is wiser than to affect a hypocritical faith. If all the lovers, and all the joyous topers, go to hell, nobody will want to go to paradise. — **McCarthy** (365)

Das Herz zu erheben durch Wein und Liebe,
Ist besser als heuchlerisch Andachtsgetriebe.
Wenn Verliebte und Trinker zur Hölle sollen,
So wird in den Himmel bald Niemand mehr wollen. — **Bodenstedt** (VII. 35)

Si j'étais libre et que je pusse user de ma volonté, si j'étais affranchi des tourments de la destinée, débarrassé du sentiment du bien et du mal de ce monde, où réside le désordre, oh! j'aimerais mieux n'y être point venu, n'y point exister, n'être point forcé d'en partir! — **Nicolas** (450)

McCarthy (317)	If I were free to use my will, if I were free from cares of good and evil in this worthless world, how willingly would I choose never to have come here, never to have lived here, never to depart hence.
Whinfield (109)	I never would have come, had I been asked, I would as lief not go, if I were asked, And to be short, I would annihilate All coming, being, going, were I asked!
Von Schack (33)	O wär' es nach meinem Willen gescheh'n Und dem Geschicke die Macht genommen, Nie wär' ich auf diese Erde gekommen, Noch braucht' ich wieder hinwegzugeh'n.

Compare Oidipous Coloneus, 1225-1227:—

μὴ φῦναι τὸν ἅπαντα νικᾷ λόγον τὸ δ' ἐπεὶ φανῇ
βῆναι κεῖθεν ὅθεν περ ἥκει
πολὺ δεύτερον ὡς τάχιστα.

" Happiest beyond compare
Never to taste of life;
Happiest in order next
Being born, with quickest speed
Thither to turn again
From whence we came."

Compare also Ecclesiastes iv. 2, 3:—

Wherefore I praised the dead which are already dead more than the living which are yet alive; yea better than them both did I esteem him which hath not yet been.

See Appendix XXX.

APPENDIX XLVI.

RUBÁ'IY CVII, 1868.

FitzGerald's expunged quatrain is a justification of murder or suicide: a finer and more ethical extravaganza is found in the following:—

Parviendrais-tu à peupler la terre entière, que cette action ne vaudrait pas celle de réjouir une âme attristée. Il serait plus avantageux pour toi de rendre esclave, par la douceur, un homme libre, que de donner la liberté à mille esclaves. — Nicolas (111)

It is better to lighten one sad soul, than to people a world. It is nobler to enslave one free man with charity, than to set free a thousand slaves. — McCarthy (318)

Better to make one soul rejoice with glee,
Than plant a desert with a colony;
  Rather one freeman bind with chains of love,
Than set a thousand prisoned captives free! — Whinfield (476)

Line 3 in Whinfield, 245 (1882), begins *Sooner one:* in the fourth line, *chained captives*.

Geläng' es, dass die ganze Erde
  Durch Deine Macht bevölkert werde:
Es zählte nicht so zu dem Grössten,
  Wie Ein unselig Herz zu trösten.
Kannst Du durch freundliches Beginnen
  Einen freien Mann zum Sclaven gewinnen,
So hast Du mehr gethan im Leben
  Als tausend Sclaven die Freiheit zu geben. — Bodenstedt (X. 20)

APPENDIX XLVII.

The preceding Rubáiyát, gathered together with a certain biographical unity, have made it evident that Omar was a man of many and often contradictory moods. A few more will help complete the picture. He never hesitates to paint his own character in the darkest hues:—

Nicolas (57)

Je ne suis digne ni de l'enfer, ni du séjour céleste ; Dieu sait de quelle terre il m'a pétri. Je suis hérétique comme un derviche, laid comme une femme perdue ; je n'ai ni religion, ni fortune, ni espérance du paradis.

McCarthy (116)

I am worthy neither of heaven nor yet of hell. God knows from what clay He fashioned me. I am as heretical as a Dervish, as ill-favoured as a harlot, I have neither faith nor wealth, nor hope of Paradise.

M. K.

Unworthy of Hell, unfit for Heaven, I be—
God knows what clay He used when He moulded me!
  Foul as a punk, ungodly as a monk,
No faith, no world, no hope of Heaven I see!

Whinfield (60)

From mosque an outcast, and to church a foe.
Allah! of what clay didst thou form me so?
  Like sceptic monk, or ugly courtesan,
No hopes have I above, no joys below.

Ich bin nicht wert, in den Himmel noch in die Hölle **Bodenstedt**
    zu kommen; (VII. 7)
Gott weiss, welchen Thon er, mich zu kneten, ge-
    nommen.
Ich bin ein Freigeist und hässlich; zwar leidlich ver-
    nünftig,
Doch glaub' ich nichts hier und hoffe nichts künftig.

Ganz unwert bin des Himmels ich, und auch die Hölle **Von Schack**
    will mich nicht, (258)
  Gott einzig weiss, aus welchem Lehm er mich ge-
    knetet haben mag.
Ein Ketzer, ein Verworfener, ein heil- und glaubensloser
    Wicht,
  Nicht denken kann ich, was mit mir geschehen soll
    am jüngsten Tag.

In the following also he may picture himself: Whinfield says the "debauchee" is "a *beshara*' or Antinomian
sufi."

J'ai vu un homme retiré sur un terrain aride. Il **Nicolas**
n'était ni hérétique, ni musulman; il n'avait ni richesses, (336)
ni religion, ni Dieu, ni vérité, ni loi, ni certitude. Qui
dans ce monde ou dans l'autre aurait un tel courage?

I saw a hermit in a desert place. He was neither **McCarthy**
heretic nor true believer, he had neither riches, nor (353)
creed, nor God, nor truth, nor law, nor knowledge.
Where is the man of like courage in this world or the
other world?

Whinfield
(375)

In a lone waste I saw a debauchee,
He had no home, no faith, no heresy,
  No God, no truth, no law, no certitude;
Where in this world is man so bold as he?

Bodenstedt
(VIII. 52)

Einen Mann sah ich ein dürres Stück Land bewohnen,
Der nichts wusste von Gesetzen und Religionen,
Nichts von Wahrheit und Gott, nichts von böse und
  gut, —
Wer im Himmel und auf Erden hätte gleichen Mut?

Von Schack
(206)

In der Wüste, wo er wohnte, traf ich einen Menschen
  an;
  Ohne Gott und Glauben war er, ohne Hab' und ohne
    Gut,
  Kein Gesetz für sich erkennend, Ketzer nicht noch
    Muselmann —
  Ist in dieser Welt und jener Einer wohl von gleichem
    Mut?

Like many another, he may have liked to shock the conservative faithful: —

Nicolas
(315)

Nous, d'une main, nous prenons le Koran, de l'autre, nous saisissons la coupe : vous nous voyez tantôt portés vers ce qui est licite, tantôt vers ce qui est défendu. Nous ne sommes donc, sous cette voûte azurée, ni complétement infidèles, ni absolument musulmans.

> We take the Koran in one hand, and the wine cup **McCarthy**
> in the other, and behold we are lured now to the law- (333)
> ful, now to the unlawful delight. Thus it comes to
> pass that underneath yon spangled bowl we are neither
> all faithful, nor all faithless.

McCarthy, 33, is almost precisely the same:—

> Take a grip of the Koran with one hand; have a clutch at
> the cup with the other, and tremble between the lawful and the
> unlawful. So shall we sit beneath the vaulted sky neither
> wholly believers nor wholly infidels.

> One hand with Koran, one with wine-cup dight, **Whinfield**
> I half incline to wrong, and half to right; (347)
>   The azure-marbled sky looks down on me
> A sorry Moslem, yet not heathen quite.

> In dieser Hand das Glas, in jener der Koran, **Von**
> Bin ich ein frommer bald, und bald ein schlechter **Hammer-**
>   Mann **Purgstall**
>   Ich bin in Weltendom, von Türkis hoch gewölbt
> Kein ganzer Giauer, und kein ganzer Musulmann.

> Den Koran in der einen, den Becher in der andern **Bodenstedt**
>   Hand, (II. 17)
> Sind wir bald dem Erlaubten, bald dem Verbot'nen
>   zugewandt.
> Sind weder ganze Ketzer, noch ganz des wahren Glau-
>   bens voll;
> So dass der Himmel selber nicht weiss, wie er es neh-
>   men soll.

Von Schack
(219)

Mit einer heb' ich den Koran, den Becher mit der an-
    dern Hand;
Bald dem Erlaubten ist mein Sinn, bald dem Verbot'nen
    zugewandt,
Auf dieser Erde dergestalt, so viel ich es ermessen
    kann,
Bin ich kein ganzer Ketzer zwar, doch auch nicht völlig
    Muselmann.

So Horace: —

" video meliora proboque."

Here is one more serious, unless, indeed, he had a sardonic mental reservation as to the meaning of the " life well spent."

Nicolas
(276)

Ne va pas croire que je craigne le monde, ou que j'aie peur de mourir, de voir mon âme s'en aller. La mort étant une vérité, je n'ai rien à craindre d'elle. Ce que je crains, c'est de n'avoir pas assez bien vécu.

McCarthy
(190)

Believe not that I fear the world, or that the thought of death and the departure of my soul fills me with terror. Since death is a truth, what have I to fear from it? All that I fear is, that my life has not been well spent.

Whinfield
(310)

Think not I dread from out the world to hie,
And see my disembodied spirit fly;
    I tremble not at death, for death is true,
'T is my ill life that makes me fear to die.

Think not I dread to see my spirit fly 　　　　　**Whinfield**
Through the dark gates of fell mortality; 　　　　(170, 1882)
　Death has no terrors when the life is true,
'Tis living ill that makes us fear to die.

Glaub nicht, dass Furcht vor der Welt mich quäle, 　**Bodenstedt**
Oder Furcht vor dem Tod und der Flucht der Seele! 　(I. 3)
Nicht fürcht' ich, als, wenn sie mich einst begraben:
Nicht würdig genug gelebt zu haben.

　　　　See Appendix VI, Nicolas, 96, etc.

———

　The "life well spent" was, literally interpreted, that spent with boon companions in the tavern. According to M. Nicolas, the tavern is only another name for the mosque: here, in either case, he obtained his inspiration:—

　Le jour où je prends dans ma main une coupe de **Nicolas**
vin et où, dans la joie de mon âme, je deviens ivre-mort, (16)
alors, dans cet état de feu qui me dévore, je vois cent
miracles se réaliser, alors des paroles claires comme
l'eau la plus limpide semblent venir m'expliquer le
mystère de toutes choses!

　The day when I hold in my hand a cup of wine, and **McCarthy**
when in the joy of my heart I drink myself drunk, (42)
then in that happy state a hundred miracles become
clear to me, and words limpid as water explain the
mystery of things.

Whinfield (19)	What time, my cup in hand, its draughts I drain, And with rapt heart unconsciousness attain, Behold what wondrous miracles are wrought, Songs flow like water from my burning brain.
Bodenstedt (IX. 42)	Wenn ich, den Becher zur Hand, froh berausche mich Und mit erhöhtem Verstand, so belausche mich; Wie erscheint mir die Welt dann so wunderbar Und alles Geheimnis der Schöpfung so klar!
Von Schack (106)	Wenn des Weines gold'ne Fluten aus dem Becher mich durchrinnen Und es mir im Freudenrausche schwindeln wird an allen Sinnen, Tausend Wunder seh' ich dann und höre Stimmen, die in klaren Worten mir das tiefste Wesen aller Dinge offenbaren.

There is in Omar none of the passion which makes the "Song of Songs" palpitate with Oriental fervor. But a few love poems may show the softer side of the old astronomer's character: these, like "the Song of Solomon," may be interpreted in a spiritual sense. The bien-aimée may be the Divinity, even as the dark but comely Shulammite is the Church:—

Nicolas (234)	Ma bien-aimée (puisse sa vie durer aussi longtemps que mes chagrins!) a recommencé à être aimable pour moi. Elle a jeté sur mes yeux un doux et furtif regard et a disparu, en se disant sans doute: Faisons le bien et jetons-le dans l'eau.

My well beloved, may her days be long as my sorrows, **McCarthy**
is kind to me again. She cast upon me a sweet and (23)
fleeting glance, and straightway vanished, saying, no
doubt, "Let me do good and cast it on the water."

My queen (long may she live to vex her slave!) **Whinfield**
To-day a token of affection gave, (273)
   Darting a kind glance from her eyes, she passed,
And said, "Do good and cast it on the wave!"

Meine Liebe (sie lebe so lange wie mein Gram!) **Bodenstedt**
War mir heut wieder freundlich ganz wundersam; (VI. 8)
Ihr Aug schoss in meines, als wollte sie sagen,
Thun wir Gutes, ohne nach Lohn zu fragen!

Mein Liebchen — möchte doch so lang ihr Leben dau- **Von Schack**
   ern, wie mein Gram! — (222)
War wieder huldvoll gegen mich, als heut sie mir
   vorüberkam;
Sie gab mir einen flücht'gen Blick, doch ging so
   schnell, wie sie genaht,
Und barg vor Allen, dass an mir geübt sie diese gute
   That.

Nicolas says that in the absence of distinctions of
gender in Persian it is a question whether the following
quatrain is to be regarded as mystic or not; still he is
convinced that the poet is addressing the divinity, and
not his mistress:—

Ô toi qui dans l'univers entier es l'objet choisi de mon **Nicolas**
cœur! toi qui m'es plus chère que l'âme qui m'anime, (2)
que les yeux qui m'éclairent! il n'y a rien, ô idole, de
plus précieux que la vie: eh bien! tu m'es cent fois
plus précieuse qu'elle.

McCarthy (122)	O you who out of all the world art dearest to my heart, more precious than the soul which quickens me or than the eyes that light my path, there is nothing, oh my Beloved, dearer than life, and yet you, ah, you are a hundred times more dear.
M. K.	Thou! chosen one from earth's full muster-roll to me! Dearer than my two eyes, than even my soul to me! — Though nothing than life more precious we esteem, Yet dearer art thou, my love, a hundred-fold to me!
Garner (II. 5)	Oh, Thou who in the Universe entire The Object art of all my fond Desire, Far dearer art Thou than my Quickening Soul, More precious Thou than Life's Consuming Fire.
Bodenstedt (I. 5)	Du in der ganzen Welt mein höchstes Ziel und Streben, Mir teurer als das Licht der Augen, Seel' und Leben: Schützt man das Leben auch als höchstes Gut, Mit Freuden hundertmal für Dich würd' ich es geben!

Nicolas (164)	Un amour ne saurait produire de reflet. Il est comme un feu à demi éteint qui n'a plus de chaleur. Un véritable amoureux ne doit connaître pendant des mois, pendant des années, durant la nuit, durant le jour, ni tranquillité, ni repos, ni nourriture, ni sommeil.
McCarthy (241)	An earthly love can seldom inspire perfection. It is like a half extinct fire which no longer gives forth heat. He who loveth in truth, should not know rest, or food, or sleep, through months, or through years, by day, or by night.

This worldly love of yours is incomplete,   **Whinfield**
And, like a half spent blaze, lacks light and heat;   (182)
  True love is his, who for days, months and years,
Rests not, nor sleeps, nor craves for drink or meat.

  Whinfield, 97 (1882), begins:—

      This love of yours is feigned and incomplete

and line 3 ends
           who through long days and nights.

Die gemeine Liebe ist verwerflich ganz,   **Bodenstedt**
Ein Glimmen in der Asche ohne Wärme und Glanz,   (VIII. 26)
Doch wo die wahre Liebe glüht,
Ergreift sie das ganze Herz und Gemüt,
Lässt keine Ruhe bei Tag und Nacht,
Weiss nicht, ob Monde, ob Jahre verbracht,
Denkt an Essen und Trinken nicht,
Ihr ganzes Wesen ist Glut und Licht.

Die laue Liebe ist ein Feuer, das ohne Glanz und   **Von Schack**
    Wärme brennt.   (195)
  Wollt ihr den ächten Verliebten erkunden, so wisst:
    ein solcher ist nur der,
  Der Monde, Jahre, zu allen Stunden, kaum seiner
    eignen Sinne Herr,
Das Weib beseufzend, das ihm teuer, nicht Rast noch
    Speise noch Schlummer kennt.

  And this is fine from either point of view:—

  Je ne vois ni le moyen de me joindre à toi, ni la   **Nicolas**
possibilité de vivre l'espace d'un souffle séparé de toi.   (451)
Je n'ai point le courage de faire part à qui que ce soit
des tourments que j'endure. Oh! quelle situation difficile, quelle étrange douleur, quelle délectable passion!

McCarthy (446)	Alas, Fate will not let me live anigh thee, yet I can not bear to live a hair's breadth apart from thee. I dare not share my woes with anyone. Oh, hard lot, strange sorrow, fair passion.
Whinfield (482)	For union with my love I sigh in vain, The pangs of absence I can scarce sustain, My grief I dare not tell to any friend; O trouble strange, sweet passion, bitter pain!
Bodenstedt (VI. 22)	Ich kann Dich nicht erlangen Und muss doch an Dir hangen, Muss das Schwerste um Dich tragen Und darf es Keinem klagen. O welch seltsames Leiden, Dich nah, wie der Hauch, zu meiden, Und mich doch selig fühlen, Während Qualen mich durchwühlen!
Von Schack (134)	Mittel nicht zu finden weiss ich, um mit dir mich zu vereinen, Aber fern von dir zu atmen, will mir auch unmöglich scheinen Und, von meinem Leid zu sprechen, fehlt der Mut mir allzumal— O der wundersamen Lage! o der süssen Liebesqual!

Théophile Gautier sees no mystic meaning in Omar's poetry. He interprets his convivial and amorous lines in the frank literalness of their confession, but how beautifully he interprets it:—

Assis sur la terrasse de sa maison pendant une de ces belles nuits d'été qu'argente la lune et que choisit le rossignol pour conter ses amours à la rose, Kéyam, seul avec quelque belle au teint nuancé des fraîches couleurs de la tulipe et relevé par un de ces grains de beauté si chers aux poêtes persans, vidait la coupe de l'amour et de l'ivresse, ou bien encore, avec des amis, qu'abreuvait un infatigable échanson, improvisait des vers qui se rhythmaient aux chants des musiciens.

D'autres fois il s'en allait dans la campagne, deployait un de ces tapis sur lesquels les Orientaux aiment à s'accroupir au bord d'un ruisseau limpide, à l'ombre des platanes ou des cyprès, et il se laissait aller au kief tout en donnant des baisers aux lèvres de la coupe pleine d'un vin couleur de rubis, préférable à tous les joyaux d'Haroun-al-Raschid.

It may be thus paraphrased:—

It is a lovely summer night; the moon pours out her jar of silvery light; the nightingale unto the rose his hopeless passion doth disclose. Sitting upon the rose-twined terrace there Khayyám alone with some fair maiden whose tulip-tinted cheek glows with fresh loveliness enhanced by the clinging caress of a mole so dear to the Persian poet's soul, empties the intoxicating cup of love and wine. Or else when his wishes to booncompanionship incline he joins his faithful friends served by the indefatigable cup-bearer and improvises verses in sweet lingering rhyme while the instruments give forth a musical merry chime.

And then again he seeks the pleasant fields and has his carpet spread where a crystalline streamlet yields a musical murmur and the cypress and the plane-tree cast their cooling shade; and he gives himself up to the blisses of languorous dreams, imprinting eager kisses on the lips of the wine-cup full of ruby wine rather to be chosen than all the jewels fine of all the Sultans or Caliphs of the East.

But the half-mocking, petulant jealousy of the following is hard to interpret except in natural literalness:—

Nicolas (111)
Oh! quel dommage que ce soient les *crus* qui possèdent le pain tout cuit, que ce soient les *incomplets* qui possèdent les richesses complètes! Les yeux des belles Turques sont la fête du cœur et ce sont de simples élèves, des esclaves qui en sont les possesseurs!

McCarthy (234)
Oh, what a misfortune that it is the ignorant or inexperienced who possess the bread well baked — the incomplete, who possess complete riches! The eyes of the beautiful girls are the joy of the heart, and it is mere knaves and slaves who are their owners.

Whinfield (111)
Ah! seasoned wine oft falls to rawest fools,
And clumsiest workmen own the finest tools,
   And Turki maids, fit to delight men's hearts,
Lavish their smiles on beardless boys in schools!

Bodenstedt (VI. 27)
Wie traurig, zu sehn, dass die edelsten Spenden
Der Erde sind meist in unwürdigen Händen!
Selbst die Schönheiten, die uns zum Höchsten begeistern:
Macht, Wahn und Rohheit dürfen sie meistern.

And this also has a humorous petulance, as of a crusty but whimsical old bachelor:—

Sur la terre, personne n'a étreint dans ses bras une charmante aux joues colorées du teint de la rose sans que le temps ne soit venu d'abord lui planter quelque épine dans le cœur. Vois plutôt le peigne : il n'a pu parvenir à caresser la chevelure parfumée de la beauté qu'après avoir été découpé en une foule de dents.
  Nicolas (150)

What dweller on this earth has ever folded in his embrace a fair one with rose-tinted cheeks, who has not first received some thorn in the heart from time? Behold this comb, before it can be suffered to touch the scented hair of beauty, it has to be hacked into a ridge of teeth.
  McCarthy (288)

Whoso aspires to gain a rose-cheeked fair,
Sharp pricks from fortune's thorns must learn to bear.
 See! till this comb was cleft by cruel cuts,
It never dared to touch my lady's hair.
  Whinfield (171)

Auf Erden hielt Niemand fest eine rosige Schöne
  umschlungen,
Ohne dass von ihr ein Dorn in's Herz ihm gedrungen.
Sieh, dieser Kamm selbst konnte der Schönheit duftige
  Strähne
Dann erst küssen, als man ihm gehörig geschnitten die
  Zähne.
  Bodenstedt (VI. 26)

And there is also a humorous but pathetic significance in these words : —

Nicolas
(143)

Bercé d'un vain espoir, j'ai jeté au vent une partie de mon existence, et cela sans avoir connu ici-bas un seul jour de bonheur. Ce que je crains maintenant, c'est que le temps ne m'empêche de saisir l'occasion de me dédommager du passé.

McCarthy
(303)

Lulled by a vain hope, I scattered to the winds a portion of my life, and that before I had known in this world a day of enjoyment. Alas! I fear now that fleeting time will not allow me to repay myself for the days that are past.

Whinfield
(166)

I wasted life in hope, yet gathered not
In all my life of happiness one jot;
  Now my fear is that life may not endure,
Till I have taken vengeance on my lot.

Bodenstedt
(IV. 21)

In eitlem Hoffen schlug ich viel Zeit in den Wind,
Ohne zu wissen, was glückliche Stunden sind,
Und nun fürcht' ich, die Zeit wird nicht mehr kommen,
Die mir giebt, was ich einst nicht selbst genommen.

Von Schack
(243)

Jetzt, wo die Rosen ihre Knospen brechen,
Bei'm Lied der Nachtigallen lasst uns zechen
  Und uns bei'm Weine, funkeln wie Rubin,
Für die vergang'nen Qualen rächen!

And now a few more specimens of Omar's wit and
wisdom: serious and serio-comic aphorisms, practical
advice, quaint conceits:—

Mets une coupe de vin dans ta main, puis mêle ta **Nicolas**
voix à celle des rossignols, car s'il était convenable de (261)
boire ce jus de la treille sans accompagnement d'aucune
voix harmonieuse, le vin ne ferait lui-même aucun bruit
en coulant hors du flacon.

Take the cup in your hand, and lift up your voice in **McCarthy**
the choir of the nightingales, for if it were seemly to (201)
drink the blood of the vine with no sweet concord of
harmonious sound, the wine itself would make no
sound in gurgling from the flagon.

Give me my cup in hand, and sing a glee **Whinfield**
In concert with the bulbuls' symphony; (301)
  Wine would not gurgle as it leaves the flask,
If drinking mute were right for thee and me!

Ô mon cœur! agis si tous les biens de ce monde **Nicolas**
t'appartenaient; imagine-toi que cette maison est pour- (197)
vue de toutes choses, qu'elle est soigneusement ornée,
et vis joyeux dans ce domaine du désordre. Figure-toi
que tu t'y es assis durant deux ou trois jours, et qu'ensuite tu t'es levé pour partir.

O! my heart, act as if all the wealth of this world **McCarthy**
were thine — think that this house is furnished with all (173)
things, that it is adorned sumptuously; and pass thy
life joyfully in this distracted sphere. Say to thyself
that thou restest here for but a few days, and wilt then
arise and depart.

Bodenstedt (V. 14)	Handle, Freund, als gehörten Dir alle Schätze der Welt, Bilde Dir ein, dieses Haus sei so schön für Dich nur bestellt; Lebe vergnügt darin, aber betrachte dies Haus Nur als Absteigequartier: bald musst Du wieder hinaus.

Nicolas (107)	Ô ami! à quoi bon te préoccuper de *l'être*? Pourquoi troubler ainsi ton cœur, ton âme par des pensées oiseuses? Vis heureux, passe ton temps joyeusement, car enfin on n'a pas demandé ton avis pour faire ce qui est.
McCarthy (280)	Oh, my friend, wherefore vex thyself with the problem of existence? Wherefore trouble thy heart and thy soul thus with idle questioning? Live thy life in joy and gladness, for after all, thy counsel was not asked in the ordering of human affairs.
Whinfield (241)	Why ponder thus the future to foresee, And jade thy brain to vain perplexity? Cast off thy care, leave Allah's plans to him, He formed them all without consulting thee.
(134, 1882)	Wherefore waste thought on fate and destiny, And vainly rack thy brain to find the key? Give respite to thy brain, and let fate be; When fate was fixed, they ne'er consulted thee.

Was sorgst Du, Freund, des Lebens Vorhang zu **Bodenstedt**
 enthüllen,   (IV. 12)
Was quälst Du Dich, den Kopf mit unnützen Gedan-
 ken zu füllen?
Leb glücklich und vergnügt. Was ist, kam zur
 Erscheinung
Einst ohne Dich, und braucht auch jetzt nicht Deine
 Meinung.

Dem Brüten über dieses Sein, ich rat' Euch, dass Ihr **Von Schack**
 ihm entsagt,   (131)
Und mit Gedanken solcher Art Euch, Freunde, nicht
 mehr nutzlos plagt;
 Sucht zu zerstreu'n Euch und seid froh! Denn, als
  der ganze Erdenkram
Erschaffen wurde, hat man Euch vielleicht um Euern
 Rat gefragt?

Si dans une ville tu acquiers de la renommée, tu es **Nicolas**
considéré comme le plus méchant des hommes; si tu (449)
vis retiré dans un coin, on te regarde comme un insti-
gateur. Ce qu'il y a donc de mieux, fusses-tu Élie ou
saint Georges, c'est de vivre de façon à ne connaître
personne, à n'être connu de personne.

If you find fame in a town you are considered evil. **McCarthy**
If you live in a nook, you are looked upon as a (347)
schemer. The best thing for any man, were he saint
or a prophet, would be to live, knowing no one, known
of no one.

Whinfield
(480)

They call you wicked, if to fame you're known,
And an intriguer, if you live alone;
  Trust me, though you were Khizer or Elias,
'T is best to know none, and of none be known.

The first two lines of Whinfield, 248 (1882), read:—

They call you " wicked " if you are widely known,
And " sly intriguer " if you live alone.

Bodenstedt
(X. 24)

Thust Du Dich in einer Stadt hervor,
  So hasst und schmäht Dich jeder Thor.
Und kommst Du nicht den Menschen näher,
  So giltst Du ihnen als heimlicher Späher.
Am klügsten bleibst Du ganz allein,
  (Magst Du Elias selber sein)!
Dass Dich kein Mensch kennt, Keinen Du:
  Dann lassen Alle Dich in Ruh!

Nicolas
(35)

Si un étranger te témoigne de la fidélité, considère-le comme un parent; mais si un parent vient à te trahir (en quoi que ce soit), regarde-le comme un malintentionné. Si le poison te guérit, considère-le comme un antidote, et si l'antidote t'est contraire, regarde-le comme un poison.

McCarthy
(50)

If a stranger serves you faithfully, think of him as close of kin. If one of your kin betray you, think of him as acting in error. If a poison cures you, call it an antidote; if an antidote works you ill, call it a poison.

Is a friend faithless? spurn him as a foe,   **Whinfield**
Upon trustworthy foes respect bestow;   (39)
   Hold healing poison for an antidote,
And baneful sweets for deadly [sic] know.

Der Mensch, dem Du am meisten schenkst Vertrauen,   **Bodenstedt**
Zeigt sich als Feind, kannst Du ihn ganz durch-   (X. 2)
   schauen.
Der Kluge sucht sein Glück im eignen Haus,
Bei vielen Freunden kommt nicht viel heraus.

   Fréquente les hommes honnêtes et intelligents.   **Nicolas**
Fuis à mille farsakhs loin des ignorants. Si un homme   (223)
d'esprit te donne du poison, bois-le; si un ignorant te
présente un antidote, verse-le à terre.

   Seek the company of men of righteousness and under-   **McCarthy**
standing, and fly a thousand leagues from a man without   (22)
wit. If a wise man giveth thee poison, fear not to
drink thereof, but if a fool offereth thee an antidote,
pour it out upon the earth.

To wise and worthy men your life devote,   **Whinfield**
But from the worthless keep your walk remote   (263)
   Dare to take poison from a sage's hand,
But from a fool refuse an antidote.

Nur mit Menschen von Geist und Gemüt geh' um,   **Bodenstedt**
Halt Dich möglichst fern von Allem, was dumm.   (X. 11)
Reicht ein kluger Mann Dir Gift, so geniess es;
Reicht ein Dummkopf Dir Gegengift, so vergiess es!

Nicolas (107)	Celui qui a posé les bases de la terre, de la roue et des cieux, que de plaies n'a-t-il pas creusées dans le cœur chagrin de l'homme! que de lèvres couleur de rubis n'a-t-il pas ensevelies dans ce petit globe de terre! que de mèches de cheveux parfumées de musc n'a-t-il pas enfouies dans le sein de la poussière!
McCarthy (168)	He who has laid the foundations of the earth, of the wheel of the heavens, what wounds has he not hollowed out in the unhappy heart of man! What ruby-coloured lips has he not buried in this little globe of earth? What musk-scented tresses has he not hidden in the bosom of the dust?
Whinfield (137) (75, 1882)	He, who the world's foundations erst did lay, Doth bruise full many a bosom day by day, And many a ruby lip and musky tress Doth coffin in the earth, and shroud with clay.
✳ (18)	The Architect of heaven's blue dome and Ruler of the wave In many a grief-laden heart doth deeper plunge the glaive, And gathers many a silken tress and many a ruby lip To fill his puppet-show, the world, and his chibouque, the grave.
Bodenstedt (X. 7)	Der die Veste der Erde gegründet Und das Licht der Sterne entzündet, Wie viel Schmerzen, Wunden und Plagen Gab er den Herzen der Menschen zu tragen! Wie viel süsse Rubinenmunde Begrub er im schmutzigen Erdenschlunde, Wie viele Locken voll holder Düfte Wurden durch ihn ein Raub der Grüfte!

Jener, der die Welt geschaffen, in der armen Menschen Von Schack
    Herzen (32)
Wie viel Wunden nicht gegraben hat er unter bitter'n
    Schmerzen!
O wie viele Locken, welche ambrasüss geduftet haben,
Wie viel Rosenlippen hat er in der Erde Schoss
    begraben!

    Nous n'avons éprouvé que chagrin et malheur dans Nicolas
ce monde qui sert un instant d'asile. Hélas! aucun (4)
problème de la création ne nous y a été expliqué, et
voilà que nous le quittons le cœur plein de regret (de
n'y avoir rien appris sur ce sujet).

    We are enduring naught but cark and care in this McCarthy
world which offers us a fleeting harbourage. Alas, not (124)
one of all creation's riddles has been read to us, and
we depart hence with sorry hearts.

Nothing but pain and wretchedness we earn in M. K.
This world that for a moment we sojourn in:
We go!—no problem solved alas! discerning;
Myriad regrets within our bosoms burning!

'Tis but a day we sojourn here below, Whinfield
And all the gain we get is grief and woe, (3)
    And then, leaving life's riddles all unsolved,
And burdened with regrets, we have to go.

    In Whinfield, 1 (1882), the second line has *life's problems*,
and the third line begins, *And harassed by regrets*.

Bodenstedt Nichts ward uns als Unglück und Weh in der Welt,
(IV. 24)   Wo wir flüchtig nur finden ein schützendes Zelt;
           Kein Rätsel der Schöpfung wird uns hier gelöst
           Und das Leben uns selbst noch im Tode vergällt.

Nicolas   Ce firmament est comme une écuelle renversée sur
(303)   nos têtes. Les hommes perspicaces y sont humiliés et
           sans force; mais voyez l'amitié qui règne entre la coupe
           et la flacon. Ils sont lèvre contre lèvre, et entre eux
           coule le sang.

McCarthy   The heaven is a bowl inverted over our heads. The
(438)   wise are shamed and feeble, but the cup and jar are
           fast friends. They are lip to lip though blood flows
           between them.

Whinfield These heavens resemble an inverted cup,
(408)   Whereto the wise with awe keep gazing up;
           So stoops the bottle o'er his love, the cup,
           Feigning to kiss, and gives her blood to sup!

(209), 1882) See how these heavens, like an inverted cup,
           Stoop down, and how mankind keep gaping up;
           So this jug, stooping o'er his love the cup,
           Drops grapeblood in her mouth, for her to sup.

Garner   Beneath the Skies each mortal undergoes
(VI. 13)   A thousand Griefs, a thousand Heartfelt Woes
           But still Love reigns between the Cup and Flask,
           And Lip to Lip pure Blood between them flows.

Wie eine umgestülpte Schale wölbt sich der Himmel **Bodenstedt**
    uns zu Haupten; (VIII. 66)
Die klugen Menschen stehn darunter kraftlos und
    ratlos gleich Betäubten.
Doch sieh, wie zwischen Kelch und Flasche die Freund-
    schaft gross ist und voll Glut.
Jetzt sind die beide Lipp' an Lippe und zwischen beiden
    fliesst der Blut.

Einer umgestürzten Schale ist der Himmel zu ver- **Von Schack**
    gleichen, (71)
Unter der, gebeugt von Leiden, machtlos hin die
    Menschen schleichen;
  Sieh dagegen, wie so zärtlich, einem jungen Brautpar
    gleich,
Krug und Becher sich die Lippen gegenseits zum
    Kusse reichen.

Comment se fait-il qu'au commencement du prin- **Nicolas**
temps le verjus des jardins soit âpre? Comment après (425)
devient-il doux? Comment ensuite le vin trouve-t-il
amer? Si d'un morceau de bois on fait une viole au
moyen d'une serpette, que diras-tu en voyant qu'au
moyen de cette même serpette on confectionne une
flûte?

How is it that grapes are sour at first, and after, **McCarthy**
sweet? How is it that wine is bitter? If a bit of wood (318)
is fashioned with a knife into a viol, how is it that the
same knife can fashion a lute?

Whinfield
(462)

Why unripe grapes are sharp, prithee explain,
And then grow sweet, while wine is sharp again?
When one has carved a block into a lute,
Can he from that same block a pipe obtain?

Bodenstedt
(VIII. 84)

Warum ist im Frühling der Rebensaft sauer?
Warum später süss und dann herb auf die Dauer!
Aus Holz schneidet man Instrumente zum Streichen
Und Instrumente zum Blasen desgleichen.

Nicolas
(411)

Résigne-toi à la douleur si tu veux y trouver un remède, ne te plains pas de tes souffrances si tu veux en guérir. Dans ta pauvreté remercie la Providence, si tu veux qu'un jour enfin les richesses deviennent ton partage.

McCarthy
(451)

Be resigned to sorrow if you wish to escape it, do not complain of your hurts if you would have them healed. If you would fain taste the joys of riches, then thank Providence for your poverty.

Whinfield
(450)

To find a remedy, put up with pain,
Chafe not at woe, and healing thou wilt gain;
Though poor, be ever of a thankful mind,
'Tis the sure method riches to obtain.

Bodenstedt
(VIII. 78)

Such durch Selbstüberwindung den Schmerz zu lindern,
Durch Klagen wirst Du ihn nicht heilen noch mindern.
In Deiner Armut danke dem Himmel auf Erden,
Sollen einst seine Schätze zu Teil Dir werden.

Il n'y a point de cœur que ton absence n'ait meurtri **Nicolas**
jusqu'au sang ; il n'y a point d'être clairvoyant qui ne (36)
soit épris de tes charmes enchanteurs, et, bien qu'il
n'existe dans ton esprit aucun souci pour personne, il
n'y a personne qui ne soit préoccupé de toi.

What heart does not bleed for your absence, what **McCarthy**
soul is not the servant of your enchanting charms? (95)
For though you pay heed to no one, there is no one
who does not pay heed to you.

No heart is there, but bleeds when torn from Thee, **Whinfield**
No sight so clear but craves Thy face to see; (40)
   And though perchance Thou carest not for them,
No soul is there, but pines with care for Thee.

Alle Herzen sind von Kummer, seit du fern bist, aufge- **Von Schack**
   rieben, (188)
Unbewegt von deinen Reizen ist kein Wesen noch
   geblieben,
   Und, wenn du auch ihrer keinen eines Blicks für
     würdig hältst,
Fühlen alle Menschen dennoch sich gedrungen, dich
   zu lieben.

Es-tu assez discret pour que je te dise en peu de **Nicolas**
mots ce que l'homme a été dans le principe ? Une (302)
créature misérable, pétrie dans la boue du chagrin.
Il a, durant quelques jours, mangé quelques morceaux
ici-bas, puis il a levé le pied pour s'en aller.

McCarthy
(420)

Art wise enough to learn in little the truth of man?
A miserable being moulded from the mud of sorrow.
A little while he eats upon this earth, then lifts his foot
to wander hence.

Whinfield
(338)

To confidants like you I dare to say
What mankind really are : — moulded of clay,
 Affliction's clay, and kneaded in distress,
They taste the world awhile, then pass away.

Bodenstedt
(IV. 23)

Darf ich Dir sagen mit leisem Munde,
Als was ich den Menschen betrachte im Grunde?
Als ein elendes Geschöpf, das geknetet aus Staub lebt,
Und so lange es lebt, nur dem Kummer zum Raub lebt.

Von Schack
(57)

Du willst, ich soll mit einem Wort dir, was der Mensch
 ist, sagen?
Ein unglückseliges Geschöpf, belastet schwer mit Plagen,
Auf Erden kurze Zeit hindurch verzehrt er ein'ge
 Bissen,
Dann bald in Eile wiederum wird er hinweggerissen.

Nicolas
(148)

Ton empire a-t-il gagné en splendeur par mon obéissance (ô Dieu!), et mes péchés ont-ils retranché quelque chose de ton immensité? Pardonne, Dieu, ne punis pas. car je le sais, tu punis tard et tu pardonnes tôt.

McCarthy
(572)

Has thy empire gained in glory by my service. O Lord my God; has thy grandeur suffered aught by my sins? Forgiveness, God, and punish not, for I know that you punish late and pardon early.

What adds my service to Thy majesty? **Whinfield**
Or how can sin of mine dishonour Thee? (169)
  O pardon, then, and punish not, I know (93, 1882)
Thou 'rt slow to wrath, and prone to clemency.

Kann mein Gehorsam Deinen Glanz vermehren? **Bodenstedt**
Kann meine Sünde Deine Macht versehren? (I. 35)
Verzeih' mir, Herr! Ich weiss, Du bist allein
Langsam im Strafen, doch schnell im Verzeihn.

Hat deines Reiches Glanz sich je durch meinen Gehor- **Von Schack**
  sam gesteigert? (171)
  Vermocht' ich irgend deine Macht durch meine
    Schuld zu mindern?
  O Gott, verzeih mir denn! Ich weiss, dass deine
    Huld den Sündern
Nicht vorschnell Strafe zuerkennt, noch die Vergebung
  weigert.

  Ce monde n'a retiré aucun avantage de ma venue ici- **Nicolas**
bas. Sa gloire et sa dignité n'ont également rien gagné (157)
à mon départ. Mes deux oreilles n'ont jamais entendu
dire à personne pourquoi l'on m'y a fait venir, pourquoi
l'on m'en fait sortir.

  This world has gained nothing by my sojourn here **McCarthy**
below, and its glory and greatness will not be lessened (105)
by my departure. I have never heard with my ears,
and have never been told by anyone the reason of my
coming or going.

Whinfield
(170)

My coming brought no profit to the sky,
Nor does my going swell its majesty;
Coming and going put me to a stand,
Ear never heard their wherefore nor their why.

> In Whinfield, 96 (1882), the first two lines read:—
>
>> Say, did my coming profit thee, O sky?
>> Or will my going swell thy majesty?
>
> And the last line has *or their why*.

Bodenstedt
(IV. 4)

Durch meine Geburt ward der Welt kein Vorteil geboren;
Durch mein Scheiden wird ihr nichts gewonnen noch verloren.
Warum ich gekommen, warum ich muss scheiden,
Vernahmen noch nie meine beiden Ohren.

Von Schack
(289)

Nichts hat es der Welt genützt, als ich auf die Erde gekommen,
Und, geh' ich wieder hinweg, wie weiter beklagte sie's?
Viel hab' ich geforscht und gelauscht, allein noch von Keinem vernommen,
Warum mich zu Leben und Tod das Schicksal hierher verstiess.

Nicolas
(23)

Ce rubis précieux vient d'une mine à part, cette perle unique est empreinte d'un sceau à part; nos différentes conclusions sur cette matière sont erronées, car l'énigme du véritable amour s'explique dans un langage à part (et qui n'est pas à notre portée.)

This captain ruby comes from an unknown mine.   McCarthy
This perfect gem is stamped with an unknown seal.   (52)
All our conclusions on the question are vain, for the
riddle of perfect love is written in an unknown tongue.

That pearl is from a mine unknown to thee,   Whinfield
That ruby bears a stamp thou can'st not see,   (27)
   The tale of love some other tongue must tell,
All our conjectures are mere phantasy.

Dieser Prachtrubin kommt aus besonderem Schacht,   Bodenstedt
Diese Perle ist von ganz besonderer Pracht;   (VI. 28)
   Aller Daseinswunder Rätsel erklärt
Sich nur aus der Liebe besonderer Macht.

   Ô khadjè, rends-nous licite un seul de nos souhaits,   Nicolas
retiens ton haleine et conduis-nous sur la voie de Dieu.   (5)
Certes, nous marchons droit, nous; c'est toi qui vois de
travers; va donc guérir tes yeux, et laisse-nous en
paix.

   Master, make lawful but one alone of all our wishes.   McCarthy
Hold your peace and guide us on the road to God.   (126)
Truly we walk straightly, it is you who go astray. Heal
your eyes and leave us to our peace.

O master! grant us only this, we prithee: M. K.
Preach not! but *mutely* guide to bliss, we prithee!
  "*We* walk not straight?" — Nay, it is *thou* who
    squintest!
Go, heal thy sight, and leave us in peace, we prithee!

Whinfield (4)	Khaja! grant one request, and only one, Wish me God-speed, and get your preaching done; I walk aright, 'tis you who see awry; Go! heal your purblind eyes, leave me alone.
Bodenstedt (VII. 48)	Komm, Frömmler, einem frommen Wunsch entgegen: Führ' schweigend uns zum Heil auf Gottes Wegen! Wir wandeln grade, aber Du siehst schief— Heil' Deine Augen, Dir und uns zum Segen!
Von Schack (127)	O Pred'ger! Einen Wunsch erfülle mir! Schweig still und lass auf Gottes Pfad mich wandeln! Quer siehst du Alles! Geh zum Augenarzt Und lass mich, wie mich gut dünkt, handeln.

Nicolas (145)	Dans les régions de l'âme, il faut marcher avec discernement; sur les choses de ce monde il faut être silencieux. Tant que nous aurons nos yeux, notre langue, nos oreilles, nous devons être sans yeux, sans langue, sans oreilles.
McCarthy (260)	In the ways of the soul thou must walk with understanding. About the things of this world thou must keep silence. Though thou hast ears, eyes and tongue, thou must be as if thou hadst them not.
Whinfield (167)	Be very wary in the soul's domain, And on the world's affairs your lips refrain; Be, as it were, sans tongue, sans ear, sans eye, While tongue, and ears, and eyes you still retain.

Im Reich des Geistes muss man Urteil zeigen,   Bodenstedt
Doch von den Dingen dieser Welt klug schweigen.   (VIII. 18)
Damit Zunge, Auge und Ohr sich bewähren,
Thun wir, als ob wir ganz ohne sie wären.

Lorsque mes péchés me reviennent à la mémoire, le   Nicolas
feu qui alors s'allume dans mon cœur fait ruisseler   (118)
mon front; et pourtant il est bien établi que, lorsqu'un
esclave se repent, le maître généreux lui pardonne.

When I recall my grievous sins to mind,   Whinfield
Fire burns my breast, and tears my vision blind;   (146)
    Yet, when a slave repents, is it not meet
His lord should pardon, and again be kind?

Steigen meine Sünden mir zum Hirne,   Bodenstedt
    Perlt der heisse Schweiss mir von der Stirne   (VIII. 4)
Von dem Feuer, das mein Herz entzündet.
    Und doch nehm' ich an als wohlbegründet:
Zeigt ein Sclave Reue seinem Herrn,
    So verzeiht der Herr dem Sclaven gern.
(Soll der Schöpfer aller Wesen minder
    Gnädig sein für seine reu'gen Kinder?)

Gedenk' ich der Sünden, die ich begangen,   Von Schack
So brennt's mir im Herzen, mir glühen die Wangen;   (202)
Doch reuigen Sklaven verzeiht der Herr;
Und wäre härter dort oben Er?

APPENDIX XLVIII.

THE VERSIONS OF H. G. KEENE.

In "Macmillan's Magazine" for November, 1887 (vol. 57, p. 27), Mr. H. G. Keene, a retired East Indiaman, familiar with Persian, had an article entitled "Omar Khayyám," in which he included a number of original versions, not with the intention, he says, of shocking the admirers of Mr. FitzGerald by an attempt to compete with his poetical treatment, but "offered as illustrative of the real Khayyám in his disjointed manner." He gives FitzGerald due credit; but while he calls his quatrains as unquestionably among the fine things in modern English verse, he avers that they "give no accurate representations of the original in any of their versions; as indeed the variations of successive editions do themselves tend to show. . . . Omar," he continues, " is no more coherent than Martial, as anyone will see who looks into Mr. Whinfield's version in Trübner's series: here is the epigram of a scoffer, there the ejaculation of a pious inquirer: the carol of the wine-bibber is followed by a stanza of tender love. In FitzGerald, on the other hand, we are not sure whether we are reminded most of Horace or of Ecclesiastes: of the flighty Persian free-thinker, eclectic and unsystematic, we see little or nothing."

After giving an historical explanation of the phenomenon of "this unparalleled figure in the usually

The real Khayyám

conventional literature of the East," he proceeds to show from his Rubáiyát what manner of man Omar was:—

"We must picture to ourselves the poet in his garden, looking out on the well-watered valley below Meshed, with vines and fruit-plots around, and a bright sky overhead assuaged by shadowy plane-trees, while streams lapsed softly through the meadow-grass. It was a retreat, yet with loop-holes, for the neighbourhood of the town afforded some choice of society. Omar's hospitality was open to pleasant persons of both sexes — to all, indeed, but zealots. He was not one to confuse belief with faith: heterodoxy is as bad in his eyes as orthodoxy; you may do what you will if you will be cheerful and undogmatic. He is the slave of freedom.

An unparalleled figure

"To drink and revel and laugh is all my art,
  To smile at faith and unfaith my Faith's part:
    I asked the bride what gift would win her love,
  She answered, 'Give me but a cheerful heart.'"

"That he is ambitious, in the vulgar sense of sighing for the perishable advantages of wealth and station, no one can believe: he may desire to influence his fellow-creatures, but it is as a friend rather than as a master. For personal comfort, he looks not to luxury, but to love: not to the blind assurance of the bigot, but to the confidence of innocence and goodness.

"If in your heart the light of Love you plant
  (Whether the mosque or synagogue you haunt),
    If in Love's court its name be registered,
  Hell it will fear not, Heaven it will not want."

His questioning

"It has been thought that Khayyám was a Sufi, and only used the language of pleasure as a symbol for pantheistic aspiration. But he can be outspoken; and such questions as the following are neither equivocal nor ambiguous:—

"This is the time for roses and repose
 Beside the stream that through the garden flows,
  A friend or two, a lady rosy-cheeked,
 With wine — and none to hear the clergy prose.

"Unless girls pour the wine the wine is naught,
 Without the music of the flute is naught:
  Look as I may into the things of life,
 Mirth is the only good — the rest is naught.

"The red wine in a festal cup is sweet,
 With sound of lute and dulcimer is sweet:
  A saint, to whom the wine-cup is not known,
 He too — a thousand miles from us — is sweet."

"Not but what he has his pious hours; for to nothing but true piety can we ascribe such thoughts as these:—

"Thou hast no way to enter the Dark Court,
 For not to mortals does it yield resort:
  There is no rest but on the lap of earth —
 Woe! that its riddle is so far from short!

"Ah, brand! ah, brand! if all that thou canst earn
 Be but to help the fires of Hell to burn,
  Why wilt thou cry, 'Have mercy, Lord, on me!'
 Is it from such as thee that He will learn?

"Of thy Creator's mercy do not hold
  Doubt, though thy crimes be great and manifold,
    Nor think that, if thou die in sin to-day,
  He from thy bones His mercy will withhold."

"Yet, convinced as he is of the need of pardon, and **His dig-** not always sure (in his human diffidence) that his Lord **nified** is anything but a magnified Sultan, who exercises man **attitude** with wilful and arbitrary caprice, he preserves his dignity in face of the appalling possibility.

"Although God's service has not been my care,
  Nor for His coming was my heart made fair,
    I still have hope to find the mercy-seat,
  Because I never wearied Him with prayer.

"Am I a rebel? then His power is — Where?
  Is my heart dark? His light and glory — Where?
    Doth He give Heaven for our obedience?
  'T is due. But then, His loving-kindness — Where?"

"These speculations bring him to the old conclusion.

"Although my sins have left me faint and fell,
  One hope I keep — the heathen have it as well —
    In dying may I clasp my girl and glass (!)
  What else to me were Paradise or hell (?)

"If I drink wine it is not for delight,
  Nor unto holiness to do despite:
    I do it to breathe a little, free from self:
  No other cause would make me drink all night.

"They say that Tophet from of old was planned,
　But that's what I could never understand:
　　If there were Hell for those who drink, then Heaven
Would be no fuller than one's hollow hand.

"With wine and music if our lives have glee,
　If grass beside the running brook wave free,
　　Better than this esteem no quenched Hell:
This is thy Heaven — if Heaven indeed there be."

Enjoy the passing moment

"He is not sure whether, even on this side of the grave, perfect bliss is to be had; and in such uncertainty it would be folly to strive. But he is quite sure of the wisdom of savouring to the utmost the passing moment; and, like Horace, he makes the precariousness of joy a reason for enjoyment.

"Since life flies fast, what's bitter and what's sweet?
　When death draws near, what matter field or street?
　　Drink wine; for after thee and me, the moon
Her alternating course will oft repeat.

"I dreamed of an old man, who said, and frowned,
　'The rose of bliss in sleep was never found;
　　Why then anticipate the work of death?
Drink rather: sleep awaits thee in the ground.'

"Ah, comrades! strengthen me with cups of wine
　Until my faded cheeks like rubies shine,
　　And bathe me in it after I am dead,
And weave my shroud with tendrils of the vine."

"But these contemplations, these delights could not always be taken, or did not always suffice. *Post prandia Callirhoe*: like his European prototypes the Per-

sian philosopher found woman essential to his scheme. Sweet companionship
His Paradise must never want an Eve with whom he
could share alike his joys and his troubles.

"Clouds come, and sink upon the grass in rain,
  Let wine's red roses make our moments fain;
    And let the verdure please our eyes to-day,
  Ere grass from our dust shall give joy again.

"Sweetheart, if Time a cloud on thee have flung,
  To think the breath must leave thee, now so young,
    Sit here, upon the grass, a day or two,
  While yet no grass from thy dust shall have sprung.

"Long before thee and me were Night and Morn:
  For some great end the sky is round us borne:
    Upon this dust, ah, step with careful foot,
  Some beauty's eyeball here may lie forlorn.

"This cup once loved, like me, a lovely girl,
  And sighed, entangled in a scented curl:
    This handle, that you see upon its neck,
  Once wound itself about a neck of pearl."

"It is to be feared that, like Anacreon, the Eastern poet found that, as old age drew on, the ladies turned to younger loves.

"Ah! that the raw should have the finished cake,
  The immature the ripest produce take,
    And eyes, that make the heart of man to beat,
  Shine only for the boys' and eunuchs' sake."

Vague but trustful hope

"But the things of Fate approach: no epicurism can do much to strip necessity of its stern aspect. Sin is sin, and the soul in the solitude of the dark valley turns to the inevitable with vague but trustful hope.

"His mercy being gained, what need we fear?
His scrip being full, no journey makes me fear:
 If, by His clemency, my face be white,
In no degree the Black Book will I fear.

"I warred in vain with Nature — what's the cure?
I suffer for mine actions — what's the cure?
 I know God's mercy covers all my sin;
For shame that He has seen it — what's the cure?"

"Yet, even here, science brings a message that is not unconsoling. He may pass, as an individual; but the moon will shine on others, and the grass be fair and odorous, and the very body that has known so much joy when it was his, will contribute to other joys hereafter.

"Is it not a shame, because on every side
 Thy curious eyes are circumscribed and tied,
  Pent in this dark and temporary cell,
 In its poor bounds contented to abide?

"O tent-maker, that frame is but a tent,
 Thy soul the king, to realms of Nothing bent;
  And slaves shall strike the tent for a fresh use,
 When the king rises and his night is spent."

" Here we come upon a stanza beautifully rendered by Fitzgerald. Speaking of the body, he makes the poet say : —

"Or is it but a tent where rests anon
  A Sultan to his kingdom journeying on,
    And which the swarthy chamberlain shall strike,
  Then, when the monarch rises to begone."
                                    [Ruba'iy XLV.]

"The difference from the original is verbally but slight; but it will be observed to seriously alter the significance. Khayyám's play on his name (Tent-maker) is sacrificed, so is the mockery of the soul's journey to an unreal kingdom. The word chamberlain is an inadequate substitute for the original *farash*, which indicates a class of slave appointed in the East for such duties, and to which the poet contemptuously likens Death.

> Slight changes make great differences

.   .   .   .   .

"A sample of Fitzgerald's manner of paraphrase may be interesting. The two metrical stanzas are his: the prose that follows gives the literal English of the original.

"O Thou who didst with pitfall and with gin
  Beset the road I was to wander in!
    Thou wilt not with Predestination round
  Enmesh me, and impute my fall to sin.

"O Thou who man of basest clay didst make,
  And who with Eden didst devise the snake!
    For all the sin with which the face of man
  Is blackened, man's forgiveness give — and take."
                              [Rubáiyát LXXX, LXXXI.]

"In my way-going Thou hast laid the snare in many a place. Thou sayest, 'I slay thee,' if I make default therein. The world is not free from Thy command a tittle. I do Thy command, and Thou callest me 'Sinner'!

"O Thou, of the sanctity of whose nature knowledge is not, and art indifferent both to our obedience and sin! I am drunk with sin, but sober with hope, in that my hope is in Thy great mercy."

Omar's philanthropy

"Khayyám mocks at circumstances. Death is a slave: even life, saving so far as it is a scene of calm enjoyment, is a mere bubble. The noise of the Franks in Syria is deadened by distance: the crimes of Hassan Sabah, the toils of Nizam-ul-Mulk, are ignored, while the poet surprises the secrets of Nature, observing her economies of matter and her recklessness of man. But, in regard to these hapless contemporaries to whom the stern stepmother shows so little pity, he infers the duty of help, urging the indulgence of a brother orphan:

"Do thou beware no human heart to wring,
  Let no one feel thine anger hotly sting.
    Wouldst thou enjoy perpetual happiness?
  Know how to suffer: cause no suffering."

"Here the veil shall fall, and our last glimpse of the poet show him in a posture of pity. He was summoned to Merv and employed in the reform of the Calendar; and he died a natural death about 1123 at Naishapoor, his old age being untroubled and his life unabridged. More than this an Oriental of that time could not hope from Fate. The rest of his happiness must come from within, as we will hope it did. One of his disciples tells us that Omar said in his old age: 'I would be buried in such a place, that the north wind may scatter roses on it.' After the poet's death the disciple visiting the grave, found that it was beneath a garden wall, 'and the fruit-trees reached their boughs over, and dropped their blossoms over his tomb, so that it was almost hidden.'

"One of the curious features of Khayyám's life and labor is the fact of such heterodox and seemingly unprofitable matter surviving, with no aid from the printing-press, through the havoc of seven stormy centuries. Of this we may be sure, that no nation preserves a work of literary art unless it has endeared itself to many minds, and found an echo in the popular feeling. Not only have Persia and Khorassan been scourged since then with fire and sword, in which the frail life of manuscripts must have been in constant danger, but the outspoken heterodoxy of the *rubáiyat* must have rendered them especially liable to the hostile pursuit of the Moslem Church. That they have, trifles as we may think them, been preserved amid all these dangers to furnish themes of enjoyment and of discussion in a state of society so unlike that in which they were born, and in which they lived so long, raises them to a position of almost scriptural dignity. And at last we behold them inspiring modern artists in the busiest centres of Western life.

"It is not at all likely that in their original amorphous state they would have pleased the generality of English readers. Mr. Whinfield has prefixed to his translation this somewhat disparaging motto from Mr. Arnold:

> . . . . 'A mind
> Not wholly clear nor wholly blind,
> Too keen to rest, too weak to find.'

FitzGerald's version and the original

"Modern Europeans do not care to be troubled with reading 'that travails sore and brings forth wind.' For the use of such it is more than probable that Fitzgerald's genius and skill have raised the only acceptable structure. Nevertheless, a sympathetic student of human history may be willing to cast a glance at the remote original, too far away in place and time, too bare and open, for permanent sojourn: a grotesque nook abounding in quaint arabesque and coloured fret-work, yet none the less a shrine of undogmatic grace and harmlessness and peace."

Mr. Whinfield's classification

In the above article Mr. Keene studiously and purposely refrains from versifying any of the quatrains used by FitzGerald. He makes only one exception. The same scholar had also in the *Calcutta Review* last year (1895) an article entitled "Loose Stanzas," in which he groups a number of translations in subject-sequence. Mr. Whinfield in his edition of 1883 classified Omar's quatrains under six heads, as follows: —

I. *Shikáyat i rozgár* — Complaints of the "wheel of heaven" or Fate, of the world's injustice, of the loss of friends, of man's limited faculties and destinies.

II. *Hajw* — Satires on the hypocrisy of the "unco guid," the impiety of the pious, the ignorance of the learned, and the untowardness of his own generation.

III. *Firákiya and Wisáliya* — Love poems on the sorrows of separation and the joys of reunion with the Beloved, earthly or spiritual.

IV. *Báháriya* — Poems in praise of Spring, gardens and flowers.

V. *Kufriya* — Irreligious and antinomian utterances, charging the sin of the creature to the account of the creator, scoffing at the Prophet's Paradise and Hell, singing the praises of wine and pleasure — preaching *ad nauseam*, "Eat and drink (especially drink), for to-morrow ye die."

VI. *Munáját* — Addresses to the Deity, now in the ordinary language of devotion, bewailing sins and imploring pardon, now in mystical phraseology, craving deliverance from "self," and union with the Truth (*Al Hakk*) or Deity, as conceived by the Mystics.

These Mr. Keene takes for his guidance. He says:

H. G. Keene's Loose Stanzas

"The object of these pages is to afford some notion of the true characteristics which distinguish the Eastern poet who has had such a paradoxical influence in recent days. The title is not intended to indicate moral laxity; if such there be, it will not come unpleasantly before us here; but some epithet had to be selected which would convey the true literary idea.

"Mr. Whinfield's first class consists of, what he calls, 'Complaints of Fortune.' All protracted lives — such as Omar's was — are full of care, ever darkening towards the end; nor were the conditions of a peaceful philosopher especially favorable under the Seljukian dynasty in Central Asia. Alp Arslan and his successor, Malik Shah, were enlightened men; and the long administration of Omar's patron, Nizam-ul-Mulk, was remarkably efficient and prosperous. Nevertheless, the ordinary current of existence must have been often ruffled for a peace-loving free-thinker surrounded by bloodthirsty fanatics, whose ideals were so opposed to his. And when the Great Minister died, — assassinated by the clients of one who had been the friend and comrade of both Omar and his patron, — the dynasty swiftly declined, and the conditions of the poet must have declined also. His pension, doubtless, ceased; and a total loss of income must needs shake a temper, however unaspiring. In such considerations we shall surely find enough to account for all the querulousness and tragic tone of such laments as these:—

I.

Complaints of fortune

"My span is but a few days, scarcely one,
  Wind on the desert blowing, quickly gone;
    Long as life lasts I care not but for two —
  The day that is not, and the day that is done.

"This vase once loved, like me, a lovely girl,
  And bent in rapture o'er a scented curl.
    This handle that you see upon its neck,
  Once wound itself about a neck of pearl.

"Be watchful! Fortune menaces deceit;
  Sharp is the sword above thee: keep thy feet;
    And if she offer thee a sugared nut,
  Forbear to taste: there is poison in the sweet.

"A hundred thousand Saints the past has seen,
  Sinai a hundred thousand Prophets seen,
    The Palatine full many an Emperor,
  Kasra a hundred thousand Shahs has seen.

"That vault of azure, and that golden bowl,
  Have rolled for ages, will for ages roll;
    Even so — the destined sons of destiny —
  We come and go, poor fragments of the whole.

"When we are gone the world will still remain,
  Yet neither name nor sign of us retain;
    In days past we were not, and no one cared,
  Nor will in future, when we are not, again.

"Ah woe! our hands must drop their garnered store,
  And Azrael's talons bathe our hearts in gore;
    While from that bourne no traveller returns,
  To tell us how they fare who went before.

"Those sons of care whom mortals call 'The Great,'
  Have lives of trouble, all at odds with Fate;
    Yet him who is not Passion's slave, like them,
  They hardly reckon as of man's estate.

"The old familiar faces! All are fled,
  Under the feet of Azrael trampled dead;
    At life's sad feast they shared the wine awhile,
  But drank too quickly, and were quickly sped.

"The wheeling zenith hides an unborn thought,
  A cup with universal meaning fraught;
    Lament not when the cup comes round to you,
  But drain with gladness what your turn has brought.

"This wheel that will to none its course explain
  Mahmud, Ayaz, a thousand such has slain;
    Drink wine! For life is given to no one twice,
  And none that once has lived comes back again.

"In circles of existence too long pent,
  And fallen from man's estate by sad descent,
    Since life can never bring us what we want
  Would God satiety could feel content!

"Pure from the void we came, impure we go;
  Welcomed with joy we came, in grief we go;
    Tempered with tears in furnace of the heart,
  Life given to the winds, to dust we go.

"Help all you may their heavy loads to bear,
  Lay waste the shrines of sacrifice and prayer.
    This soothsay of Khayyám receive, O friend,
  Drink wine, take purses, but be kind to care.

"This pile whose gables wooed the smile of day,
  And on whose floor kings wont their brows to lay,
    We saw a dove upon its battlements,
  And all she said was—'Where, Ah! Where are they?'"

"The weariful monotone of Pessimism rises to a climax, in the last of our samples, where the cry of Sophocles is unconsciously repeated:—

"Since all man gathers in this waste below
  Feeds him on ashes and then bids him go,
    Happiest is he who soonest takes his leave,
  Or he who never saw this world of woe."

Satires on his opponents
"So far our poet might pass for a confirmed hater of life and all its gifts. But let us turn to another of his aspects, and see how he handles the unsympathetic men who are the main causers of his sadness, and their depressing tenets:—

II.

"Temple and Kāba both are fanes of prayer,
  Bells and Müazzins call alike to prayer;
    Churches and mosques, crosses and rosaries,
  What are they all but instruments of prayer?

"In fane or cloister, mosque or school, one lies
  Adread of Hell, one dreams of Paradise;
    But none that know the secrets of the Lord,
  Will sow their hearts with such absurdities.

"If in your heart the lamp of Love you plant,
  Whether the mosque or synagogue you haunt,
    If in Love's Court your name be registered,
  Hell you will fear not, Heaven you will not want.

"Pity! the raw should win the well-cooked cake,
  And prentice-bunglers mar the plans we make;
    Sweet eyes that bid the hearts of men to beat
  Shine but for schoolboys, or for eunuchs' sake.

"If roses fail, my fate is thorns you see;
  And, if light fails, why darkness does for me,
    And if I find no place for Muslim prayer,
  I must make shift with Christian heresy."

"Ah! heedless race: the world's affairs are naught,
  Foundation of the wind; whereof comes naught;
    The bounds of being are two negatives,
  One on each side and, midway, you, too, naught.

"Seek not to do the people harm by night,
  Lest they appeal to God from thee by night;
    Lean not on strength or beauty of thine own,
  For this and that will leave thee soon by night.

"The red wine in a festal cup is sweet,
  With sound of lute and dulcimer is sweet;
    A holy man who does not think it so,
  He, too, a thousand miles from us is sweet."

"But our poet is too genial to be satisfied with satire; he could love; and his love-notes have a tender pathos not common in Eastern literature. M. Nicolas, indeed, was led to believe that both Omar and Hafiz — whose treatment of the subject is most like Omar's — were Sufis with whom women and wine were but symbols put to indicate desire for God and spiritual absorption. On this point, however, attention is surely due to the opinion of contemporaries. Now, it so happens, that Shahrastáni, author of the "Philosophical Biography," lived between A. D. 1086 and 1153, and must have known in what light Omar was regarded. He mentions him as a great scholar, versed especially in Greek, but *in no respect a Sufi:* his strong point was astronomy, his weak one want of self-control. With his testimony we may combine a few specimens of Omar's epicurean poetry, and leave judicious readers to draw their own conclusions : —

Omar no Sufi

His epicurean verses

III.

"On Love's sweet path pursue the offering heart,
  In Love's own precinct seek a perfect heart,
    A hundred temples are but beaten clay,
  Let be the temple, so thou find a heart.

"Arise! Where is the song you used to sing?
  Your little mouth my spirit's food can bring;
    But pour me wine as rosy as your face,
  My heart is like your ringlet's broken wing.

"These compasses resemble you and me
    Whose heads are two, though one the body be,
      About the centre, like a circle, twined;
    But in one point they meet at last, you see.

"A jug of wine, a book of poetry,
  For stay of life a crust of bread give me,
    And thou beside me, in the wilderness!
  The Sultan's Kingdom better cannot be.

"I cannot see the form mine eyes require,
  Nor can I bear the frustrated desire,
    Nor yet relate my pain to any one,—
  Hard suffering, strange grief, delightful fire!

"Your love-nets hold my hair-forsaken head,
  For which my lips with wine are always red;
    Repentance born of reason you have wrecked,
  And bid time tear the robe that patience made."

"Akin to these amatory yearnings are the apprecia- Omar and
tions of spring and out-door life:— springtime

IV.

"Now that new joy to earth the Zephyrs bring,
  And every living heart goes forth to spring,
    On every bough the hand of Moses gleams,
  The voice of Jesus quickens everything.

[or, elsewhere, the same thought in varied phrase;—

"It is the season when the land grows green,
  And Moses's hand upon the boughs is seen:
    The breath of Jesus rises from the ground,
  And weeping clouds above the landscape lean.]

"'I am Joseph's flower from Egypt,' said the Rose,
  'My ruby mouth such glittering jewels shows,'
    I asked her to produce another sign,—
  'See,' she replied, 'with blood my raiment flows.'"

"Here is a quatrain of which the original defies representation in English:—

"Look where I may, I see on every side
  Fresh fountains springing in the champaign wide,
   And lawns that once were called the plains of Hell
Now smile like Heaven, with ladies heavenly eyed."

Reasons for Omar's revolt

"The most characteristic, however, of all Omar's moods is unhappily that of remonstrance or revolt. The religion in which he was born and nurtured was one of which we can easily see the central doctrine, and how it leads to antinomianism, by thinking of the Puritans and the influence of Calvinism in Europe. The origin of Evil has never been an easy department of theology; and the purely Semitic view of the Deity gives much emphasis to the problem. Omar had inherited that view; and could never quite shut it out, however he might shift and turn. If Allah was a Mighty Sultan, having all human powers in their extremest dimensions, his foreknowledge must be equalled by all his other attributes. He knows what crimes a man will commit before that criminal is born; why then does He punish him for what he cannot help doing? Nay, the very materials and machinery of evil must be of Divine origin or creation: how then can man be held answerable for the inevitable result? These bewilderments must palliate, if they may not wholly excuse, a spirit of criticism which the enemies of our poet called "rebellious blasphemy," and which we cannot but deplore as needlessly flippant in some instances of expression. Yet there is a sincerity about them which goes a great way towards accounting for the tenacity with which human admiration has preserved these little poems. It will be hardly necessary to add that their author was no Atheist, not even an Agnostic. His addresses to the Deity, even when most audacious, are those of a convinced believer; sometimes offering the advice of an intrepid subject to his sovereign, sometimes throwing out the shrewd comments of a court jester; always recognizing supremacy, often implying goodness. But let us hear:— **Omar's "rebellious blasphemy"**

V.

"If I go right, Thy guiding hand is — WHERE?
 If I go darkling, Thy clear-light is — WHERE?
  Dost Thou give Heaven for my obedience?
 'T is due; but Thy benevolence is — WHERE?

"The impress of His hand the vessels keep,
 Who makes and throws them on the rubbish heap,
  But if they turn out well why are they broken?
 If ill, the blame is surely His to reap.

"He makes Earth bear the firmamental thrust,
 He scars our hearts with sorrow, fear and lust,
  And many a ruby lip and perfumed lock
 Garners in clay and coffers in the dust.

"When shame for sin committed stirs the heart,
 Hot from the breast the scalding eye-drops start
  And surely when the slave laments his fault
 Complete forgiveness is the master's part.

"I drink, and every wise man does like me,
 Which God, no doubt, regards indulgently —
  Foreseen before the making of the world,
 If I did not, where would His prescience be?

"To keep from what is ordered beats our skill,
  'Bid' and 'forbid' are masters of our will;
    Helpless we stand between their 'Yea' and 'Nay,'
  Like guests advised to tilt, but not to spill.

"Thou settest in my pathway snare and gin,
  Saying, — 'I slay thee if thou fall therein,'
    The world is free from Thy command no jot,
  Thine the command, but mine is still the sin."

"A similar complaint was made by a forgotten English poet of the time of Shakespeare.

"Is it the mask or Majesty of power
  To make offences, that it may forgive?
  Nature herself doth her own self deflower
    To hate those errors she herself doth give."

      [GREVILLE, LORD BROOKE, *Mustapha*."

Poems of submission and prayer

"The last class named by Mr. Whinfield is that containing poems of submission and prayers for pardon. Without being a strong or persistent pietist, and, indeed, kept by his audacious humour from association with any school of mystics, Omar turned to his Lord in moments of dejection : —

VI.

"As we know Thee, the Zealot knows Thee not,
  Like faithful followers strangers know Thee not,
    Thou sayest — 'The wicked shall be sent to hell;'
  — Say so to some of those that know Thee not!

" Better in wine shops for Thy secrets yearn,
   Than patter praises that by rote we learn;
     Ah! Thou art Alpha and Omega still,
   Whether thou please to cherish or to burn.

" His mercy gained, what cause have we for fear?
   His scrip being full, what journey need we fear?
     If by his grace my face be once made white,
   In no degree the black-book will I fear.

" I war in vain with nature — what is the cure?
   I suffer for my doings — what is the cure?
     I know his mercy covers all my sin,
   For shame that He has seen it — What is the cure?

" I weep, because I am of evil fame,
   Defiled with many a lust and taint of shame;
     Commanded things undone, forbidden done,
   I weep to find my life so full of blame."

"Here the tone resembles that of *Job*: despondent, but **Omar and** not without faith and self-respect. This class of quatrain **Job** also reminds us of the old Hebrew poet in another way. A few of the stanzas, however they have found their way into the text, are evidently hostile commentors' attempts to answer Omar out of the resources of scandalized orthodoxy. The limits of space will only allow of one example. The poet had declared his trust — quite in the spirit of the man of Uz: —

" I grovel to appease the Heavenly will,
   I found no claim by good to atone for ill,
     Whereso Thy bounty pleases, there will come
   Undone as done, and done as undone still."

Abu Said's quatrain

"But there was a contemporary poet, who wrote opposition quatrains. His name was Abu Said Fazl Ullah, and one of his pious comments has found life on the margin of Omar's manuscript. This is it:—

"Ah! ne'er-do-well, that workest nought but ill,
 Yet grovellest to appease the Heavenly will;
  Hope not for absolution; evermore
 Good will be good, and evil, evil still."

"But before we close the book, let us take a hasty glance at one more of the poet's chameleon phases, hardly included in any of the recognized classes, yet rightly noticed by Mr. Whinfield as characteristic of Omar. Readers of Horace recollect the attitude of which so strong an expression is to be found in the ode to Dellius,— the friends reclining on the grassy bank of a stream, quaffing their wine under the shade. In that attitude the astronomer of Khurasan is often to be seen; sometimes careless, at others a little agitated by the anticipations of death and judgment. Here are a few random samples:—

The dilettante Omar

"At dawn a voice came from the house of wine;
 'Ho! reckless wastrels lying there supine,
  Rise! let us fill our measures full of drink
 Before they fill your measures, yours and mine.'

"I'll drink till such a scent of wine shall rise
 Out of the earth where my dead carcase lies,
  That cup-sick revellers, passing by the place,
 Shall from that scent receive new enterprise.

"Ah! comrades strengthen me with draughts of wine
  Until my sallow cheeks like rubies shine;
    And wash me in it after I am dead,
  And stitch my shroud with tendrils of the vine.

"If I drink wine it is not for delight,
  Nor unto holiness to do despite;
    I drink to breathe a moment free from self.
  No other cause would make me drink all night.

"Unless girls pour the wine the wine is naught,
  Without the music of the flute is naught.
    Look as I may into the world's affairs,
  Mirth is the only good, the rest is naught.

"Clouds come, and soon will feed the grass with rain,
  Let Life's glad moments make our senses fain;
    Rest thee, dear friend, a while, and drink with me,
  Till, of our clay fresh grass shall grow again."

"We have found in European writing many diverse parallels for Omar's varying moods, and have seen that he had no plan, or 'principle,' no set intention of writing a continuous *Apologia pro vitâ suâ*. Perhaps this very fitfulness it is that has endeared him to the fitful sons of men, and has given to the fugitive scraps of an Eastern astronomer's lost moments a charm which the world would not willingly let die. The general spirit is one of freedom and cheerfulness; and everything is tolerated but intolerance. Mr. Stokes has admirably caught this in a stanza which, if not exactly answer-

His undying charm of fitfulness

ing to any of Omar's, yet sums up his entire teaching:—

'This is the time for roses and repose
  Beside the stream that through the meadow flows.
    A friend or two, a rose-like lady love,
  With wine ; and not to hear the clergy prose.'

Or, perhaps, the only explanation of these 'loose stanzas,' in their inconsistency, is that we see Japhet dwelling in the tents of Shem, and observe the Aryan uneasiness under the yoke of an alien orthodoxy."

APPENDIX XLIX.

BIBLIOGRAPHY OF OMAR KHAYYAM.

I.

Persian originals

"J. E. C." (Mrs. H. M. Cadell), in "Fraser's" for May, 1879 (Vol. 99, p. 651), writing of the Rubáiyát,— a word which she derives from the Arabic numeral "*arba*," four, — says :—

Rarity of MSS.

"The MS. copies are rare, both in Europe and the East, though some of the oldest MSS. are so short that they could be transcribed in a few hours by an apt penman. Still they are not so rare as Mr. FitzGerald seems to consider. We have seen eleven MS. copies, of which seven are in England and four in Paris. Then there is M. Nicholas' [*sic*] edition of his text, published in Paris, 1868 [*sic*]. Of these collections the smallest contains 158 rubáis, the largest 516. Some of the rubáis are mere paraphrases one of another, and some, not many, are repetitions; but after all possible weeding has been done, there will remain at least a thousand which we have collected from these MSS., and a few minor sources, claiming to be the work of Khayam. The opinion of those best qualified to judge would place the number of undoubtedly genuine quatrains at about 250 to 300. . . . Beside Manuscript evidence, the tests most to be trusted are simplicity of language, perfection in rhythm and sound, and epigrammatic completeness. Khayam was a clear-headed person, and master of his own language in its best days, and we may discard rubáis at once when there is looseness of grip in the thought."

Manuscripts and Original Text.

For MSS. in the Royal Library at Berlin see Wilhelm Pertsch's "Verzeichniss der persischen Handschriften der königlichen Bibliothek zu Berlin," 1888. See p. 1180 b. ('Umar Khayām). **MSS. at Berlin**

MS. 35 (fol. 80) contains 238.
MS. 666 has 65; No. 1 = Nicolas, 459.
MSS. 671 and 673 have also a number.
MS. 672 contains 40 Rubáiyát.
MS. 674 (49, fol. 794ᵇ) contains 380.
MS. 697 contains 43 (in late and very fluent Shikastah script, the first corresponding to Nicolas 211, Whinfield 252).

The Catalogue of the Persian MSS. in the British Museum, edited by Charles Rieu, Ph. D. (London, 1881), in 3 large quarto volumes, records on p. 546 col. a. "Or. 330 Foll. 109, with gold-lined margins," 423 Rubá'iyát of 'Umar Khayyām, ending with Nicolas, 400. Another: 330, imperfect, containing 540 Rubá'iyát, the first, Nicolas 11, the last, Nicolas 426. Also Add. 27, 261; a sort of pocket library written by a grandson of Timúr, Jalal ud-Din Iskander B. 'Umar Shaikh, containing in Section XV some Rubáiyát of Omar's. **MSS. at British Museum**

Professor Ed. Sachau, Ph. D., began, and Hermann

MSS. at the Bodleian Library

Ethé, Ph. D., completed, the Catalogue of the Persian, Turkish, Hindûstânî, and Pushtû MSS. in the Bodleian Library. Part I (1150 pp.) contains that of the Persian MSS. Many of these are in the Ouseley Collection.

MS. 524 contains 405 'Rubâ'iyyât-i-'Umar Khayyâm' ("breaks off in the last letter with the first bait of the 406th.")

MS. 525: a shorter collection, containing 158 (finished "in the residence Shiraz" in Dec. 1460). No. 140 in Ouseley Coll.

MS. 1210 described as "a brouillon of a collection of various authors" containing on ffs. 88^b and 89^b–90^b a number of Omar's quatrains.

MSS. at Gotha

In the Herzogliche Bibliothek at Gotha there is a MS. and a Turkish Version by Dewletschah. This contains a number of quatrains not in Nicolas (Bodenstedt).

Whinfield catalogues:—

Calcutta Asiatic Society's MS. No. 1548, containing 516 quatrains.

India Office MS. No. 2420, ffs. 212–267, containing 512.

India Office MS. No. 2486 ffs. 158–194, containing 362.

Two MSS. in Paris both of the Xth Cent., containing one, 175, the other 213 quatrains.

A MS. at Cambridge, Eng. (modern), containing 801.

First printed edition

The first edition printed is that of Calcutta, 1836, containing 438 quatrains, with an appendix of 54 more, found in a Bayáz or common-place-book.

Rubáiyát: A Selection of the Rubais of Omar Khayyâm, Baba Thâhri, 'Attar, and a tarjí of Shams Tabrizi, Teheran A. H. 1274 (1857).

The Teheran (Tihran) Edition of 1274 A. H. (1857) is said by Whinfield to be the same as that afterwards printed by M. Nicolas, and contains 464 quatrains.

Pertsch mentions another Tihran edition of 1278 [that of Abdallah Ansári? 1277?] A. H. (1861).

That of Sir Gore Ouseley (London, 1846) contains two.
That of Garcin de Tassy (Paris, 1857) contains ten.
That of Nicolas (Paris, 1867) contains 464.
That of P. Whalley (1877) contains 9.
That of E. H. Whinfield, London, 1883, contains 500.

Pertsch also mentions the Lakhnau (Lucknow) edition of 1878 [edited by Mulvi Muhammad Sadik Ali], which contains 763 quatrains, an edition or fragment of an edition by the late Professor Blochmann containing only sixty-two quatrains, and an edition edited by C. J. Lyell [for the Calcutta Asiatic Society]. Also Lucknow Editions of 1882, and 1883; and a Recension by P. de La Garde in Göttingen, 1870.

Graf von Schack includes in his authorities those that he found "in the great Persian Lexicon ('Heft Kulzum')."

Omar's life in Persian Omar's life may be read in the original Persian in the Bodleian MS. No. 384: Alashkada or "The Fire Temple" by Hâji Lutf 'Alîbeg of Isfahân, called Âdhur; in the part entitled "The First Firebrand."

II.

TRANSLATIONS.

Thomas Hyde, D. D., one Latin quatrain
VETERUM ‖ PERSARUM ‖ ET ‖ PARTHORUM ‖ ET ‖ MEDORUM ‖ RELIGIONIS ‖ HISTORIA ‖

Autor est THOMAS HYDE, S. T. D. Linguæ *Hebraicæ* in ‖ Universitate *Oxon.* Professor *Regius*, & Linguæ *Arabicæ* Professor *Laudianus*.

EDITIO SECUNDA.

Oxonii ‖ e Typographeo Clarendoniano, MDCCLX. 580 pp. quarto, plates, &c. The first edition appeared in the year 1700.

The second title-page begins : —

HISTORIA ‖ RELIGIONIS ‖ VETERUM ‖ PERSARUM ‖ EORUMQUE ‖ Magorum. ‖ Ubi etiam nova ABRAHAMI, & MITHRÆ, & VESTÆ, & ‖ MANETIS, &c. Historia; atque ANGELORUM Officia & ‖ Præfecturæ ex Veterum Persarum Sententiâ. ‖ ITEM ‖ Persarum Annus *Antiquissimus* tangitur,

and ends : —

Dantur VETERUM PERSARUM Scripturæ & Linguæ (ut ‖ hæ jam primò *Europæ* producantur & Literato Orbi postliminio ‖ reddantur) Specimina.

De Persiæ ejusdemque Linguæ Nominibus; déque hujus Dialectis, & à ‖ Modernâ Differentiis, strictim agitur.

Professor Cowell, in his article on Omar Khayyám, in the *Calcutta Review*, refers to Dr. Thomas Hyde, and quotes from the "Veterum Persarum Religio" an anecdote borrowed by FitzGerald to enliven his rather meagre Introduction.

It may interest classical students to have at hand the original reference to Omar (probably the first ever made by a European, certainly the first by an Englishman) and the extract from the appendix which contains the quaint Latin translation of the Rubá'iy given in the various versions in the note to Cowell's version.

The first extract, which may be found on p. 187 of the beautifully printed folio, describes Omar's efforts in revising the calendar, he being "one of the Eight who settled the Jaláli era in 1709" : —

"Interim verò *Persæ* veteribus Mensium & Dierum nominibus utebantur; sed cum Intercalatione quâdam, quippe ad quam cogebant victores. Illorum enim tunc *Martius* incipiebat circa medium *Piscium*, donec Calendarium reformaret Rex *Gjelâleddîn Melicshâh*, qui Anni initium (facto XVIII dierum Embolismo, ut in sequentibus monstrabitur,) ad initium *Arietis* retrahebat, ex cogitatâ novâ Anni formâ quæ Solis motui quàm maximè responderet. Id autem non fecit primo suo anno, sed (ut puto) postquam aliquot annos regnaverat; idque suasu insignis Astronomi *Omar Cheiyâm*, cujus Propositionem de emendandâ Epochâ omnes statim tanquam oraculum pronis auribus animisque exceperunt. . .

"Deinde eo [Yézdegherd] occiso, post aliquod temporis intervallum, in Persidem introductus est *Civilis Annus Solaris fixus*, incipiens à medio *Piscium*. Quis certò hoc fecerit, nondum reperi. Videtur autem id fecisse *Selgjûk*, qui Persiam occupavit et longævus usque ad CIX annos vixit; vel aliàs, id fecit aliquis *Selgjukidarum* ex ejus familiâ; cum ea esset Anni Solaris forma quâ in patriâ suâ *Chorasân* utebantur dicti *Selgjukidæ*."

The anecdote is found in the sixth appendix, pp. 529, 530.

"In Libro *Persico* D. *Bunelei*, Num. 44, de Morte Celeberrimi *Astronomi Omar Cheiyâm*, sequente modo legitur." [Then comes more than a full page of Persian text quoted, followed by Dr. Hyde's Latin translation]: —

"In Chronico memoratum & exaratum est, quòd Mors Regis Sapientum & Principis Doctorum atque Exemplaris Excellentium, Doctissimi Chogja Omar Cheiyâm accidit anno 517 in Urbe Neishâbur. Atque in omnibus Scientiis ac Sapientiis unicus & scientissimus sui temporis fuit Chogja Nezâmi Versificator Samarcandensis, qui sui temporis Doctissimus atque unus ex Discipulis dicti Chogja Omar fuit : & is mortem Chogja Omar sequente modo narrat. Mihi in Urbe Balch acciderunt Conversationes quædam, & habuimus consessum, ubi ille verbum effatus est, *Meum Sepulchrum erit in Loco, in quem quovis tempore verno ventus septentrionalis Flores spargit.* Ego autem miratus mecum dixi, *Certe iste homo futilia non loquitur.* Donec tandem, post Mortem ejus, cùm aliquoties ad Urbem Neishâbur consesseram, sepulchrum ejus inveni : & observavi ipsius Sepulchrum esse propè murum Horti, ubi arborum fructiferarum Malogranatorum Summitates, extra Hortum exporrectæ, tam affatim super ipsius caput effuderunt Flores, ut illo tempore Sepulchrum ejus non comparuerit. Ego propter Sermonem Chogjæ Omar mirabundus, expetivi Domum ejus adire. Cúmque ejus domum adiveram, postquam de eo interrogaveram, dixi, *Voluntas ejus sic fuit :* & deinde veram ipsius Notitiam dedi. Mater ejus respondit, *Ego quoque post mortem ejus vidi quiddam mirandum, quod hoc est, sc. Nocte quâdam, cùm pro Omaro meo à Deo precarer Peccatorum Remissionem, et exorarem atque Supplicationes effunderem, mox in Somnum incidi, & in Somnio vidi Omarum mihi recitantem Tetrastichum. Cúmque evigilarem, illud Tetrastichum in Memoriâ meâ haesit.* Ejus quoque extant multa Tetrasticha Sapientiâ referta. Pauca quædam in initio Sermonum ejus exciderunt : ast unum Tetrastichon scripto mandatum est, quod mater ejus post Mortem ipsius in Somnio vidit. Ipsa quæsivit, *O fili, quid Deus tecum fecit ?* Tum ille dictum Tetrastichon Matri suæ recitavit. Et cùm Mater Cheiyâmi à Somno evigilaret, ipsa memoriâ retinuit illud Tetrastichon, quod etiam jam celebre est. Tetrastichon itaque, quod in Somnio vidit, hoc est.

Marginalia:
Flowers shall scatter their petals on his grave

His apparition to his mother

The quatrain his mother dreamed

> O combustus combustus Combustione!
> Væ, à te est Ignis Gehennæ Accensio!
> Quousque dicis, *Omaro misericors esto?*
> Quousque Deum, *Caput Misericordiæ*, docebis?"

Dr. Hyde adds:—

"Et deinde posteà in eodem Codice Persico sequuntur alia Tetrasticha fortè ducenta."

Von Hammer-Purgstall, 1818

GESCHICHTE ‖ DER ‖ SCHÖNEN REDEKÜNSTE PERSIENS, ‖ MIT EINER ‖ BLÜTHENLESE ‖ AUS ‖ ZWEYHUNDERT PERSISCHEN DICHTERN ‖ VON ‖ JOSEPH VON HAMMER, RITTER DES ST. ANNEN-ORDENS ZWEYTER, UND DES DANEBROGS DRITTER CLASSE, WIRKLICHEM K. K. HOFRATHE UND HOFDOLLMETSCHE AN DER GEHEIMEN-HOF- UND STAATSKANZELLEY ‖ &c. &c.

MIT DEM PORTRÄT DES VERFASSERS, EINEM NOTENBLATTE UND EINEM SACHREGISTER. ‖ WIEN, 1818, BEY HEUBNER UND VOLKE, BUCHHÄNDLER.

xii + 433 pp.   P. 80 § 20 Omar Chiam: 1 p. of introduction, 2 pp. of quatrains.

This work of Von Hammer-Purgstall is based on Daulatsah ibn 'Alá al-daulah ibn Bakhtisah al Gází alsamarkandi's great collection of Biographies of the Persian poets.

The Voltaire of Persian poetry

Von Hammer in his introduction speaks of Omar as being unique for the irreligious character of his poetry: he calls him "der Dichter der Freygeister und Religionspötter," the Voltaire of Persian poetry. He says that to understand him, one must be master of the mystic terminology, of the Sufis,—'the part' and 'the whole,' 'being' and 'not being.'

His words are:—

"Er ist der Dichter der Freygeister und Religionsspötter, und darf in dieser Hinsicht füglich der Voltaire persischer Dichtkunst geheissen werden. Es ist merkwürdig, dass wie überall so auch in Persien, die Freygeisterey die Vorlauferinn der Mystik war, und dass das Zeitalter von dem tiefsten Unglauben zu dem höchsten Aberglauben überging."

And here are all the quatrains, the quaint old-fashioned spelling retained:—

I.

Von Hammer-Purgstall's versions

Du wünschest, dass zu Theil dir werde Licht:
Zuerst thu' deinem Nächsten Böses nicht,
Denk' an den Tod, und an die Nahrung nicht,
Denn Beydes kömmt von selbst als Loosgericht.

II.

Thu' auf das Thor! denn der Eröffende bist Du,
Zeig' mir den Weg! denn der Wegweisende bist Du,
Ich lege meine Hand in keines Führers Hand,
Weil sie vergänglich sind, der Ewige bist Du.

[Ap. XXXIV, Nicolas, 409, etc.]

III.

In dieser Hand das Glas, in jener den Koran,
Bin ich ein frommer bald, und bald ein schlechter Mann.
Ich bin im Weltendom, von Türkis hochgewölbt,
Kein ganzer Giaur, und kein ganzer Musulman.

[Ap. XLVII, Nicolas, 315, etc.]

IV.

Bereit bin ich den Kopfbund zu verkaufen,
Den Stab für Flötentöne zu verkaufen,
  Den Rosenkranz der hundert Nahmen Gottes
Für einen Becher Weines zu verkaufen.
               [Ap. XXII, Nicolas, 279, etc.]

V.

Im Weinhaus wo mein Liebchen glühend steht,
Verrichte ich mit ihm mein Stossgebeth.
  Wer sich mit Liebeswein gereinigt hat,
Verrichte vor dem Liebchen sein Gebeth.

VI.

Bin ich von Lieb' und Wein berauscht, so bin ich's;
Bin ich ungläubig Götzen hold, so bin ich's;
  Die Leute sprechen Vieles über mich:
Ich bin derselbe der ich bin, so bin ich's.
               [See p. 481, Nicolas, 297, etc.]

VII.

Ich schaute gestern einem Töpfer zu,
Der schlug auf frischen Lehm gewaltig zu.
  Da sprach der Lehm mit seinem eignen Wort:
Schlag' mich nicht so; bin ich denn nicht was du?
               [XXXVII, p. 74]

VIII.

Ich bin an's Rosenantlitz von Natur gebunden,
Und meine Hand ist an den Becher Wein's gebunden.
  In jedem Theilchen wird ein Antheil mir erfunden
Doch an das Ganze sind die Theilchen all gebunden.
               [Nicolas, 163.]

IX.

Im Frühling, wenn mir ein Hurisgesicht
  Die Kanne Weines schäumend reicht als Schenke,
(So schändlich dies auch däucht gemeinem Wicht)
  Bin ich ein Hund, wenn ich ans Paradies gedenke.*

[XII, p. 24.]

X.

Die Nacht verjaget schon des Morgens Heer,
Steh auf geschwind, gib Wein der Maghen her,
Schliess auf die schlummertrunkenen Narcissen,
Steh auf, zu lang liegst du zu meinen Füssen.

XI.

Chiam! bist trunken du, bist du verliebt, sey froh!
Hast ein Paar Tage du den Wein verehrt, sey froh!
  Wie lange wirst du dich noch kümmern ob ich bin,
Da du nicht bist, wie wohl du bist, so lebe froh.

[Nicolas, 242.]

XII.

Ich sprach: mein Herz soll Wissenschaft verstehen,
Und wenig war, was ich nicht eingesehen:
Doch wenn ich's schaue reiferen Gesicht's:
Das Leben ist vorbey — und ich weiss Nichts.

[Ap. XI, Nicolas, 113, etc.]

XIII.

Ich trinke Wein, doch siehst du mich berauschet nicht,
  Ich strecke aus die Hand nach einem Glas;
  Warum ich Wein anbethe? weisst Du das?
Damit ich nicht wie du anbethe mein Gesicht.†

[Nicolas, 301.]

---

* Im Original: Bin ich schlechter als ein Hund.
† Wörtlich: Damit Ich nicht mein Ich anbethe.

XIV.

Ich bin nun eingesperrt im Käfichte des Daseyns,
Und wittre Duft des Nichts im Farbenlicht des Daseyns,
  Ich will dem Nichts gern hundert Dankesopfer bringen,
Wenn es den Nahmen rettet mir vom Schimpf des Daseyns.

XV.

Da Nichts nach unserm Wunsche geht im Leben,
Was nützen Müh', Gedanken und Bestreben!
Ich sitz gedankenvoll darob in Wehen,
Dass ich seit langem kam, und schnell muss gehen.

                [Ap. XII, Nicolas, 41, etc.]

XVI.

Wo Tulpen auf den Feldern sprossen,
Trank jeder Fleck das Blut der Grossen.
Die Veilchen, die auf Wiesen prangen,
Sind Muttermaale schöner Wangen.*

XVII.

Wird mir die Rose nicht, sich Dornen da!
Wird mir der Lichtstrahl nicht, sie Gluthen da!
  Sind Kloster, Kutte, Scheich nicht bey der Hand,
Ist Christenkirch, und Glock' und Gürtel da.

                [Nicolas, 253.]

* Translated by Emerson: —

    Each spot where tulips prank their state
    Has drunk the life-blood of the great;
    The violets yon field which stain
    Are moles of beauties Time hath slain.

See p. 38, FitzGerald, XIX.

XVIII.

Ich trinke Wein und jeder trinket der gescheit,
Verzeihung ist dafür mir bey dem Herrn bereit.
Von ewig wusste Gott, ich würde trinken Wein,
Drum wenn ich ihn nicht tränk, Gott müsst' unwissend
  seyn.   [Nicolas, 182.]

XIX.

Du der dich viel mit Vier und Sieben,
Von Sieben und von Vier viel hast geschrieben,
Trink Wein, ich sag dirs tausendmahl und immer:
Wer fort ist, der ist fort, und kommet nimmer.
      [XXXV, p. 70.]

XX.

Zu einem Greiss, den ich sah in der Schenke,
Sprach ich: Der Abgeschiedenen gedenke.
Er sprach: O trinke Wein auf gutes Glück!
Sie gingen all', doch keiner kam zurück.
 [LVIII, p. 112, and Appendix XXII, Nicolas, 412.]

XXI.

Es führt von hier kein Weg in höh'res Land,
Nur ich und du, wir haben noch Verstand.
Verzicht' auf was du glaubst: es ist, es war;
Denn Alles ist nur Schatten, nichts ist wahr.
      [LXIII, p. 122.]

XXII.

Du sprichst mir von Huris, vom Paradiese,
Von Edens lusterfüllter goldner Wiese.
Geh nimm den Pfennig hin und lass mich geh'n,
Von ferne hört sich die Trommel schön.
      [XIII, p. 26.]

XXIII.

In dem unendlichen Bezirk hienieden,
Sind zweyerley Personen nur zufrieden,
  Der, so was gut und bös ist wohl erkennt,
Und der, dem ganz Unwissenheit beschieden.

[Nicolas, 320.]

XXIV.

Die Seelen sind im Schweiss, die Herzen sind voll Blut,
Zu wissen was hienieden wahr sey und was gut.
Vor deiner Kenntniss, Gott! vergeht des Menschen
    Sinn,
Es ging von Dir heraus die Welt, Du bist darin.

XXV.

O du! vom Loos getrieben wie vom Schlägel Ballen,
Der du in Lust des Wein's und der Huris gefallen,
Du bist gefallen auf des Ewigen Geheiss;
Er ist es, der es weiss, der's weiss, der's weiss, der's
    weiss.

[LXX, p. 136.]

Ralph Waldo Emerson's translations

    Ralph Waldo Emerson was, as he himself confessed, principally indebted to Baron von Hammer-Purgstall for his knowledge of Persian literature, and the translations which appear in his article on "Persian Poetry" in "Letters and Social Aims" were made through the medium of the German. In the index to Emerson's collected works, translations from Omar Khayyám are referred to volume vi. 11, viii. 231, and ix. 247. The first reads:—

> "On two days, it steads not to run from thy grave,
>   The appointed and the unappointed day;
>   On the first, neither balm nor physician can save,
>   Nor thee, on the second the Universe slay."

The one in the ninth volume corresponds to Fitz-Gerald's nineteenth stanza, and may be found in the quatrains of Von Hammer following that from which it was translated, the sixteenth.

The third, corresponding to the twenty-third stanza of Von Hammer, follows, with comparative versions:—

Ralph Waldo Emerson
On earth's wide thoroughfares below—
Two only men contented go:
Who knows what's right and what's forbid,
And he from whom is knowledge hid.

Nicolas (320)
Si tu sais à quoi t'en tenir sur la marche de ce cercle sans fin, tu dois reconnaître deux classes d'hommes: ceux qui connaissent parfaitement son bon et son mauvais côté, et ceux qui n'ont de notion ni d'eux-mêmes ni des choses d'ici-bas.

McCarthy (412)
If thou canst understand the circuit of this wheel, thou must perceive two kinds of men, those knowing good and evil, and those that know neither themselves nor aught else.

Whinfield (363)
In this eternally revolving zone,
Two lucky species of men are known;
  One knows all good and ill that are on earth,
One neither earth's affairs, nor yet his own.

Bodenstedt (VIII. 40)
In diesem endlos kreisenden Erdenrund
Werden Dir zwei Arten von Menschen kund:
Die, welche Gutes und Böses zu scheiden wissen,
Und die, welche gar nichts von beiden wissen.

There is still another included in his poems, but it is questionable whether, together with the one in the sixth volume of his works, it is not by another author: —

He who has a thousand friends has not a friend to spare,
And he who has one enemy will meet him everywhere.

GRAMMATIK, POETIK UND RHETORIK DER PERSER, VON FRIEDRICH RÜCKERT, HERAUSGEGEBEN VON W. PERTSCH. GOTHA, 1874.

Friedrich Rückert

Von Hammer's Persian mantle descended upon Friedrich Rückert, who was born May 16, 1788, at Schweinfurt-am-Obermain; he studied at Jena, then at Heidelberg, lived afterwards at Stuttgart and in Italy, and then again at Koburg. As Professor and student of Oriental Literature he became imbued with the Philosophy of the East, and the long array of volumes which bear his name are filled with poems either translated from Persian and Arabic sources or inspired by Eastern subjects. He is best known to English readers by his "Wisdom of the Brahmin," in twenty books, — "a poetic treasury" of which, says Dr. Beyer, the German nation may well be proud. While he was collaborating with Von Hammer-Purgstall in Oriental investigation, he wrote a long and careful review of the seventh part of the King of Oude's Dictionary and Grammar of the Persian Language ("The Seven Seas," by Abul-Musaffer Muiseddin Shah seman Ghasieddin Haider Padishah Ghasi, Lekhneo, 1822). This article appeared in vol. 40 of the "Wiener Jahrbücher der Literatur" (1827), and was, after his death (in January, 1866), published as above. I know of no copy in America.

His two unrhymed versions

But from the original article, entitled "Persiche Philologie," may be quoted his two unrhymed versions illustrating the Rubá'iy (as the fifth stream flowing into the second sea of the Seventh Kolgûm!) accompanied by the transliteration from Omar mentioned in the Introduction, as follows:—

ez bâdi śabâ dilem ćn bôjí tu gireft
bugdhâsht' merâ u ġust u ġust u gôjí tu ġerift
eknûn zi mení khaste nemí âred jâd.
bôjí tu girift' bûd khôjí tu girift.

Da vom Morgenwind mein Herz hatte deinen Duft
    ergriffen,
Hat es mich verlassen, und hat das Suchen nach dir
    ergriffen.
    Nun mag es meiner, des Kranken, nicht weiter
        denken;
    Es hatte deinen Duft ergriffen, so hat es nun auch
        deine Art ergriffen.

Beyspiel eines Rubá'ijiterane

bí bâde mebâsh' tâ tuwânî jekdem
kiz bâde shewed 'akl u dil ú dín moh'kem
   iblís' 'eger bâde bukhordê jekdem
kerdê du hezâr' seġde pêshí âdem.

Ohne Wein bleibe, so sehr du vermagst, keinen Augen-
    blick;
Denn durch Wein wird Verstand und Herz und
    Glauben befestiget.
Iblîs (der gefallene Engel), wenn er Wein getrunken
    hätte einen Zug,
Würde er zweytausend Fussfälle vor Adam gemacht
    haben.

Compare: —

Applique-toi à n'être jamais un moment privé de vin, car c'est le vin qui donne du reflet à l'intelligence, au cœur de l'homme, à la religion. Si le diable en avait goûté un seul instant, il aurait adoré Adam et aurait fait devant lui deux mille génuflexions. — Nicolas (270)

See that thou art never left without wine, for it is wine which fills the heart of man with wisdom and with knowledge of religion. If the Devil had tasted one drop thereof, he would have adored Adam, and would have bowed himself down before him two thousand times. — McCarthy (198)

Ne'er for one moment leave your cup unused!
Wine keeps heart, faith, and reason too, amused;
   Had Iblis swallowed but a single drop,
To worship Adam he had ne'er refused! — Whinfield (343)

Sei, so viel als möglich, ohne Wein nicht einen Augenblick,
Denn er stärkt Verstand und Glauben, er nur schafft des Menschen Glück.
Wenn des Weines einen Schluck auch Iblis nur gekostet hätte,
Tausendmal vor Adam wär er huld'gend hingekniet, ich wette. — Von Schack (170)

BIOGRAPHICAL NOTICES ‖ OF ‖ PERSIAN POETS: ‖ WITH ‖ CRITICAL AND EXPLANATORY REMARKS ‖ BY ‖ THE LATE RIGHT HONOURABLE ‖ SIR GORE OUSELEY, BART. ‖ To which is prefixed ‖ A MEMOIR ‖ OF ‖ THE LATE RIGHT HON. SIR GORE OUSELEY, BART., ‖ SOMETIME AMBASSADOR EXTRAORDINARY AND PLEN- — Sir Gore Ouseley, 1846

IPOTENTIARY [AT THE COURT OF PERSIA. | BY | THE REV. JAMES REYNOLDS, M.R.A.S. [&c., &c.] LONDON | PRINTED FOR THE ORIENTAL TRANSLATION FUND [OF GREAT BRITAIN AND IRELAND ;] SOLD BY] W. H. ALLEN AND Co., LEADENHALL STREET ; | AND | B. DUPRAT, Paris. | M.DCCC.XLVI.

First prose translation of Omar

Sir Gore Ouseley deserves the credit of having made the first prose translations from Omar Khayyám. They are only two in number, but none the less they deserve their acknowledgment, and warrant the insertion of the memorial volume in the Bibliography. The two versions, which he calls "sentences," are these: —

"My inclination leads me constantly to the enjoyment of pure wine, my ears are always filled with the soft tones of the flute and harp. When turned to clay and fashioned into a jar by the potters, O that the jar be for ever filled with pure wine."

"I saw a potter in the market place, who incessantly stamped upon a piece of fresh clay that he might fashion it into a vessel, when the clay raised its voice and said, 'I, too, was once a man like thee, therefore be gentle with me.'" (See Rubá'iy XXXVII.)

The first, numbered IV, on p. 384, has, in parentheses, "From Omar Kheiam." This Rubá'iy appears to have been omitted by McCarthy and Whinfield. French and German versions are as follows : —

Nicolas
(20)

Je suis constamment attiré par la vue du vin limpide, mes oreilles sont sans cesse attentives aux sons mélodieux de la flûte et du rubab. Oh, si le potier fait une cruche de ma poussière, puisse cette cruche être constamment pleine de vin !

Immer hält mich der Zauber des rosigen Weines umfangen, **Bodenstedt**
Immer trag' ich nach Klang der Flöten und Harfen Verlangen. (IX. 90)
Macht einen Krug einst der Töpfer aus meinem Staube:
Mög' er voll immer sein vom edelsten Safte der Traube!

Stets hält die Blicke mir gebannt des Weines zarte Röte, **Von Schack**
Im Ohre hallt mir immerdar der süsse Klang der Flöte. (154)
Formt einst der Töpfer einen Krug aus meines Leibes Staube,
O stets sei dieser Krug gefüllt mit feur'gem Saft der Traube!

L'ALGÈBRE ∥ D'OMAR ALKHAYYÂMÎ ∥ PUBLIÉE, TRA- **Woepcke,**
DUITE ET ACCOMPAGNÉE ∥ D'EXTRAITS DE MANU- **1851**
SCRITS INÉDITS, ∥ PAR ∥ F. WOEPCKE ∥ DOCTEUR
AGRÉGÉ À L'UNIVERSITÉ DE BONN, MEMBRE DE LA
SOCIÉTÉ ASIATIQUE DE PARIS. ∥ PARIS ∥ BENJAMIN
DUPRAT, LIBRAIRE DE L'INSTITUT, ∥ DE LA BIBLIO-
THÈQUE NATIONALE, DES SOCIÉTÉS ASIATIQUES DE
PARIS, DE LONDRES ET DE CALCUTTA. ∥ RUE DU
CLOÎTRE-ST.-BENOIT, 7 ∥ M DCCC LI. Paris. —
Typographie de Fermin Didot Frères, rue Jacob, 56.
[Introduction, xxi pp. Translation, 127 pp. Arabic,
52 pp., plates, &c.]

M. Woepcke says:—
"Alkhayyâm signifies 'fabricant des tentes.' It is
scarcely probable that the celebrated astronomer himself exercised this profession; but probably it was his
father's or one of his ancestors', and consequently of
the two readings Alkhayyâmî seems to be the one to
be preferred.

"Alkhayyâmî himself informs us," continues Woepcke, "that he also had composed a treatise on the extraction of roots of higher degrees; and the little which he tells us is sufficient to reveal to us the same generalizing spirit which, as we shall soon see, led him to a systematic theory of cubic equations."

And here is a specimen of his writing in the original:—

Unjust charges against Omar

"Alkhayyâmî était poëte. Mais ses vers, écrits en persan, lui ont valu une réputation d'athée et de libertin. Rappelons-nous, cependant que les mêmes accusations furent portées contre Descartes par un turbulent théologien, le recteur Voët, de l'université d'Utrecht. Ne nous empressons donc pas de souscrire à un jugement qui a peut-être sa source uniquement dans les haines religieuses que les poésies satiriques et spirituelles d'Alkhayyâmî devaient susciter contre lui."

"Ce morceau," he says, "est extrait du manuscrit No. 481, supplément arabe, de la Bibliothèque nationale, qui contient un abrégé du Târîkh-Alhogamâ, terminé en 647 de l'hégira, et dont l'auteur s'appelait Alzoûzenî:—

Woepcke's translation

"*Omar Alkhayyam, imâm du Khorâçân, le grand savant du temps, était versé dans les sciences des Grecs. Il exhortait à chercher le Dieu unique, gouverneur du monde, par la purification des mouvements corporels, de manière à rendre l'âme humaine exempte de toute impurité. Il recommandait aussi une étude persévérante de la politique, fondée sur les bases de cette science établies par les philosophes grecs. Les Soûfis des temps postérieurs ont accueilli le sens apparent d'une partie de ses poésies, et puis les ont accommodées à leurs doctrines de sorte qu'ils en font l'objet de discussions dans leurs assemblées et dans leurs réunions privées. Mais le sens caché de* les poésies consiste en axiomes de la religion universelle, et en principes généraux embrassant les devoirs pratiques. Comme les hommes de son temps blâmaient ses opinions religieuses, et mettaient à découvert ce qu'il cachait en secret, il craignit pour sa vie, et mit un frein aux écarts de sa langue et de sa plume. Il fit le pèlerinage, grâce plutôt à une rencontre fortuite que par piété ; et son extérieur trahit ses pensées secrètes, bien que rien n'en parût dans ses paroles. Lorsqu'il fut arrivé à Bagdâd, les personnes qui s'étaient livrées aux mêmes études que lui en fait de sciences anciennes accoururent auprès de lui ; mais il leur ferma sa porte, en homme qui avait renoncé à ces études, et non pas en homme qui fût resté leur confrère. Après être retourné de son pèlerinage dans son pays, il se rendait au lieu des prières le soir et le matin, et cachait ses secrets, qui pourtant ne pouvaient pas manquer de se révéler. Il était sans pareil dans l'astronomie et dans la philosophie ; et sa capacité éminente dans ces sciences aurait passé en proverbe s'il avait reçu en partage le respect des convenances. On a de lui des poésies légères dont le sens caché perce à travers leurs expressions voilées, et dans lesquelles la veine de la conception poétique est troublée par l'impureté de l'intention cachée. Poésie : —

Omar charged with hypocrisy

'Comme mon âme se contente d'une aisance modeste et facile à obtenir, que toute fois ma main et mon bras ne me procurent qu'avec effort.

'Je suis à l'abri de toutes les vicissitudes de la fortune, et dans mes malheurs, ma main et les projets que je forme sont mon refuge.

'Les sphères dans leur mouvement n'ont-elles pas prononcé l'arrêt, que toutes les étoiles heureuses finissent par décliner vers une position funeste ?

'Persévérance donc, ô mon âme, dans ton repos ! Tu en fais seulement crouler le sommet, en voulant en consolider les bases.'"

Charles J. Pickering gives of the above quotation from the Tarikh-ul-Hukamá of Jamálu'd-dín 'Alí the following translation from the original Arabic:—

Pickering's translation

"'Umar al-Khayyám, Imám of Khurásán, and the profoundest *savant* of his time, was learned in the science of the Greeks (*Yúnán*). He was ever urging the quest of the one only Judge by means of the purification of bodily motions and the sublimation of the human soul. And he enjoined the zealous study of political science according to the principles of the Greek philosophic school. The moderns of the Súfí sect have adopted and adapted to their own system the exoteric sense of part of his makings, and bring it up for discussion in their assemblies and private gatherings. But their esoteric sense consists of axioms of comprehensive religion (*sharí'atu'l-wási*) and maxims of universal obligation. But since the people of his day reviled him for his belief, and exposed to view the secrets he had veiled from them, he feared for his blood, and reined in the bridle of his tongue and pen.

"He made the pilgrimage, not from piety, but as the result of a chance *rencontre*; wherein also he betrayed the secrets of his heart's ungodliness. When he got to Baghdád the men of his own method of ancient science beset him, but he shut on them his door with the shutting of compunction and not of companionship (*sadda 'u-ná limi lá sadda 'n-nadími*). And he returned from the Hajj unto his city, to repair morning and evening to the place of worship, concealing his secret thoughts; and yet they could not but out. He was unparalleled in astronomy and natural philosophy (*hikmat*) and his pre-eminence in these provinces would have passed into a proverb, had he only safe-guarded his good name (*lau razaqa'l-'asmata*). By him there

are fugitive verses whose secret sense pierces their
veil of concealment, and whose fount of conception is
troubled by the turbidness of their hidden intent.

'Since my soul is content with an easy enough
(Tho' that little *sans* toil palm nor arm may procure)
From the turns and revulsions of Time it is safe:
Guard me hand and heart's aim in my life's darkest hour.
In their dizzying whirl hath the heavens not decreed
That all fortunate stars to disaster should lower?
Then patience, O soul, in thy noonday repose:
Build the base in too deep, thou o'ertopplest the tower.'"

"This characterization," says Woepcke in conclusion, "is evidently not by a friendly hand. One would judge from it that Alkhayyâmî's character was only a mixture of impurity and hypocrisy. But in spite of all efforts to impugn our author's morality, the homage which it is impossible to withhold from the philosopher comes out in all the brighter light. He is a detestable man, but an unequalled astronomer; he is perhaps a heretic, but surely he is a philosopher of the first order. Three hundred years later passions had had time to calm. The knowledge, or at least the rumor of Alkhayyâmî's discoveries had spread even to Spain, and Ibn Khaldoûn refers to him in his prolegomena. Now he is no longer either the hypocrite or the libertine Alkayyâmî; he is simply 'Un des plus grands géomètres de l'Orient.'" **The characterization by an unfriendly hand**

A leading article in the *Saturday Review* for August 20, 1892, says:—

"The wise and excellent Giyâth ed Dîn Abûl Fath Omar ben Ibrâhîm Alkhayyâmî of Naishâpûr was

Omar as a mathematician

unequally treated by his prophet FitzGerald. While he made of the rapt and staring *Rubáiyát* a possession forever, the notice which he prefixed thereto is scant both of material and of workmanship. For example, — a minor example, — he flings aside one of Omar's (unpoetical) works in this clause of a sentence: 'and the French have lately republished and translated an Arabic treatise of his on Algebra.'

Omar's Algebra discovered in 1742

"This was F. Woepcke's production, which was assisted into the book-world by Prince Friedrich of Anhalt Dessau in 1851. But the scientific world had been advertised of the 'discovery' of Omar's Algebra nine years and a hundred years previously by Gerard Meerman in his (Latin) *Specimen of the Fluxions* — a Calculus, wherein he mentioned an Arabic manuscript of Omar's treatise which had been left to the Leiden Library by Warner. [M. Libri discovered a complete MS. in the Bibliothèque royale.] Natheless Colebrooke, in writing of the Algebra of the Hindûs, did not know of Omar, or he would never have asserted that algebra had remained almost stationary among the Mussulmans from Mahomet ben Moussa to Behâ ed Dîn. . . .

The peculiarities of his Algebra

"The peculiarities of his Algebra were that he dealt with four media, — the line, surface, solid, and time (which last had, he said, not heretofore been touched), — and tho' in the solving of every equation he gave both the arithmetical and the geometrical demonstrations. These last, too, were all written out laboriously in the interminable Arabic, without any diagrams. His equations of the third degree were best, and Woepcke said positively that Diophantus had been indebted to Omar. Another peculiarity that differentiates his treatise from those now generally published 'for the use of schools' is the incessant way in which he rounds off a solu tion with a *laus Deo*, instead of some barren Q. E. D. He begins, like a pious Moslem (atheist and libertine though he was proclaimed): 'In the name of Allah the Clement and the Merciful; praise be to Allah, lord of the worlds, and a happy end to those who fear him, [and no enmity, unless to the unjust. May the divine benediction rest on the Prophets, and particularly Muhammad and all his holy family.'] And then, as he warms to his work, you read: 'I lay hold of the rope of divine assistance, and with the precious help of Allah I declare that Algebra is a scientific art!' 'Now,' he goes on elsewhere, 'am I about to discuss and demonstrate one by one all the twenty-five kinds of equations; and I implore the aid of Allah. Whosoever faithfully relieth upon him, Allah directs him, and it sufficeth.' And he winds up at the very end by acknowledging with simple humility that 'it is Allah who has made plain the solution of these difficulties by his benefits and his generosity.'

Omar calls on Allah

"These phrases can scarcely have been due to scribes or transcribes, but they may of course have been used as mere common forms, like the notorious, 'In the name of the Prophet, Figs,' of the pseudo-Johnson; and even that might easily be outdone with the cry of the Cairene hawker of parched melon-seeds, — 'O consoler of the embarrassed, Pips!' Such clichés of the Arabic treatises must have been caught up long ago in a Moorish University by the thirteenth-century physician Gilbert the Englishman, who, in his *Compendium Medicinæ* describing his marvellous treatment of one of the eyes of one Bertrand de Giblet, wrote down, ' By the mercy of the Lord, I squeezed a turnip.' It is on folio cxxxvii of his book (Lugduni, 1510.)"

Garcin de Tassy, 1857

Note ‖ sur ‖ les Rubá'iyát de 'Omar Khaïyám, ‖ par M. Garcin de Tassy, ‖ Membre de l'Institut. ‖ Paris ‖ Imprimerie Impériale ‖ M DCCC LVII.

Verso of Bastard title: Extrait No. 9 de L'Année 1857 ‖ du Journal asiatique. Paper, 5 - 11 pp. last three devoted to the Persian and French Rubáiyát.

Garcin de Tassy, whose full name was Joseph Héliodore Sagesse Vertu, begins with a slender account of Omar's life. He considers the old poet's style as pure and masculine, and for the most part free from those far-fetched ideas and expressions which so often injure the later compositions of the Persians. He criticises his involuntary pantheism, and remarks upon the foundation of the belief that the author of the Rubáiyát was a materialistic atheist, if not also an impious infidel. He makes no pretence to decide this mooted point, but adds that examples give a better idea of Omar's bent of mind and his poetry than any description could do. Accordingly he prints at the end of his article ten Rubáiyát transcribed by Edward FitzGerald, though he does not say so, from a MS. presented to the Bodleian Library by the late Sir W. Ouseley. "This MS.," he says "unfortunately contains only one hundred and fifty-eight quatrains, yet is excellent, and very ancient, having been written at Shiraz in 866 (1460-1461)." **Reason for rarity of manuscripts** As for MSS., he says those of Omar are very rare, there being only one in Paris, and he attributes this scarcity, and the limited number of quatrains admitted, to the audacity of the poet's expressions, which the copyists — good Mussulmans — were probably unwilling to reproduce.

As Garcin de Tassy's article is not easily accessible, an extract from it and the ten quatrains, which he says "'n'ont jamais été publiés ni traduits," will prove interesting:—

"Il y a, en effet, de belles et de remarquables choses dans ces quatrains. Le style en est pur et mâle, et généralement exempt de cette recherche d'idées et d'expressions qui gâte souvent les compositions persanes plus modernes. Malheureusement les vers de 'Omar sont empreints, non-seulement de ces idées spiritualistes qui dédaignent la religion positive, et qui, sans s'occuper du culte extérieur, se rapportent uniquement à Dieu, que le poëte voit en tout et partout, ce qui le fait tomber dans un panthéisme involontaire; mais, en prenant à la lettre quelques-uns de ces *Rubá'iyát*, on croirait même que l'auteur est athée et matérialiste; et, en effet, quoique quelques-uns de ses coreligionnaires l'aient considéré comme un saint, d'autres l'ont regardé comme un auteur impie et mécréant. Partant de ce point de vue, de Hammer le nomme le Voltaire de la poésie persane; mais il se hâte d'ajouter, cependant, pour excuser les vers quelquefois mal sonnants de notre auteur, qu'il ne faut pas toujours les condamner absolument; car ce qu'il attaque, c'est la religion telle qui l'entendent les *uléma* et la morale des casuistes musulmans; plutôt que la religion et la loi naturelle. . . .

Purity and strength of Omar's style

"Tant que tu peux n'afflige personne, ne fais subir à personne le feu de ta colère. Si tu veux jouir du bonheur éternel, sache souffrir patiemment, et ne fais souffrir personne. [See Whitley Stokes's Versions, (10).]

"La joie règne dans le monde; mais le spiritualiste se retire dans le désert. Là, chaque branche fleurie lui représente la blanche main de Moïse, et chaque souffle de vent l'haleine vivifiante du Messie. [See Rubá'iy IV.]

Garcin de Tassy's version

"Khayâm, pourquoi ce deuil pour tes fautes, et quel avantage trouves-tu à dévorer ton chagrin? Celui qui n'a pas péché n'a pas été non plus l'objet de l'absolution divine. Le pardon est pour les fautes, pourquoi donc te livrer à la douleur? [Appendix XXV, Nicolas, 43, etc.]

"Dans l'oratoire du cloître, dans la mosquée, dans la pagode, dans l'église, on éprouve la crainte de l'enfer et on recherche le paradis. Mais celui qui connaît les secrets de Dieu n'a jamais jeté dans son cœur une telle semence. [Appendix XXV, Nicolas, 46, etc.] *

"Voici la saison des roses et du repos au bord du ruisseau et sur la lisière de la prairie, avec deux ou trois amis et une belle de nature angélique. Qu'on apporte aussi des coupes de vin, et ne nous mettons en peine, ni de la mosquée, ni de l'église. [Rubá'iy XII.]

"Suivons le chemin du pur amour avant d'être saisi par les étreintes de la mort. Charmant échanson, ne reste pas inactif, donne-moi de l'eau à boire en attendant que je devienne de la terre. [Appendix XXXVII.]

"C'est parce que ton amour a attiré dans ses filets ma tête chauve, que je tiens dans ma main la coupe de vin. Tu as anéanti le repentir que ma raison m'avait inspiré, et le temps a déchiré le vêtement que la patience avait cousu. [Whitley Stokes's Version, 19.]

* In the pamphlet reprint this Rubá'iy begins: "Dans le cloître et dans le collège, dans la pagode et dans l'église."

"Un amour superficiel n'est pas honorable; il est pareil au feu à demi éteint, qui est sans force. L'amant véritable doit n'avoir de repos et de tranquillité ni dans l'année, ni dans le mois, ni la nuit, ni le jour. [Appendix XLVII, Nicolas, 164, etc.] *Garcin de Tassy's version*

"Ne laisse pas la colère s'emparer de toi, ni une douleur insensée se saisir de ton existence. Reste avec tes livres et ton ami au milieu des champs verdoyants, avant que la terre t'enserre. [Rubá'iy XII.]

"Nous devons considérer comme une lanterne magique ce monde mobile où nous vivons dans l'étourdissement. Le soleil en est la lampe, et le monde la lanterne où nous passons comme les figures qu'on y montre." [Rubá'iy LXVIII.]

RUBAIYÁT ‖ OF ‖ OMAR KHAYYÁM ‖ THE ASTRONOMER-POET OF PERSIA ‖ TRANSLATED INTO ENGLISH VERSE. ‖ **FitzGerald's first edition, 1859**

LONDON ‖ BERNARD QUARITCH, ‖ CASTLE STREET, LEICESTER SQUARE ‖ 1859 ‖

On the verso:
G. Norman, Printer, Maiden Lane, Covent Garden, London.

Brown paper, xiii + 21 pp., 22 notes occupying 5 pp. "In beggarly disguise as to paper and print, but magnificent vesture of verse."

Nicolas, 1867

LES ‖ QUATRAINS DE KHÈYAM ‖ TRADUITS DU PERSAN ‖ PAR J. B. NICOLAS, ‖ EX-PREMIER DROGMAN DE L'AMBASSADE FRANÇAISE EN PERSE ‖ CONSUL DE FRANCE À RESCHT. ‖ PARIS ‖ IMPRIMÉ PAR ORDRE DE L'EMPEREUR ‖ À L'IMPRIMERIE IMPÉRIALE ‖ M DCCCLXVII.

xv, 229 pp. 8vo. 464 Rubáiyát, with notes.

He says in his preface: —

"J'ai longtemps pensé, durant mon séjour en Perse, qu'une traduction française des quatrains de Khèyam pouvait offrir quelque intérêt pour l'Europe littéraire. Ce vieux grande poète qui florissait au XIe siècle et qui faisait dans le Khoraçan les délices de la cour des Seldjoukides, continue encore de nos jours à charmer **Difficulties in the way** les loisirs du palais des Kadjars à Téhéran. Mais, d'un côté, la difficulté de traduire un écrivain si essentiellement abstrait dans ses pensées philosophiques, si étrangement mystique dans ses expressions figurées (trop souvent présentées sous des formes d'un matérialisme repoussant); d'un autre côté, les embarras que j'entrevoisais pour la correction des épreuves à une si grande distance de Paris, et par-dessus tout le sentiment de mon incapacité pour entreprendre un tel travail, m'avaient toujours empêché de le publier jusqu'à présent.

The urgency of friends "À mon dernier passage à Paris, j'y ai rencontré des amis avides de nouveauté en fait de littérature orientale, parmi lesquels j'aime à citer ici Mme Blanchecotte, connue par plusieurs publications vives et passionées de moraliste et de poète. Après avoir entendu les citations orales que j'ai pu leur faire succinctement de quelques quatrains du poète qui nous occupe, ils m'ont si fortement conseillé d'en publier une traduction complète, ils ont mis tant d'insistance dans leurs conseils, tant de bienveillance dans leurs offres de service, que je me suis décidé à me conformer à leurs désirs en éditant aujourd'hui cet ouvrage.

"Cependant je le considérerais encore comme au-dessus de mes forces, sans la coopération de Hassan-Ali-Khan, ministre plénipotentiaire de Perse près la cour des Tuileries, qui a poussé l'obligeance jusqu'à m'aider de sa profonde érudition et de ses précieux avis."

The rest of the preface is devoted to a sketch of the life of Omar. It ends with the anecdote elsewhere told of the broken wine-jar and the blasphemous quatrain, but as Nicolas translates it from another Rubá'iy than that given in his text, it may be interesting to quote it here:— *The broken wine-jar*

"Tu as brisé ma cruche de vin, mon Dieu! tu as
"ainsi fermé sur moi la porte de la joie, mon Dieu!
"c'est moi qui bois, et c'est toi qui commets les dés-
"ordres de l'ivresse! Oh! (puisse ma bouche se
"remplir de terre!) serais-tu ivre, mon Dieu?"

"Le poète, après avoir prononcé ce blasphème, jetant les yeux sur une glace, se serait aperçu que son visage était noir comme du charbon. C'était une punition du ciel. Alors il fit cet autre quatrain non moins audacieux que le premier, et qui exprime d'une manière absolue la répulsion du poète pour la doctrine des peines futures, décrites dans le Koran, et prêchées si chaleureusement par les moullahs. Les soufis considèrent cette doctrine, non-seulement comme le renversement de la leur, mais encore comme indigne de la miséricorde et de la clémence de la Divinité. Voici ce quatrain:—

"Quel est l'homme ici bas qui n'a point commis de péché, dis? Celui qui n'en aurait point commis comment aurait-il vécu, dis? Si, parce que je fais le mal, tu me punis par le mal, quelle est donc la différence qui existe entre toi et moi, dis?"

"Mais arrivons au livre lui-même, à la pensée complète du poète qui se déduit si énergiquement et avec tant d'unité à travers les fantaisies ou les rudesses de ses quatrains."

Gautier's review

In "Le Moniteur" of December 8, 1867, Théophile Gautier reviewed the French prose translation of Nicolas. It was afterwards included in tome second of his "L'Orient" (pp. 57-72), under the title "Poésie persane." It begins with a brief sketch of Omar's life, includes the passage already quoted (page 392), and has also the following eloquent estimate of his poetry:

"Rien ne ressemble moins à ce qu'on entend chez nous par poésie orientale, c'est-à-dire un amoncellement de pierreries, de fleurs et de parfums, de comparaisons outrées, emphatiques et bizarres, que les vers du soufi Khèyam.

Symbolic language

La pensée y domine et y jaillit par brefs éclairs, dans une forme concise, abrupte, elliptique, illuminant d'une lueur subite les obscurités de la doctrine, et déchirant les voiles d'un langage dont chaque mot, suivant les commentateurs, est un symbole. On est étonné de cette liberté absolue d'esprit que les plus hardis penseurs modernes égalent à peine, à une époque où la crédulité la plus superstitieuse régnait en Europe, aux années les plus noires du moyen âge.

Hamlet's soliloquy anticipated

"Le monologue d'Hamlet est découpé d'avance dans ces quatrains où le poète se demande ce qu'il y a derrière ce rideau du ciel tiré entre l'homme et le secret des mondes, et où il poursuit le dernier atome d'argile humaine jusque dans la jarre du potier ou la brique du maçon, comme le prince de Danemark essayant de prouver que la glaise qui lute la bonde d'un tonneau de bière peut contenir la poussière d'Alexandre ou de César. Comme il s'écrie avec une mélancolie amère : Marche avec précaution ; la terre que tu foules est faite avec les joues de rose, les seins de neige, les yeux de jais de la beauté ; dépêche-toi de t'aller asseoir près de ces fleurs avant qu'elles soient fanées ; va, car bien souvent elles sont sorties de terre et bien souvent elles y sont rentrées. Hâte-toi de vider ta coupe, car tu n'es pas sûr d'exhaler le souffle que tu aspires, et du limon dont tu es composé on fera tantôt des coupes, tantôt des bols, tantôt des cruches ! quel profond sentiment du néant des hommes et des choses, et comme Horace, avec son *carpe diem* de bourgeois antique et son épicuréisme goguenard est loin de cette annihilation mystique qui cherche dans l'ivresse l'oubli de tout et l'anéantissement de la personnalité !"

Bitter melancholy

The insignificance of man

Professor Charles Eliot Norton in volume cix of "The North American Review" takes the lately published edition of Nicolas under consideration, together with Edition II of FitzGerald. He translates a number of Nicolas's quatrains into such beautiful English that it is a pleasure (with his kind permission) to reproduce them here :—

Professor Norton's translation from Nicolas, 1869

In this world, which for an instant serves us as an asylum, we have experienced naught but trouble and misfortune. Alas! no problem of creation has been solved for us; and yet we quit this earth with hearts full of regret.

(4)

Professor Norton's translation

(8) Since no one can assure us of to-morrow, hasten to rejoice thy sad heart. Drink, O beloved! drink from the ruby cup; for the moon shall long turn around the earth without again finding us.

(16) When I take in my hand a cup of wine, and in the joy of my heart am drunken, then in the fire that consumes me — behold! — a hundred miracles become real, and words clear as limpid water seem to explain the mystery of the universe.

(20) Unbelief is divided from faith but by a breath. Pass gayly over the dividing line.

(22) My life runneth out in a brief space: it passeth as the wind of a desert. Therefore while a breath remaineth to me, there are two days concerning which I will not disquiet myself, — the day that hath not come, and the day that hath gone.

(38) Who can believe that he who fashioned the cup meaneth to break it to pieces? All these fair heads, these beautiful arms, these delicate hands, — by what love are they made? by what hate are they destroyed?

(43) O Khayyám! why grievest thou because of thy sin? What solace findest thou in thus tormenting thyself? He who hath not sinned shall not taste the sweet of forgiveness. It is for sin that forgiveness exists. How then canst thou fear?

(50) That day when the heavens shall melt, and the stars be darkened, I will stop Thee on Thy way, and, seizing Thee by the hem of Thy garment, will require of Thee to tell me, Why, having given me life, Thou hast taken it from me.

I asked of the world — the bride of man — what was her dowry; and she answered me, My dowry is the joy of thy heart.	Professor Norton's translation (56)	

The heart on whom the light of love hath shone, whose name is written in the book of love, that heart, whether it frequenteth mosque or synagogue, is free from fear of hell, or hope of heaven.   (60)

If I drink wine it is not for mere delight of the taste, nor that I should become disorderly and renounce religion and morality: no, it is that I may for one moment exist outside myself.   (63)

I know not whether He who created me belongeth to paradise or to hell; but this I know, that a cup of wine, my beautiful love, and a lute on the edge of a meadow, are three things which I enjoy to-day, while thou livest on the promise of a paradise to come.   (92)

At this moment, when life is not yet gone out of my heart, it seemeth to me there are few problems that I have not solved. But when I appeal to my understanding, and turn inward on myself, I perceive that my life hath flowed away, and as yet I have defined nothing.   (113)

O Thou! in whose eyes sin is of no account, order the wise to proclaim this truth: for there is no folly equal to that of making the divine foreknowledge the accomplice of iniquity.   (116)

My being was given me without my consent, so that my own existence is a wonder to me. Yet I leave the world with regret, having comprehended neither the object of my coming, of my stay, nor of my departure.   (117)

Professor Norton's translation
(120)

They who by their learning are the cream of the world, who by their understanding traverse the heights of heaven, even they, in their search after knowledge of the divine, have their heads turned, whirling in vertigo, like the firmament itself.

(138)

Give thyself to joy, for grief will be infinite. The stars shall again meet together at the same point of the firmament; but of thy body shall bricks be made for a palace-wall.

(154)

The day when I shall be a stranger to myself, and when my name shall be as a tale that is told, then make of my clay a wine-jar for use in the tavern.

(175)

The secrets of existence no man hath penetrated; a step beyond himself no man hath taken. From the scholar to the master I behold only incompetence, the incompetence of all of woman born.

(177)

Who hath found access behind the curtain of destiny? Who hath knowledge of the secrets of Providence? Night and day, for three score years, have I meditated, yet have I learned nothing; the riddle remaineth unsolved.

(179)

Drink wine! for wine putteth an end to the disquietudes of the heart, and delivereth from meditations on the two-and-seventy sects. Abstain not from this alchemy, for if thou drinkest but one jarful, a thousand infirmities shall fall away from thee.

(190)

The devotee comprehendeth not as we the divine mercy. A stranger knoweth thee not so well as a friend. If Thou sayest, "Behold, if thou committest sin I will cast thee into hell,"—go, say it unto one who knoweth Thee not.

The rolling heavens do naught but multiply our woes. What they set upon earth they quickly snatch away. Ah! if they who have not yet come knew what suffering the world inflicts, they would take good heed how they came.

Professor Norton's translation
(105)

O friend! why busy thyself concerning *existence*? Why trouble thy heart and soul with idle thoughts? Live happy; pass joyful days; for in truth thy advice was not asked concerning creation.

(107)

O Thou, in quest of whom the whole world hath gone astray and is in distress, neither prayers nor riches avail to find thee out: Thou takest part in every conversation, but all are deaf; Thou art before the eyes of all, but all are blind.

(204)

Though I have not pierced the pearl of obedience that is due to Thee, though never with my heart have I swept up the dust of Thy steps, yet I despair not of reaching the sill of Thy throne of mercy, for never have I importuned Thee with my complaints.

(229)

We are puppets with which the heavens amuse themselves; we are pieces on the chess-board of being, whence we are laid aside, one by one into the coffin of nothingness.

(231)

I saw on the walls of the city of Thous a bird, with the skull of Kay-Kavous before him. The bird said to the skull, Where now is the noise of thy glory? where now is the sound of thy clarion?

(237)

If the rose be not ours, yet have we not its thorns? If the light reach us not, have we not the fire? If Heaven refuse me peace, am I not ready for war?

(251)

Professor Norton's translation

(256) All things that the world contains are images and illusions, and he hath little wisdom who includeth not himself among these images. Be quiet, then, O friend! drink, and deliver thyself from vain fancies and thoughts that cannot reach their goal.

(267) If I am drunken with old wine, so be it. If I am infidel, or idolater, so be it. Let each man think of me as he will, what matters it? I belong to myself, and I am that which I am.

(304) The circle of the universe is a ring of which you and I are the graven gem.

(321) Lift Thou from my heart the weight of the vicissitudes of life. Hide from men's eyes my faults. Give me happiness to-day, and to-morrow deal with me according to thy mercy.

(339) I beheld a man withdrawn into a desert place. He was neither heretic nor Mussulman; he possessed neither riches nor religion, nor God, nor truth, nor law, nor certitude. Who is there in this world or in the other who hath such courage?

(348) The wheel of heaven runs to thy death and mine, O beloved! it conspires against thy soul and mine. Come, come, sit beside me on the grass, for little time remaineth before the grass shall spring from my dust and thine.

(356) Tell me what man is there who hath not fallen into sin. Can man exist and not sin? If because I do ill Thou punishest me with ill, say, what difference is there between Thee and me?

> Thou hast set a hundred snares around about us. Thou sayest, "If ye fall into them ye shall surely die! It is Thou that spreadest the net, and if a man be taken in it Thou condemnest him, Thou deliverest him to death, Thou callest him rebel!"

Professor Norton's translation (390)

> A sheikh said to a harlot: "Thou art drunken; thou art taken in the net of whoso will." And she answered: "O Sheikh! I am that which thou sayest; but thou, art thou what thou professest thyself to be?"

(410)

> At times Thou art hidden, disclosing Thyself unto no one; then again Thou revealest Thyself in all the images of the universe. Verily, it is for Thyself and for Thine own pleasure that Thou workest these marvels, for lo! Thou art both the show and the spectator.

(413)

"Such passages as these," Professor Norton goes on to say, "suffering from the accumulated injuries of a double translation and reproducing neither the poetic form nor the style of the original verse, while they but imperfectly render the substance, can hardly fail in spite of all these drawbacks to leave a strong impression on the mind of the reader, especially if he be a little versed in the usual manner of the Persian poets — of the originality of Omar's genius, and of the vigor of his character as shown in the independence of his attitude toward the popular belief and predominant opinions of his time. The individual quality of the poet's imagination, the clear, defined precision of his expression, the spiritual insight of his speculation, and the realistic truth of his rendering of feeling, unite to give him a high place among the poets of his country, while his direct dealing with subjects of universal import, and

The originality of Omar's genius

his grasp of thoughts and moods common to the latest generation, set him among the few poets who have more than a mere historic or literary interest for men of different race, of different language, and of another age than his."

Hungarian edition

KELETI GYÖNGYÖK. ‖ EGY CYNIKUS PERSA KÖLTÖ ‖ OMER CHEJJAM ‖ KÖLTEMÉNYEI. ‖ PERSÁBÓL FORDI-TOTTA ÉS ISMERTETTE ‖ ÉKÖDI HARRACH BÉLA ‖ PEST ‖ AIGNER LAJOS ‖

Which being interpreted means : —

Eastern Pearls ‖ by the Persian Cynic Poet ‖ Omar Khayyám ‖ Poems ‖ from the Persian, translated and published ‖ by Bela Harrach ‖ Budapest ‖ Lajos Aigner.

16mo. 130 pp. No date. Follows Nicolas ; as, *e. g.*, No. 43.

Ugyan Chejjam, mért töprengsz egy bűn miatt?
As a bánat s töprengés tán javithat?
Ki nem bűnös, kegyelmet sem várhat az ;
Bűnért van a kegyelem; mért hát panasz? l

FitzGerald's second edition, 1868

RUBÁIYÁT ‖ OF ‖ OMAR KHAYYÁM ‖ THE ASTRONO-MER-POET OF PERSIA ‖ RENDERED INTO ENGLISH VERSE ‖ SECOND EDITION ‖ LONDON : ‖ BERNARD QUARITCH, ‖ PICCADILLY ‖ 1868. (John Childs and Sons, Printers.)

xviii + 30 pp. 25 notes, occupying 5½ pp.

This is also a paper-bound quarto pamphlet and is now almost as much of a rarity as the princeps.

RUBÁIYÁT ‖ OF ‖ OMAR KHAYYÁM, ‖ THE ASTRONO-MER-POET OF PERSIA, ‖ RENDERED INTO ENGLISH VERSE [Old Eng. type] ‖ THIRD EDITION ‖ LONDON : ‖ BERNARD QUARITCH, ‖ PICCADILLY. ‖ 1872. xxiv + 36 pp. quarto, half Roxburghe, maroon cloth. *FitzGerald's third edition, 1872*

A few years ago at a trade sale in New York, a number of copies of this edition consigned by Quaritch were sold by auction for fifty cents each. They now bring about a guinea.

SAME: FIRST AMERICAN ‖ FROM THE THIRD LONDON EDITION ‖ BOSTON : ‖ JAMES R. OSGOOD AND COMPANY ‖ LATE TICKNOR & FIELDS, AND FIELDS, OSGOOD & CO. ‖ 1878. (78 pp. versos blank ; red line.) 23rd Edition, 1894, Houghton, Mifflin & Co. *First American edition (1877 ?) 1878*

In 1877 "The Journal of the Asiatic Society of Bengal" published nine "Metrical Translations from the Quatrains of 'Umar Khayyam" by P. Whalley, C. S., Muradabad. They were accompanied by the Persian originals. They are as follows :— *P. Whalley's nine quatrains, 1877*

I.

There's not a heart but bleeds for thy disdain ;
   There's not a sage but has gone mad for thee ;
And though for love thou giv'st no love again,
   There's not a brain that from thy love is free.
                [App. XLVII, Nicolas, 36, etc.]

II.

Drink, drink! Like quicksilver I see with ruth
   Life from thee slide :
And false is fortune, hope a dream, and youth
   Ebbs, like a tide.

P. Whalley's versions

III.

Come and ere sorrows swarm up to harry us,
  Idol mine, blithely the wine-cup we'll drain.
We are not gold that the rough hands that bury us
  Ever should care to exhume us again. [Rubá'iy XV.]

IV.

We are but puppets danced by juggling fate,
To trim the phrase no jot of truth I bate,
On Being's board we serve to dress a play,
And, played our little game, — we're packed away.
                                [Rubá'iy LXIX.]

V.

Though steeped in sin, let no vain qualms be thine,
  Nor fear to meet thy maker. Death atones,
Die drunk and reprobate. His sun will shine
  As bland as ever on thy rotting bones.

Compare Nicolas, 262, with V: —

Garde-toi de désespérer jamais, pour un crime commis, de la clémence du souverain Créateur, de ce maitre miséricordieux ; car mourrais-tu, aujourdhui, dans l'état de la plus complète ivresse, que demain il pardonnerait tout à tes os putréfiés.

Also McCarthy, 200: —

Never despair, for all thy sins, of the divine mercy of the merciful Master, for if you were to die to-day, dead drunk, to-morrow, he would pardon your corrupted bones.

Also Whinfield, 305: —

Allah, our Lord, is merciful, though just;
Sinner! despair not, but His mercy trust!
  For though to-day you perish in your sins,
To-morrow He'll absolve your crumbling dust.

Also Bodenstedt, II, 4:—

Verzweifle nie in Deiner Sündenpein.
An des Allmächtigen Gnade und Verzeihn!
  Gingst Du im tollsten Rausche heut zu Grunde,
Gott strafte morgen doch nicht Dein Gebein.

P. Whalley's versions

VI.

Earth, water,—such is the sum of us:
  Monk, priest, Thou hast made us the same,
Fame, shame,—all that may come of us,—
  Thine is the honour,—and thine is the blame.
          [App. XXXII, Nicolas, 346, etc.]

VII.

I am drunk with old wine? So I am.
  A rank libertine? So I am.
Let them think of me what they will,
  I am mine: As I am, so I am.

Compare Nicolas, 297:—

Si je suis ivre de vin vieux; eh bien! je le suis. Si je suis infidèle, guèbre ou idolâtre; eh bien! je le suis. Chaque groupe d'individus s'est formé une idée sur ma compte. Mais qu'importe, je m'appartiens, et je suis ce que je suis.

Also Whinfield, 334:—

Am I a wine-bibber? What if I am?
Guerber or infidel? Suppose I am?
  Each sect miscalls me, but I hear them not,
I am my own, and, what I am, I am.

VIII.

Lighten my cares and my sorrow,
  Hide from my fellows my guilt,
Keep me happy to-day,—and to-morrow
  Deal with me as Thou wilt.

Compare McCarthy, 407:—

Make the conditions of this world easy unto my heart, and make my evil actions secret from creation. Give me to-day my pleasure, and to-morrow inflict on me whatever thy liberality deems meet.

Also Whinfield, 364:—

Make light to me the world's oppressive weight,
And hide my failings from the people's hate,
   And grant me peace to-day, and on the morrow
Deal with me as Thy mercy may dictate!

IX.

Some trust their church or creed to bear them out,
Some pray for faith, and tremble at a doubt.
Methinks I hear a still small voice declare
'The way to God is neither here nor there.'

                              [Rubá'iy XXV.]

Graf Von Schack, 1878

STROPHEN ‖ DES ‖ OMAR CHIJAM. ‖ DEUTSCH ‖ VON ‖ ADOLPH FRIEDRICH GRAFEN V. SCHACK ‖ STUTTGART. ‖ VERLAG DER J. G. COTTA'SCHEN BUCHHANDLUNG. ‖ 1878.

8vo; paper covers; 124 pp. inc. 4 pp. Anmerkungen.

Von Schack became acquainted with Omar Khayyám in the Calcutta version of 1836. Of Nicolas's version he says:—

"Mr. Nicolas's interpretation seems to me rather a thick veil of mist concealing the Persian text, than a guide to the understanding of it; the way in which the Frenchman after the manner of the Persian Súfis finds mysticism in everything and understands Divinity under the terms Wine, Wine cup, Cypress etc., comes near being burlesque."

Graf von Schack marked with an asterisk the strophes which he collected from the great Persian Lexikon (Heft Kulzum) and other sources; he says in one of his notes, "Some of the starred quatrains I have found only in an English translation of 110 Rubáiyát which appeared anonymously at London published by Quaritch in 1868." Graf von Schack comments on the extraordinary variation of the readings from which this English translation was made!

Mr. John Leslie Garner writes: "I understood that Schack did his partially from FitzGerald's Version,—but nevertheless they are wonderfully fine."

RUBÁIYÁT ‖ OF ‖ OMAR KHAYYÁM ‖ AND THE ‖ SALÁMÁN AND ABSÁL ‖ OF ‖ JÁMÍ; ‖ RENDERED INTO ENGLISH VERSE ‖ BERNARD QUARITCH; 15 PICCADILLY, LONDON, 1879. Bastard Title: RUBÁIYÁT ‖ OF ‖ OMAR KHAYYÁM, THE ASTRONOMER-POET OF PERSIA ‖ RENDERED INTO ENGLISH VERSE. ‖ Fourth Edition. *FitzGerald's fourth edition, 1879*

4to. xv and 112 pp. (of which the Rubáiyát and notes occupy 35).

DIE LIEDER UND SPRÜCHE ‖ DES ‖ OMAR CHAJJÂM ‖ VERDEUTSCHT ‖ DURCH ‖ FRIEDRICH BODENSTEDT. ‖ BRESLAU, 1881. ‖ SCHLETTER'SCHE BUCHHANDLUNG (E. FRANCK). *Friedrich Bodenstedt, 1881*

[Printed in blue and red] small 8vo; xxii + 217 pp. cloth. Also zweite Auflage; same year. Dritte Auflage, 1882; vierte Auflage ‖ Breslau. ‖ A. Kurze & W. Zemsch ‖ (Schletter'sche Buchhandlung) ‖ (Franck & Weigert) With "Vorwort zur vierten Auflage" dated Wiesbaden, Mitte Oktober, 1889. 467 Rubáiyát in ten Books thus divided:—

I. Die Gottheit des Dichters.[38] II. Der Gott des Koran und sein Prophet.[23] III. Schein und Wesen.[18] IV. Die Grenzen der Erkenntniss.[21] V. Schicksal und Freiheit.[15] VI. Lenz und Liebe.[3] VII. Der Dichter und seine Gegner.[45] VIII. Welt und Leben;[34] IX. Der Dichter beim Pokale.[17] X. Verschiedene.[40]

Bodenstedt first read before the Wissenschaftlicher Club of Vienna in April, 1878, fifty translated from the Calcutta Collection of 1836. Then he printed the first samples of his work in Spemann's annual " Für Kunst und Leben." Then when he had completed his work, which he claims to be the first attempt made in Germany to translate or rather imitate (*nachbilden*) the whole of Omar's poetic remains, he sent the manuscript of the " Lieder und Sprüche " to Hofrat von Barb, director of the Oriental Academy, in Vienna, who, together with the learned Orientalist, Freiherr von Schlechta-Wessehrd, compared the poems with the original. Herr von Barb wrote the author in December, 1878: " Die Original-Gedichte haben sich im Geiste des Dichter-Übersetzers sinn- und formgetreu wiedergespiegelt, sind von diesem, sozusagen, mit empfunden und mit der vollendetsten Meisterschaft wiedergegeben worden."

Bodenstedt's versions declared masterly copies of form and spirit

It is hardly correct to call Bodenstedt's versions faithful to the form of the original, for only a few make any claim to reproduce the form of the original Rubáiyát, and Bodenstedt confesses to have taken many poetic liberties, but tried to be true to the sense of the original. Only occasionally does he try to follow the rhythm of the original. Rearranging the poems according to their significance, he claims to give a fairer idea of Omar than is to be found in FitzGerald, who, he thinks, scarcely does justice to the old Persian's "göttlicher Humor."

Poetic liberties

He says:—

"I have good ground for the assertion that out of a thousand readers scarcely one knows anything of the remarkable man whose poetical remains form the content of this book; but I have equally good ground to assert that out of a thousand readers scarcely one will forget old Omar Khayyám, when once they shall have learned to know him in his significance. . . .

"Many of his quatrains might be taken for newly discovered verses of Goethe, rather than the utterances of a poet who lived eight hundred years ago, and yet he stood on a height of speculation, and cast such deep glances into Nature, as if he had the prophetic penetrating knowledge of all our philosophic hypotheses and speculations and our modern Natural Science. He may be compared to Lucretius among the Romans. . . .

The modernness of Omar's thought

"He wrote little, but his remains may be regarded as the very quintessence of all Oriental poetry, certainly in regard to the highest questions that have puzzled men. . . .

"The poet," says Bodenstedt, "is inexhaustible in his coinage of new expressions, striking metaphors, witty conceits, and surprising turns of thought. A clear, investigating eye, which always searches into the heart of things; an enlightened mind, which is yet always in search of more light; a keen understanding, which finds the stereotyped scholastic expressions insufficient to designate the unusual; deep feeling, and love for the truth are united in him with a lively and rich fancy, which enables him to make the clearness of his thought become evident in the picture. . . .

"It speaks well for Malek Shah that he clung to him. Malek Shah is remembered only on account of a poet who never sang his glory or even mentioned his name!"

A few passages in the German may prove of interest : —

"Soviel steht fest, dass viele der Verse des Omar Chajjam, welche nicht in lokalen Beziehungen wurzeln, ebenbürtig verdeutscht und unbefangenen Hörern ohne Nennung des Dichters vorgetragen, eher würden für neuentdeckte Göethe'sche Verse genommen werden als für diejenigen eines alten Persers der achthundert Jahre vor uns lebte und doch schon damals auf einer Höhe der Weltanschauung stand und so tiefe Blicke in die Natur that, als ob er alle Resultate und Hypothesen unserer philosophischen Speculation und modernen Naturwissenschaft mit prophetischem Geist vorausgekannt hätte. Schon hierdurch ist er unter den persischen Dichtern eine ebenso merkwürdige Erscheinung wie Lucrez unter den römischen Dichtern. . . . Seine Muse war ihm eine treue Begleiterin durch's Leben, der er in guten wie in trüben Stunden alle Geheimnisse seines Geistes und Herzens anvertraute, in einer schönen, wohlklingenden Sprache, die damals ihre beste Zeit hatte und die er so meisterlich beherrschte, dass seine Verse noch mustergültig sind.

"Allein, obwohl ein Dichter von Gottes Gnaden, war er doch keiner von Profession. Dem Umfang nach schrieb er nur wenig, aber er wusste in dem Wenigen soviel zu sagen, dass sein poetischer Nachlass als die Quintessenz der ganzen orientalischen Poesie betrachtet werden kann, soweit sie sich um die tiefsten und höchsten Fragen dreht, welche die denkende Menschheit immer bewegt haben und immer bewegen werden. Darin liegt seine Grösse. Er suchte nicht nach Stoffen, um sie zu bearbeiten; er schrieb nur wenn er von innen dazu gedrängt wurde und seine Verse entsprossten ihm dann so natürlich wie einem in gutem Boden wurzelnden Baume Blüten und Früchte.

His modernness

A notable apparition

A poet by the grace of God

Was er schrieb, schrieb er nur für sich, allein es kam oft vor, dass er in lebhafter Unterhaltung über Dinge, die ihm tief gingen, seinen Gedanken in improvisirten Versen Ausdruck gab, die dann von Freunden wie Feinden festgehalten und niedergeschrieben wurden, meist um ihm zu schaden und die Priester gegen ihn aufzubringen, über deren heuchlerisches Treiben er sich lustig machte. So kam manches in die Öffenlichkeit und verursachte ihm manche Ungelegenheit, ohne jedoch den furchtlosen Mann im Geringsten vorsichtiger in seinen Ausdrücken zu machen. . . .

"Ob diese in Omar's junge oder alte Tage gefallen, liesse sich nur feststellen, wenn seine poetischen Bekenntnisse chronologisch geordnet wären. Da dies nicht der Fall ist und das Ganze blos äusserlich nach den Reimbuchstaben der ersten Verse geordnet, innerlich bunt durch einander gewürfelt und völlig verwirrend erscheint, so bleibt, um einen klaren Überblick zu gewinnen, nichts übrig als mit Sorgfalt eine neue Ordnung zu schaffen durch Zusammenstellung des innerlich Zusammengehörigen, wie ich es in meiner Übersetzung gethan habe. Da wird der unbefangene Leser dann von dem ganzen Omar Chajjam, den er hier in allen Phasen seiner Entwicklung kennen lernt, einen ganz anderen Eindruck erhalten als durch eine Sammlung aus dem Zusammenhange gerissener Proben, wie sie auch FitzGerald bietet, der zudem in seinen Versen dem göttlichen Humor des alten Omar nicht ganz gerecht wird. . . . *No chronological arrangement possible*

"Der Dichter ist unerschöpflich an Gedanken von neuem Gepräge, schlagenden Gleichnissen, witzigen Einfällen und überraschenden Wendungen. Ein klares Forscherauge, das immer den Kern der Dinge sucht; ein erleuchteter Geist, der doch immer nach mehr Licht verlangt; ein scharfer Verstand, der die gewöhn- *Omar's inexhaustible invention*

lichen Schulausdrücke unzulänglich findet, um das
Ungewöhnliche zu bezeichnen; tiefes Gefühl und Liebe
zur Wahrheit vereinen sich in ihm mit einer so leb-
haften wie reichen Phantasie, die ihn befähigt, die
Klarheit seiner Gedanken im Spiegel des Bildes ein-
dringlich anschaulich zu machen. Darum findet man
in seinen Versen weder eine Phrase noch ein Flick-
wort. Dass es übrigens darin an dunklen Ausdrücken
nicht fehlt, zu deren Erklärung das Lexikon nicht
ausreicht und über welche die Gelehrten streiten können, versteht sich, auch abgesehen von den Irrungen
der Abschreiber, wohl von selbst bei einem Dichter,
der acht Jahrhunderte von uns gelebt hat. Hier ist der
kritischen Forschung ein weiter Spielraum geboten und
eine der dankbarsten Aufgaben gestellt, denn kein den-
kender Kopf wird sich ohne reichen Gewinn in das
Studium des Omar Khajjam versenken."

The introduction ends with the usual sketch of
Omar's life, and a few words about other German
translations. It is dated, Wiesbaden, Mitte Oktober,
1880.

In the Introduction to his "Fourth Impression" he
says:—

The goal for which he aimed

"Über den poetischen Wert meiner Verdeutschung des
genialsten und witzigsten Spruchdichters, welchen die
ganze orientalische Literatur aufzuweisen hat, selbst
ein Urteil zu fällen, würde mir nicht geziemen: ich
kann hier nur das Ziel bezeichnen, dem ich nachstrebte:
die fremden Dichtungen bei treuer Wiedergabe ihres
eigenartigen Inhalts unserer heimischen Sprache so
anzueignen als ob sie darin geboren wären und ihr
Schöpfer, auf der Höhe seiner Kunst stehend, heute
noch lebte. . . .

"In England und Amerika erfreut sich der alte Perser

einer Volkstümlichkeit wie etwa Heinrich Heine in Deutschland; er ist in jedem Hause zu finden, wo man überhaupt Bücher kauft. Den Hauptanlass dazu hat ein überaus verlockend ausgestattetes Büchlein gegeben, welches vor ein Par Jarzehnten unter dem Titel 'Rubaiyat of Omar Khayyām, the Astronomer-Poet of Persia' anonym erschien und eine geschmackvolle Auswal seiner Gedichte in freier aber talentvoller Nachbildung enthielt. . . . Ich habe in Deutschland den ersten Versuch gemacht, den ganzen poetischen Nachlass Omar Chajjâms, so weit das schwer zu beschaffende Material zugänglich war, nachzubilden. . . ."

His vogue in England and America

THE QUATRAINS ‖ OF ‖ OMAR KHAYYÁM. ‖ TRANSLATED INTO ENGLISH VERSE ‖ BY ‖ E. H. WHINFIELD, M. A. ‖ LATE OF THE BENGAL CIVIL SERVICE. ‖ LONDON: ‖ TRÜBNER & CO. LUDGATE HILL. ‖ 1882. [All rights reserved.]

Whinfield's first version, 1882

8vo. cloth; 91 pp. including 13 pp. of notes. 253 quatrains arranged under Alif, Be, Te, He and Khe, Dal, Re, Ze, Sin, Shin, Káf and Lám, Mim, Nun, Wau, He, Ye, with numbered references to Nicolas and generally following the order of Nicolas.

The notes are collected in an appendix. On p. 2 the lines:—

> "An aching body, and a mind
> Not wholly clear, nor wholly blind,
> Too keen to rest, too weak to find,
> That travails sore, and brings forth wind."
> M. ARNOLD.

Mr. Whinfield in his Introduction gives a summary of the authorities regarding Omar's life:—

The authorities for Omar's life

I. The Wasíyat or Testament of Nizám ul Mulk, Minister of Alp Arslan and Malik Shah, written about 480 A. H. [1085 A. D.], preserved in part in Mirkhond's Rauzat us Safa, which may be found, with a French translation, in vol. xi. p. 143 of "Notices et Extraits des MSS.," and also in the Dabistan i Mazahib, which exists in Shea and Troyer's Translation, vol. ii. p. 423.

II. The Tarikh ul Hukama written about 647 A. H. [1252 A. D.], given in full in Woepcke's "Algébre," préface, p. v. [This passage has already been given, see above.]

III. Géographie d'Abulfeda; prolegomena, p. ci., translated by Reinaud.

Abulfeda lived 1287–1347 A. D. He records that Omar Khayyám was placed by Nizám ul Mulk in charge of the Royal Observatory, and while holding that post superintended the reform of the old calendar. Abulfeda remarks that "Omar was too much addicted to poetry and pleasure, and seemed not to set much store by his astronomical labors."

The typical Rubá'iy

Mr. Whinfield says of the quatrain: "What may be regarded as the normal line consists of thirteen syllables, seven long and six short. But whenever two short syllables come together, they may be contracted into one long syllable, and the result is that German prosodians reckon no less than twenty-four different variations of the line, the shortest of which consist of ten syllables, all long. But, as may be supposed, this last form of the line is of very rare occurrence. The nearest English equivalent to a normal Rabái line would be such an Alexandrine as the following of Mr. Matthew Arnold, with accents on the second, fifth, tenth, and twelfth syllables: —

"We márk not the wórld's course, but would have *it* take *oúrs*."

And he ends by commending the decasyllable as used in FitzGerald's "brilliant translation," a metre approved by Mr. Swinburne, and also additionally suitable as being " the meter of the Elizabethan sonnet, which is perhaps the nearest English equivalent to Omar's verse."

THE QUATRAINS ‖ OF ‖ OMAR KHAYYÁM. ‖ THE PERSIAN TEXT WITH AN ENGLISH VERSE ‖ TRANSLATION ‖ BY ‖ E. H. WHINFIELD, M. A. ‖ LATE OF THE BENGAL CIVIL SERVICE ‖ LONDON : ‖ TRÜBNER & Co., LUDGATE HILL. ‖ 1883 ‖ [All rights reserved.] *Whinfield's second version, 1883*

xxxii + 335 pp. cloth. 500 quatrains; brief notes, mainly concerning the Persian scansion, at foot of each page.

Whinfield's introduction gives a sketch of the life of Ghiás uddin Abul Fath Omar bin Ibrahim al Khayyám and quotes the passage of Sharastáni from Woepcke.

In regard to the difficulty of establishing a standard text for Omar, he says: "Many of the quatrains ascribed to Omar are also attributed to other poets. I have marked a few of these in the notes, and doubtless careful search would bring many more to light. It might be supposed that the character of the language employed would be sufficient to differentiate the work of Omar, at any rate from that of poets writing two or three centuries after his time; but . . . the literary Persian of eight hundred years ago differs singularly little from that now in use. Again, if, as has been supposed, there were anything exceptional in Omar's poetry, it might be possible to identify it by internal evidence; but the fact is that all Persian poetry runs very much in grooves, and Omar's is no exception. The poetry of rebellion and revolt from orthodox opinions, *Tests of genuineness* which is supposed to be peculiar to him, may be traced in the works of his predecessor Avicenna, as well as in those of Afzul Ká-hi, and others of his successors."

In warrant of the form which Mr. Whinfield chose for his translation, he says:—

<small>Warrant for verse translations</small>

"Omar is a poet who can hardly be translated satisfactorily otherwise than in verse. Prose does well enough for narrative or didactic poetry, where the main things to be reproduced are the matter and substance; but it is plainly contra-indicated in the case of poetry like Omar's, where the matter is little else than 'the commonplaces of the lyric ode and the tragic chorus,' and where nearly the whole charm consists in the style and the manner, the grace of the expression, and the melody of the versification. A literal prose translation of such poetry must needs be unsatisfactory, because it studiously ignores the chief points in which the attractiveness of the original consists, and deliberately renounces all attempts to reproduce them. . . .

<small>The choice of metre</small>

"As regards metre, there is no doubt that the quatrain of ten-syllable lines, which has been tried by Hammer, Bicknell, and others, and has been raised by Mr. FitzGerald almost to the rank of a recognized English metre, is the best representative of the *Rubá'í*. It fairly satisfies Conington's canon, viz., that there ought to be some degree of metrical conformity between the measure of the original and the translation, for though it does not exactly correspond with the *Rubá'í*, it very clearly suggests it. In particular, it copies what is perhaps the most marked feature of the *Rubá'í*,—the interlinking of the four lines by the repetition in the fourth line of the rhyme of the first and second. Mr. Swinburne's modification of this metre, in which the rhyme is carried on from one quatrain to the next, is not applicable to poems like Omar's, all of which are isolated in sense from the context. Alexandrines would, of course, correspond more nearly than decasyllables with *Rubā'ī* lines in number of syllables, and they have been extensively used by Bodenstedt and other German translators of *Rubā'īs*; but, whatever may be the case in German, they are apt to read very heavily in English, even when constructed by skilful verse-makers, and an inferior workman can hardly hope to manage them with anything like success. The shorter length of the decasyllable is not altogether a disadvantage to the translator. Owing to the large number of monosyllables in English, it is generally adequate to hold the contents of a Persian line a syllable or two longer; and a line erring, if at all, on the side of brevity, has at any rate the advantage of obliging the translator to eschew modern diffuseness, and of making him try to copy the 'classical parsimony,' the archaic terseness and condensation of the original. *[Alexandrines too heavy]*

... Much of Omar's matter, when literally translated, seems very trite and commonplace, many of the 'conceits,' of which he is so fond, very frigid, and even his peculiar grotesque humour often loses its savour in an English replica. The translator is often tempted to elevate a too grovelling sentiment, to 'sharpen a point' here and there, to trick out a commonplace with some borrowed modern embellishment. But this temptation is to be resisted as far as possible." *[The temptation to trick out the triteness of a literal version]*

Mr. Whinfield thinks it possible that after the death of his patron, Nizam ul Mulk, Omar may have lost his stipend of 1200 gold miskals, and been reduced to poverty; he certainly thinks it remarkable that Omar should have lived to such a ripe old age in a city in which the *odium theologicum* raged with such violence. He attributes the bitterness of his satire to the same cause. *[Omar's poverty]*

Speaking of his love-poems he says:—

Omar's love poems

"The love-poems are samples of a class of compositions much commoner in later poets than in Omar. Most of them, doubtless, probably bear a mystical meaning, for I doubt if Omar was a person very susceptible of the tender passion. He speaks with appreciation of 'tulip cheeks' and 'cypress forms,' but apparently recognizes no attractions of a higher order in his fair friends.

"The poems in praise of scenery again offer a strong contrast to modern treatment of the same theme. The only aspects of nature noticed by Omar are such as affect the senses agreeably,— the bright flowers, the song of the nightingale, the grassy bank of the stream and the shady garden associated in his mind with con-

Omar's scenery

vivial parties. The geographer translated by Sir. W. Ouseley says of Nishapur: 'The city is watered by a subterranean canal, which is conveyed to the fields and gardens, and there is a considerable stream that waters the city and the villages about it; this stream is named

Nishapur

Saka. In all the province of Khorasan there is not any city larger than Nishapur, nor any blessed with a more pure and temperate air.' No doubt it was some of these gardens that called forth Omar's encomiums."

Whinfield takes the sensible view of the contradictory Antinomian quatrains and the pious aspirations. He says:—

The chronology of the poems

"His poems were obviously not all written at one period of his life, but from time to time, just as circumstances and mood suggested, and under the influence of the thoughts, passions, and desires which happened to be uppermost at the moment. It may be that the irreligious and Epicurean quatrains were written in youth, and the *Munájat* in his riper years. But this hypothesis seems to be disproved by Sharastáni's account of him, which is quite silent as to any such conversion or change of sentiment on his part, and also by the fact that he describes himself from first to last as a '*Dipsychus*' in grain, a halter between two opinions, and an '*Acrates*,' or backslider, in his practice."

Mr. Whinfield thinks it more likely that he was early indoctrinated in the great Semitic conception of One God which excludes any opposing evil Power. God alone is responsible for "all the evils in the world, the storms and the earthquakes, the Borgias and the Catilines." He compares Omar's expostulations with those of Job, and with the pessimism of the "weary king Ecclesiast." "Of course," he says, "the manner in which the serious Hebrew handles these matters is very different from the levity and flippancy of the volatile Persian, but it can hardly be denied that the Ecclesiast and Omar resemble one another in the double and contradictory nature of their practical conclusions." Omar and the Hebrew poets

Whinfield thinks he was not a Sufi, though he must have been affected by the mysticism of some of his predecessors: his philosophical studies, he says, would naturally stimulate his sceptical and irreligious disposition, while his mystical leanings would operate mainly in the contrary direction. He therefore denies the connection between Omar and Lucretius. "Whatever he was, he was not an atheist." Nor does he feel satisfied with Hammer's comparison between Omar and Voltaire:— Omar not to be compared with Lucretius

"In reality he is a Voltaire, and something more. He has much of Voltaire's flippancy and irreverence... But Omar also possessed what Voltaire did not, strong religious emotions, which at times overrode his rationalism, and found expression in those devotional and mystical quatrains which offer such a strong contrast to the rest of his poetry." Omar and Voltaire

The "Post's" review of Whinfield

The New York *Evening Post* of Saturday, April 21, 1883, reviewing the 1882 edition of Mr. Whinfield, says: "Those who have carefully examined the great variations in the successive editions of FitzGerald's translation, and, still more, those who have compared his striking version of the 'Agamemnon' of Æschylus (see *Nation*, vol. xxiv, p. 310 [reviewed by Col. T. W. Higginson]) with the original, must own that he belongs to the very loosest school of translators, and that it is very hard to tell whether, in any given case, he is offering a translation or a paraphrase. The trouble is, that when the result is so fine, the reader does not much care whence it come. If Whinfield best represent the poet Omar, we can only say that we prefer the poet FitzGerald. . . . Yet this disparity does not destroy the interest of the comparison, but rather enhances it. The translators illustrate each other; and it may be, after all, that neither is Omar, just as neither Pope nor Chapman is Homer. Even if the two only give between them the maximum and the minimum of the poet's quality, it is something to know what that range is; and we fortunately have now the German version of Bodenstedt with which to compare them both. It must be said, in justice to Mr. Whinfield, that his work seems to grow stronger as it goes on, and that the powerful closing quatrain is rendered with a vigor worthy of FitzGerald himself."

Advantages of comparative versions

The pirated edition of FitzGerald, 1883

OMAR KHAYYÁM, THE RUBÁIYÁT translated into English Verse. Royal 4to. Title printed on the covers. Bds. 10 s. London, John Campbell, Jun. MDCCC-LXXXIII.

"A pirated edition; the first leaf bears the following inscription: 'To the Translator, with the Printer's thanks and apologies. Henry Quilter.' It is word for word an exact reprint of Mr. FitzGerald's translation." [Extract from B. Quaritch's Catalogue.]

Justin Huntly McCarthy, M. P., tells about this edition:—

"At Harry Quilter's house one night, the house that Godwin built and that Whistler inhabited, and over which such a war of epigram has been waged, at Mr. Quilter's house one night, where half a dozen were gathered together in the name of good fellowship, some one suggested that it would be a pleasant thing to have a privately-printed edition of Omar Khayyám. Mr. Quilter, then as now governed by an indomitable energy, immediately and warmly took the notion up, and carried it out with all speed. The result was an enormous quarto volume, naturally exceedingly slender, and printed upon a curious coarse paper full of blots and blemishes, and which looked exceedingly like tea paper. Why this particular paper had been chosen remained a mystery. But it was presumed that it lent some odd bibliophilic charm to the book. It certainly was not an attractive book; it was much too big, and print and paper recalled the comments of Browning's degenerate detestable priest; but it had two advantages: it gave FitzGerald's text without any notes, and it was a literary curiosity. It is indeed a very rare book, and if a copy of it ever gets into the market it goes at a high figure." [In 1887 Quaritch advertised a copy of Quilter's pirated edition for sale at ten shillings].

Justin Huntly McCarthy relates "the biggin' o't"

The Vedder edition

RUBÁIYÁT ‖ OF ‖ OMAR KHAYYÁM ‖ THE ASTRONO-MER-POET OF PERSIA ‖ RENDERED INTO ENGLISH VERSE BY ‖ EDWARD FITZGERALD ‖ WITH ‖ AN ACCOMPANIMENT ‖ OF ‖ DRAWINGS ‖ BY ‖ ELIHU VEDDER ‖ HOUGHTON, MIFFLIN AND COMPANY ‖ BOSTON ‖ COPYRIGHTED BY HOUGHTON, MIFFLIN & CO. 1884 ‖

Quatrains in slightly different order. Illustrations: cover, lining paper, frontispiece, title-page, publisher's mark, Dedication, Omar's Emblem, 47 designs, artist's signature. XXXI — XXXVII = (XXXVII — XLIII), XXXIX — LII = (XLV — LVIII), LIII = (XXXII), LIV = (XXXIII), LV — LXXII = (LIX — LXXVI), LXXIII = (LXXVIII), LXXIV = (XXXI), LXXV — LXXVII = (XXXIV — XXXVI). Notes: FitzGerald's Introduction, unpaged folio, cloth, gilt top, $25.00.

The same: *Édition de luxe*; 100 copies on Japan vellum, bound in full morocco, satin linings, $100.00. 1884.

The same; Phototype edition, reduced plates; 4to; cloth; gilt top; $12.50. 1886.

The same; Popular edition; Life of Author and Sketch of FitzGerald by M. K. Followed by Rubáiyát in First Ed. etc. 61 pp.; small 4to; cloth; gilt top, $5.00.

Vedder's designs

The London *Athenæum* called Mr. Vedder "the latest follower of Michael Angelo," and said he was "an admirable and energetic, if not too refined draughtsman, whose 'inventions' are allied to Blake's, though they are not, like his, inchoate or indefinite, and have something of the muscular vigor and mental fibrousness of Ghirlandajo."

Mr. Vedder went to Rome early in 1883: he began his work in May of that year, and finished the last plate in March, 1884. Photographs of these drawings were exhibited at the rooms of the Tile Club in New York, and were spoken of as "entirely characteristic, weird, grotesque, and fantastic, very admirable in their symbolism and direct significance."

RUBÁIYÁT ‖ OF ‖ OMAR KHAYYÁM ‖ THE ASTRONOMER-POET OF PERSIA. ‖ RENDERED INTO ENGLISH VERSE ‖ BY ‖ EDWARD FITZGERALD. ‖ THE GROLIER CLUB OF NEW YORK. MDCCCLXXXV. Second title: RUBÁIYÁT ‖ OF OMAR KHAYYÁM. THE ASTRONOMER-POET OF PERSIA. ‖ REPRINTED FROM THE EDITION OF ‖ BERNARD QUARITCH, LONDON, 1879 ‖ HEADBANDS FROM EXAMPLES IN ‖ OWEN JONES'S GRAMMAR OF ORNAMENT. COVER FROM AN EXAMPLE IN AUDLEY'S OUTLINES OF ORNAMENT.

The Grolier Club edition, 1885

Each copy had this advertisement: —

"One hundred and fifty copies on Japan paper, and two copies on vellum. Printed from type, for the Grolier Club of New York, in the month of May, 1885, of which this is number — "

Octavo; xx + 51 pp.

The Japan paper copies were issued to members of the Club at $3.00. The price has enormously enhanced: $92.50, $110, and $150 have been paid for single examples.

In *The Academy* of Jan. 17, 1885, Whitley Stokes, the celebrated Keltic scholar, published a metrical translation of eighteen quatrains from Omar Khayyám without comment. They were arranged under four headings: —

He evidently gives a mystic rather than a literal interpretation to the love-quatrains.

I.—DEATH.

Whitley Stokes's versions, 1885

I dashed my clay-cup on the stone hard-by:
The reckless frolic raised my heart on high:
   Then said a shard with momentary voice:
"As *thou* have *I* been; thou shalt be as I." *
               [App. XIV, Nicolas, 404, etc.]

Annihilation makes me not to fear:
In truth it seems more sweet than lingering here:
   My life was sent me as a loan unsought:
When pay-day comes I'll pay without a tear.

   Compare Whinfield, 214:—

I am not one whom Death doth much dismay,
Life's terrors all Death's terrors far outweigh:
   This life, that Heaven hath lent me for a while,
I will pay back, when it is time to pay.

Has God made profit from my coming? Nay.
His glory gains not when I go away.
   Mine ear has never heard from mortal man
This coming and this going, why are they?
             [App. XLVII, Nicolas, 157, etc.]

* Compare the common country epitaph:—
    Stranger, pause as you pass by:
    As you are now so once was I.
    As I am now so you must be,
    Prepare for death and follow me!

I 'd not have come, had this been left to me:
Nor would I go, to go if I were free:
  Oh! best of all, upon this lonely earth
Neither to come nor go — yea, not to be!
              [App. XLV, Nicolas, 450, etc.]

Whitley Stokes's versions

Oh! that there were some place where men could rest,
Some end to look for in this lonely quest,
  Some hope that in a hundred thousand years
Our dust might blossom on the Mother's breast!
              [Rubá'iy XCVII.]

Alas for me! the Book of Youth is read:
The fresh glad Spring is now December dead:
  That bird of joy whose name was Youth is flown;
Ay me, I know not how he came or fled! *
              [Rubá'iy XCVI.]

II. — GOD.

Thou art the Opener, open Thou the door:
Thou art the Teacher, teach my soul to soar:
  No human masters hold me by the hand:
They pass away — Thou bidest evermore.
              [App. XXXIV, Nicolas, 409, etc.]

I cannot reach the Road to join with Thee:
I cannot bear one breath apart from Thee:
  I dare not tell this grief to any man:
Ah hard! Ah strange! ah longing sweet for thee!
              [App. XLVII, Nicolas, 453.]

---

* The translator compares this to Bion's πόθος δέ μοι ὡς ὄναρ ἔπτη. ['Επιτάφιος 'Αδώνιδος · Εἰδύλλιον α'. "But my love has fled like a dream"; Idyllion I. l. 58.]

III. — CONDUCT.

Whitley Stokes's versions

In school and cloister, mosque and fane, one lies
Adread of Hell, or dreams of Paradise;
  But none that know the secrets of the Lord
Have sown their hearts with suchlike phantasies.
[App. XXV, Nicolas, 46.]

Ah, strive amain no human heart to wring:
Let no one feel thine anger burn or sting:
  Wouldst thou be lapt in long-enduring joy,
Know how to suffer: cause no suffering.

Whinfield 15: —

  What e'en thou doest, never grieve thy brother,
  Nor kindle fumes of wrath his peace to smother;
    Dost thou desire to taste eternal bliss,
  Vex thine own heart, but never vex another!

While sinew, vein and bone together blend,
Outside the path of Doom we cannot wend.
  Bow not thy neck, though Rustam be thy foe:
Be bound to none, though Hátim be thy friend.
[Rubá'iy X.]

IV. — CONSOLATION.

This is the time for roses and repose
Beside the stream that by the meadow goes:
  A friend or two, a sweetheart like a rose,
With wine, and none to heed how Mullas prose.
[Rubá'iy XII.]

Come, bring that Ruby in yon crystal bowl,
That brother true of every open soul:
  Thou knowest overwell this life of ours
Is wind that hurries by — O bring the bowl!

Whitley Stokes's versions

  Compare Nicolas, 203 : —

Apporte de ce rubis balais dans une simple coupe de crystal, apporte cet objet habituel et chéri de tout homme généreux. Puisque tu sais que tous les êtres ne sont que poussière, et qu'un vent qui souffle pendant deux jours les fait disparaître, apporte du vin.

  McCarthy, 225 : —

Bring hither the Captain ruby in a cup of Crystal, bring hither the desired and beloved of all generous men. Since thou knowest that all the dwellers on the earth are but dust, and that when the wind passeth over them they are no more, bring hither the wine.

  Von Schack, 194 : —

Bring her den flüssigen Rubin, den Liebling aller edlen
    Seelen!
Da Staub nur alle Wesen sind,
Ziemt uns, ihn zum Begleiter uns auf diesem Erdengang zu
    wählen,
Eh uns von dannen weht der Wind.

With loving lip to lip the bowl I drain,
To learn how long my soul must here remain,
  And lip to lip it whispers, "While you live,
Drink, for, once gone, you come not back again."
        [Rubá'iy XXXV, Whinfield, 274.]

  The translator compares this with Olivier Basselin's *Vaux de Vire*, XVII : —

    "Les morts ne boivent plus dedans la sepulture."

Whitley Stokes's versions

Sweet airs are blowing on the rose of May:
Sweet eyes are shining down the garden gay:
   Aught sweet of dead Yestreen you cannot say —
No more of it — so sweet is this To-day!

   Compare Whinfield, 112: —

     Sweet is the breath of Spring to rose's face,
     And thy sweet face adds charm to this fair place;
       To-day is sweet, but yesterday is sad,
     And sad all mention of its parted grace.

When Death uproots my life-plant, ear and grain,
And flings them forth to moulder on the plain,
   If men shall make a wine-jug of my clay,
And brim with wine, 'twill leap to life again.
            [App. XXXIX, Nicolas, 115.]

This jar was once a lover like to me,
Lost in delight of wooing one like thee;
   And, Lo! the handle here upon the neck
Was once the arm that held her neck in fee.
            [Rubá'iy XXXVI.]

Your love-nets hold my hair-forsaken head:
Therefore my lips in warming wine are red:
   Repentance born of Reason you have wrecked,
And Time has torn the robe that Patience made.

   Compare Whinfield, 212: —

Ah! thou hast snared this head, though white as snow,
Which oft has vowed the wine-cup to forego;
   And wrecked the mansion long resolve did build,
And rent the vesture Penitence did sew!

THE DIALOGUE ‖ OF ‖ THE GULSHAN-I-RÁZ ‖ OR **An**
MYSTICAL GARDEN OF ROSES OF ‖ MAHMOUD SHA- **Anony-**
BISTARI ‖ WITH SELECTIONS FROM ‖ THE RUBAIYAT **mous**
OF OMAR KHAYAM. [No author.] LONDON ‖ TRÜB- **version**
NER & CO., LUDGATE HILL, ‖ 1887. 8vo. 64 pp.

This volume includes a selection of twenty-two Rubáiyát from Omar Khayyám. Some of them will be found in the preceding pages marked with a numbered *. The rest follow:—

Thy ruby lips pour fragrance into mine, (5)
  Thine eye's deep chalice bids me drink thy soul;
As yonder crystal goblet brims with wine,
  So in thy tear the heart's full tide doth roll.

To those who know the truth, what choice of foul or fair, (7)
Where lovers rest; though 't were in Hell, for them 't is
    Heaven there.
  What recks the Dervish that he wears sackcloth or
    satin sheen,
Or lovers that beneath their head be rocks or pillows
    fair.

  Compare Whinfield, 128:—
    To lover true, what matters dark or fair?
    Or if the loved one silk, or sackcloth wear,
      Or lie on down or dust, or rise to heaven?
    Yea, though she sink to hell, he'll seek her there.

Whinfield considers this quatrain mystical; his 1882 version numbered 50 begins. *To lover's eyes*, and ends, *he seeks her there*.

Though with the rose and rosy wine I dwell, (9)
Yet time to me no tale of joy doth tell;
  My days have brought no sign of hopes fulfilled;
'T is past! the phantoms fly, and break the spell.

(10) Though sweet the rose, yet sorely wounds the thorn;
Though deep we drink to-night, we rue the morn;
   And though a thousand years were granted, say,
Were it not hard to wait the last day's dawn.

(12) Oh, joy in solitude! of thee well may the poet sing;
Woe worth the heart that owns no soil wherein that flower may spring;
   For when the wassail sinks in wailing and traitor friends are gone,
Proudly through vacant hall the sturdy wanderer's step shall ring.

(13) If grief be the Companion of thine heart,
Brood not o'er thine own sorrows and their smart;
   Behold another's woe, and learn thereby
How small thine own, and comfort thy sad heart.

(14) Oh, swiftly came the winter wind, and swiftly hurried past;
So madly sought my longing soul the rest she found at last;
   Now faint and weak as weakness' self, she waits but for the end;
The bowl is broke, the wine remains, but on the ground is cast.

(18) Though I be formed of water and of clay,
And with the ills of life content for aye,
   Ever thou bid'st me shun the joyful cup.
My hand is empty: wherefore bidst me stay?

(20) Lo, blood of men slain by the stroke of doom!
   Lo dust of men strewn on the face of earth!
   Oh, take what life may give of youth and mirth;
Full many an opening bud shall never bloom.

XLIX] *Appendices.* 507

WORKS OF ‖ EDWARD FITZGERALD ‖ TRANSLATOR OF Memorial
OMAR KHAYYÁM ‖ REPRINTED ‖ FROM THE ORIGINAL edition
IMPRESSIONS, WITH SOME CORRECTIONS ‖ DERIVED FROM
HIS OWN ANNOTATED COPIES ‖ IN TWO VOLUMES ‖

NEW YORK & BOSTON   LONDON
HOUGHTON, MIFFLIN & CO. BERNARD QUARITCH ‖
1887.

With dedication: — TO THE ‖ AMERICAN PEOPLE, ‖ WHOSE EARLY APPRECIATION OF THE GENIUS OF ‖ EDWARD FITZGERALD ‖ WAS THE ‖ CHIEF STIMULANT OF THAT CURIOSITY ‖ BY WHICH HIS NAME WAS DRAWN FROM ITS ANONYMOUS ‖ CONCEALMENT AND ADVANCED TO THE POSITION ‖ OF HONOUR WHICH IT NOW HOLDS, ‖ THIS EDITION OF HIS WORKS IS DEDICATED ‖ BY ‖ THE EDITOR.

2 vols. 8vo, $10.00; large paper copies issued at $25.00.

Vol. I. begins with a Biographical Preface, followed by a memorial poem, a letter from the artist William Simpson concerning Omar's Grave, then the Rubáiyát: the 1st and 4th editions facing each other, with Fitz-Gerald's notes followed by 12 pages of notes by the editor, M.K. vi + 90 pp. octavo. Portrait; sketch of Omar's grave at Nishâpûr.

This edition is the basis of the Houghton, Mifflin & Co. Comparative Edition; also of the Mosher Bibelot Edition. The editor contributes a poem signed Mim-kaf, in which his initials are hidden under the Persian letters. The poem is as follows: —

> "Though still the famous Book of Kings Mr. Michael
>   With strange memorial music rings, Kerney's
> Firdausi's muse is dead and gone   verses
> As Kai-kobad and Feridon,

And Rustum and his pahlawan
Are cold as prehistoric man.
— KHAYYÁM still lives: his magic rhyme
Is forged of spells that conquer Time.
The hopes and doubts, the joys and pains,
That never end while Man remains;
The sin, the sorrow, and the strife
Of good and ill in human life:
Such themes can ne'er grow stale and old.
— Nor can the verse in which they're told,
Reflecting as it does each phase
Of human thought and human ways.
The world may roll through ages yet,
New stars may rise, old stars may set,
But like the grass and like the rain
Some things for ever fresh remain,
Some poets whom no rust can touch
— KHAYYÁM and HORACE are of such.
But while we knew the Roman's tongue,
Khayyám in vain for us had sung,
Till One arose on English earth
Who to his music gave new birth.
Henceforth, so long as English speech
Shall through the coming ages reach,
The name of KHAYYÁM will go down
With such a glory of renown
As ne'er on Eastern poet's brow
Has poured its radiance until now.
— And Who has wrought this spell of might
That brings the hidden gem to light?
'T was One who touched his harp, unseen,
Who never wished to lift the screen
That hid him from the outer throng,
But blameless lived and sang his song
In modest tones, not over-loud,

> To shun the plaudits of the crowd,
> Now that we know him — now, at last,
> When o'er the threshold he hath passed —
> We 'll love with love that knows no change
> The Hermit-bard of Little Grange. — MIMKAF."

In a note to Mr. Edward Clodd, president of the Omar Khayyám Club of London, Mr. Bernard Quaritch, in response to my inquiry as to the personality of the mysterious M. K. who furnishes this edition with translations in the metre of the original, writes: —

"The name of the scholar in my establishment is Mr. MICHAEL KERNEY. He edited for me, under my inspiration, the edition of FitzGerald, in 2 vols. 8vo, now out of print."

THE ROSE GARDEN OF PERSIA, BY LOUISA STUART COSTELLO: AUTHOR OF "SPECIMENS OF THE EARLY POETRY OF FRANCE," &c. LONDON: GEORGE BELL AND SONS, MDCCCLXXXVII. xvi, 193 pp. (with ornamental borders in gold and colors in Persian style). 66-76 pp. are devoted to Omar Khiam.

In a brief introduction the author says: "Omar was one of the most remarkable, as well as the most distinguished, of the poets of Persia, at the latter end of the twelfth century. He was altogether unprecedented in regard to the freedom of his religious opinions; or rather, his boldness in denouncing hypocrisy and intolerance, and the enlightened views he took of the fanaticism and mistaken views of his countrymen. He may be called the Voltaire of Persia, though his writings are not calculated to shock European notions so much as those of the followers of the Prophet . . . It is asserted by his ill-wishers, that instead of his studies leading him to the acknowledgment of the power of the Supreme Being, they prompted him to disbelief. The result of his reflections on this important subject is given in a poem of his, much celebrated, under the title of Rubajat Omar Khiam. . . . He was the friend of Hassan Sabah, the founder of the sect of the Assassins; and, it has been conjectured, assisted him in the establishment of his diabolical doctrines and fellowship. Some allowances must, however, be made, for the prejudices of his historians, who would, of course, neglect nothing calculated to cast odium on one so inimical to their superstitions.

"The following will give an idea of his compositions:—

<small>Miss Costello's paraphrase</small>

'Ye who seek for pious fame,
And that light should gild your name,
Be this duty ne'er forgot,—
Love your neighbour — harm him not.
To Thee, Great Spirit, I appeal,
Who can'st the gates of truth unseal;
I follow none, nor ask the way
Of men who go, like me astray;
They perish, but Thou can'st not die,
But liv'st to all eternity.
Such is vain man's uncertain state,
A little makes him base or great;
One hand shall hold the Koran's scroll,
The other raise the sparkling bowl —
One saves, and one condemns the soul.

'The temple I frequent is high,
A turkis-vaulted dome — the sky,
That spans the world with majesty.
Not quite a Moslem is my creed,

Nor quite a Giaour; my faith, indeed,
May startle some who hear me say,
I'd give my pilgrim staff away,
And sell my turban, for an hour
Of music in a fair one's bower.
I'd sell the rosary for wine,
Though holy names around it twine.
And prayers the pious make so long,
Are turned by me to joyous song;
Or, if a prayer I should repeat,
It is at my beloved's feet.

'They blame me that my words are clear;
Because I am what I appear;
Nor do my acts my words belie —
At least, I shun hypocrisy.
It happened that but yesterday
I marked a potter beating clay,
The earth spoke out — " Why dost thou strike?
Both thou and I are born alike;
Though some may sink and some may soar,
We all are earth, and nothing more.'

" His verses in praise of beauty and wine are much esteemed " : —

GAZEL.

Nature made me love the rose,
   And my hand was formed alone
Thus the wine cup to enclose;
Blame then — ye, the goblet's foes, —
   Nature's fault, and not my own.
When a Houri form appears,
Which a vase of ruby bears,
Call me Giaour if then I prize
   All the joys of Paradise!

IN PRAISE OF WINE.

Morn's first rays are glimmering [,]
From the skies the stars are creeping;
Rouse, for shame, the goblet bring,
All too long thou liest sleeping:
Open those narcissus eyes,
Wake — be happy — and be wise?

Why, ungrateful man, repine,
When this cup is bright with wine?
All my life I've sought in vain,
Knowledge and content to gain;
All that nature could unfold,
Have I in her page unrolled;
All of glorious and grand
I have sought to understand.
'T was in youth my early thought,
Riper years no wisdom brought,
Life is ebbing, sure though slow,
And I feel I nothing know.
Bring the bowl! at least in this,
Dwells no shadowed distant bliss;
See; I clasp the cup whose power
Yields more wisdom in an hour
Than whole years of study give,
Vainly seeking how to live.
Wine dispenses into air,
Selfish thoughts, and selfish care.
Dost thou know why wine I prize?
He who drinks all ill defies:
And can awhile throw off the thrall
Of self, the God we worship — all!

THE VANITY OF REGRET.

Nothing in this world of ours
   Flows as we would have it flow;
What avail, then, careful hours,
   Thought and trouble, tears and woe?
Through the shrouded veil of earth,
   Life's rich colours gleaming bright,
Though in truth of little worth,
   Yet allure with meteor light.
Life is torture and suspense;
Thought is sorrow — drive it hence!
With no will of mine I came,
With no will depart the same.
Know'st thou whence the hues are drawn
Which the tulip's leaves adorn?
'T is that blood has soaked the earth,
Where her beauties had their birth.
Know'st thou why the violet's eyes
Gleam with dewy purple dyes?
'T is that tears, for love untrue,
Bathed the banks where first she grew

If no roses bloom for me,
Thorns my only flowers must be:
If no sun shine on my way,
Torches must provide my day,
Let me drink, as drink the wise:
Pardon for our weakness lies
In the cup — for Heaven well knew,
   When I first to being sprung,
I should love the rosy dew,
And its praise would oft be sung.

'T were impiety to say
We would cast the cup away,
And be votaries no more,
Since it was ordained before.

The translator continues: "The latter part of the poem seems intended to ridicule the belief in predestination, carried to so absurd an extent by Mahommedans in general." Then after making several illustrative quotations from other authors, she continues: —

"The poem which follows, by Omar Chiam, is in a strain of philosophy of a higher order": —

THE WISDOM OF THE SUPREME.

All we see — above, around —
Is but built on fairy ground:
All we trust is empty shade
To deceive our reason made.
Tell me not of Paradise,
Or the beams of houris' eyes;
Who the truth of tales can tell,
Cunning priests invent so well?
He who leaves this mortal shore,
Quits it to return no more.

In vast life's unbounded tide
  They alone content may gain,
Who can good from ill divide,
Or in ignorance abide —
  All between is restless pain.
Before thy prescience, power divine [.]
What is this idle sense of mine?
What all the learning of the schools?
What sages, priests, and pedants? — Fools!

The world is thine, from thee it rose
By thee it ebbs, by thee it flows.
Hence, worldly lore! By whom is wisdom shown?
The Eternal knows, knows all, and *He* alone!

LES ‖ ORIGINES ‖ DE ‖ LA POÉSIE PERSANE ‖ PAR ‖ M. J. DARMESTETER ‖ PARIS ‖ ERNEST LEROUX, ÉDITEUR ‖ 28, RUE BONAPARTE, 28, ‖ 1887. 91 pp.

Darmesteter, after considering the work of Abou Saïd, goes on to speak of Omar Khayyám: —

"Son grand imitateur Omar Kheyyam, l'algébriste poète, aura la force de la certitude implacable ; mais c'est une force qui, en poésie, est presque une faiblesse, car elle est mortelle à l'émotion. La souffrance humaine est l'écueil du panthéisme. Il essaye en vain du stoïcisme et du silence : — **Omar and Abu Said**

"'O mon cœur, quand la séparation de la bien-aimée fait éclater les veines de ton âme, ne montre à personne tes haillons tachés de sang. Gémis sans qu'on entende ta plainte. Consume-toi, sans que la fumée en sorte.'

"Mais, en dépit de lui, ce n'est pas la fumée, c'est la flamme même qui éclate du volcan."

After this quotation, which is interesting to compare with at least three of Omar's, he goes on: —

"Un soir qu'Omar Kheyyam s'entretenait avec ses amis, au clair de lune, sur la terrasse, la coupe en main et dans les chansons, un coup de vent éteignit les lampes et renversa la cruche qui se brisa. Le poète irrité lança ce quatrain au Dieu qui troublait ses plaisirs : —

"'Tu as brisé ma cruche de vin, Seigneur :
Tu as fermé sur moi la porte du plaisir, Seigneur,
Tu as versé à terre mon vin pur :
(Dieu m'étrangle!) — mais serais-tu ivre par hazard,
Seigneur!'

"À peine le blasphème lancé, le poëte, jetant les yeux sur la glace, vit sa face noir comme le charbon : il s'écria : —

"'Quel est l'homme ici-bas qui n'a point péché, dis? Celui qui n'aurait point péché, comment aurait-il vécu, dis?

"'Si parce que je fais le mal ; tu me punis par le mal,

"'Quelle différence y a-t-il entre toi et moi, dis?'"

See Appendix LI.

Dr. Hermann Ethé, 1888

DIE ∥ MYSTISCHE, DIDAKTISCHE UND LYRISCHE POESIE ∥ UND DAS ∥ SPÄTERE SCHRIFTTHUM DER PERSER. ∥ VON PROF. DR. HERMANN ETHÉ. ∥ HAMBURG. ∥ VERLAG VON L. F. RICHTER ∥ 1888. (In the Neue Folge der Sammlung gemeinverständlicher wissenschaftlicher Vorträge.)

After briefly recounting his life and describing his scientific labors Dr. Ethé continues : —

"Inmitten all dieser aufreibenden wissenschaftlichen Thätigkeit fand 'Omar noch Musse genug, auch dem poetischen Genius, der in ihm wohnte, vollauf genüge zu thun und sich in kurzer Frist einen Dichterruhm

zu erringen, vor dem selbst sein Gelehrtenruf in den
Hintergrund treten musste. Etwa 500 Rubâ'is sind es,
in denen er den ganzen aufgehäuften Schatz seiner
Welt- und Menschenkenntnis niedergelegt hat, und
wenn auch einzelne darunter von echt çûfischem Geiste
durchweht sind, so tragen doch bei weitem die meisten
— und diese sind auch zugleich die künstlerisch vollendetsten — ein völlig verschiedenes Gepräge zur Schau.
Man kann sie mit Recht das Andachtsbuch eines
radikalen Freigeistes nennen, denn wie sie auf der
einen Seite mit den scharfen Waffen der Satire gegen
die engherzige Frömmelei und den fanatischen Eifer
der 'Ulamâs oder orthodoxen Theologen des Islams
zu Felde ziehen, so überschütten sie auf der anderen
Seite mit der Lauge schadenfrohen Spottes auch den
scheinheiligen oder vor Verzückung ausser sich geratenen
Mystiker, und das ganze sprachliche Rüstzeug des
Çûfî dient dem genialen 'Omar, gerade so wie dem
drei Jarhunderte später blühenden Hâfiz, nur dazu,
den Çûfismus selbst, besonders in seinen krankhaften
Auswüchsen, lächerlich zu machen. Man hat ihn daher
oft als den Voltaire des Morgenlandes bezeichnet, und
soweit es sich um glänzende Sprache, bestechenden
Witz, beissende Ironie und ein warmes Mitgefühl mit
der ganzen leidenden Menschheit handelt, ist der Ver-
gleich auch wirklich zutreffend, weiter aber nicht.

The prayer-book of a radical free-thinker

" Voltaire hat nichts geschrieben, was sich mit 'Omar's
glühenden Rapsodien zum Preis des Weins, der Liebe,
und des Vollgenusses irdischer Freuden, oder mit
seinen tiefinnersten Herzensergüssen messen kann, in
denen sich Zartheit des Gefühls mit sinniger Gedan-
kenanmut und kerniger Lebensweisheit part. Ein
par Epigramme, die vorwiegend den beiden letzge-
nannten Gattungen angehören, mögen hier ihre Stelle
finden ". —

Omar and Voltaire

Nicht das Morgen ist's, das hülfreich deinem *Heute*
   Glück beschert,
Durch das Grübeln um das Morgen wird die Galle nur
   genährt;
Lass nicht unbenutzt das Heute, ist dein Herz nicht
   ganz verkehrt,
Denn was sonst noch bleibt vom Leben ist nicht einen
   Heller wert.

Weh' dem Herzen, doppelt wehe, das in Flammen nie
   entbrannt,
Nie der Herz-Entzünd'rin Liebe heisse Leidenschaft
   empfand;
So verloren ist kein Tag wohl, als der eine letzte dir,
Da du scheiden musst von hinnen und nicht fühlst der
   Liebe Hand.

Ach, wie schön, wenn Neujarslüfte Rosen wehn um's
   Angesicht,
Ach wie schön, wenn süsse Wangen des Jasmines
   Blüt' umlicht!
Doch gefallen will mir's nimmer, sprichst du von
   Vergangnem mir,
Fröhlich sei und lass das *Gestern* — strahlt das *Heut*
   doch hell und licht!

Zum Beginn gleich wollt' ergründen, strebend über
   Himmel fort,
Tafel, Schreibrohr, Paradies ich und der Hölle
   Marterort.
Da mit wohlverständ'gem Sinne sprach mein Meister
   dieses Wort:
Rohr und Tafel, Höll und Eden — sie sind *in dir*, such'
   sie dort!

Dann erst, wenn des Atmens ledig, du beginnst die
 Wanderschaft,
Schaust du die Mysterien Gottes frei von jedes
 Schleiers Haft.
 Nicht, von wannen du gekommen, weisst du — sei
  drum frohgelaunt;
Nicht, wohin du gehn wirst, weisst du — schlürfe drum
 den Rebensaft!

Pfeilschnell, wie der Sturm durch's Blachfeld, pfeilschnell wie im Strom die Wogen,
Ist der Lebenstage einer wieder mir dahingezogen.
Aber um *zwei* Tage dennoch hab' ich nie des Grams
 gepflogen,
Um *den* Tag, der fern noch weilet, und um *den*, der
 schon verflogen.

Weil du viel gesündigt, 'Omar, giebst du solchem Leid
 dich hin?
Immerdar am Grame zehren, bringt dir das wohl je
 Gewinn?
 Wer sich nie der Sünd' beflissen, dem wird Gnade
  nie zu teil,
Gnade folgt allein der Sünde, hat dein Grämen also
 Sinn?

Wein — der flüssige Rubin ist's, und der Humpen ist
 sein Schacht,
Körper ist des Bechers Höhlung, drin sein Saft als
 Seele wacht;
Und das Glas dort das krystall'ne, das vom Trunke
 rosig lacht,
Eine Träne ist's, drin Herzblut niederträufelt heimlich
 sacht.

RUBÁIYÁT OF ‖ OMAR KHAYYÁM ‖ IN ENGLISH VERSE ‖ EDWARD FITZGERALD. ‖ THE TEXT OF THE FOURTH EDITION, FOLLOWED BY THAT OF THE FIRST; ‖ WITH NOTES SHOWING THE EXTENT OF HIS INDEBTEDNESS ‖ TO THE PERSIAN ORIGINAL ‖ AND ‖ A BIOGRAPHICAL PREFACE. ‖ NEW YORK AND BOSTON ‖ HOUGHTON, MIFFLIN AND COMPANY ‖ THE RIVERSIDE PRESS, CAMBRIDGE, 1888.

This is practically a reprint of the two-volume memorial edition of 1887. The editor Mr. Michael Kerney's contributions consisting of a biographical introduction and notes, the translations in the original metres of fifty of the Rubáiyát, most of which are reproduced in the present edition. 128 pp. 12 mo. boards ½ vellum.

John Leslie Garner, 1888

THE STROPHES ‖ OF ‖ OMAR KHAYYÁM ‖ TRANSLATED FROM THE PERSIAN ‖ BY ‖ JOHN LESLIE GARNER ‖ WITH AN INTRODUCTION AND NOTES. ‖ MILWAUKEE. ‖ THE CORBITT & SKIDMORE CO. ‖ 1888. Square 12 mo. xii + 76 pp. cloth.

In his introduction Mr. Garner begins with a brief sketch of Omar's life. As to his philosophy he says: "He probably suffered periodic attacks of metaphysics, with accompanying changes in his beliefs; but unfortunately the arbitrary arrangement of the original, which is in accordance with the alphabetical order of rhymes, offers no clew to the chronological development of his ideas. It is well-nigh impossible for an Occidental to accept the mystic interpretation of M. Nicolas, and, judging by his notes, it seems as if he too had grave misgivings regarding poor Omar's character. However, while the old Tent-maker doubtless was human, it is not likely that he was past redemption. He drank wine as he sang of it, and it is probable that his morals were little, if any, in advance of his age and country, but his vices go hand in hand with great virtues; throughout his *Rubáiyát* there breathes a spirit of charity and toleration towards his opponents, and an independence in thought, unusual in his time and in an Oriental land. . . . Insomuch as there is a vein of Pantheism in his poems, he may be regarded as a Súfi; but his Súfism is not the kind which the professors of the creed would have us believe, and his wine, woman, and song are doubtless no less real than were the material inspirations of Anacreon, Horace, and Beranger. . . . By his contemporaries he was regarded as a Freethinker and a Scoffer, and it was not until long after his death, probably when the examples furnished by his way of living had ceased, that the Súfis discovered the deep spiritual meaning of his Bacchanalian verses. That they did make this discovery, however, need not surprise us, for the Oriental mind, like the Oriental languages, as Mr. Huxley has remarked, is exceedingly subtle, and the Súfi of the East, as an expounder of the obscure, is no less adroit than the Theologian of the West. . . . His appreciation of the unavoidable separation from things mundane, and the fewness of his wants, led him to disregard wealth and honors. Frequently a vein of pessimism crops out in his writings; but it is of a healthy aggressive sort, very different from the article which the pseudo-pessimists of the day, in their solemn seasons of reflection upon their individual ills, are wont to style truth; Omar was a precursor of Schopenhauer, rather than of Leopardi. . . ."

Omar as a wine drinker

Healthy pessimism

Mr. Garner's translation, which is now out of print,

has one hundred and forty-two quatrains, distributed in eleven books, introduced by quotations from Bourne's "Anacreon," Leconte de Lisle, Giordano Bruno, Goethe, Alfred de Musset, Paul Bourget, Marcus Antoninus, St. James, Sully-Prudhomme, Edmund Waller, and Escriva.

Justin Huntly McCarthy, 1889

RUBAIYAT OF OMAR ‖ KHAYYAM, TRANSLA ‖ TED BY JUSTIN HUNTLY ‖ MCCARTHY, M. P. ‖ PUBLISHED BY DAVID NUTT ‖ IN THE STRAND, MDCCCLXXXIX.

The printing of this book was begun by ‖ the Chiswick Press, Tooks Court, Chan ‖ cery Lane, in January, MDCCCLXXXIX, ‖ and was finished in May of the same ‖ year. Five hundred and fifty copies ‖ were printed on small paper and sixty ‖ on large paper. Foolscap, 8 vo. LXII + CLVI pp. [Copies exist printed on vellum.] The whole book is set in capitals.

Mr. McCarthy says in his introduction:—

McCarthy's enthusiasm for Omar

"I shall never forget the day when I first made acquaintance with Omar Khayyam. It was years ago, 'I shall not say how many,' that FitzGerald's translation was lent to me to read by a young lady who has since been found 'dear to the Muses,' and whom Destiny had evidently marked out for sympathy with Persian scholarship, Miss Mary Robinson, the charming poetess, who is now the wife of the distinguished Orientalist, Mr. Darmestetter [*sic*]. She had herself, if I remember rightly, been introduced to Omar by the late Mr. E. W. Godwin, a man whose rare abilities have inexplicably left less mark upon the time than

might have been expected. To say that the Rubaiyat
were a revelation to me and that I adored the revelation, would be but to convey a pitiful and meagre sense
of my enthusiasm. I drank the red wine of Omar from
the enchanted chalice of FitzGerald, and gloried as joy-
ously as Omar himself in the intoxication. The book
was not mine to keep, but I knew it almost by heart
before I parted with it; and I speedily had an Omar of
my own. From this Omar with infinite pains I made
a small copy which I carried about with me, carried with
me in wanderings to Italy and read and re-read; read in
all manner of fair Italian cities, till even now the winds
of Verona and the waters of Venice and 'praeceps Anio'
seem to bear the burden rather of the dear old Persian
singer than any echo of Romeo, or Tasso, or Horace. I
made myself a kind of little religion out of Omar; I became a burden to my friends; my writings — for I wrote
even in those days — seemed with the persistency of Hut-
spur's starling to do little save echo the name of Omar.

"From the Omar of FitzGerald's incomparable verse
to Omar himself, the real Omar in his native Persian
was but a step, but a hard step. I plunged into Persian for Omar's sake; I struggled with the strange
script of the East; I became possessed of Mr. Whinfield's edition first, then of Nicolas's, the one accompanied by a rendering in English verse, the other by
a translation in French prose. With these, in such
leisure as I could find, and at long intervals, I grap-
pled. My Persian of to-day is at the best but beggarly,
but such as it is it has given me infinite pleasure. I
have got a little nearer to the great poet of Naishapur;
I dare not say I know him better, I could not say I
love him better; shall I say that I have read more of
him? The result of scattered studies and efforts re-
newed at long intervals lies at my hand, a mass of

Mr. McCarthy studies Persian for the sake of Omar

translation, here brought together not so much for what it is worth as for what it would be worth. 'Take the will for a better deed.' Such as it is it sets forth the meaning of Omar as I could best fathom it. It is no 'crib' to the Persian text, no hard-and-fast literal translation. I have sought to convey the meaning of my poet as it appeared to me; I have set it down in prose, because, firstly, prose can give the meaning more nearly than any verse can give it, secondly, because it has never been done in English prose, thirdly, because it has been done in English verse once and for ever, and to attempt verse again is but to put oneself in comparison with FitzGerald, which, in the pithy phrase of the great Hellenic humourist, 'is absurd.' Think then of these poor renderings but as rose petals gathered hastily from the grave of Omar, and pardon the faded trophies for the sake of the living tree."

Mr. McCarthy devotes several pages to the history of FitzGerald's translation; then he thus speaks of its influence upon the thought and literature of the day:

The Rubáiyát form naturalized

"Mr. Swinburne, who has so largely influenced the literary form of the generation, was himself profoundly influenced by Omar, and the influence may be easily seen in his earlier works. He was the first English poet, after Edward FitzGerald, to make use of the Rubaiyat form of verse in 'Laus Veneris,' introducing into it an exquisite artistic amplification by which the third unrhymed line of the Persian form rhymed with the third line of the next stanza. Mr. Edmund W. Gosse was, I think, the next to use the form in the charming introduction to his first independent volume of verse 'On Viol and Flute.' Since then it has practically taken its place as one of the recognized forms of English verse, and one, too, of the most beautiful. . . There is no evidence that I can trace of any Omar

influence in Rossetti's work, and, curiously enough, his
brother William Rossetti, in his interesting preface to
the collected edition of Dante Gabriel's writings, does
not even mention the fact of his either reading or ad-
miring 'Omar Khayyam.' . . . Those who have ever
enjoyed the felicity of hearing Sir Richard Burton
recite Rubaiyat of Omar in their sonorous Persian,
know best his admiration for the Astronomer Poet
and the estimation in which he holds him.

"Only an admirer of Omar Khayyam could have
written the Kasidah — couplets — of that Haji Abdu el
Yezdi, who must rank in the shadow-land of mythical
Orientals with Mirza Schaffy, and whose 'Lay of the
Higher Law,' known to the fortunate, represents, in
verse of intensely Eastern aroma, the creed of El Hich-
makani, a surname of Haji Abdu, signifying of 'No
Hall Nowhere':— *(margin: Sir Richard Burton's Orientalism)*

The hour is nigh: the waning Queen walks forth to rule
    the later night;
Crowned with the sparkle of a star and throned on orb
    of ashen light:

The wolf-tail sweeps the paling East to leave a deeper
    gloom behind,
And dawn uprears her shining head, sighing with sem-
    blance of a wind.

"It opens as Khayyam opens, with the False Dawn,
the wolf-tail; here are some verses that have something
of the resolute independence of Khayyam in them: -

Do what thy manhood bids thee do, from none but self
    expect applause,
He noblest lives and noblest dies who makes and keeps
    his self-made laws.

Lay of the Higher Law

All other life is living death, a world where none but phantoms dwell,
A breath, a wind, a sound, a voice, a tinkling of the camel-bell.

How then shall man so order life that when his tale of years is told,
Like sated guest he wends his way, how shall his even tenour hold?

Despite the writ that stores his skull; despite the table and the pen,
Maugre the Fate that plays us down, her board the world, her pieces men."

Omar in France

After disclosing the open secret that "Haji Abdu" was Sir Richard Burton, Mr. McCarthy goes on to speak of other versions of Omar. He says that he "found a similar fate in France to that which he experienced in England. He was at once recognized and welcomed by men of genius."

This statement is apparently based on the fact that Théophile Gautier "recognized the genius and the beauty of Omar Khayyam." It is quite true that "Théophile Gautier is as enthusiastic about the Omar known to him through Nicholas [sic] as Swinburne is about the Omar known to him through FitzGerald." But it is a question whether M. Nicolas's translation made any impression at all in France. M. Garcin de Tassy could not even find it, and FitzGerald had to send him one of his. Nevertheless, Mr. McCarthy gives a very pretty paraphrase of Gautier:—

His words, he says, "help to conjure up a characteristic, delightful picture of Omar Khayyam seated on some wide white terrace at the cool of the day, with friends and dancing-girls about him, with cups and jars at hand, with some book of verses hard by, the fair fine Persian script black upon the ivory-tinted vellum all gorgeous with blues and reds and powdered with gold. Here the Skimmer of the stars set free his soul, laughed at the mollahs, sang his divine songs, and 'loosed his fingers in the tresses of the cypress-slender minister of wine.' Or we may imagine him walking in some garden red with roses and noisy with nightingales, and meditating upon the doom of youth and beauty and the grinding wheel of heaven which reduces Jamshid and Kai Khosrou to potter's clay and bids tulips spring from the cheeks of perished loveliness. Or, yet again reclining in some green place where the lilies blow like the lazy Horatian child of genius, 'by the smooth head of some sacred stream,' with wine and rhymes and a delicious friend. But always melancholy, as melancholy as Koheleth yesterday, Schopenhauer or Julius Bahnsen to-day, filled indeed with what Renan calls 'la grande curiosité,' but wholly unable to gratify it or stifle it. For my own part," he continues, " I can never accept the Omar whom some would have us believe in — the Omar whose verses are all a juggle of mysticism, whose love of wine is but a cheating cant, whose phrases of passion are but the overstrung and most unseemly utterances of the unhinged devotee. . . . He was no sheer sensual worshipper of wine, women, and song, like some of the children of Golias, but we may take it for granted that he shared the opinions of Martin Luther on the three, and that his writings have nothing in common with the golden book of Molinos, or the Quietism of Madame Guyon."

 Mr. McCarthy then speaks of Emerson's acquaintance with Omar, and quotes one of his Von Hammer

<small>Gautier paraphrased</small>

<small>Omar no Quietist</small>

renderings, passes on to the German translations of Bodenstedt, Von Hammer, and Rückert, but not mentioning Ethé's or Wollheim's, or Graf von Shack's, the best; he compliments the size and appearance of the Hungarian translation, and after erroneously stating that "you may search in vain through Gore Ouseley's attractive volume on the Persian Poets for a hint as to his (Omar's) existence," he describes the genesis of the "pirated edition" quoted above. He then pays his compliments to Whinfield and Garner, and quotes from D'Herbelot the brief and curiously mistaken account of Omar and "the lovely legend." This is followed by the usual biographical sketch, and then come these interesting quotations from Hafiz:—

Omar and Hafiz

"Hafiz was in many ways distinctly a follower of Omar Khayyám. There are passages in the Ghazels of Hafiz which resemble certain Rubáiyát of Omar Khayyám too closely for mere chance similarity. Thus this verse: 'One morning an unseen voice in friendly tone calls to me from the wine-house, "Come back thou who hast so long served at the threshold,"' is exceedingly Khayyámesque. Again, 'The chant of the bird is heard once more, but where is the wine-flask? The nightingale is lamenting, who will withdraw the veil from the rose?' And again: 'I will cast into the fire my rags, stained like the rose with wine.' And this especially: 'A twain of clever friends, a flagon of old wine, quiet, and a book and a corner of the lawn; I would not exchange this condition either for this world or that which is to come.' And once again: 'To-morrow our draught may be from the river of Paradise and amidst the Houris: but to-day enjoy the radiant looks of the cup-bearer and a goblet of wine.' And yet again: 'Hafiz, leave thou the "How and the Wherefore," and drink for the moment thy wine. His wisdom hath withholden from us what is the force of the words "How and Wherefore."' Once more: 'In this world of clay there is no real man! We must make a new world and create a new Adam.' All these parallels were noted by me long since from the delightful little volume of translations from Háfiz by the late S. Robinson, long, alas, out of print and hard to find, and might no doubt easily be multiplied."

Mr. McCarthy ends his introduction with a rather sentimental wish that "some wanderer to the East, some Burton, some Kinglake, some Warburton, might carry this little book in saddle-bags, and ride through Khorassan till he came to Naishapur, and cast it down in the dust before the tomb of Omar Khayyám."

The Rubáiyát are prefaced by the following stanzas:—

OMAR KHAYYAM.

Omar, dear Sultan of the Persian song,
Familiar friend whom I have loved so long,
*   Whose volume made my pleasant hiding-place*
From this fantastic world of right and wrong.

My youth lies buried in thy verses: lo,
I read, and as the haunted numbers flow,
*   My memory turns in anguish to the face*
That leaned o'er Omar's pages long ago.

Alas for me, alas for all who weep
And wonder at the silence dark and deep
*   That girdles round this little lamp in space*
No wiser than when Omar fell asleep.

[McCarthy's verses to Omar Khayyám]

> Rest in thy grave beneath the crimson rain
> Of heart-desired roses. Life is vain,
>   And vain the trembling legends we may trace
> Upon the open book that shuts again.

Criticism upon Mr. McCarthy and Omar

Mr. Justin Huntly McCarthy's version was thus criticised by the London *Spectator* of Aug. 17, 1889:

"If this book were the work of a very young writer, we should forgive its affectations and conceits, in the belief that they only came of a mistaken but not unworthy desire to follow in the steps of the great masters of former generations, and that more experience would teach him to distinguish the permanent forms of the English language which are for all time, from those which are only good for their own day, and would drop off in succession like the yearly leaves on a great oak. But when the writer claims to be a man of mature intellect and culture, acquainted with many lands and many people, we are justly irritated by such affectations and conceits. Not content with calling Persian writing 'the strange script of the East,' the whole book from the title on the cover to the last page is printed in the still more strange and disagreeable 'script' which printers call 'Small Caps,' and which makes the book look as if it were in type-writing of the earlier and less readable kind. . . .

"Notwithstanding the preference hinted by Mr. Fitzgerald, and avowed by Mr. McCarthy, for Omar to Saadi and Hafiz, we must declare our own opinion that the Quatrains of Omar can no more claim precedence over the Diwan of Hafiz, than can the Epigrams of Martial or of the Greek Anthology over the Odes of Horace and Anacreon. We share their high appreciation of the vigorous thought and picturesque imagery in which Omar so often embodies the scepticism with which he mocks the Sphinx whose riddle he despairs of solving; but not only do we prefer the only half-intelligible mysticism with which Hafiz takes the place of such scepticism, but we must think that in all that constitutes poetry, Hafiz is far superior. And still less can we agree with our critics that Omar's Quatrains can be even compared for imagination, any more than for moral philosophy, with the Bustan and Gulistan of Saadi. Nothing, indeed, can surpass the epigrammatic wiseness and vigour and imagery of some of those Quatrains, as represented by Mr. Fitzgerald. But a larger — we suspect, though without counting, a far larger — number of the whole, have little of these qualities. This is true even of the limited number which Mr. Fitzgerald has given us; and still more is it apparent in the complete collection of Mr. McCarthy. . . . Dry and shrivelled specimens of the Quatrains of Omar Khayyám are all that Mr. McCarthy has given us. Notwithstanding the enthusiasm which he expresses, and no doubt feels, for his author, they are sadly wanting alike in the poetic and epigrammatic qualities, no less than in the 'accomplishment of verse.'

Hafiz superior to Omar

"The contrast with Fitzgerald's translations is very great. Fitzgerald saw — as all successful translators have seen — that a certain amplification and paraphrase are necessary in order to give side meanings, and associations, and shades of thought which belong to the word in the original, but which are not carried with it by the mere verbal representation of the corresponding word in the other language. He puts himself into the place of his author, drinks of his spirit till he can say, —

> 'I see no longer, I myself am there,'

and then pours forth in English verse what Omar would have said had he been an Englishman, or Fitzgerald had he been a Persian.

"No one, we believe, will agree more readily than Mr. McCarthy himself in this estimate of Fitzgerald's merits as a translator: we only regret that he should have persuaded himself that his own bald prose can help us to a better knowledge of Omar."

Fitz-Gerald's collected works

LETTERS ‖ AND LITERARY REMAINS ‖ OF ‖ EDWARD FITZGERALD ‖ EDITED BY ‖ WILLIAM ALDIS WRIGHT ‖ IN THREE VOLUMES. LONDON: ‖ MACMILLAN AND CO. ‖ AND NEW YORK. 1889. [All Rights reserved.]

Vol. I contains frontispiece: engraved portrait of Fitzgerald. Life and Letters.

Vol. II, "Euphranor," "Six Dramas from Calderon," "The Bird Parliament," "The Two Generals." (Frontispiece: The "Little Grange.")

Vol. III: Translations: "The Mighty Magician," "Such Stuff as Dreams are Made of," the three Œdipus dramas, "Agamemnon," The Rubáiyát of Omar Khayyám, pp. 333-366, notes, pp. 367-372, Reprint of First Edition, pp. 373-386, Note by the Editor, beginning, "It must be admitted that Fitzgerald took great liberties with the original in his version of Omar Khayyám. The first stanza is entirely his own, and in stanza XXXI. [sic] of the fourth edition (XXXVI. in the second) he has introduced two lines from Attár." Variations between the second, third, and fourth editions of Omar Khayyám, pp. 387-393. Stanzas which appear in the second edition only, pp. 394-395. Comparative table of stanzas in the four editions, pp. 395, 396. "Salámán and Absál," "Bredfield Hall," "Chronomoros," "Virgil's Garden," "Preface to Polonius," "Introduction to Readings in Crabbe," "Written by Petrarch in his Virgil." Frontispiece: the Persian picture of the Royal Game of Chugán, "Horse-hockey," or Polo, which accompanied Ed. IV of the Rubáiyát.

RUBÁIYÁT | OF OMAR KHAYYÁM || THE || ASTRON‑ OMER-POET OF PERSIA || RENDERED INTO ENGLISH VERSE || LONDON || MACMILLAN AND CO. || AND NEW YORK. || 1890 || All rights Reserved. *FitzGerald's fifth edition, reprint, 1890*

Fifth Edition. Reprinted separately from preceding. iv, 112 pp. Notes; 1st Edition; Variations between the Second, Third, and Fourth Editions of Omar Khayyám. Comparative table of stanzas in the four editions. [Edited by W. Aldis Wright.]

RUBÁIYÁT OF OMAR KHAYYÁM: Pamphlet Edition. Green Wrapper. 12 mo. 48 pp. 20 cents. San Francisco, 1891. *Pamphlet edition, 1891*

RUBÁIYÁT OF OMAR || KHAYYÁM || THE ASTRON‑ OMER-POET OF PERSIA || RENDERED INTO ENGLISH VERSE || BY EDWARD FITZGERALD || PRINTED FOR THOMAS V. MOSHER || AND PUBLISHED BY HIM AT || 37 EXCHANGE STREET, PORTLAND, || MAINE MDCCCXCIIIJ. *Bibelot edition, 1894*

Narrow Fcap. 8vo. 80 pp. Contains Andrew Lang's Poem to Omar from "Letters to Dead Authors," Fitz‑ Gerald's Introduction; text of 1st and 4th Editions on opposite pages; notes; quatrains printed in 2nd Edition only; List of English Versions and Justin Huntly

McCarthy's poem as L'Envoy. 725 copies on Van Gelder paper ($1.00) and 25 on Japan vellum ($2.50). Out of print.

St. Paul edition, 1895

RUBÁIYÁT OF OMAR ∥ KHAYYÁM ∥ THE ASTRONOMER-POET OF PERSIA ∥ RENDERED INTO ENGLISH VERSE ∥ BY EDWARD FITZGERALD ∥ PRINTED FOR E. W. PORTER ∥ COMPANY, PUBLISHERS 100 EAST ∥ FOURTH STREET, SAINT PAUL, ∥ MINNESOTA MDCCCXCV. Reprint of 1st and 4th Editions, with omitted stanzas from 2nd Ed. Cover and title-pages from drawings by W. Robert Pike. 750 copies printed from type; $1.25.

Old World edition, 1895

RUBÁIYÁT ∥ OF OMAR KHAYYAM ∥ [red] RENDERED INTO ENGLISH VERSE ∥ BY EDWARD FITZGERALD PORTLAND, MAINE ∥ THOMAS B. MOSHER ∥ MDCCCXCV.

Narrow Fcap. 8vo. 125 pp. Contains: Rosamund Mariott Watson's Sonnet: "Omar Khayyám to A. L.;" Toast to Omar Khayyám by Theodore Watts; Biography of Edward FitzGerald by W. Irving Way; FitzGerald's Introduction; text of 1st and 4th editions; notes; variations; quatrains printed in 2nd edition only; Bibliography; "To the Winds" by Theodore Watts; Designs and headbands by Charles M. Jenckes. First edition, 950 copies, $1.00. Japan vellum, 100 copies, $2.50.

TWO SUFFOLK FRIENDS ∥ BY ∥ FRANCIS HINDES GROOME ∥ WILLIAM BLACKWOOD AND SONS ∥ EDIN. & LONDON. ∥ 1895. XII. + 135 pp. [pp. 67-133 devoted to Edward FitzGerald].

III.

MAGAZINE LITERATURE.

"Journal Asiatique." No. 9, 1857. Garcin de Tassy. See above. "Note sur les Rubà'iyât de 'Omar Khaïyâm."

"Calcutta Review": Vol. XXX. Jan. 1858. Professor E. B. Cowell: see FitzGerald's Introduction, p. cxxxiv, and Editor's Introduction, p. xvii.

"Le Moniteur," Dec. 8, 1867. "Les Quatrains d'Omar:" Review of Nicolas's Version: Théophile Gautier: see "L'Orient." Vol. II.

"North American Review." CIX: 565-584. Oct. 1869. Review of Nicolas's Translation and FitzGerald's (Ed. II.), by Charles Eliot Norton.

Professor Norton, from whose article extracts have been already quoted, says of Omar:—

"There is much in the quality of his verse to render it unacceptable to the generality of orthodox readers of poetry, and to those who read only *with* and not *through* their eyes. The transcendental character of much of his poetry takes it out of the range of common appreciation, and that it may be understood at all it requires to be read with something of the same spirit with which it was written." *[Transcendental character of Omar's work]*

"Fraser"* (LXXXI, 777-784), June, 1870. Reviews FitzGerald's Ed. II. (Author anonymous, but said to be Thomas W. Hinchcliff.)

---

* The article on Omar, in "Fraser" (LXXXIII, p. 487), April, 1871, by W. G. Palgrave, catalogued in Poole's Index, concerns not Omar Khayyám, but the Arabian Poet Omar-Ebn-Abee Rabee'ah, "the Mogheree."

The reviewer says:—

"It would be difficult to find a more complete example of terse and vigorous English, free from all words of weakness or superfluity. The rhythm of his stanzas is admirable and that with which the poem begins may be taken as a fair specimen of the pointed force with which he expresses himself.... The scepticism of Omar is but the 'old old story' clad in a more than usually poetic dress: it reminds us of the saying of a Frenchman, Royer-Collard, that philosophy is the art of tracing back human ignorance to its fountain-head: it has flowed down to us from the days of *vanitas vanitatum*, in a continued succession till the day when our own Laureate set the great battle of the human soul before us in his form of The Two Voices. The doubts and difficulties of thinking and intelligent man, are there set forth in much the same way as in the verses to the old Tentmaker. Tennyson there says, through the medium of the evil voice which tempts man to despair and suicide, in consequence of his inability to arrive at the absolute knowledge of truth:—

 'To which he answered scoffingly:
  Good soul! suppose I grant it thee,
  Who'll weep for *thy* deficiency?

 'Or will one beam be less intense,
  When *thy* peculiar difference
  Is cancelled in the world of sense?'

"What Omar Khayyám said by way of anticipation seven centuries ago is the scepticism of a man who, after working through all the fields of science open to him, finds himself disposed to weep despairingly over the unsatisfactory result of human knowledge. Tennyson, in the masterly poem alluded to, was as unable as Omar to untie the knot in a logical manner; but, with the better light of modern thought to guide him, he cut it by an assertion of faith in the beauty and life and happiness of the world around him.

"To the old Persian sage such a lofty stage was perhaps impossible: he knew the difficulty equally well, but he was not prepared for such a happy solution of it. We must be content to admire his verses for their intrinsic beauty. The vigour of his thought and expression, and their harmony with much that is now going on around us, inspire us with a strange feeling of sympathy for him who in the darkest ages of Europe filled himself with all knowledge accessible to him before he went to his last sleep under the roses of Naishápúr." *The intrinsic beauty of his verse*

"Old and New": (V: p. 611) May, 1872. The Poems of Omar Khayyám: FitzGerald Ed. II. reviewed by (the Rev.) John W. Chadwick.

Mr. Chadwick says:

"The poetry of Omar Khayyám has had much less fame in the west than that of Firdusi and Saadi and Hafiz; but mainly, it must be, because there has been less knowledge of it. He is quite able to match the strongest winged of those great singers in his flights. Emerson had found him out, and given us a taste of his quality, but not a mouthful and still less a meal. Now a feast is spread. . . . *Omar the equal of any Persian poet*

"It is his poetry, not his science that, makes him interesting to us. It is the poetry of an epicurean, but not of a merry one. It is too deeply interested in the problems of life, death and futurity for that. The epicureanism is a transparent mask through which we see a very sober countenance. Some one has called

Sadder than Ecclesiastes

Ecclesiastes 'the saddest of all sad books.' He had never read Omar Khayyám. These verses are far sadder than Ecclesiastes. For one reason, because they are so much sweeter; for another, because they are so much more desperate; for another, because we feel behind the written word a far, far nobler spirit. . . .

A contribution to our faith

"After all, this book, and every such book is a real contribution to our faith. It is only indifference that begets in us any permanent doubt. Only let the interrogation be earnest and passionate enough, and its earnestness and passion assure us that there is, there must be, some adequate reply."

"Contemporary Review" (XXVII: pp. 559-570). March, 1876. H. Schütz-Wilson reviews Ed. III, FitzGerald: indirectly claims to make the first public announcement of the translator's name:—

"I am now permitted to state publicly that the translator of Omar is Mr. Edward Fitzgerald." Also prophesies coming vogue of the Rubáiyát. "There will be, I think, more editions yet."

Speaking of FitzGerald's work, he says:—

The beauty of Fitz-Gerald's work

"The translation may justly be termed masterly; the preface and notes are decidedly the work of a thoughtful scholar. . . . The translation, indeed, reads like an original work, and that work the work of a poet. Eastern scholars vouch for its fidelity (!); every competent reader can certify the beauty of the thing translated, as of the translation itself."

The article goes on to consider Omar's philosophy.

The London "Spectator," commenting on this article, said:—

"It should, we think, take rank rather as the poem of Revolt and Denial, the song of speculative Nihilism and cynical Sensualism, than as a poem of the stamp which the *Contemporary Review* claims for it,— namely, one which 'denies divinely the divine,' and is full of 'the unconscious faith which complains to the Deity of its inability to comprehend the Divine.' Of this character, we confess we cannot find a trace in Mr. Edward Fitzgerald's magnificent translation, — a translation which confessedly selects all the finest verses of the Oriental poem, and leaves only the most sensual still under the veil of the Persian original. With something of the cynical force of Byron, and something, too, of the humourous and familiar ease of Goethe, the writer of this poem (though a contemporary as Mr. Schütz-Wilson reminds us, of Henry II. and Fair Rosamond) expends his whole power in showing what a mockery of man is implied in irreversible laws of creation; and he accomplishes his task with all the grasp of a thinker of first rate calibre, and all the bitterness of a defiant heart."

"Journal of the Asiatic Society of Bengal," XLVI, 158-160. Calcutta: 1877. Metrical translations from 'Umar Khayyam, accompanied by the Persian original by P. Whalley, C. S., Murádábád. See above.

"Atlantic Monthly": (XLI, p. 421). April, 1878: Thomas Bailey Aldrich reviews the Osgood edition of 1878: He speaks of "the exquisite quatrains," and thus defines a Rubá'iy: —

"The quatrain, as exemplified by the masters of it, occupies a field of its own, like the sonnet, and though not fettered by so involved laws as the latter, it has laws which are not to be broken with impunity. It is a surprisingly difficult species of composition. The quatrain is an instrument on which one may strike the lightest or the deepest note, but it must be a full note. It is imperative that the single thought, fancy, or mood with which it deals should find complete expression. If

Mr. Aldrich defines the quatrain

your statement exceeds the austere limit of four verses and requires one or more additional stanzas to complete itself, you have written a poem of eight, twelve, or fourteen verses, as the case may be, but not a quatrain. Then again, a trifle too much point or snap turns your poem into an epigram. A perfect quatrain is almost as rare as a perfect sonnet. There is nothing of sustained effort here: the poems are not of long breath; they are not to be measured with a yard-stick; but so exquisite is their workmanship, so firmly and cleanly are they cut, that they are a part of the world's precious things, retaining their freshness and their subtilty through corroding centuries, like those intaglios turned up from time to time in Roman earth. Omar Khayyám has shown us once more that a little thing may be perfect, and that perfection is not a little thing.

The thought cuts deep

"But are these poems in any sense little things? Here and there the poignant thought in them cuts very deep. It is like a crevasse in an Alpine glacier, only a finger's breadth at the edge, but reaching down to unfathomable depths.

"The mysteries of life and death and the problem of future existence occupied the good Omar Khayyám very much in his soft nest at Naishápúr. In vain broodings over these matters, his supply of Moslem faith gave out; he became a sceptic, a Pantheist; destiny took the place of Providence. . . .

"Many of his verses are in praise of the wine-cup; but I suspect that he praised more wine than he drank, and that the epigram which English Herrick wrote upon himself would be an excellent fit for the Persian's tombstone:—

'Jocund his Muse was, but his life was chaste.'

"Aside from the admirable technique of the quatrains, the most striking feature is their intensely modern spirit. Some of them deal with the questions which **Their** assail and defeat us to-day, so that it would be easy to **modern** imagine them the work of a poet of the period, if any **spirit** poet of the period could have written them.

"There is a Singer sleeping in the English Burying **Landor** Ground at Florence who might have written certain of **and Omar** them. It is to praise both poets to say their quatrains are alike in grace, repose, and consummate finish. . . . The compact, flexible stanza in which Mr. FitzGerald has reset the Persian's jewels is a model for young poets of the 'howling dervish' school."

"Fraser's," "The True Omar Khayyám," 1879. See Introduction.

"The Daily Telegraph," Aug. 15, "The Scotsman," Sept. 12, and "The Academy," Sept. 20, 1879, review FitzGerald's Edition IV.

New York "Evening Post," April 21, 1883. Reviews Whinfield's 1882 Version of "The Quatrains of Omar Khayyám."

"The Academy" (XXVI, 361). London, Nov. 29, 1884. Amelia B. Edwards reviews the FitzGerald Version, particularly with reference to the illustrations of Elihu Vedder.

"The Academy," (XXVI, p. 44). London, Jan. 17, 1885.

A. Houtum-Schindler takes exception to Miss Edwards's statement regarding the uncertainty of the dates in Omar's life. He asserts that Omar left Nishâpûr College in 1042, corrected the calendar 1072-1092, and died at Nishâpûr in 1124, over a century old.

"The Academy" (XXVII, p. 63). London, Jan. 24, 1885. 18 quatrains from Omar translated into verse by Whitley Stokes. See above. [Also reprinted in New York "Critic," Feb. 7, 1885.]

"The Times" of London, Dec. 29, 1885. Reviews briefly Mr. Vedder's Illustrations.

A curious misjudgment "Magnificently got up, a master-piece of American engraving;" speaking of the poet, it says: "The sage who immortalized himself as a man of science might have been expected to write in a serious strain. But, on the contrary, the Rubáiyát is [*sic*] sensually epicurean, advising mortals to make the most of the passing hour, since life is short and death is certain. We look confidently for some sudden turn towards a higher moral, in the vein of Solomon [?] in Ecclesiastes, but it never comes. The poem trips off in light quatrains. We know not of course whether the translation be free or literal, but it is assuredly easy and graceful."

"Macmillan's" (LXVII: 27), Nov. 1887. H. G Keene. See Appendix XLVIII.

"The Spectator" (LXIII). Aug. 17, 1889. Criticism.

"National Review" (XVI, 506), 1890. C. J. Pickering. See Introduction.

"Saturday Review," Aug. 20, 1892. Omar (Al) Khayyám (i.) (Brief Review of Woepcke's translation of Omar's "Al-gebr.")

"The Nation" (LVII, p. 304). Oct. 26, 1893. "The Omar Khayyám cult in England." Moncure D. Conway. See Appendix L.

"English Illustrated," Feb. 1894. Article on Edward FitzGerald by Edward Clodd.

"Calcutta Review," 1895. H. G Keene. See Appendix XLVIII.

NOTE.— Mr. Willard Austin, Assistant Librarian of Cornell University, in 1891 prepared for the University Omar Khayyám Club "a complete Bibliography of the Rubáiyát, comprising the text editions, translations, book and magazine literature of the subject."

A complete bibliography on any subject is a very difficult matter to predicate. The present is by no means complete, though it is the fullest ever printed. I have not succeeded in finding that there are translations in Spanish or Italian, or in the Scandinavian languages. In 1888 a Persian edition, from a MS. transcribed by Mir Husein in Tebris in 1285 A. H., is said to have been published at St. Petersburg under the editorship of A. Sobrievsky, with the approval of A. V. Zhukovsky, who is an authority on the Persian language. Other Persian authors have been admirably translated into both Italian and Russian, and it is altogether likely that Omar Khayyám has found interpreters in these tongues, both of which are so well adapted for metrical versions. *The Petersburg lithographed edition*

One German translation is not represented in the Bibliography, — that of Dr. Wollheim, the Chevalier da Fonseca. It is not in the Boston Public Library, the Boston Athenæum, the Columbia College Library, or the Astor Library; and the copy belonging to Harvard College happened, unfortunately, to be in temporary exile, together with sixty or seventy thousand other books, pending the completion of the addition to Gore Hall. The following extract from Kayser's Bücher Lexicon was kindly sent to me by Mr. F. Saunders of the Astor Library: —

Die National-Literatur sämmtlicher Völker des Orient's. Eine prosaische und poetische Anthologie aus den besten Schriftstellern des gesammten Orients mit erläuternden, kritischen, literarischen und biographischen Notizen.

   Lex. = 8. (1. Bd. VIII u. 683 S. und
     2. Bd. XIII. u. 859 S.)
   Berlin, 1869-73. Hempel.

NOTE. — It was issued in fascicules numbering 1-28, at a price of 1 Mark each.

Not being able to indicate the number of quatrains translated, I have omitted it from the body of the Bibliography. Nor was I able to discover how many of the Rubáiyát, if any, were translated into German by Professor Blochmann. No small amount of periodical literature had to be omitted for reasons of space — notably, interesting extracts from "Le Journal Asiatique." The whole field of German criticism remains to be explored. If, as Mr. Andrew Lang says in his letter permitting me to print his Omar Khayyám poem, "The connection between Omar, Jemmy Jawkins, and Tearlach Righ nan Gael, needs a volume to elucidate," certainly all the extant references to Omar in all languages would require a lifetime, and make a library in itself.

APPENDIX L.

The Omar Khayyám Club of London

The Omar Khayyam Club of London was organized in London in 1892: among its early members were Mr. Clement Shorter, Editor, "Illustrated News;" Mr. Edward Clodd, the author; Mr. William Simpson, the artist; George Whale, Solicitor, V. P.; Frederic Hudson, Secretary; Arthur Hacker; Justin Huntly McCarthy, M. P.

On the 7th of October, 1893, the club went to Boulge (which Mr. Conway says is pronounced *Bowidge*) and took part in the ceremony of planting at FitzGerald's grave two little rose-trees.

The roses were planted at the head of the slab of rosy granite which marks FitzGerald's resting-place, and a bronze plate was infixed containing this inscription:—

The inscription at FitzGerald's grave

"THIS ROSE-TREE, RAISED IN KEW GARDENS FROM SEED BROUGHT BY WILLIAM SIMPSON, ARTIST-TRAVELLER, FROM THE GRAVE OF OMAR KHAYYÁM AT NAISHÁPÚR, WAS PLANTED BY A FEW ADMIRERS OF EDWARD FITZGERALD IN THE NAME OF THE OMAR KHAYYÁM CLUB, 7 OCTOBER, 1893."*

At the ceremony poems were read by Mr. McCarthy and Mr. Edmund Gosse. Mr. Grant Allen sent the following quatrain:—

Mr. Grant Allen's quatrain

"Here on FitzGerald's grave from Omar's tomb
  To lay fit tribute pilgrim singers flock;
Long with a double fragrance let it bloom,
  The rose of Iran on an English stock."

These Rubáiyát were also read as a sort of litany:

"Diversity of worship has divided the human race into seventy-two nations. From among all their dogmas I have selected one — the Divine Love.

"The morning hath already thrown off the veil of darkness. Wherefore thy sadness? Rise up; let us breathe again the morning air before having to long for it. For alas! long enough will the morning breathe when we breathe not.

"The entire world shall be populous with that action of thine which saves a soul from despair.

---

* According to Mr. Conway the hips were sent to Mr. Thistleton Dyer; but Mr. Simpson, in his letter to Mr. Quaritch, dated Nishapur. 27th October, 1884, says:—

"From the association of your name with that of Omar Khayam I feel sure that what I enclose in this letter will be acceptable. The rose-leaves I gathered to-day, growing beside the tomb of the poet at this place, and the seeds are from the same bushes on which the leaves grew."

Rubáiyát read at Fitz-Gerald's tomb

"A thousand chains of thine own broken by thee are less than to have chained to thee by sweetness the heart of a free man.

"The dogmas admit only what is obliging to the deity. But refuse not thy bit of bread to another, guard thy tongue from speaking evil, and seek not the injury of any being, and I undertake on my own account to promise thee paradise. Since from the beginning of life to the end there is for thee only this earth, live at least as one who is on the earth and not buried under it.

"O my heart, thou wilt never penetrate the mysteries of the universe; thou wilt never reach that culminating wisdom which the intrepid omniscients have attained. Resign thyself, then, to make what little paradise thou canst here below; for, as for that one beyond, thou shalt arrive there, or thou shalt not."

If by McCarthy, they are a different translation from that in his book. Mr. McCarthy's poem was published in the "Pall Mall Gazette."

Mr. Gosse's "Inscription" was printed in the London "Athenæum" of Oct. 7: —

"Reign here, triumphant rose from Omar's grave,
  Borne by a fakir o'er the Persian wave;
    Reign with fresh pride, since here a heart is sleeping
  That double glory to your Master gave.

"Hither let many a pilgrim step be bent
  To greet the rose re-risen in banishment;
    Here richer crimsons may its cup be keeping
  Than brimmed it ere from Naishápúr it went."

Mr. Theodore Watts wrote a sonnet for the same occasion. It was entitled:—

HEAR US, YE WINDS.

My tomb shall be on a spot where the North-Wind may strow roses upon it. — *Omar Khayyám to Kwájah Nizámi.*

Hear us, ye winds!
    From where the North-wind strows
Blossoms that crown "the King of Wisdom's" tomb,
The trees here planted bring remembered bloom
Dreaming in seed of Love's ancestral Rose
To meadows where a braver North-wind blows
O'er greener grass, o'er hedge-rose, may, and broom,
And all that make East England's field-perfume
Dearer than any fragrance Persia knows:—

Hear us ye winds, North, East, and West, and South!
This granite covers him whose golden mouth
Made wise ev'n the word of Wisdom's King:
Blow softly o'er the grave of Omar's herald
Till roses rich of Omar's dust shall spring
From richer dust of Suffolk's rare FitzGerald.

Theodore Watts's sonnet

In connection with this ceremony it may be proper here to quote a part of Mr. Simpson's letter to Mr. Quaritch, describing his visit to Omar's tomb, where he got the rose-hips so successfully transplanted to English soil. Mr. Simpson was sent to accompany Sir Peter Lumsden and the Afghan Boundary Commission, as special artist of the "Illustrated London News." On Oct. 8, 1884, he reached Nishâpûr and wrote:—

"For some days past, as we marched along, I have been making inquiries regarding Omar Khayam and Nishapur; I wanted to know if the house he lived in

William Simpson's letter from Naishápúr

still existed, or if any spot was yet associated with his name. It would seem that the only recognised memorial now remaining of him is his tomb. Our Mehmandar, or 'Guest-Conductor,'—while the Afghan Boundary Commission is on Persian territory it is the Guest of the Shah, and the Mehmandar is his representative, who sees that all our wants are attended to,—appears to be familiar with the poet's name, and says that his works are still read and admired. The Mehmandar said he knew the tomb, and promised to be our guide when we reached Nishapur. We have just made the pilgrimage to the spot; it is about two miles south of the present Nishapur; so we had to ride, and Sir Peter, who takes an interest in the matter, was one of the party. We found the ground nearly all the way covered with mounds, and the soil mixed with fragments of pottery, sure indications of former habitations. As we neared the tomb, long ridges of earth could be seen, which were no doubt the remains of the walls of the old city of Nishapur. To the east of the tomb is a large square mound of earth, which is supposed to be the site of the Ark, or Citadel of the original city. As we rode along, the blue dome, which the Mehmandar had pointed out on the way as the tomb, had a very imposing appearance, and its importance improved as we neared it; this will be better understood by stating that city walls, houses, and almost all structures in that part of Persia, are built of mud. The blue dome, as well as its size, produced in my mind, as we went towards it, a great satisfaction; it was pleasing to think that the countrymen of Omar Khayam held him in such high estimation as to erect so fine a monument, as well as to preserve it,—this last being rarely done in the East,—to his memory. If the poet was so honoured in his own country, it was little to be wondered at that his fame should have spread so rapidly in the lands of the West. This I thought, but there was a slight disappointment in store for me. At last we reached the tomb, and found its general arrangements were on a plan I was familiar with in India: whoever has visited the Taj at Agra, or any of the large Mohammedan tombs of Hindostan, will easily understand the one at Nishapur. The monument stands in a space enclosed by a mud wall, and the ground in front is laid out as a garden, with walks. The tomb at Nishapur, with all its surroundings, is in a very rude condition; it never was a work which could claim merit for its architecture, and although it is kept so far in repair, it has still a very decayed and neglected appearance. Even the blue dome, which impressed me in the distance, I found on getting near to it was in a ruinous state from large portions of the enamelled plaster having fallen off. Instead of the marble and the red stone of the Taj at Nishapur,—with the exception of some enamelled tiles producing a pattern round the base of the dome, and also in the spandrils of the door and windows,—there we find only bricks and plaster. The surrounding wall of the enclosure was of crumbling mud, and could be easily jumped over at any place. There is a rude entrance by which we went in and walked to the front of the tomb; all along I had been under the notion that the whole structure was the tomb of Omar Khayam; and now came the disenchantment. The place turned out to be an Imamzadah, or the tomb of the Son of an Imam. The Son of an Imam inherits his sanctity from his father, and his place of burial becomes a holy place where pilgrims go to pray. The blue dome is over the tomb of such a person, who may have been a brute of the worst kind,—that would not have affected his sanctity,—instead of the poet whom

The tomb of Omar Khayyám

The "Poet's Corner" at Naishápúr

we reverence for the qualities which belonged to himself. When we had ascended the platform, about three feet high, on which the tomb stood, the Mehmandar turned to the left, and in a recess formed by three arches and a very rude roof, which seemed to have been added to the corner of the Imamzadah, pointed to the tomb of Omar Khayam. The discovery of a 'Poet's Corner' at Nishapur naturally recalled Westminster Abbey to my mind and revived my spirits from the depression produced by finding that the principal tomb was not that of the Poet. The monument over the tomb is an oblong mass of brick covered with plaster, and without ornament,—the plaster falling off in places; on this and on the plaster of the recess are innumerable scribblings in Persian character. Some were, no doubt, names, for the British John Smith has not an exclusive tendency in this respect; but many of them were continued through a number of lines, and I guessed they were poetry, and most probably quotations from the Rubaiyat. Although the 'Poet's Corner' was in rather a dilapidated state, still it must have been repaired at no very distant date; and this shows that some attention has been paid to it, and that the people of Nishapur have not quite forgotten Omar Khayam.

"The Imamzadah — this word, which means Son of an Imam, applies to the person buried as well as to the tomb — was Mohammed Marook, brother of the Imam Reza, whose tomb at Meshed is considered so sacred by the Shias; — the Imam Reza was the eighth Imam, and died in 818; this gives us an approximate date for his brother, and it is, if I mistake not, a couple of centuries before the time of Omar Khayam; and the Imamzadah — here I mean the building — would have been erected, most probably, about that number of years before the poet required his resting-place. Behind the Imamzadah is a Kubberstan, or 'Region of Graves,' and the raised platform in front of the tomb contains in its rough pavement a good many small tomb-stones, shewing that people are buried there, and that the place had been in the past a general grave-yard. All this is owing to the hereditary sanctity which belongs to the Son of an Imam, and we are perhaps indebted to Mohammed Marook, no matter what his character may have been, for the preservation of the site of Omar Khayam's burial-place; the preservation of the one necessarily preserved the other.

"In front of the Imamzadah is the garden, with some very old and one or two large trees, but along the edge of the platform in front of Omar Khayam's tomb I found some rose bushes; it was too late in the season for the roses, but a few hips were still remaining, and one or two of these I secured, as well as the leaves,— some of which are here enclosed for you; I hope you will be able to grow them in England,— they will have an interest, as in all probability they are the particular kind of roses Omar Khayam was so fond of watching as he pondered and composed his verses. *Omar's rose-bushes*

"It may be worth adding that there is also at Nishapur the tomb of another poet who lived about the same time as Omar Khayam,— his name was Ferid ed din Attar; according to Vambéry, he was a 'great mystic and philosopher. He wrote a work called "Mantik et Teyr, the Logic of Birds." In this the feathered creatures are made to contend in a curious way on the causes of existence, and the Source of Truth. "Hudhud," the All-Knowing magical bird of Solomon, is introduced, as the Teacher of Birds; and also Simurg, the Phœnix of the Orientals, and Symbol of the Highest Light.' In this it is understood that the Birds represent humanity, Hudhud is the Prophet, and the Simurg stands for Deity. This tomb I shall not have time to visit."

The sketch which Mr. Simpson sent to the London "News" was reproduced, and serves as the frontispiece to the memorial or first comparative edition of the "Rubáiyát."

At the July, 1895, meeting of the Omar Khayyám Club, which took place at the Burford Bridge Hotel, a still larger number were present: among them Thomas Hardy, William Sharp, and Mr. George Meredith. Mr. Meredith received an ovation. Mr. Gosse's verses for the menu were —

Mr. Gosse's verses

"One cup in joy before the banquet ends,
  One thought for vanished, for transfigured friends,
    Stars on the living cope of heaven embossed,
The heaven of Love that o'er us beams and bends!

"Roses and bay for many a phantom head!
  Death is but what we make it — for the dead;
    Held hard in memory, those we loved and lost
Shall live while blood is warm and wine is red."

Andrew Lang's memorial poem

It was in that poetic locality that Keats wrote a large part of "Endymion," and there Robert Louis Stevenson once stayed. Mr. Andrew Lang's poem to "Omar's friends at Burford Bridge" was a memorial to Stevenson. It began: —

"Not mid the London dust and glare,
  The wheels that rattle, the lamps that flare,
    But down in the deep green Surrey dingle,
You drink to Omar in fragrant air.

Poem in memory of R. L. Stevenson

"He who sleeps on the Vaea crest
  Came to your tavern for work or rest,
    There he lingered, and there, he told us,
  Was by the Shade of a Sound possessed!

"Men in the darkling inn that meet,
  Heard the sound of a horse's feet,
    Hooves that scatter the flying pebbles,
  And a warning whip on the casement beat.

"*Boot and saddle!* was then the cry,
  Mount and ride, for the foe is nigh!
    Over the water, or high in the heather,
  Thither the friends of the king must fly.

"Such was the sound that Louis heard,
  Out of the silence a single word,
    Out of the dust of the withered ages,
  Something that wakened, and beat, and stirred!

"Here, he said, was a tale to tell
  Of Burford Bridge in the lonely dell,
    A tale of the friends of the leal White Roses,
  But he told it not, who had told it well.

"Drink to him then, ere the night be sped!
  Drink to his name while the wine is red!
    To Tearlach drink, and Tusitala,
  The King that is gone, and the friend that's dead!

"Out of the silence if men may hear,
  Into the silence faint and clear,
    The voice may pierce of loving kindness,
  And leal remembrance may yet be dear."

A few more of the poems inspired by Omar Khayyám may appropriately bring this appendix to a conclusion. And first Mathilde Blind's graceful quatrains from "Birds of Passage" (p. 72), entitled :—

ON READING THE RUBÁIYÁT OF OMAR KHAYYÁM IN A KENTISH ROSE GARDEN.

Mathilde Blind's quatrains

Beside a Dial in the leafy close,
Where every bush was burning with the Rose,
  With million roses falling flake by flake
Upon the lawn in fading summer snows:

I read the Persian Poet's rhyme of old,
Each thought a ruby in a ring of gold —
  Old thoughts so young, that, after all these years,
They're writ on every rose-leaf yet unrolled.

You may not know the secret tongue aright
The Sunbeams on their rosy tablets write;
  Only a poet may perchance translate
Those ruby-tinted hieroglyphs of light.

And then :—

ANDREW LANG TO OMAR KHAYYÁM.
(In his "Letters to Dead Authors.")

Wise Omar, do the Southern Breezes fling
Above your Grave, at ending of the Spring,
  The Snowdrift of the petals of the Rose,
The wild white Roses you were wont to sing?

Far in the South I know a Land divine,
And there is many a Saint and many a Shrine,
  And over all the shrines the Blossom blows
Of Roses that were dear to you as wine.

You were a Saint of unbelieving days,   Andrew
Liking your Life and happy in men's Praise;   Lang to
   Enough for you the Shade beneath the Bough,   Omar
Enough to watch the wild World go its Ways.   Khayyám

Dreadless and hopeless thou of Heaven or Hell,
Careless of Words thou hadst not Skill to spell,
   Content to know not all thou knowest now,
What's Death? Doth any Pitcher dread the Well?

The Pitchers we, whose Maker makes them ill,
Shall He torment them if they chance to spill?
   Nay, like the broken potsherds are we cast
Forth and forgotten, — and what will be will!

So still were we, before the Months began
That rounded us and shaped us into Man.
   So still we *shall* be, surely, at the last,
Dreamless, untouched of Blessing or of Ban!

Ah, strange it seems that this thy common thought —
How all things have been, ay, and shall be nought —
   Was ancient Wisdom in thine ancient East,
In those old Days when Senlac fight was fought,

Which gave our England for a captive Land
To pious Chiefs of a believing Band,
   A gift to the Believer from the Priest,
Tossed from the holy to the blood-red Hand!

Yea, thou wert singing when that Arrow clave
Through helm and brain of him who could not save
   His England, even of Harold Godwin's son;
The high tide murmurs by the Hero's grave!

Andrew Lang to Omar Khayyám

And *thou* wert wreathing Roses — who can tell? —
Or chanting for some girl that pleased thee well,
   Or satst at wine in Nashâpúr, when dun
The twilight veiled the field where Harold fell!

The salt Sea-waves above him rage and roam!
Along the white Walls of his guarded Home
   No Zephyr stirs the Rose, but o'er the wave
The wild Wind beats the Breakers into Foam!

And dear to him, as Roses were to thee,
Rings long the Roar of Onset of the Sea;
   The *Swan's Path* of his Fathers is his grave:
His sleep, methinks, is sound as thine can be.

His was the Age of Faith, when all the West
Looked to the Priest for torment or for rest;
   And thou wert living then, and didst not heed
The Saint who banned thee or the Saint who blessed!

Ages of Progress! These eight hundred years
Hath Europe shuddered with her hopes or fears,
   And now! — she listens in the wilderness
To *thee*, and half believeth what she hears!

Hadst *thou* THE SECRET? Ah, and who may tell?
'An hour we have,' thou saidst. 'Ah, waste it well!'
   An hour we have, and yet Eternity
Looms o'er us, and the thought of Heaven or Hell!

Nay, we can never be as wise as thou,
O idle singer 'neath the blossomed bough!
   Nay, and we cannot be content to die;
We cannot shirk the questions 'Where?' and
    'How?'

Ah, not from learned Peace and gay Content   Andrew
Shall we of England go the way he went —   Lang to
   The Singer of the Red Wine and the Rose —   Omar
Nay, otherwise than *his* our Day is spent!   Khayyám

Serene he dwelt in fragrant Nashâpûr,
But we must wander while the Stars endure,
   He knew THE SECRET: we have none that knows,
No Man so sure as Omar once was sure!

And earlier still are the late Christopher P. Cranch's quatrains, which appeared in the "Independent."

OMAR KHAYYÁM.

Reading in Omar till the thoughts that burned
Upon his pages seemed to be inurned
   Within me in a silent fire, my pen
By instinct to his flowing meter turned.

Vine-crowned free-thinker of thy Persian clime —
Brave bard, whose daring thought and mystic rhyme
   Through English filter trickles down to us
Out of the lost springs of an olden time —

Baffled by life's enigmas, like the crowd
Who strove before and since to see the cloud
   Lift from the mountain pinnacles of faith —
We honor still the doubts thou hast avowed;

And fain would round the half-truth of thy dream;
And fain let in, if so we might, a beam
   Of purer light through windows of the soul,
Dividing things that are from things that seem.

C. P. Cranch's quatrains

True, true, brave poet, in thy cloud involved,
The riddle of the world stood all unsolved;
   And we who boast our broader views still grope
Too oft like thee, though centuries have revolved.

Yet this we know. Thy symbol of the jar
Suits not our Western manhood, left to mar
   Or make, in part, the clay 'tis molded of;
And the soul's freedom is its fateful star.

Not like thy ball thrown from the player's hand,
Inert and passive on a yielding strand;
   Or, if a ball, the rock whence it rebounds
Proves that the ball some license may command.

But though thy mind, which measure Jove and Mars,
Lay fettered from the Unseen by bolts and bars
   Of circumstance, one truth thy spirit saw —
The mystery spanning life and earth and stars.

Dervish and threatening dogma were thy foes.
The question though unanswered still arose,
   And through the revel and the wine-cups still
The honest thought: "Who knows, but One — who knows?"

As I read again each fervent line
That smiles through sighs, and drips with fragrant wine —
   And Vedder's thoughtful Muse has graced the verse
With added jewels from the Artist's mine —

I read a larger meaning in the sage —
A modern comment on a far-off age;
   And take the truth, and leave the error out
That casts its light stain on the Asian page.

And last of all Theodore Watts's "East Anglian Echo-Chorus," which appeared in the "Athenæum."

TOAST TO OMAR KHAYYÁM.

CHORUS.

In this red wine, where Memory's eyes seem glowing
  Of days when wines were bright by Ouse and Cam,
And Norfolk's foaming nectar glittered, showing
What beard of gold John Barleycorn was growing.
We drink to thee whose law is nature's knowing,
        Omar Khayyám!

I.

Star-gazer, who canst read, when night is strowing
  Her scriptured orbs on Time's frail oriflamme,
  Nature's proud blazon: "Who shall bless or damn?
Life, Death, and Doom are all of my bestowing!"

CHORUS.

    Omar Khayyám!

II.

Master whose stream of balm and music, flowing
  Through Persian gardens, widened till it swam —
  A fragrant tide no bank of time shall dam —
Through Suffolk meads where gorse and may were blowing.

CHORUS.

    Omar Khayyám!

III.

<small>Watts's Echo-Chorus</small>

Who blent thy song with sound of cattle lowing,
   And caw of rooks that perch on ewe and ram,
   And hymn of lark, and bleat of orphan lamb,
And swish of scythe in Bredfield's dewy mowing?

CHORUS.

Omar Khayyám!

IV.

'T was Fitz, "Old Fitz," whose knowledge, farther going
   Than lore of Omar, "Wisdom's starry Cham,"
   Made richer still thine opulent epigram:
Sowed seed from seed of thine immortal sowing.

CHORUS.

Omar Khayyám!

In this red wine, where Memory's eyes seem glowing
   Of days when wines were bright by Ouse and Cam,
And Norfolk's foaming nectar glittered, showing
What beard of gold John Barleycorn was growing,
We drink to thee whose lore is nature's knowing,
      Omar Khayyám!

APPENDIX LI.

The following quatrain, to which reference is made on page lxvii of the Introduction, appears in a slightly different form in the Bibliography, p. 469. There is also a variant of it under Darmesteter, on p. 516.

It is said that one evening as Omar was sitting with some friends a sudden wind sprang up and extinguished the candles, and in the confusion ensuing the jug of wine was broken and spilt; whereupon the poet immediately composed the irreverent Rubá'iy: —

Tu as brisé ma cruche de vin, mon Dieu! tu as ainsi fermé sur moi la porte de la joie, mon Dieu! tu as versé à terre mon vin limpide. Oh! (puisse ma bouche se remplir de terre!) serais-tu ivre, mon Dieu?   **Nicolas** (388)

Thou hast broken my wine-jug, O Lord, thou hast closed against me the door of delight, O Lord, thou hast spilt upon the earth my clear wine; earth be in my mouth unless thou art drunk, O Lord.   **McCarthy** (101)

Oh! Thou hast shattered to bits my jar of wine, my Lord!
Thou hast shut me out from the gladness that was mine, my Lord!
Thou hast spilt and scattered my wine upon the clay —
O dust in my mouth! if the drunkness be not Thine, my Lord!   **M. K.**

"According to the testimony of an old MS., according to Nicolas, the third line of this stanza ought to run thus:

'*I* drink the wine; 't is Thou who feel'st its power — '"

Bodenstedt
(II. 21)

Meinen Weinkrug hast Du mir zerschlagen, o Herr!
Der Wein floss in den Staub statt in den Magen,
   o Herr!
Die Pforte des Genusses hast Du mir verschlossen,
Ich blieb nüchtern: kannst Du das auch sagen,
   o Herr?

The legend runs that, after uttering this blasphemy, he chanced to look into the glass, and saw that his face had turned black as coal. Whereupon he composed another equally audacious, expressing his detestation of the doctrine of future punishment, to the effect that if the Almighty punished him for his sins, there would be no difference between them! [See Appendix XXXVI, Nicolas, 256, etc.]

And he more than once refers to the clemency of God in washing his face white, and erasing his evil record from the Black Book in which the Angel Sehel (al Sijil, or Sijjil) keeps an account of each man's sins:—

Nicolas
(275)

Ta miséricorde m'étant acquise, je n'ai point peur du péché. Avec les provisions que tu possèdes, je n'ai pas à m'inquiéter des embarras du voyage. Ta bienveillance rendant mon visage blanc, du livre noir je n'ai aucune crainte.

McCarthy
(244)

Seeing that thy mercy is vouchsafed to me, I have no fear for my iniquities; since thou possessest all goodness, I need not be anxious to provide myself for the journey. The leaves of the book have no terrors for me, since thy clemency has cleared my countenance.

Sure of Thy grace, for sins why need I fear? Whinfield
How can the pilgrim faint whilst Thou art near? (318)
  On the last day Thy grace will wash me white,
And make my "black record" to disappear.

Deine Barmherzigkeit macht keine Furcht in mir Bodenstedt
    rege, (l. 15)
Deine Fürsorge schützt mich vor Mangel allerwege,
Deine Gnade macht weiss mein Angesicht,
Und vor dem schwarzen Buche erschreck' ich nicht.

APPENDIX LII.

OMAR AND HIS OPPONENTS.

It was inevitable that with all the stir which Omar has made in the modern world of thought and literature, there should be some who could see nothing in him; who would regard his Rubáiyát, especially in the narrower limits of FitzGerald's paraphrase, as dangerous and heretical. There would still remain some of the *odium theologicum* which, as we have seen, did not cease to pursue him during his life, and while his memory was still green. To many also, out of sheer opposition, so characteristic of certain orders of mind, the popularity of Omar would savor of affectation: on hearing so much of his greatness, they would echo Horace's words: — *The opposition to Omar's philosophy*

    "Persicos odi, puer, apparatus."

Some expression of this has appeared; and I may be pardoned for quoting two or three anonymous poems which embody this cavilling spirit. It is rather remarkable that there is not more sarcastic or flippant reference to Omar and his philosophy:—

To Omar Khayyám.

A sarcastic appeal to Omar

Late from thy face the veil of darkness clears;
Thy name now rings forever in our ears;
 So that we wonder as we listen, how
We've done without thee this eight hundred years.

We wonder if thy critics bade thee take
Thy rhymes elsewhere, and hint that thou wouldst make
 A good vine-dresser, or might'st guide the plough;
And bid thee sing no more for pity's sake.

Thou hadst a secret, so our young men say,
World-weary youths who writhe and groan that they
 Were born to solve the "Where," the "How," but tell
Us nought besides of thy strange-titled lay.

Hadst thou of that red wine a famous brand,
Sinless of aching head or trembling hand?
 Couldst thou unpricked a rosy wreath entwine?
Lies here the riddle, Omar, thou hadst planned?

What loss if thou hadst laid its answer bare!
One theme the less! one passion less to tear!
 And he who sips the monthly draught of rhyme
Will know that themes are getting somewhat rare.

Thou art a store-house for our rhymester crew.
They read thee not — that were too much to do —
  But cull thy telling bits and quote them free,
Till men believe that they are poets too.

For folk uncultured know not of thy song.
Thou art too high, too deep, perchance too long.
  But to the spouters of thy sample lines
They give high place the bardic ranks among.

And so these win a name. Wise Omar, say,
Old man, hadst thou a secret that would pay
  So well as this? The world is for the West,
And Eastern secrets now have had their day.

The second appeared in the "Saturday Review,"
and pretends to be from Omar's ghost to his new
translators.

RECENT RUBÁIYÁT.

Down in the Grave the dead Men drink no more,
Alas! nor e'er ajar is here a Door,
  And over-baked, my Brother, is the Clay,
Wherein the amber wine we used to pour!

Rubáiyát by Omar's ghost

Nay here, among the dusky Groves of Death,
There comes no Moon the Dusk that lighteneth,
  And here the Nightingale hath Naught to say,
And here the Rose hath lost her scented Breath!

So were the Blossom blowing on the Tree,
And now the Dust about the Roots are We,
  And seldom cometh now a kindly Soul
To drench the thirsty Lips of Thee and Me!

Rubáiyát by Omar's ghost

About the old Mahogany they sit,
Our Friends, and dream themselves the Mouth of Wit.
   Doth one remember us and spill the Bowl
For us beneath the Daisies? Out on It!

Alas! were We alive, and They were dead,
A kind Libation to their Dust I'd shed:
   We are the white, that were the purple Rose,
Their Burgundy might lend us of its red.

Suppose I sent them up a Telegram,
Much would they care for Omar, called Khayyám?
   Nay You, that might be more polite, you doze,
As I were boring you — perchance I am?

When once one gets the Hang of it, I think
That rhyming is as easy as to drink.
   Alas! give Me the Cup, and spare the Pen;
Alas! give me the Wine, and take the Ink!

Translating and translating me they go,
Philologists and Women, even so,
   Fitzgerald, Thou alone of later Men,
Who try the Trick, the Trick didst really know!

Omar in "Punch"

In "Punch" for Aug. 17, 1895, there were five mock Rubáiyát entitled "A Query. By Omar Khayyám." But the humor of them depended largely on the accompanying picture, and the travesty was merely of the

form, not of the matter of Omar. They referred to
an advertisement in "the Times" calling for "An Up-
and-down Girl; aged 16, English, strong." The first
stanza ran : —

"Tell me mysterious maiden, when and whence
  And where and wherefore and on what pretence,
    You 're ' up-and-down ' — this riddle rede I pray,
  And rid my bosom of a care immense!"

and the last : —

"What though I 've never met you in the throng,
  I 'm glad you 're English-born sixteen and strong;
    Life has its ups and downs (more downs than ups),
  And you 're a *new* sort — hence this idle song.

Omar in "The Philistine"

That very delightful "Magazine of Protest," "The Philistine," which, like Herakles in his cradle, began its career by choking the various serpents of modern Conceit and Decadentism, had a sarcastic reference to Omar in its fourth number (September, 1895). It says : "What we are coming to in poetry is always a fascinating theme. . . But what we are going away from is more satisfactory to contemplate. It is pleasant to think that Homer, the blind minstrel, and Omar, the tent maker, are fixed facts. They are the poles of verse — one standing for the heroic and romantic, self-unconscious and buoyant, the other for vampire introspection and fatalism which mistakes interior darkness for an eclipse of the universe."

In the same number occurred some mock quatrains by Mr. William McIntosh, managing editor of "The Buffalo News." They were entitled : —

The Rubaiyat of O'Mara Khayyan.

Erin (Iran?) Year of the Hegira 94—Via Brooklyn.

Wake! for the night that lets poor man forget
His daily toil is past, and in Care's net
   Another day is caught to gasp and fade;
Oh, but my weary bones are heavy yet!

Wake! son of kings that bears a hod on high,
And builds the world. The red sun mounts the sky
   And circles squares in the cot's every chink
And gilds ephemeral motes that whirl and die.

Wake! for the bearded goat devours the door!
And now the family pig forbears to snore,
   And from his trough sets up the Persian's cry—
"Eat! drink! To-morrow we shall be no more!"

Eat, drink and sleep! Aye, eat and sleep who can!
I work and ache. The beast outstrips the man;
   And when oblivion bids the sequence end,
Which shall we say has best filled nature's plan?

When on Gowanus' hills the whistle blows
What dreams are mine of Hafiz' wine-red rose?
   And when I drag my leaden feet toward home
No sensuous bulbul note woos to repose.

I envy the dull brute my hand shall slay.
He lifts no stolid eye above the clay.
   I, longing, on the cloud-banked verge discern
"Unborn To-morrow and dead Yesterday."

What is the Cup to lips that may not drain?
Or fleeting joy to lives conceived in pain?
   Toil and aspire is still the common lot,
Stumbling to rise and rising fall again.

And is this all? Shall skies no longer shine,
Or stars lure on to themes that seem divine?
   Ah, Maker of the Tents! is this thy hope —
To feed and grovel and to die like swine?

Rabelais and the bottle

Probably Rabelais never heard of the Persian poet, but the verses which Babbuc, the Priestess of the Holy Bottle, whispers in Panurge's ear, for him to repeat, sound almost like a travesty on Omar's worship of wine: —

> "Bottle! whose mysterious deep
>   Does ten thousand secrets keep,
>   With attentive ear I wait;
>   Ease my mind and speak my fate.
> Soul of joy like Bacchus we
> More than India gain by thee:
>   Truths unborn thy juice reveals
>   Which futurity conceals.
> Antidote to fraud and lies,
> Wine that mounts us to the skies,
>   May thy father Noah's brood
>   Like him drown but in thy flood."

La fist Babbuc, la noble pontife, Panurge besser et baiser la marge de la fontaine, puis le fist lever, et autour danser trois Ithymbons. Cela fait, luy commanda s'asseoir entre deux scelles, le cul à terre la préparées. Puis desploya son Livre rituel, et, luy soufflant en l'oreille gausche, le fist chanter une epilenie, comme s'ensuit : —

<pre>
                    O
                BOUTEILLE
                  PLEINE
                  TOUTE
               DE MISTERES,
             D'UNE   OREILLE
           JE   T'ESCOUTE;
          NE   DIFFERES,
        ET   LE   MOT   PROFERES
      AUQUEL   PEND   MON   CUEUR.
        EN LA TANT DIVINE LICQUEUR,
        QUI EST DEDANS TES FLANS RECLOSE,
      BACHUS, QUE FUT D'INDE VAINCQUEUR,
      TIENT   TOUTE   VERITÉ   ENCLOSE.
     VIN TANT DIVIN, LOING DE TOY EST FORCLOSE
      TOUTE   MENSONGE   ET   TOUT   TROMPERYE;
       EN JOYE SOIT L'AME DE NOÉ CLOSE,
       LEQUEL DE TOY NOUS FEIST LA TEMPERYE.
        SONNE LE BEAU MOT, JE T'EN PRYE,
         QUI ME DOIBT OSTER DE MISERES.
          AINSI NE SE PERDE UNE GOUTTE
              DE TOY, SOIT BLANCHE OU
                 SOIT VERMEILLE,
                   O   BOUTEILLE
                 PLEINE   TOUTE
                   DE MISTERES.
</pre>

Sancho Panza and the mole

And the Persian's celebration of the mole (*la mouche*, Pope's "Happy spot") as an accessory of female beauty finds a lovely echo in Don Quixote, where Sancho Panza, speaking of the beauty of Don Quixote's mistress, Dulcinea del Toboso, declares that it was enhanced by the mole which she had on her right lip:

"Nunca yo ví su fealdad, sino su hermosura, á la cual subia de punto y quilates un lunar que tenia sobre el labio derecho, á manera de bigote, con siete ú ocho cabellos rubios como hebras de oro, y largos de mas de un palmo."

Sancho, by the way, makes very effective use of the fine comparison of man to the figure on the chessboard: — *Sancho's comparison of the game of chess*

"'Brava comparacion!' dijo Sancho, 'aunque no tan nueva que yo no la haya oido muchas y diversas veces, como aquella del juego del ajédrez, que mientras dura el juego cada pieza tiene su particular oficio, y en acabándose el juego todas se mezclan, juntan y barajan, y dan con ellas en una bolsa, que es como dar con la vida en la sepultura.'" *Rubá'iy LXIX.*

APPENDIX LIII.

TRANSLATIONS FROM OMAR KHAYYAM, BY FRANK SILLER.

Mr. Frank Siller, of Milwaukee, is favorably known both in Germany and the United States as a poet. His translation of Longfellow's "Evangeline" into German hexameters very greatly pleased the old poet himself, and has, since its first publication in 1879, taken its place in German literature as a classic. It is

Frank Siller

used in the University of Berlin as the best version of that poem. Many other admirable translations from English into German, and from German into English verse, have proceeded from his pen, and a few years ago he collected into a volume a representative selection of his poetry under the title, "The Song of Manitoba ‖ and other ‖ Poems," ‖ which was published by the T. S. Gray Company of Milwaukee (1888). It is now, unfortunately, out of print.

The late Friedrich Bodenstedt, in the winter of 1880–81, both before and after his visit to California, visited Milwaukee, and Mr. Siller, at whose house he stayed, using his German explanation of the Persian original, as well as the MS. of his complete translation of the Rubáiyát, made an English version of a baker's dozen of them, which were published in "The Literary World" for February 26, 1881 (vol. xii, p. 71). The same also appear in Mr. Siller's volume of poems. He has been kind enough to copy these thirteen stanzas for me, and to permit me to reproduce them. The rubric number refers to Bodenstedt's version:—

X. 17
A potter near his modest cot
Was shaping many an urn and pot;
He took the clay for the earthen things
From beggars' feet and heads of kings.

V. 29
Know ye why the Cypress tree as freedom's tree is known?
Know ye why the Lily fair as freedom's flower is shown?
Hundred arms the Cypress has, yet never plunder seeks;
With ten well developed tongues, the Lily never speaks!

With mine own heart I am in constant strife, what   I. 2
    shall I do?
Remembrance of past errors blights my life, what shall
    I do?
  Though kindly Thou, O Lord, my sins forgivest,
Their memory still within my heart is rife, what shall
    I do?

Like wind flies Time 'tween life and death;   VIII. 90
Therefore, as long as thou hast breath,
Of care for two days hold thee free:
The day that was and is to be.

No fear have I of life nor death —   I. 3
That dreaded flight of soul and breath;
But not to do my duty here
And die — shall be my constant fear!

Attempt not to fathom the secrets of heaven,   IX. 18
But gratefully use what to thee is here given:
For none have returned from that realm of bliss,
To tell how those fared who have prayed much in this.

I doubt whether those who through every clime   VIII. 10
  Have wandered and sought, in peace and in strife,
For gold and for treasures, have ever found time
  To study the genuine value of life.

Many of our leading men are rotten cores in glittering   VIII. 12
    shells;
Wealth, position may be theirs, but in their hearts no
    comfort dwells;
So perverted are they oft that only those they can
    respect
Who, like them, for sordid causes all the higher aims
    neglect.

V. 44   To-morrow's fate, though thou be wise,
        Thou canst not tell nor yet surmise;
        Pass therefore not to-day in vain,
        For it will never come again!

I. 24   The Prophet's followers seek Kaba's shrine;
        Bells call the Christian host in prayer to join —
            Cross, rosary and pulpit will I praise,
        If they but prove safe guides to Truth Divine!

X. 5   The heart that has no power of self-denial
        Severely suffers, suffers many a trial;
        The unselfish heart feels bliss without alloy
        In causing others happiness and joy!

VIII. 9 The world will turn when we are earth
            As though we had not come nor gone;
        There was no lack before our birth,
            When we are gone there will be none!

II. 12 Friend! believe of dogmas only such as lift the soul
            to God:
        If thy neighbor should be needy, go, alleviate his lot;
        Shun deceit, be just and kind, and cause no fellow-
            being pain,
        Then wilt thou contentment here, hereafter life eternal
            gain!

APPENDIX LIV.*

Dr. Wollheim da Fonseca's "Literature of the Persians"

The fourth part of "Die Classiker aller Zeiten und Nationen," edited by Adolph Wolff, is entitled: Die National-Literatur ‖ sämtlicher Völker des Orients.‖ Eine prosaische und poetische Anthologie ‖ aus den besten Schriftstellern des gesamten Orients ‖ mit ‖ erläuternden, kritischen, literarischen und biographischen Notizen ‖ Herausgegeben ‖ von ‖ Dr. A. E. Wollheim, Chevalier da Fonseca, ‖ Berlin, 1873. ‖ Verlag von Gustav Hempel.

In the second volume of this immense work, four pages (206–209) are devoted to "Ômar Chijâm." After giving a few meagre and dubious details of his life, and speaking of his astronomical tables and Woepcke's edition of his algebra, of the Calcutta edition of his Rubáiyát of 1836, of Nicolas's edition, which he says was published under the title, "Les quatrains de Chyâm," "with almost ludicrous attempts to explain his verses in a mystical way," and of Fitzgerald's second edition, which he mistakenly says contained one hundred strophes, Wollheim da Fonseca copies nineteen of Von Hammer's tetrastichs, in order that the reader may be able to determine whether Omar Khayyám was a mystical or an Epicurean and Anacreontic poet. The rest of the article, which includes seventeen of Wollheim da Fonseca's own metrical translations, num-

---

* After page 543 had been already cast, I was enabled to get the great work of Wollheim da Fonseca from the Harvard University Library, and add as a final appendix his brief and interesting contribution to the literature of Omar Khayyám.

bered in accordance with the text of Nicolas, I copy *in extenso*, notes and all, since the original book is not easy of access: —

Ill arrangement and inaccuracy of Von Hammer's version

"Ich bemerke," says the Chevalier, "dass diese Hammer'sche Uebertragung die Strophen Omar's nicht nur ausserhalb ihrer Reihefolge auf Geratewohl herausgegriffen hat, sondern auch *sehr* frei ist, ja oft nicht einmal den Sinn wiedergiebt, und dem persischen Dichter seine poetische Eigentümlichkeit oder Deutlichkeit raubt. Ich lasse hier noch einige Strophen aus dem Anfang der Omar'schen Tetrastichen folgen:

(1) "Ein Zauberruf aus unser'm Weinhaus scholl:
Auf Schlemmer! Schwärmer![1] seyd vom Wein Ihr toll?
Erwacht! lasst uns das Mass der Becher füllen,
Bevor noch unser eignes Mass[2] ist voll!

(2) "O Du, vor allen Erdbewohnern auserlesen,
Bist werter mir als Aug' und Seel' gewesen!
Zwar Herrlich'res nichts als das Leben gibt's,
Doch Du bist's hundertfach, geliebtes Wesen![3]

[1] *charâbâti*, Besucher von Weinhäusern und Bordellen.

[2] hier ist im Text das Wort *peimânch*, welches sowol: Becher, wie Mass heisst, zweimal gebraucht. Ich habe die letztere Bedeutung gewählt, weil im Persischen die Redensart *peimânch pur schoden*, "das Mass vollseyn" so viel wie: dem Tode verfallen seyn, heisst. Der Vers lautet: *berchis kih pur kunim peimânch semei, sân pîsch keh pur kunend peimânci mâ*, wolauf, lasst uns den Becher mit Wein füllen, ehe man unser Mass füllt, d. h. ehe wir sterben.

[3] Der Französische Übersetzer bezieht dieses "geliebte Wesen" auf die Gottheit, was aber augenscheinlich eine erzwungene und falsche Deutung ist, wie die folgende Strophe, die sich offenbar auf die bezieht, beweist.

"Wer führte Dich zu uns berauscht heut Nacht? (3)
Wer hat entschleiert Dich hierher[1] gebracht?
 Hat ihm, der fern von Dir im Feuer brannte,
Dich Jemand zugeführt wie Sturmesmacht?[2]

"Die Zeit ist nur ein kurz Karwânserai,[3] (4)
Versuchung sint und Kummer stets dabei;
 Nicht ward der Rätsel Lösung uns gegeben;
Wir gehn — im Herzen Sorgen vielerlei.

"Erfüll'[4] ein wünschend Wort das uns entfuhr, (5)
Sonst schweig' und lass' uns ziehn auf Gottes Spur;[5]
 Wir gehen g'rad, doch Deine Blicke schielen,
D'rum heil' Dein Augenpar, und lass' uns nur!

"Auf! komm! das Herz zu stillen,[6] magst Du sagen (6)
Die Lösung *einer* nur der Ratselfragen!
 Sonst bring' zum Trunk uns einen Krug mit Wein,
Eh Krüg' aus unsern Staub zu drehn sie wagen.

---

[1] wörtlich: "in diese Einöde" (*bedin descht*); die Taverne wird oft so genannt, vgl. weiter unten Strophe 19.

[2] Der Sinn ist: hat Dich Jemand mir, der ich schon in Deiner Abwesenheit glühte, wie ein Wind zugeführt, und so das Feuer noch heftiger angefacht?

[3] *in dehr keh bûd mu-ldati mensili mâ*, diese Zeit (oder Welt) ist für uns nur eine Zeit lang (ein augenblickliches) ein Karwân-Serai; *mensil* bedeutet auch Poststation, ein Ziel und ein Tagereise.

[4] der Dichter redet hier mit den Worten *ei châdschch*, einen pedantischen Lehrer oder Prediger an, den er verspottet.

[5] *kâri chodâ*, Beschäftigung mit Gott, gottgefälliges Thun.

[6] *berâi dili mâ*, für unser Herz, zum Besten unserer Herzen.

(7) "Wenn ich gestorben bin, wascht mich mit Wein [1]
Von Wein und Kelch singt mir in's Grab hinein.[2]
Und wollt Ihr mich zum Auferstehungstage,
So sucht im Staub der Schenke mein Gebein!

(8) "Die Bürgschaft leistet Niemand für das Morgen,
Befrei' Dein Herz darum von schwarzen Sorgen!
Leer', Mond, den Glanzkelch d'rum! Nie sieht der Mond
Und mehr, ob er nun scheint, ob er verborgen.[3]

(9) "Der Liebende sei trunken stets und toll,
Von Wahnwitz sei er und von Schande voll![4]
Bei klarem Sinn geniessen wir nur Kummer;
Sind wir berauscht, dann komm', was kommen soll!

[1] statt mit dem Wasser, mit welchem die Leichen gewaschen werden.

[2] *telqin sescheráb u dschám gûjid merâ*, als Belehrung sprecht mir (nämlich statt der Totengebete) von Wein und Becher.

[3] wörtlich: trinke Wein aus hellem Kelche, o Mond! (d. h. hier die Geliebte, deren Antlitz wie bei allen orientalischen Dichtern diesem Gestirne verglichen wird.) denn der Mond (d. h. der am Himmel) wird vielmals sich drehen und uns nicht mehr finden — *mei nûsch benfirbádch ai máh kih mâh biçjár begerded u nijábed mará*.

[4] *âschiq hemeh çâlch mest u scheidâ bádâ, diwânch u schûrideh uruçwâ (ruçijáh?) bádâ*; der Liebende möge das ganze Jahr hindurch betrunken und verrückt (dumm), er möge toll und (vor Liebe) wahnsinnig und ehrlos (verbrecherisch, einen schlechten Ruf habend) seyn.

"So viel will Wein ich trinken, dass sein Duft, (14)
  Werd' ich zu Staub, vom Staub steigt in die Luft,
    Und dass vom Weindunst tiefberauscht, die Trunk-
      nen
  Auf meinem Staub tot sinken in die Gruft.

"Erstrebst Du etwas, suche einen Nützer, (15)
  Bist im Besitz Du, suche einen Schützer [1]
    Ein Herz wiegt hundert Lehm- und Wasserkâba's,
  Was soll die Kâba? such' ein Herz als Stützer! [2]

"Ich, Sänger, Wein der wüste Raum — Gewand, (19)
  Pokal, Herz, Seel' weihn wir dem Wein als Pfand; [3]
    Der Gnadenhoffnung und der Straffurcht ledig,
  Was sind uns Erde, Wasser, Wind und Brand?

---

[1] *der kôi nijâs her derilâ derjâb, der kôi hus'ûr muqbilirâ derjâb*, wörtlich: in dem Gebiet des Bittens (der Bedürftigkeit) suche jedes Herz (nämlich: zu gewinnen); im Gebiete des Gekommenseyns (d. h. der Ruhe, der Behäbigkeit, wenn man in den Besitz der Erbetenen gelangt ist) suche einen Begünstigenden (zu finden).

[2] *kâba tscheh rewî, berew delirâ derjâb*, was soll der Weg zur Kâba? (der bekannte Tempel zu Mekka) komm und suche ein Herz.

[3] *mâjim umei umuthrib wer în gundschi charâb, dschân u dil u dschâm u dschâmeh der rehini scherâb*, wir (oft poetisch statt: ich) und Wein und Sänger (oder: Tänzer) und dieser verwüstete Raum, wir (geben hin) als Pfand für den Wein die Seele und das Herz und den Becher und das Gewand, d. h. wir alle in diesem jetz leeren Raum der Schenke oder der Erde, opfern Alles für den Wein. Der französische Herausgeber übersetzt: *ce trésor en ruine*, indem er statt *gundsch* "Raum, Platz, Ort" *gendsch* "geheimer Schatz" liest.

(22) " Ein, zwei, drei Tage — und das Leben flieht,
Dem Winde gleich, der durch die Wüste zieht.
  Weg, Gram! Zwei Tage ja geniess' ich nimmer:
Den der entflohn, und den man noch nicht sieht!¹

(24) " Da meiner Jugend noch das Heut geweiht ist,
Trink' Wein ich, weil das meine Seligkeit ist;
  Gut ist er, ob Ihr ihn gleich herbe schimpft.
" Herb" nur, weil er wie meine Lebenszeit ist.²

(28) " Der Krug hier ist, gleich mir, in Liebe bangend,
Nach einer Schönen Locken heiss verlangend;
  Der Henkel, den an seinem Hals Du schaust,
Ist eine Hand, der Freundinn Hals umfangend.

(38) " Wer einem Becher schöne Form verlieh
Ihn zu zerbrechen wünschet er wol nie;—
  So schöne Häupter, Beine, Füss' und Hände,³
Wess Liebe schuf, wess Hass zerstörte sie?

---

¹ *rûsî kih niâmedest rûsî kih gudsescht*, den einen Tag, der (noch) nicht gekommen ist und den einen Tag, der (schon) vorüber ist.

² *üibesch mekunid es ânkch telch est, chôsch est; telch est ânkch sindegânî men est*, thut ihm keinen Schimpf an, dass er herbe (bitter) sei; er ist bitter, weil er (wie) mein Leben (d. h. bitter) ist.

³ *kef*, welches ich hier durch " Füsse" übersetzt habe, heisst eigentlich: " die innere Fläche der Hand, die untere Fläche des Fusses; die Fusssohle." Dass dies Wort hier für Fuss steht, beweist das folgende " *u dest*, und Hand."

" Lenztulpengleich greif' zum Pokal geschwind,[1]
Kredenzt ihn Dir ein tulpenwangig Kind;
Trink fröhlich Wein! denn dieser blaue Himmel
Kann plötzlich Dich hinschmettern, wie ein Wind."[2]

(40)

[1] *tschûn lâleh benewrûs qadeh gîr bedest*, " wie die Tulpe am Newrus (das persische Neujahr, welches mit dem Frühling anfängt) ergreife den Pokal mit der Hand." Der Tulpenkelch wird sehr häufig von den orientalischen Dichtern seiner Form wegen mit einem Becher verglichen.

[2] *tscheri kebûd nâgâh terâ tschû bâd girdâned pest*, urplötzlich wie ein Wind zerschmettert. Dich (oder : " verdreht Deine Achse." denn *gerdaniden* heisst : " etwas verändern, umdrehen, verwandeln in etwas, zu etwas umschaffen, und *pest* bedeutet sowol " niedrig, elend, zerschmettert " wie auch : " die Achse ;" Beides gibt hier einen passenden Sinn) das blaue Himmelsgewölbe ; *tschereh* heisst die Himmelskugel mit ihrer kreisförmigen Bewegung, oder überhaupt jedes Ding, welches sich in einem Kreise dreht, und bedeutet hier das Kreisen der Himmelskörper. welche, nach der Meinung der Perser, durch ihre Bewegung das Schicksal der Menschen bestimmen.

APPENDIX LV.

COMPARATIVE TABLE

Showing the number-relationship of the FITZGERALD *versions of the* Rubáiyát, *together with those of* NICOLAS, MCCARTHY, WHINFIELD, BODENSTEDT, GRAF VON SCHACK, KERNEY, *and the translator of the* "Gulshani-Ráz."

In the case of MCCARTHY's version the page and number on the page are given. In any case when it is desired to find the page of a MCCARTHY Rubá'iy (there being three to a page, except on page i, where there are only two), add one and divide by three. This locates it approximately.

FitzGerald, Eds. III., IV., V., 1872, 1879, 1889.	FitzGerald, Ed. I., 1859.	FitzGerald, Ed. II., 1868.	Nicolas, 1867.	McCarthy, 1879.	McCarthy, Page and No.	Whinfield, 1883.	Whinfield, 1882.	Garner, 1888.	Bodenstedt, 1881.	Graf von Schack, 1878.	1887.		
i.	i.	i.	...	...	lxii. 1	233	...	Ms.	ix. 34	...	1	...	
ii.	ii.	ii.	...	183	cxl. 3	1	...	i. 34	x. 1	139	2	M. K.	
iii.	iii.	iii.	426	419	xxxi. 2	463	...	i. 14	vi. 2	224	...	...	
iv.	iv.	iv.	186	91	...	201	...	...	...	...	...	...	
v.	v.	v.	...	...	...	133	...	...	...	...	...	...	
vi.	vi.	vi.	...	...	...	174	94	i. 3	viii. 23	284	6	M. K.	
vii.	vii.	vii.	153	247	lxxxiii. 2	81	73	i. 21	x. 4	214	...	M. K.	
viii.	viii.	viii.	79	167	lvi. 3	134	...	...	vii. 15	6	...	M. K.	
ix.	ix.	ix.	105	148	l. 2	414	235	...	v. 38	82	...	M. K.	
x.	x.	x.	370	463	clv. 2	455	234	i. 8	x. 16	...	...	M. K.	
xi.	xi.	xi.	416	390	cxxxi. 1	452	39	i. 20	ix. 59	125	...	M. K.	
xii.	xii.	xii.	413	449	cl. 3	84	61	iii. 6	...	151	...	M. K.	
xiii.	xiii.	xiii.	82	177	lx. 1	94	189	...	...	245	...	VON H.	
xiv.	...	xv.	92	314	cv. 3	352	95	i. 33	vi. 5	...	...	VON H.	
xv.	xiii.	xvi.	...	4	ii. 2	175	...	...	...	...	...	...	
xvi.	xiv.	xviii.	156	277	xciii. 2	243	34	vii. 2	viii. 5	48	...	M. K.	
xvii.	xv.	xviii.	67	140	xlvii. 3	70	35	i. 10	viii. 6	199	...	M. K.	
xviii.	xvi.	xix.	69	151	li. 2	72	58	...	...	101	...	M. K.	
xix.	xviii.	xxiv.	...	...	...	104	31	i. 5	vi. 24	84	...	M. K.	
xx.	xix.	xxv.	59	123	xiii. 1	62	167	v. 7	viii. 35	308	...	M. K.	
xxi.	xx.	xxi.	269	194	lxv. 3	312	...	i. 17	...	300	...	M. K.	
xxii.	xxi.	xxiii.	70	156	liii. 1	219	205	iii. 3	viii. 92	50	...	M. K.	
xxiii.	xxiii.	xxvi.	348	353	cxx. 2	73	198	...	viii. 58	252	...	M. K.	
xxiv.	xxiv.	xxvii.	337	434	cxlv. 3	399	82	...	viii. 53	8	...	M. K.	
xxv.	xxv.	xxix.	120	252	lxxxv. 1	376	141	...	iv. 3	...	...	M. K.	
xxvi.	...	xxix.	225	40	xiv. 2	147	185	...	v. 18	143	...	M. K.	
xxvii.	xxviii.	xxxi.	132	211	lxxi. 2	264	...	...	iii. 13	...	...	M. K.	
xxviii.	...	...	...	...	...	353	...	...	...	...	...	...	
xxix.	xxix.	xxxii.	22	51	xviii. 1	26	12	i. 24	viii. 90	113	11	M. K.	

...	...	...	...	...	VON H.	...	...	...	...	...	VON H.
...	...	...	...	M. K.	...	...	...	...	...	...	M. K.
...	...	...	...	{146 12}	...	...	...	22	...	...	{21 19}
...	...	190 235	5	4	87 23	79	59 200 296 276	...	172 23	153	187	...	41 117 07 315 162
viii. 3	iii. 11	i. 12	viii. 44	iii. 3 x. 9 viii. 7 ix. 83 ix. 48 ix. 88 iv. 2	viii. 28	viii. 94 viii. 13 viii. 9 ix. 66 i. 38	v. 19 j. 8 iv. 2 ix. 97	iv. 8	v. 4 viii. 46 x. 80	i. 18	iv. 14 x. 40
...	...	ix. 3 xi.	...	vii. 5 viii. 9 vii. 7	...	v. 11	xi. 8 vi. 10 iv. 3 viii. 10	...	ix. 2	vi. 5 i. 26	viii. 4	i. 27	ii. 7 vi. 8
64 80 161 203 136	149	17 137 110	...	28 139 218	37 90 83	...	10	213 244 28	166	105	...	60 141 116
{110 145} 303 389 271 247	{274 431} 12 252 493 203	44 332 52 251 {436 187}	82 161 150 136	24	416 475 52 453 196	181 386 370 194	...	265	107 258 209
lxiii. 3	xxii. 1 i. 2 xxii. 2 lxxvi. 2	cxvi. 1	xxv. 2 lxxxiii. 3 xci. 1 lvii. 3	xxxv. 2 xcv. 2 xxiv. 1	xc. 2	lvii. 2 lxxix. 2 lxxxi. 1 lvi. 1 xvi. 2	clv. 1 cxvi. 2 xxiv. 1 cx. 2 vii. 3 xciii. 1.	vi. 3. cxxi. 1 xcvii. 2	xxix. 1. xc. 1	liv. 2	...
188	...	2 63 226	345	73 245 270 170 102 283 69	268	169 235 210 165 46	462 346 69 328 20 276 17 360 289 119	84 267	160	...
117	...	232 204	389	28 211 119 188 40 294 49	171	80 137 123 106 20	73 443 49 414 181 165 42 329 179	226 169	217 464
xxxiii.	xxxiv. xxxv. xxxvi. xxxvii.	xxxviii.	xxxix. xl. xli. xlii. xliii. liv. xlv. xlvi.	lxix.	lxx. lxvii. lxviii. xlix.	l. li. lii. liii. liv. lvi. lv. lvii. lviii. lix.	lx. lxi. lxii. lxiii. lxiv.	lxvi. lxvii. lxviii.
xxx.	xxxi. xxxii. .... xxxiii. xxxiv.	xxxv. xxxvi.	.... xlvii. xlviii.	Preface.	Preface.	.... xxxviii. .... xxxix. xl. xli. xxxvii. xliii. xliv.	xxvi.	....
xxx.	xxxi. xxxii. xxxiii. xxxiv.	xxxv.	xxxvi. xxxvii. xxxviii. xxxix. xl. xli. xlii. xliii.	xliv.	xlv. xlvi. xlvii. xlviii. xlix.	l. li. lii. liii. liv. lv. lvi. lvii. lviii. lix.	lx. lxi. lxii. lxiii. lxiv.	lxv.

	FitzGerald, Eds. III., IV., V., 1872, 1879, 1889.	FitzGerald, Ed. I., 1859.	FitzGerald, Ed. II., 1868.	Nicolas, 1867.	McCarthy, 1879.	McCarthy, Page and No.	Whinfield, 1883.	Whinfield, 1883.	Garner, 1888.	Bodenstedt, 1881.	Graf von Schack, 1878.	1887.		
	lxvi.	....	lxxi.	....	....	xxxiii. 3	114	68	....	i. 31	335	15	....	....
	lxvii.	xlvi.	lxxii.	90	98	lxxvii. 3	92	....	vii. 12	iii. 10	269	....	M. K.	....
	lxviii.	xlix.	lxxiii.	267	230	xxi. 2	310	165	ix. 4	x. 39	1	....	M. K.	G. DE T
	lxix.	l.	lxxiv.	231	61	....	270	148	iv. 2	v. 19	144	....	....	....
	lxx.	li.	lxxv.	....	....	liv. 1	401	204	MS.	v. 17	....	....	....	....
	lxxi.	lii.	lxxvi.	216	159	xiv. 1	257	140	iv. 4	v. 8	191	....	M. K.	VON H.
	lxxii.	liii.	lxxviii.	95	39	xxix. 3	76	45	x. 11	ix. 62	83	....	....	....
	lxxiii.	....	lxxix.	31	86	lxi. 1	35	20	....	v. 1	....	....	....	....
	lxxiv.	liv.	lxxx.	85	180	lxxix. 1	87	40	viii. 7	ix. 11	207	....	....	....
	lxxv.	lv.	lxxxi.	110	219	iii. 1	140	77	iv. 1	vii. 2	264	....	M. K.	VON H.
	lxxvi.	lvi.	lxxxii.	182	6	xxx. 1	197	107	iv. 5	i. 17	287	....	....	....
	lxxvii.	....	lxxxiii.	222	87	xxxviii. 2	262	142	ii. 3	v. 10	17	....	....	....
	lxxviii.	....	lxxxiv.	....	112	....	100	46	iv. 3	i. 14	213	....	....	....
	lxxix.	lvii.	lxxxv.	99	189	lxiv. 1	93	42	....	ii. 22	288	....	....	....
	lxxx.	lviii.	lxxxvi.	91	296	xcix. 3	432	224	ii. 1	i. 20	168	....	M. K.	....
	lxxxi.	lix.	lxxxvii.	390	49	xvii. 2	276	152	viii. 3	x. 17	....	....	....	....
	lxxxii.	....	lxxxviii.	236	393	cxxxii. 1	466	240	....	viii. 59	49	....	....	....
	lxxxiii.	....	lxxxix.	431	....	....	....	....	viii. 8	iii. 5	....	....	....	....
	lxxxiv.	lxi.	xc.	363	100	cxxiii. 1	391	22	....	....	6	....	....	....
	lxxxv.	lxii.	xci.	38	....	xxxiv. 2	42	242	....	ii. 6	61	....	....	....
	lxxxvi.	lxiii.	xcii.	349	344	cxv. 3	{471 126}	52	xi. 4	iv. 16	291	....	....	....
	lxxxvii.	....	xciii.	436	115	xxxix. 2	283	156	....	ii. 3	226	....	....	....
	lxxxviii.	lx.	xciv.	243	281	xcii. 3	193	....	....	vii. 6	75	....	M. K.	....
	lxxxix.	lxiv.	xcv.	178	125	xlii. 3	330	175	....	....	309	....	....	....
	xc.	lxv.	xcvi.	290	47	xvi. 3	218	76	v. 10	ix. 67	306	....	....	....
	xci.	lxvi.	xcvii.	94	154	lii. 2	139	....	i. 16	ix. 3	275	....	M. K.	....
	xcii.	lxvii.	xcviii.	109	27	xi. 1	17	....	....	ix. 41	98	....	....	....
	xciii.	lxix.	c.	14	....	....	....	....	....	....	....	....	M. K.	....
	....	....	ci.	142	287	xcvi. 3	165	....	....	ix. 74	279	....	....	....

xciv.	lxx.	cii.	{162, 133}	v. 1	425	....	....	....	278	....	....
xcv.	lxxi.	ciii.	{12, 113, 255}	lxxxvi. 1 / xxxviii. 3	....	....	....	....	....	....	M. K.
xcvi.	lxxii.	civ.	463	....	208	115	vi. 14	ix. 3	62	....	M. K.
xcvii.	....	cv.	128	lxxv. 2	155	86	vii. 6	vi. 1	{182, 170}	....	M. K.
xcviii.	....	cvi.	223	cxlvii. 3	412	229	....	v. 36	238	....	M. K.
xcix.	lxxiii.	cvii.	400	cl. 2	486	251	ii. 8.	x. 31	11	....	M. K.
c.	lxxiv.	cviii.	457	cxxvii. 1	379	200	v. 8.	v. 25	96	3	M. K.
ci.	lxxv.	cix.	340	iv. 1	7	2	....	....	203	....	M. K.
		cx.	8	xxxv. 1	234	112	....	ix. 5	102		
		xiv.	192	clvi. 1	411	....	....	viii. 68	189		
		xx.	366	cxxii. 2	392	206	i. 9	viii. 60	176		
		lxv.	350	xliv. 1	67	33	i. 19	ii. 11	28		
		cvii.	64	xix. 1	29	14		v. 43			
			25	54							

NOTE.— Rubáiyát xxxvii and xlv of Ed. I. are not found in the body of the later editions. Rubáiyát xiv, xx, xxviii, xliv, lxv, lxxvii, lxxxvi, xc, xcix, and cvii of Ed. II. are not found in the text of later editions.

INDEX.

(The transliteration of Persian and Arabic words varies in the practice of various scholars. Thus Omar Khayyám may be found spelled in upwards of a dozen different ways. But where the spelling is obvious, no attempt is made, in the following index, to make distinctions, unless the initials differ. Some of the typical phrases and catch-words of FitzGerald's quatrains are introduced for the sake of facilitating ready reference. The references to FitzGerald, Nicolas, McCarthy, Bodenstedt, and Graf von Schack, do not comprise the quotations from their several versions included in the body of the book.)

ABBAS the Great, xxix.
Abû Nasr, ci.
Abu Saïd, 290, 291, 436, 515.
"Academy," liv, lxvii, lxxviii, 268, 541.
Addison (Vision of Mirza), xi, lvi.
Adhèm, 291.
Æschylus, lxviii.
Afrasiab, 290, 293.
"After wrath," 164.
"Agamemnon" (Fitzgerald's translation), lvii, 496.
Agnosticism, cxxiii.
Alchemist, the sovereign, clxix, 114.
Aldrich, Thomas Bailey, 539.
Alexander the Great, 216, 471.
Algebra of Omar, cxxxviii, 457, 458, 462, 463, 490.
Alif, clxvii, 98.
Al-Khayyám. *See* Omar Khayyám.
Allah's secrets, 141.
Allen, Archdeacon, xxxiv, xxxv.
Allen, Grant, quatrain, 515.
Alp Arslan, cxxxiii, cxxxv, 425.
Amir Muizi, cii.
Anakreon, cxxiii, cxxix, 214, 419, 530.
"Angel of the darker Drink," xc, clxvi, 86.
"Angel Shape," clxix, 112, 282.
"Annihilation's Waste," clxvii, 96.

Antoninus, cxvii.
Anvári Soheili, 330.
Aristophanes, quoted, 359.
Aristotle, xviii, 217, 218.
Arnold, Matthew, cxxv, 423. 489, 490.
Artisan, the heavenly (Architect of heaven), 266, 402.
Assassin, origin of the word, cxxxvi.
Astrology, 317.
"Athenæum, The," xxxvi, l, 498, 546.
"Atlantic Monthly," 539.
Attâr, xiv, lxvi, lxxxiv, cxxii, cxxxvii, cxxxix, clv, 67, 217, 236, 238, 256, 270, 551.
"Aureate earth," xxxii, clx, 30.
Aurelius, Marcus, lxiv.
Austin, Willard, 542.
Avicenna, cvi, 492.
Ayaz, 327.
Azrael, 87.
Azrael's talons, 427.

BAGDAD, xx, xxix, 460.
Bahnsen, Julius, 527.
Bahrám, king, xxx, clxi, 34, 36, 217, 234, 236.
Balkh, xx, 17.
Ball, the, clxxii, 136.

"Balm of Life," clxx, 120.
Bang (Bhang), 233.
Barb. Hofrat von, lxxv, 484.
Barbauld, Mrs., cxxvi.
Barbier de Meynard, cxxx.
"Barren Reason," clxviii, 106.
Barton, Bernard, lv.
Base metal, clxxiii, 114, 146, 287, 373, 421.
"Baser Earth," cxiv, clxxiv, 158.
Basselin, Oliver, cli, 214, 503.
Ben Sabbáh, cxxxiv.
Berlin, Omar MSS. at, 439.
Bibelot Edition of Fitzgerald, 507, 533.
Binning, Mr., quoted, 213, 235.
Bion, quoted, 274, 501.
Bird of Joy, xxxi, cxi, 186, 501; of Time, clviii, 14.
Bird-Parliament, 129, 217, 236, 238, 256, 270, 551.
Blacken'd Face of Man, xcviii, cxiv, 158, 340, 420, 435, 469, 516, 562.
Blake, Swinburne's Essay on, cxxv.
Blasphemy of the wine, 301.
Blind, Mathilde, quatrains, 554.
Blochmann, Professor, 544.
"Blood of the vine," 262.
Bodenstedt, Friedrich (von), lxxiv, lxxv, lxxvi, cxl, cxlviii, 483–489, 493, 496, 528, 572.
Bodleian Library, x, clv.
Bodleian MSS., cxliv, cliii, clv.
Bodleian quatrain, xcix, cxlviii.
"Book of Fate," clxxviii, 190.
"Book of Youth," xxxi, cxi, clxxviii, 186, 501.
Borák (Muhammad's steed), 53.
Bou-Saïd. See Abu Saïd.
Bouzourdjméhr, 217.
"Bowl we call the Sky," 140, 317.
Bread (crust, Loaf of) xxv, xlviii, cxviii, cxxxviii, clix, 23, 24, 221, 222, 223, 394, 431.
Breath of 'Isa, lxxxvi, cxxi, cxxii, 8, 215, 431, 465.
Brevity of human life, 52, 122, 242, 246, 253, 272, 319, 427.
British Museum, Omar MSS. at, 439

Broken wine-jar, 469.
Browning, Robert, lvi, cxxix, 360.
Bulbul. See Nightingales.
Bull, the, 270, 329.
Burford Bridge, 552.
"Buried Ashes," clxxvii, 178.
Burton, Sir Richard, 525.

CADELL, Mrs., lxxxii; her article on the "True Omar Khayyám," lxxxiii–xcix, cxiv, 438.
Cæsar, clxii, 38, 217, 365, 471.
"Calcutta Review," xv, xvii, lxxxi, lxxxii, cxxxiv, cxliv, clii, 316, 424, 442, 535.
Calcutta text, cxlvi, clii, cliv, 236, 440, 484, 575.
Calderon's Six Dramas, xxxvii, l, lvii.
Calendar, cxxxviii, clxix, 110, 213, 422, 442, 541.
Calvinistic Creed, 318, 432.
Caravan (of life), xxiv, clxvii, 96.
Caravanserai (the world), clx, 34, 577.
Carlyle, Thomas, liii, liv, cv, 328, 359.
Catullus, lxx.
Caucasus, Mt., 208.
Cervantes, cxxx, 571.
Chadwick, John W., 537.
Charlemagne, 293.
Chehl-minar (Forty Columns), 235.
"Chequer-board of Nights and Days," clxxii, 134.
Chessmen, xxxi, 475, 480.
Cicero, cxliii.
"Clay Suburb," clxxi, 88.
"Clod of saturated Earth," clxv, 76.
Clodd, Edward, 509, 542, 544.
Cockcrow, clvii, 6, 209.
Comb quatrain, 395, 430.
"Common Earth," clxxv, 162.
Compass poem, 278.
Complaints of Fortune, 425, 426.
"Conscious Something," clxxiv, 152.
"Contemporary Review," 538.
Conway, Moncure D., 542, 544.
"Coo, coo, coo," clxi, 236–238, 428.
Cook, Captain, cxlii.
Costello, Louisa Stuart, 509.

Index.

"Couch of Earth," clxi, 46.
Cowell, Professor E. B., xv, xvi, xvii, xxxv, xxxviii, xxxix, xl, xli, xlii, xliii, xlvi, lviii, cxxvi, cxxxvi, cxlvi, clii, 67, 159, 214, 220, 316, 442, 535.
Cowell's article, xviii–xxxii, cxxxiv–cxliii.
Crabbe, the Rev. George, lviii.
Cranch, Christopher, quatrains to Omar Khayyám, 557
Creation's summary (man), 318.
Crescent, the little, clxxvi, 174.
"Critic, The," 541.
Crusaders, xxix.
Crust of bread, xxv, 23, 24, 221, 222, 223, 394, 431.
Cup, xxxii, xlviii, xc, xcvi, cvii, 16, 30, 42, 44, 78, 80, 82, 86, 97, 106, 112, 118, 120, 148, 259, 303, 317, 363, 397, 404, 480.
Cupbearer, xvii, xxiv, xxx, lxxxix, cii, civ, cxlv, clvi, 31, 60, 92, 104, 196, 220, 230, 242, 275, 287, 377, 466.
Cup of Jamshed, 11, 216, 217, 245.
Cynicism of Omar, xlix.
Cypress, 263–267, 268, 482, 572.
Cypress form, 73, 82, 266, 494.
"Cypress slender Minister of Wine," clxviii, 82.
Cyrus, 293.

Dante, lxviii, lxxiii, cii.
Darmesteter, James, lxxi, lxxii, 515, 522, 561.
"Daughter of the Vine," clxviii, 106, 277.
Daulatsah (Dewletschah), 440, 445.
David's strain, 116.
Dawn, cix, cxxi, 1, 5, 208, 209, 210, 375, 436, 545.
"Dawn's Left Hand," 4.
Death, xxxii, lxxii, lxxxix, cvii, cxiii, cxx, cliv, 44, 172, 176, 215, 311, 367, 387, 418, 422, 427, 437, 446, 500, 504, 573.
"Debt and not mercy," 154.
"Debt we never did contract," clxxiv, 154.
D'Herbelot, cxix, cxl, cxli.
Denham, Sir John, li.

"Desert of nothingness," 271.
Destiny, xcii, cxiii, clii, 110, 134, 138, 142, 146, 173, 190, 230, 251, 317, 392, 402, 420, 426, 433, 474, 526.
Dice box, 317.
Dies Iræ, 214.
Divan (Diwan) of Fate, 146.
"Divine high piping Péhlevi," clviii, 12.
Diviner Drink, the hope of, 120.
Divorce, clxviii, 106, 276, 356.
Djemshid. *See* Jamshýd.
Dondeauville, Duc de, xlii.
Donne, Dr., xxxii, 278.
Don Quixote, 570.
"Door of Darkness," lxxxv, clxiii, clxx, 54, 64, 124, 446, 501.
Dream quatrain, cxlvii, 445.
"Drowsy Worshipper," clvii, 4.
Drums, clix, 26, 218, 219, 224, 450.
Drunkenness, lxvi, 297, 305, 349, 374, 377, 422, 436, 447, 472, 476, 481, 578.
Dyer, Thistleton, 545.

"Earth's first Clay," clxxiii, 142.
Eastwick's "Gulistan," xxxix, 267.
Ecclesiastes, lii, lxvii, cxxiii, 243, 252, 275, 354, 380, 495, 538, 542.
Edwards, Amelia B., lxvii, 541.
Elias, 399.
Emerson, Ralph Waldo, xiii, cxix, 449, 451, 527, 537.
Empty Glass, the, 196.
Ennius, 67.
Epictetus, cxvii.
Epicurean Eclogue, xliv.
Epicureanism, xix, xxiii, cvi, cxlix, 430, 431, 494, 537.
Epicurus, lxviii, cxlix, cliii.
Esdras, cviii.
"Eternal chain," clxxii, 139.
"Eternal Sáki," the, clxvi, 92.
Ethé, Hermann, 439, 440, 516–520, 528.
"Euphranor," xxxvii, lvii.
Euripides, lxx.
"Evening Post," 496.
"Everlasting Penalties," clxxiv, 152.
Evil, origin of, 432.

"Fainting Traveller, the," clxxviii, 188.
Falcon (Sparrow Hawk), cxii, 55, 244.
"False and True," clxvii, 98.
False Dawn, clvii, 4, 207, 208, 525.
False money, 286.
Fate, xcii, xciii, clii, 110, 134, 138, 142, 146, 173, 190, 230, 251, 317, 392, 402, 420, 427, 433, 474, 526.
Feridun, 257, 292, 293, 507.
Ferrash (the dark), clxxi, 90, 421.
Ferukh Khan, xlii.
Firdusi, xv, lxxvii, lxxxiv, ci, cxliv, cxiv, 117, 537.
"Fire of Anguish," clxv, 78.
"First Morning of Creation, clxxiii, 142.
Fish and Moon. *See* "Mah to Mahi."
FitzGerald, ix, xvi, xxiv, xxxiii–liv, lxxii, lxxxii, lxxxiii, lxxxv, xc, xci, xcvii, xcviii, c, cxxiii, cxxv, 67, 214, 220, 270, 330.
FitzGerald's Latin Version, xliv.
FitzGerald's notes (in order), 3, 207, 213, 11, 13, 21, 27, 29, 234, 43, 63, 65, 256, 260, 87, xxiv, 270, 278, 115, 117, 316, 137, 147, 359, 175.
FitzGerald's translation of Omar, c, 496, 524, 536; Ed. I., xliii, xlv, xlvii–li, 467; Ed. II., xlvi, li, clvii–clxxix, 478; Ed. III., 479; Ed. IV., 483; Pirated Ed., 497.
"Flaming Foal," 148.
Flood of Anguish, the hoarse, 202.
Flute, the, 226, 232, 294, 437, 447, 456.
"Forbidden wine," 60.
Foreordination, 152.
Forgiveness, xcvii, cxiv, cxxvi, clxxiv, 14, 158, 182, 339, 413, 421, 433, 472, 480, 573.
Fountain in the Desert, clxxviii, 188.
"Fraser's Magazine," xvii, xliv, liii, lxxxii, 438, 535, 541.
French, Frederick W., lix, cxxxi.
Friedrich of Anhalt-Dessau, Prince, 462.
Friendship, 321.

Frivolous women, 314.
"Fruitful Grape," clxviii, 104.
Futility of human wisdom, 52, 242, 243, 244.
Futteh Ali, Shah of Persia, xii.
Future's Riddle, the, 195.

Gabriel, the angel, 291.
Garcin de Tassy, xl, xli, xlii, 133, 441, 464–467, 526, 535.
Garden, the, 10, 176, 194.
Garner, John Leslie, lxxiii, lxxix, lxxx, cxxvi, cxxxi, cxi, cxl, 3, 5, 7, 9, 12, 23, 25, 27, 31, 35, 37, 41, 44, 17, 49, 69, 73, 75, 77, 88, 91, 92, 97, 98, 101, 105, 107, 115, 118, 124, 130, 133, 135, 136, 139, 141, 144, 157, 161, 165, 169, 177, 179, 185, 186, 193, 195, 212, 215, 218, 219, 220, 237, 239, 258, 259, 269, 285, 300, 315, 318, 338, 362, 370, 371, 404, 483, 520, 521, 522, 528.
Gautier, Théophile, quoted, 362, 393, 470, 526, 535.
Gaveh, the blacksmith of Ispáhán, 292.
Gazna, 117.
Gibbon, cxxxviii.
Gibb's Rendering from Jalál, cxv.
Glory drown'd in a Shallow Cup, clxxvii, 180, 373.
Godwin, E. W., 522.
Goethe, lxviii, cii, cxxix, cxxx, 485, 539.
Gold, xxxii, clxix, clxxiv, 154, 480.
"Golden Eastern lay," lx.
"Golden grain," clx, 30.
Goodwin, Professor W. W., 67.
Gosse, Edmund W., 524, 545, 546, 552.
Gotha, Omar MSS. at, 440.
Grape (the fruitful), clxvii, clxix, 104, 112, 176.
Gray, Thomas, xix.
Greville, Lord Brooke, 434.
Grolier Edition of Fitzgerald, 499.
Groome, Francis Hindes, lxxiii, 534.
Guerchasp, 290.
"Guests Star-scatter'd on the Grass," clxxix, 196.
Gulistan, quoted, 267.

Index.   591

Gulshan-i-Râz, lxvi, lxxviii, 99, 107, 131, 525.
Guyon, Madame, 527.

Hâfiz, xv, xxiii, xxxix, xl, c, cxxiii, cxliv, clii, clv, 13, 99, 235, 260, 300, 301, 430, 517, 528, 530, 537.
Haji Abdu, 525.
"Hamlet," quoted, 365, 470.
Hammer, Joseph (Freiherr von H. Purgstall, xiv, xcix, c, ciii, cvi, cxlvi, cliii, 415–454, 495, 528, 575.
Haroun-al-Raschid, 393.
Harp, the, 220, 232, 261, 375, 456.
Hasan al Sabbáh, cxxxiii, cxxxiv, cxxxv, 422, 510.
Hashish, cxxxvii, 233.
Hatim Tai, clix, 20, 290, 502.
Heaven and hell, xci, civ, clxx, 26, 122, 128, 308, 309, 379, 382, 418, 425, 426, 433, 473, 502, 505, 518.
"Heaven's unopening Door," clxvii, 102.
Heft Kulzum (Seven Seas) 94, 441, 453, 483.
Heine, Heinrich, lxvii, cxx, cxxx, 489.
"He knows," clxxii, 136.
"Helpless pieces of the game," 134.
Hemzeh (Hamzah), 305.
Herald of the Morn, 3, 6, 7, 209.
Herbelot, D', xcix, cxl, cxli, 528.
Herbert, Freiherr von, xiv.
Hermit bard of Little Grange, 509.
Herrick, Robert, quoted, 540.
Heywood, John, quoted, 274.
Higginson, Thomas Wentworth, liv, cxxxi, 496.
Hinchcliff, T. W., liii, 535.
Homer, lxviii, 67.
"Hope of some Diviner Drink," clxx, 120.
Horace, xxiii, lxiii, lxviii, lxx, cxi, cxii, cxxix, 228, 388, 418, 436, 471, 508, 523, 530, 563.
Houris, xcv, 24, 27, 111, 221, 225, 287, 450, 514, 528.
Houtoum-Schindler, A., 541.
Hugo, Victor, quoted, 252.

Humor of Omar Khayyám, cxx, cxlix, 179, 294, 396, 397, 484.
Hungarian Version, lxxiv, cxxix, 290, 478, 528.
"Hunger stricken Ramazan," clxxiv, 160.
Hunt, Leigh, civ.
Huxley, Thomas H., 521.
Hyde, Dr. Thomas, ix, x, cxl, cxlvii, 441, 442.
Hypocrisy, clvi, 294, 343, 424, 511, 573.

Illusion, xxv, xxxi.
Imâm Muwaffiq (Mowaffak), cxix, cxxxiv, cxxxv.
"Imitation," quoted, 339.
"Impotent Pieces of the Game," clxxii.
"Independent, The," lxiv, 557.
Inevitableness of the Past, xxv, lxxxv, clxx, 122, 319.
"Infinite Pursuit," 104.
"Inverted Bowl we call the Sky," clxxii, 140. See also 404.
Invisible, the, clxxi, 128.
Irak, flute of, 229.
Iram' lute, 230.
Ismaîlians, Sect of the, cxxxvi.
"Isolation's fulness," cxvii.
Istakhr (Takht-i-Jamshed), 216.

Jalal ('Asad Bardi), cxv. cxxxviii, 349, 442.
Jalâlu'd-dîn (Jelaluddin), cvi, cxxxviii. clv.
Jâmi, xiii, xxiii, xxxviii, lxxvii, cxix, clv, 212.
Jamshid (Jamshed, Jamshýd), xxx, clix, clxi, 10, 11, 18, 34, 36, 213, 216, 220, 235, 245, 290, 527.
Ján-ibn-Ján, 235.
"J. E. C." See Mrs. Cadell.
Jenckes, Charles M. (designs), 534.
Jesus, lxxxvi, cxxi, cxxii, clviii, 8, 215, 431, 465.
"Jewel of Good deed," cxlviii.
Jihun, 130.
Job, lxviii, cxxvii, 353, 435, 495.
Johnson, Samuel, xl.

Jones, Sir William, xi, xxxix, lxx, 220.
Joseph (Yúsuf), 216, 217.
"Journal Asiatique," xli, 544.
Joy in solitude, 506.
Justice, cxix, 341.

KAABAS, cxvi, 334, 335, 428, 574, 579.
Kai-Kaius (Key-Kavous), 218, 219, 289, 290, 475.
Kai-Khosru, xlviii, clix, 3, 20, 216, 218, 220, 257, 258, 292, 293, 527.
Kai-Kobad, xxx, xlviii, clix, 18, 20, 216, 219, 289, 290, 507.
Kaunitz, Prince, xiv.
Keats, John, xxii, 234, 552.
Keble, John, lxviii.
Keene, H. G., lxxxi, cxxvi, 414, 438, 542.
Kemble, Fanny, xxxiv, lvi.
Kerney, Michael, lxxxi, lxxxii, 4, 16, 19, 21, 22, 24, 26, 30, 34, 36, 40, 48, 49, 50, 52, 54, 58, 71, 90, 106, 113, 124, 127, 132, 134, 138, 168, 173, 176, 184, 186, 190, 192, 194, 196, 210, 211, 222, 228, 268, 272, 282, 301, 308, 338, 339, 340, 353, 363, 376, 382, 390, 403, 509, 520, 562.
Khankah (monastery), cxviii.
Khurasan, ci.
Khusrau, Amír, 236.
Kitchen of Life, 281.
Koheleth, lii, lxvii, cxxiii, 243, 252, 275, 354, 380, 495, 527, 538.
Kouucer (Kausar), The, 121, 226.
Koran, lxxii, xcv, cvii, cxxxiv, cxli, 213, 276, 291, 305, 306, 348, 373, 384, 446, 469, 510.
Kuza-nama (Book of Pots), xlix, 160, 259, 354, 359.
Kwájah Nizámi, cxlii.

LAMB, Charles, xxxvi.
"Lamp amid the Darkness," 68.
Lamp of love, 309.
Landor, Walter Savage, 541.
Lang, Andrew, lxiii, 533, 544, 552, 554.
Lantern, xxxi, clxxi, 132, 315, 467.
"Last Dawn of Reckoning," clxxiii, 142.

"Last Harvest," clxxiii.
Latin Versions, xi, xlii, xliv, 214, 445.
"Leaves of life," clviii, 16.
Leopardi, lxviii, 521.
Life, brevity of, 52, 122, 242, 246, 253, 272, 319, 397, 407, 427.
Life's illusion, xxv, xxxi, 132, 316, 450.
"Life's leaden metal," clxix, 114, 146, 287, 373, 421.
Lion and lizard, clxi, 36.
Lion, the, clxi, 36, 269.
Liszt, cxxiii.
"Literary World," the, 572.
"Little Hour of Grace," clxvi.
"Logic absolute," clxix, 114.
Long Journey (Road), 124.
"Long Oblivion," clxxvi, 172.
"Loquacious Lot," 168.
Love Rubáiyát, lxxxvii, 387, 388, 389, 411, 419, 424, 494, 518.
Luckless Pots, 170.
Lucknow (Lakhnau) MS. cxlvi, 441.
Lucretius, xix, xxv, xxvi, xxvii, lxiii, lxviii, cxxiii, cxlviii. cliii, 214, 485, 495.
Lumsden, Sir Peter, 548, 549.
Lute, the, xxx, cx, 26, 82, 230, 405, 429, 473.
Luther, Martin, 527.

MCCARTHY, Justin Huntly, xlvi, lxxviii, lxxix, cxxv, cxxvi, cxxxix, cxli, cxlvii, 175, 497, 503, 522–532, 534, 544, 546.
McIntosh, Wm. (mock quatrains), 568.
"Macmillan's Magazine," 414, 542.
"Magic Shadow Shapes," 132.
Máhmúd the Great. cxxxiii, clix, clxix, 22, 116, 117, 300, 427.
"Mah to Mahi," clxvii, 100, 268, 270, 330.
Málik Shah, cii, cxxxiii, cxxxvii, cxxxviii, 425, 485.
"Man's forgiveness give and take," 158, 330.
Mantik-ut-tair (et Teyr, Bird-Parliament), xl, 129, 217, 236, 238, 256, 270, 551.
Manuscripts of Omar, lxxxiv, cxlvi, 423, 438.

Manuscript of Youth, cxi, 186.
Marlowe, Christopher, li.
Martial, 416, 530.
Mary (Miriam), 291.
"Master knot of human Fate," clxiv, 62.
"Master of the Show," clxxi, 132.
Meaning of Life, xxviii, xciv, 409, 473.
Meninski's Lexicon, xiv.
Mercy, 357, 409, 420, 422, 434, 435, 466, 474, 519.
Merdasht, Plain of, 235.
Meredith, George, 552.
Merv, lxiii, cxxxvii.
Meynard, C. Barbier de, cxxx.
"M. K." *See* Kerney, Michael.
Milton, John, xxiii, lxviii, 208.
"Mimkaf's" memorial verses, 507.
Mirkhond's History of the Assassins, cxxxiv, 400.
"Misbelieving and black Horde," clxix, 116.
Mohammed (Muhammad), xxiv, cxvii, clv, 111, 115, 121, 300, 303, 304, 305, 327, 328.
Mole of beauty, xx, xc, 38, 351, 449, 570, 571.
Mollahs, the, xcvi, 221, 277, 502.
"Moniteur, Le," 470.
Moon, xx, xxiv, xxxi, l, cx, clxvi, clxxvi, 16, 174, 175, 184, 194, 211, 270, 418, 472.
Moore, Thomas, lxvi, 207.
Moses, lxxxvi, clviii, 8, 213, 214, 291, 431, 465.
Mosher's Bibelot Ed. of Fitzgerald, 507, 533.
Mosque, the, civ, 150, 308, 332, 364, 428, 466, 473, 502.
"Moving Finger, The," clxxii, 138.
Mowaffak (Muwaffiq), Imâm, cxix, cxxxiv, cxxxv.
"Muezzin from the Tower of Darkness," clxii, 50.
Musæus, li.
Mustapha (Mostafa), 303, 305.
Mysticism, xxi, xxiii, xxvii, xxix, lii, lxv, lxix, lxxxvii, cviii, cxv, cliii, cliv, clv, 482.
Mystic license explained, lxvi.

NAISHÂPÛR, xlvii, cii, cxxxiii, cxxxiv, cxxxvii, cxli, cxliii, 16, 219, 422, 443, 494, 529, 540, 545.
"Nation" (N. Y.), 496, 542.
"National Review," xcix, 542.
Newton, Sir Isaac, xviii.
New World, A, 192.
Nicolas, J. B., lxiv, lxix, lxxiii, lxxix, lxxxv, cii, cviii, cxvi, cxxvi, cxxix, cxxxix, cxlvii, cli, clii, cliii, 115, 159, 175, 179, 216, 229, 242, 260, 288, 300, 315, 347, 373, 389, 430, 438, 468 478, 482, 489, 503, 523, 526.
Niebelungenlied, lxviii.
Nightingales, xxx, lxv, lxxx, lxxxvi, lxxxviii, cix, cx, clviii, clxxviii, 12, 19, 179, 186, 291, 292, 397, 528.
Nirvana, cxvi.
Nizâm ul Mulk, cxxxiii, cxxxvii, cxxxix, cxli, 422, 425, 444, 490, 493, 547.
Noah, 376.
Noorouz (Nuruz, Naw Rooz), 81, 213, 216.
Noouzer, 290.
"North American Review," li, 471, 535.
Norton, Professor Charles Eliot, li, liii, lix, cxxxi, 279, 535; his translation from Nicolas, 471–477.

OBEDIENCE, xcix, 344, 345.
Ocean, the, ciii, cxx, 254.
Oidipous Coloneus, quoted, 380.
"Old and New," 537.
"Old barren Reason," clxviii, 106.
Old Clomeface, 360.
"Old familiar Juice," the, clxxvi, 172.
Old Man of the Mountains, cxxxvi.
"Old Mortality," 360.
"Old World Edition" (variorum), 534.
Omar's dream quatrain, cxlvii.
Omar Khayyám, ix, xii, xiii, xv, xvii, xxi, xxv, xxvi, xxvii, xxviii, xxix, xxxii, xxxviii, xl, xlviii, li, liv, lvii, lxviii, lxix, lxxi, lxxiii, lxxvi, lxxxix, xcii, xcv,

xcvii, xcix, c, ci, ciii, civ, cv, cvi, cx, cxiii, cxiv, cxv, cxix-cxxii, cxxiii, cxxvi, cxxvii, cxxix, cxxxiii-clvi, 92, 94, 122, 196, 213, 221, 294, 310, 311, 316, 346, 365, 382, 415-438, 439, 443, 457, 458, 477, 484, 485, 491, 492, 493, 507, 509, 520, 536.
Omar Khayyám Club, lv, 544.
Omar the Mogheree, 535.
"One True Light," clxxiii, 150.
"Oriental Collection," xiii.
Oriental poetry, xiii.
Origin of evil, 432.
Ouseley, Sir Gore, xi, xii, 441, 455, 456, 528.
Ouseley, Sir William, xii, cliii, 404, 494.
Ouseley MSS. (Oxford), lxx, cxlvi, 440.
Oxus, The, xci, 131.

Painter, the heavenly, 265.
"Pall Mall Gazette," 516.
Pamphlet Edition (San Francisco) of FitzGerald, 533.
Pantheism, 359.
Paradise, xcv, civ, clix, 24, 26, 111, 208, 221, 225, 305, 358, 379, 382, 384, 418, 419, 448.
Parwin, cxiii, clxxiii, 146, 328.
Pascal, lxviii.
"Pastime of Eternity," clxvii, 100.
Patient endurance, 320, 321, 465, 502.
Paul, St., cxxviii.
Pearl of obedience, xcix, 344, 345, 475.
"Pearson on the creed," quoted, 359.
"Peevish Boy," clxxv, 164.
Persepolis, 216, 235.
Persian language, xix, lxxxiv, cxxiv, 13, 236, 454, 523.
"Persian Miscellanies," xiii.
Pertsch, W., xvi, 439, 440.
Peshdadian dynasty, 219, 235, 290.
Petersburg (St.) Lithographed text, 543.
Phantasmagoria of things, 66.
Phantom Caravan, the, 96.
"Phantom of False morning," clvii, 4.
"Philistine, the," 567.
Pickering, C. J., xi, lxxxi, xcix; his article on 'Umar of Nishâpûr, xcix-cxxii, cxxvi, 460, 542.
Pike, W. Robert (designs) 534
Plane (the quivering), clxxix, 194.
Plato, 67.
Plato's School of Philosophy, cxlv.
Pleiades, 330.
Plumtre, the Rev. E. H., lxvii.
Plutarch, 67.
Pocock's specimens, 115.
Poe, Edgar Allen, cxxiv.
Poison and antidote, 297, 298, 299, 400, 401.
Pollock, Sir Frederick, lix.
"Polonius," xxxvii.
Poole's Index, 535.
"Porter's shoulder-knot," clxxvi, 174.
Potter, the, xxxi, lxxiii, lxxxix, xc, cx, clxv, clxxv, 74, 76, 160, 166, 168, 174, 258, 353, 359, 362, 447, 456, 511, 572.
Poverty, xxv, 406.
Predestined Evil, xcvi, clxxiv, 156, 337, 421, 433, 453.
"Predestin'd Plot of Dust and Soul," clxxiii, 146, 148.
Present enjoyment, lxxxviii, xciii, cix, clvi, 70, 82, 224, 227, 241, 398, 418, 448, 474, 476, 518, 574.
Problem of Existence, 398.
Prometheus (Bound), 131.
"Prophet's Paradise," clix, clxx, 26, 200, 305.
Pulsatilla, 237.
"Punch," 566.
Punishment, 354, 408, 476.
Puppets of the Sky, 135.
Purgstall, Joseph von Hammer, xiv, xcix, ciii, cvi, cxlvi, cliii, 75, 137, 445-456, 495, 528, 575.
Purple, the mourning color, 67.
Pushkin, Alexander, lxxiv.

Quaritch, Bernard, xxxvii, xlv, lvi, lxxxii, 479, 509, 545.
Quicksilver, cx, clxvii, 100, 268, 269, 479.
Quietism, civ, 527.
Quilter, Harry, 497.

RABELAIS, 569.
Ramazán (Ramadan), xlix, clxxv, 160, 175, 348-353.
Reason, cxii, clxviii, 106, 362, 504.
Reincarnation, 188.
Renan, Ernest, cxxix, 527.
Repentance, xcvii, cxiv, clviii, clxxvii, 14, 158, 182, 310, 311, 339, 413.
Reputation sold for a Song, clxxvii, 180.
"Retreating whisper," 123.
"Revelations of Devout and Learn'd," clxx, 126.
Rieu, Charles, 439.
Ring dove quatrain, clxi, 236, 237, 238, 428.
River's Lip, the, 40.
"Robe of Honour," clxvii, 184.
Robinson, S. (Háfiz), 529.
Roman Theatre, cxlix.
Roses, lxxx, lxxxvi, cix, cxi, cxvii, cxlii, clviii, clix, clx, clxii, 10, 13, 18, 28, 30, 38, 182, 220, 236, 269, 423, 429, 444, 449, 466, 505, 513, 545, 551, 554.
Rossetti, Dante Gabriel, xlv, 525.
Royer-Collard, quoted, 536.
Rubáiyát, story of, xliii, xliv, xlv.
Rubá'iy, definition of, lxxi, lxxii, lxxxiv, cl, 490, 492, 539.
Rückert, Friedrich, xv, 453-455, 528.
Rúdagí, protopoet of Iran, ci.
"Rule and Line," clxviii, 108.
"Rumble of a distant Drum," clix, 26.
Rustum (Rustem), clix, 20, 21, 290, 502, 508.

SAADI (Sadi), xv, lxxxiv, cvi, cxxiii, 267, 530, 537.
Sachau, Ed., 439.
Sage, the, cix, 52, 282-287, 298, 331, 479
"Saints and Sages," clxiii, 52.
Saki. *See* Cupbearer.
"Salámán and Absál," xxxvii, xxxix, cxix, 3, 212, 302, 330.
Sale, George, 213, 276, 306.
Sancho Panza, quoted, 571.
"Saturday Review," xlvi, lxxviii, 461, 542, 565.

Saturn, xix, xcv, clxiv, 62.
Saunders, F., 543.
Schack, Friedrich von, lxxvi, lxxvii, cxl, 117, 175, 482.
Schopenhauer, cxiii, 521, 527.
Schütz-Wilson, H., xxxvii, 538.
"Scotsman, the," 541.
"Scroll of Universe," clxxviii, 202.
"Seas that mourn," clxiv, 66.
Secret, the, 98.
"Secret of my Life," 70.
"Secret Well of Life," clxiv, 68.
"Seed of Wisdom," clxiii, 56.
"Senseless Nothing," clxxiv, 152.
Sevenfold heaven, 71.
Seven Heavens, 236, 246.
Seven Seas (Heft Kulzum), 91, 441, 453, 483.
Seventy-two nations (sects), cxviii, cliii, clxix, 114, 115, 299, 474, 545.
Shaddad, King, 11.
"Shadow of a Soul of Fire," clxxi, 131.
Shah-nama (Book of Kings), 21, 235.
Shakespeare, lxviii, cv, cxii, cxxix.
Sharastani, 300, 430, 491.
Shelley, xx, cxix.
Shiraz, cliv.
"Silken Tassel," clx, 28.
Siller, Frank, 571-574.
Simpson, William, 507, 541, 547-552.
Simurgh, cxviii, 129, 552.
Sinai, Mt., 213.
Skepticism, cvi.
"Sleeve of Night and Morn," clxiv, 66.
Smith, G. C. M., 268.
"Smoke of Hell," clxxvi.
Snake, the, xcviii, cxiv, cxxvi, clxxiv, 158, 421.
"Snare of Vintage," clxxvii, 178.
"Snow upon the Desert's dusty Face," clx, 32.
Sobrievsky, A., 543.
Solomon's ring, xix.
Song of Solomon, 302, 388.
Sophocles, lxviii, 380, 428.
"Sorry Scheme of Things," l, clxxviii, 192.

Sorry trade, the, clxxiv, 154.
Soul, the, 88, 128.
Southey, Robert, 13.
"Sovereign Alchemist," clxix, 114.
"Spangle of Existence," clxvii, 98.
Sparrow-hawk comparison (Falcon), cxii, 54, 55, 244.
"Spectator" on McCarthy's Version, 530, 542; on Schütz-Wilson, 538.
Spedding, James, xxxiv.
Spemann's "Für Kunst und Leben," lxxv, 484.
Spiritual Liberty, cxviii.
Sprenger, Dr., cxlvi, cliii.
Spring, clxxvii, clxxviii, 182, 186, 298, 405, 406, 424, 448, 504.
Stern Recorder, the, 190.
Stevenson, Robert Louis, 552.
Stokes, Whitley, lxxxi, 234, 437, 465, 499-504, 544.
"Strip of Herbage strown," clix, 22.
"Stubborn Floor of Earth," 102.
Subhány, Rubáiyát of, lxxi.
Subhi Khazib (False Dawn), 4, 207, 208, 525.
Sufism, xxiii, xxvii, lxv, cii, cxii, cxxi, cxxii, cliii, 148, 430, 482, 517, 521.
Suicide advocated, clxxi, 88, 381.
"Sultan of the Persian Song," 529.
"Sultan's Turret," 2.
"Sun-illumin'd Lantern," clxxi, 132.
"Sup of Heavenly Vintage," clxv, 80.
Surly master (Tapster), xlix, clxxvi, 170.
Swinburne, A. C., cxxv, 491, 524.

TAJ MAHAL, 549.
Takhallus, lxxiii, cxxxviii.
Tassy, Garcin de, xl, xli, xlii, 133, 441, 464, 467, 526, 535.
Tavern, the, xxxix, cvii, clvii, cxlv, clxix, clxxiii, clxxiv, 4, 5, 6, 112, 150, 182, 283, 296, 332, 367, 368, 369, 370, 378, 387, 436, 450, 474, 575.
Taylor, Bayard, quoted, 366.
Teheran text, lxiv, cxiv, cli, cliv, 440.
Tekhté-Djemshid (Takht-i-Jamshid), 216, 235.

Tennyson, Alfred, xxxiv, xxxvii, lix, lxviii, c, cv, 536.
Tent Quatrain, cxxxix, clxxi, 90, 420.
"Terror of his wrathful Face," clxxiv.
Thackeray, W. M., xxxiv.
Thaxter, Levi S., liv.
Theognis, 240.
Thompson, W. H., xxxiv, xlv.
Thorwaldsen, cxliii.
Thoughtful Soul, the, clviii, 8.
Thous (Tús), 218, 219, 289, 290, 475.
"Thread-bare Penitence," clxxvii, 182.
"Thread of Present Life," the, clx, 198.
"Threats of Hell," clxx, 122.
Thugut, Freiherr von, xiv.
"Times, The," 542.
"Time's vintage," 44.
Tir (Tyr) and Dai, 220.
"Tiresias," Proem to, lx.
Toghrul Beg, cxxxiii.
Tomb of Omar, 549.
"To-Morrow's Silence, Triumph, or Despair," clxxiii, 144.
"To-morrow's tangle," clxviii, 82.
"Tower of Darkness," clxii, 50.
Transitoriness of Life, 52, 122, 217, 242, 246, 253, 272, 319, 397, 407.
Tree of existence, 367.
Tregenna, James Hamley, 360.
Trübner's "Oriental Catalogue," lxxxi.
Truth, the, cxxi, 288.
Tulip-cheeks, 40, 221, 222, 266, 494, 581.
Tulip, the, xxx, lxxxvii, xc, cxi, clxv, 80, 122, 265, 449, 513, 527.
"Twisted tendril," clxix, 118.
Two and seventy Creeds (sects), cxviii, cliii, clxix, 114, 299, 474, 545.
Two Worlds, 52.

'UMAR. See Omar.
"Unborn To-morrow," clxix, 110.
"Unfolded Roll of Fate," 190.
"Unfrequented Gardenside," clxxvi, 176.
"Unpermitted Pleasure," clxxiv, 152.

VAMBÉRY. 551.
Vault of heaven, 248.

Vedder, Elihu, lxii, 498, 542.
Veil, the, lxxxv, cv, clxiv, clxvi, 64, 68, 94, 144, 249-252, 312, 519.
Venus, 184, 185.
Vergil, lxviii, 67, 322.
Vespæ (Wasps) of Aristophanes, 359.
"Vessel of a more ungainly Make," clxxv, 166.
"Veterum Persarum Religio," x, cxl, 441, 442.
Victor Hugo, quoted, 252.
Vienna "Jahrbücher der Literatur," xv.
Vine, xlix, 10, 146.
"Vine and Love-abjuring Band," clxx, 200.
Virgil, 67.
"Visionary shapes," clxxi.
"Vision of fulfill'd Desire," clxxi, 130.
Voltaire, 445, 465, 495, 503, 517.
Von Hammer. *See* Hammer.
Von Schack. *See* Schack.

WALTON, Bryan, x.
Walton, Izaak, xxxii, 278.
War with passions, 342.
Waring, Scott, quoted, 207.
Watts, Theodore, Sonnet, 547; toast, 534, 559.
Way, W. Irving, 534.
Well of Life, cviii, clxiv, 96.
Westminster Abbey, 550.
Whalley, P., lxxxi, 441, 479-482, 539.
Wheel of heaven (of Fortune), xx, xcii, xciii, xcvi, cxxi, 48, 80, 92, 110, 133, 140, 146, 322-326, 363, 424, 426, 452, 476.
"Whether at Naishapur or Babylon," xlvii.
Whinfield, Edward Henry, lxxviii, lxxix, cxxxix, cxlviii, 115, 300, 424, 434, 489-496, 504, 505, 528.
"Whirlwind Sword," clxix, 116.
"White Hand of Moses," clviii, 8, 214.
"Wiener Jahrbücher der Literatur," 453.
"Wilderness were Paradise enow," clix, 24.
Williams, Talcott, cxxiii.
Wilson, C. E., lxxviii.

"Wind along the waste," clxiii, 58, 426, 472, 519, 580.
Winding sheet of Vine-leaf, 176.
Wine, xxiv, xxv, xxx, xxxi, lx, lxxx, lxxxv, lxxxvii, lxxxviii, xc, xciv, civ, cvii, cviii, clii, cliii, clviii, clxviii, 12, 22, 24, 30, 46, 60, 78, 84, 104, 108, 114, 144, 148, 172, 176, 180, 184, 208, 210, 217, 218, 221, 226, 228, 230, 232, 233, 242, 260, 268, 282, 286, 287, 288, 289, 292, 294, 295, 296, 297, 301, 332, 346, 348, 362, 367, 372, 374, 375, 376, 405, 430, 434, 448, 450, 454, 466, 472, 473, 482, 503, 511, 512, 517.
Wine-laving, cvii, cliv, clxxvi, 176, 367, 418, 437, 578.
"Wine of Life," clviii, 16.
"Winter garment of Repentance," clviii, 14.
Wisdom of Solomon, quoted, cxxviii.
Woepcke, F., xi, 457-463, 490, 542.
Wolff, Adolph ("Classiker aller Zeiten"), 575.
Wollheim, A. E., 528, 543, 573-581.
Wood-pigeon, 137.
Wordsworth, William, quoted, 275.
"Worldly hope turned ashes," clx, 32.
Wotton, Sir Henry, cxvii.
Wright, W. Aldis, xlvii, lviii, 67, 159, 532.

"YESTERDAY'S sev'n thousand Years," clxi, 42.
"Yoke of unpermitted Pleasure," 152.
"Youth's sweet-scented manuscript," clxxviii, 186.
Yusuf flower, 29, 431.
Yúsuf, 216, 217, 238.

ZACHARIAS, 291.
Zal, 20, 21, 290.
Zamzam (the fount of life), 57.
Zohak the Cruel, 293.
Zerduscht, cxlv.
Zhukovsky, A. V., 543.
Zoroastrianism, cxvi.

* 3, 5, 17, 59, 97, 122, 128, 195, 225, 249, 402, 505, 506.